The 100 MOST NOTABLE *Cornellians*

The 100
MOST
NOTABLE

Cornellians

Glenn C. Altschuler

Isaac Kramnick

R. Laurence Moore

CORNELL UNIVERSITY PRESS   *Ithaca and London*

First published 2003 by Cornell University Press
Printed in the United States of America

Library of Congress Cataloging-in-Publication Data

Altschuler, Glenn C.
   The 100 most notable Cornellians / Glenn C. Altschuler, Isaac
Kramnick, R. Laurence Moore.
      p.   cm.
Includes bibliographical references and index.
   ISBN 0-8014-3958-2 (cloth : alk. paper)
   1. Cornell University—Alumni and alumnae—Biography.   I. Title: One
hundred most notable Cornellians.   II. Kramnick, Isaac.   III. Moore, R.
Laurence (Robert Laurence), 1940–   IV. Title.
   LD1362 .A48 2003
   378.747′71—dc21

                                                           2002154681

Photographs of notable Cornellians are credited on page 249.

Cornell University Press strives to use environmentally responsible suppliers and materials to the fullest extent possible in the publishing of its books. Such materials include vegetable-based, low-VOC inks and acid-free papers that are recycled, totally chlorine-free, or partly composed of non-wood fibers. For further information, visit our website at www.cornellpress.cornell.edu.

Cloth printing 10 9 8 7 6 5 4 3 2 1

To the Cornell undergraduates we have taught

and from whom we have learned

Contents

Preface

THIS BOOK WAS conceived early one winter morning at the YMCA in Ithaca after a vigorous game of racquetball. Larry Moore mentioned to Isaac Kramnick that John R. Mott—whose pivotal role in YMCA history Isaac had just been reading about in the "Y" newsletter posted on the bulletin board—was a graduate of Cornell and that Mott had won the Nobel Peace Prize as well. Surely, Isaac mused, there were many other "notable" Cornellians whose connection to the institution was unknown to the vast majority of alumni. Isaac and Larry enlisted Glenn Altschuler in the project, and three good friends set out to research and write *The 100 Most Notable Cornellians*.

By "notable" we mean remarkable and therefore worthy of notice. Our one hundred Cornellians have left their mark on the American or international scene in their fields of endeavor. We decided against using the term "great" to emphasize that our choices are, as our social science colleagues say, "value free." In the overwhelming number of cases, but not in every one, the imprint left by our notables has been positive. Readers will notice one or two characters and charlatans on our list—Clifford Irving, for example, who is remarkable for activities few of us would applaud. And we have included Leo Frank, whose fame is linked not to his own willful activity but to the terrible tragedy that beset him.

Compiling our list took some work. We surveyed a wide range of biographical encyclopedias and who's whos, sifted through Cornell's archives and alumni records, and consulted knowledgeable people in various Cornell colleges and academic and nonacademic departments and offices. A large number of our one hundred were immediate and obvious choices to all three of us: we decided, for example, to include all the Nobel laureates we found. Where we were uncertain or disagreed, we decided by majority rule. We recognize that, at bottom, our choices represent our subjective preferences, including a desire to reflect the wide diversity of distinction that has characterized Cornell since the first class graduated in 1869. And we understand that many eminently notable Cornellians do not appear in this book.

We did make one decision rule that profoundly affected our selection process. Our notables are women and men who completed an undergraduate degree program at Cornell (the one exception is William Alanson White, who completed four years and all requirements except for trigonometry). We did not consider members of the Cornell faculty and thus denied ourselves the pleasure of writing biographical sketches of, among others, Frances Perkins, secretary of labor under President Franklin Roosevelt and the first woman appointed to a cabinet-level position in the United States; the novelist Vladimir Nabokov; and the astronomer Carl Sagan. Nor do any of the names of those Cornellians whose degrees come only from the graduate or professional schools appear in this volume. Included among these notables are Edmund Muskie, the United States senator from Maine and secretary of state under President Carter; William Rogers, President Nixon's secretary of state; Nobel Prize–winning novelists Pearl S. Buck and Toni Morrison; Robert Moog, inventor of the synthesizer that bears his name; C. Everett Koop, the surgeon general of the United States; Mae Jemison, the astronaut; Jimmy Smits, the actor; and Lee Teng-Hui, the president of Taiwan.

Our decision rule also excludes luminaries who attended Cornell as undergraduates but left without a degree. Because a B.A. or a B.S. was not a sine qua non for professional employment until World War II, many extraordinary men and women fall into this category. The list includes Colonel Edward House, principal advisor to President Wilson; Henry Morgenthau, secretary of the treasury in the administration of Franklin D. Roosevelt; Robert Trent Jones, the preeminent designer of golf courses (including one in Ithaca); Billy Evans, the Hall of Fame umpire; David Burpee, the seed innovator and tycoon; the suave, mustachioed actor Adolphe Menjou; the publisher John S. Knight; the writer Kurt Vonnegut; the pioneer feminist Susan Brownmiller; and the civil rights activist Michael Schwerner, who was murdered in Mississippi before he could complete his senior year.

Our one hundred notable Cornell undergraduates span a bit more than the first hundred years of the university, concluding with several who got their degrees in the first half of the 1970s. In compiling our list, we have tried to be sensitive to accomplishments in all walks of life. Among the one hundred are architects, artists, athletes, biologists, business leaders, chemists, engineers, inventors, journalists, judges, labor leaders, movie stars, winners of the Nobel and Pulitzer Prizes, philanthropists, photographers, physicians, physicists, politicians, psychiatrists, psychologists, reformers, religious leaders, senators, service workers, singers, TV personalities, university presidents, veterinarians, and writers.

Cornell has not always been hospitable to women, but it has often been more hospitable than other colleges and universities. And there are notable African Americans on our list, most of whom have had to overcome prejudice on the Cornell campus as well as in society at large. What struck us most was the large number of notables, men and women, whose accomplishments were in the applied physical and social sciences. This feature, we suspect, reflects the emphasis on the practical that was the founding legacy of Ezra Cornell, the farmer-entrepreneur who was enthralled with the telegraph and the steam engine and who was also an elected member of the New York State Senate.

Cornell is unique among American research universities and in the Ivy League. It had its origin in the Morrill Land Grant Act, which prescribed a curriculum in agriculture and the mechanic arts. It aspired to the ideals of Ezra Cornell, who would "found an institution where any person can find instruction in any study." And, at the same time, it was shaped in accordance with the high intellectual vision of its first president, Andrew Dickson White, who sought a "center and a school for new Literature" and "an asylum for Science, where truth shall be sought for truth's sake," an institution, in short, "to turn the current of mercantile morality which has so long swept through this land." A world-class institution with an egalitarian soul, Cornell has played a distinctive role in democratizing higher education, while helping to shape the American university's post–Civil War commitment to useful service to American society and to the world. The undergraduate experience has been the heart of life on East Hill, "far above Cayuga's waters." Its undergraduates have lived the ideals carved into the Eddy Street gate: "So enter that daily thou mayest become more learned and thoughtful. So depart that daily thou mayest become more useful to thy country and to mankind." It is our privilege and honor to single out and, in most cases, pay tribute to Cornell's most distinguished sons and daughters.

Identifying and writing about the one hundred most notable Cornellians has been instructive and enjoyable. We have had lots of help along the way. We are especially grateful to the many biographers and the authors, signed and unsigned, of obituaries and entries in biographical dictionaries, from whom we learned so much about these notables. *American National Biography, Current Biography,* and *Notable American Women* have proved especially valuable in our work. Tammy Lee, Susan McAvoy, Stefan Osdene, and Emily Parise gathered biographical material on the one hundred Cornellians in this book as well as many others who are not on the final list. Thanks as well to the many people in Alumni Affairs and Development and at the *Cornell Alumni Magazine,* especially its former editor John Marcham, who helped us identify useful material. We made the final selections as guests at the fishing lodge of Tom and Dottie Litwin in Roscoe, New York. We are grateful for their hospitality and for their memories of Cornell student life. Our colleague Sherman Cochran was of invaluable help in preparing the biographies of Cornell's notable graduates from China.

As he has done for years, Michael Busch deciphered Isaac Kramnick's indecipherable handwriting and entered it into a computer. Esther Tzivanis, executive assistant to Glenn Altschuler, has lived with the notables for two years, and she has been indispensable every step of the way. She has done research and word processing, tracked down photographs, and secured permissions. She has mastered working for three masters. One of the most competent and intellectually curious people we know, she has been a joy to work with. John Ackerman, director of Cornell University Press, understood immediately that this book would be informative, interesting, and fun. He kept us and his staff on a tight production schedule.

Finally, we wish to thank the institution that has been home to each of us for thirty years. Cornell is a wonderful place to live and work. It is a community of scholars enriched by its superb faculty and excellent students and sustained by an active alumni body who have left their mark on every conceivable endeavor both in the United States and around the world. Ezra Cornell knew what he was doing.

The 100 MOST NOTABLE *Cornellians*

Launching Cornell, 1868–1900

When Cornell University celebrated its Inauguration Day on October 7, 1868, Ezra Cornell, its founder, and Andrew Dickson White, its first president, had already articulated radical ideas that would shape the distinctive greatness of this very complex institution. Taking encouragement from the impetus given to "practical" education by the Morrill Land Grant Act, signed into law in 1862 during the Civil War, Cornell dreamed of founding a university where students could find instruction in any subject. He was a wealthy man, having had the vision to work with Samuel F. B. Morse in developing telegraph communication. With a willingness to endow such a place with a large amount of his own cash and a substantial tract of farmland in Ithaca, Cornell teamed with White, his learned colleague in the New York State Senate, to complete the financing of Cornell's dream with college land grant monies. On Cornell University's opening day, President White reiterated his wish that men and women of all races would have the option to study agriculture and the

President Andrew Dickson White. (Reprinted from Kermit Carlyle Parsons, *The Cornell Campus: A History of Its Planning & Development*. Copyright 1968 by Cornell University. Used by permission of the publisher, Cornell University Press.)

I

mechanic arts at Cornell, confident that these pursuits had the same academic dignity as the study of Latin and Greek. Cornell students would have exceptional freedom to "elect" their subjects of study—the first university to allow electives—the only significant exception being religion, which both Cornell and White believed was best left out of the curriculum.

The Cornell University that opened on that beautiful fall day had a long way to evolve before it resembled the modern research university it aimed to be. Only a single building, Morrill Hall (called South Building), was complete, and it lacked hinges to attach the doors. White Hall (called North Building) was under construction. Nine bells given to the university by Miss Jeannie McGraw, which would first be placed in the tower of the third campus building, which was financed by her lumber-magnate father John McGraw, sat on a rough wooden structure located, appropriately enough, where the famous campanile attached to the University Library would rise later in the century. The 332 students in the first freshman class and the 80 others admitted with advanced standing were an unremarkable group of white males, mostly from the local area. They were at least distinct from the applicants who had not passed the entrance examination. Along with an unhappy group of faculty, they were crowded into primitive housing at Cascadilla Hall. White called it an ill-ventilated, ill-smelling, uncomfortable, ill-looking almshouse.

The twenty faculty members could not have had an entirely clear idea of their mission. They did not have advanced degrees, which American universities including Cornell were only beginning to confer, and in some cases they were not especially learned in the subjects they were supposed to teach. The most distinguished of Cornell's early faculty were eight nonresident professors who traveled to Ithaca to give a special set of lectures. They included Louis Agassiz, America's best-known naturalist; James Russell Lowell, one of the country's most celebrated men of letters; and Theodore Dwight, a distinguished Columbia University jurist who taught constitutional law. Goldwin Smith came from a bit farther off. Having recently resigned as the Regius Professor of History at the University of Oxford, he was captivated by President White's vision of a university even though he believed White was failing in his mission to design a quadrangle comparable to those of Oxford's great colleges. Of the original trio of buildings that still define the west side of the Arts Quad, Smith commented, "Nothing can redeem them but dynamite."

White got good value from his visiting appointments. (The idea behind them inspired the university in 1965 to establish the Andrew Dickson White Professors-at-Large program, which at any one time affiliates twenty outstanding intellectuals from around the globe with Cornell.) However, White also began

McGraw Hall. (Reprinted from Kermit Carlyle Parsons, *The Cornell Campus: A History of Its Planning and Development.* Copyright 1968 by Cornell University. Used by permission of the publisher, Cornell University Press.)

to assemble a resident faculty that would build departments of academic distinction—Isaac P. Roberts in agriculture and chemistry, Burt Green Wilder in comparative anatomy and natural history, James Law in veterinary medicine, Daniel Willard Fiske in European languages (and Cornell's first librarian), William Cleveland in civil engineering, William Anthony in physics. The first students chose courses from the several degree programs that were offered: one in classics that was similar to the core curriculum then offered at most American colleges; one in science; one in philosophy that resembled what we now call a liberal education; and ones devoted to a specific vocational field, including engineering, agriculture, and architecture.

If the first students were free in their academic choices, they were less free in their personal lives. They followed a military regimen. Reveille sounded in Cascadilla between 5 and 6 A.M., the time depending on the season, and the students, decked out in military uniforms, were marched in to breakfast after they had made their beds, cleaned their quarters, and submitted themselves to inspection. The rest of the day followed a fixed schedule, including a stint of manual labor that Ezra Cornell deemed an essential part of education, with lights out at 10 P.M.

The military discipline relaxed along with the requirement of manual labor after a few years, although military training was off and on made mandatory. Students moved into town away from Cascadilla, and the dormitory rooms that were once in Morrill and White Halls were put to other purposes. A more dramatic change in life at Cornell came with the fulfillment of its founder's pledge to admit women. It was a controversial move, opposed by most male students and many of the faculty. Nonetheless, in September 1870 Miss Jennie Spencer of Cortland became the first woman to attend Cornell classes. A hard winter and long trudges up what became Libe Slope broke her will, and she returned home. Three more women took her place in 1871, and the following year Henry Sage, a wealthy business partner of John McGraw, gave the university money to build a women's dormitory. When Sage College for Women opened in 1875 (a renovated Sage Hall is now the Johnson School of Management), 37 women were enrolled at Cornell compared with 434 men. The women attended classes with the men. For the rest of the nineteenth century Cornell's women, a distinct minority of the student population, complained about their isolation, the condescension shown them by men, and the university's restrictions on how they lived. They also recognized that Cornell opened to them educational opportunities almost unique at the time at American and European universities.

Henry Sage was not only a university benefactor but also a powerful trustee whose influence on university policy has never been equaled by any subsequent member of the board of trustees. He did not always see eye to eye with President White. For one thing, Sage chafed at Cornell's reputation as a "godless university," and he did what he could to chart a different course for it as a Christian institution. In the same year that Sage College for Women opened, 1875, another Sage-endowed building graced the university landscape, one also designed by Cornell's first professor of architecture, Charles Babcock. Sage Chapel was a Christian-inspired building trying to look interdenominational. White at least blocked Sage's proposal to appoint a permanent university chaplain, and compulsory chapel failed to become a Cornell tradition. Cornell never built a divinity school, and most students who were religious worshipped, as White wished, in the various churches in Ithaca.

Not all Cornell students found the splendid isolation and physical beauty of the campus stimulating. To fill their hours when they were not attending classes or studying, they formed organizations—glee clubs, bands, dramatic groups, and social fraternities. They threw parties and, with the approval of President White and the condemnation of local ministers, danced. A temporary wooden building served as a gymnasium, and Cornell students, at least the men, participated in sports, sometimes in competition with other colleges. They played early

Morrill Hall in 1868. (Reprinted from Kermit Carlyle Parsons, *The Cornell Campus: A History of Its Planning & Development.* Copyright 1968 by Cornell University. Used by permission of the publisher, Cornell University Press.)

versions of baseball and American football, but the prestige athletic activity was rowing. Cornellians also very early developed a passion for student publications. The *Cornell Sun* first appeared in 1880, but before that there were the *Cornell Era* and the *Cornell Review* (renamed the *Cornell Magazine*). Later, students added a humor magazine, the *Cornell Widow.*

Before he stepped down from the presidency in 1885, White, in addition to the buildings already named, had overseen the construction of the west section of Sibley Hall (to house mechanical engineering), Franklin Hall (now Tjaden Hall and originally the home of physics and chemistry), and an armory that served as the university gymnasium. He and his family lived in a splendid mansion that White built and later donated to Cornell. It served as the President's House for many years. In 1953 it became the University Art Museum and now is the home of the Society for the Humanities. As his term wore on, however, White showed signs of becoming bored with the running of his Cornell fiefdom. He took a leave of absence in 1876 and again in 1879, the latter time to serve as the American minister to Germany. William C. Russel, one of Cornell's original faculty members, tried to run Cornell but managed to please almost no one. The board of trustees insisted in 1881 that White come home. He did, but his innovative vision for Cornell was being upstaged by innovations at other universities, most notably at Harvard and at the newly created Johns Hopkins University. It was time for a change.

Change came in the person of Charles Kendall Adams, who had once been White's student at the University of Michigan. A historian like White, Adams proved to be an administrator of vision but a poor politician. In his seven-year tenure as Cornell's president, from 1885 until 1892, he alienated powerful members of the faculty, many students, and Henry Sage, who doubted Adams's religious orthodoxy even more than he had White's. Yet it was Adams who began to reorganize Cornell into the collection of separate colleges that it is today. In 1888 and in 1891 respectively, the Department of Agriculture and the Department of Civil Engineering became colleges. In 1892 Boardman Hall became the home of the new law school, a two-year undergraduate program that was arguably the least distinguished of Cornell's degree programs but one that attracted a first-rate faculty. Charles Evans Hughes, the future Supreme Court justice, taught for two years at Cornell.

In addition to Boardman Hall, Adams added to Cornell's physical plant Barnes Hall (originally for the very active Cornell YMCA movement), Lincoln Hall (for civil engineering), and Morse Hall (for chemistry, an ill-fated building that suffered heavy damage from several fires before its final demolition in 1954 left its magnificent site vacant until the construction of the Johnson Museum of Art). More important was the University Library, another gift of Henry Sage, which opened in 1891 with a first-rate research collection, thanks in part to what White had sent back during his travels abroad. In 1962, it was renamed Uris Library when a generous gift from Harold and Percy Uris allowed the university to refurbish it for undergraduate use. Cornell's enrollment rose from 573 in the last year of White's presidency to 1,537 in the last year of Adams's presidency. Yet Adams resigned under pressure. From Ithaca he went to Madison, Wisconsin, where he served with distinction and with far more appreciation as president of the University of Wisconsin.

Adams's replacement was Jacob Gould Schurman, who came to Cornell as a professor of Christian ethics and moral philosophy and in 1890 was named head of the Susan Linn Sage School of Philosophy. Henry Sage had at last found a real Christian to run Cornell. Yet Schurman, whose tenure as Cornell's president was to extend through the first two decades of the twentieth century, had no plans to disturb Cornell's secular character. He turned his considerable oratorical skills instead toward securing more state aid for Cornell. In 1894 that aid made

President Jacob Gould Schurman. (Reprinted from Kermit Carlyle Parsons, *The Cornell Campus: A History of Its Planning & Development*. Copyright 1968 by Cornell University. Used by permission of the publisher, Cornell University Press.)

possible the construction of a portion of what eventually became Goldwin Smith Hall. It rounded out the Arts Quad and served as the dairy husbandry building. In 1895, again with full financial support from New York State, Cornell established a College of Veterinary Medicine on the site of what is now the Industrial and Labor Relations School. Cornell Medical College opened in New York City in 1898, although it did not require a college degree for admission until 1908. A branch of the medical college on the Ithaca campus allowed some students to do two years of their medical training in Stimson Hall, a state-of-the-art facility that was opened on the south end of the Arts Quad in 1903. Women were required to do their early medical training at the Ithaca division of the medical school, which did not close until 1938.

In the last year of the nineteenth century, Cornell had over two thousand undergraduate students and almost two hundred graduate students. Of the undergraduates, most were enrolled in engineering programs. Arts and Sciences students made up the next largest group, followed by law students (now a three-year program), architecture students, and, in last place, agricultural students. Scientific farming, which was intended as the centerpiece of Ezra Cornell's institution, had not yet taken off, but Liberty Hyde Bailey, who came to Cornell in 1888, would soon change that. A single faculty no longer ruled Cornell.

Undergraduate students who enrolled in the College of Law, the College of Architecture, the College of Civil Engineering, the College of Mechanical Engineering, the College of Agriculture, and the various departments that made up Arts and Sciences developed separate identities. Many of them lived off campus or in fraternities. With the exception of Sage College for Women, Cornell had not since its first years tried to house students in dormitories.

Even so, teaching was then carried out in a compact space, certainly compared with the expansion that took place in subsequent decades. Cows roamed the campus quad, a reminder to all students of their common connection to a university not quite like any other. And despite the changes in the organization of Cornell since its founding, the university was culturally homogeneous. There was no racial diversity, and only a few of the children of Catholic and Jewish immigrants to the United States made their way to Ithaca. Women were never more than 15 percent of the student population in the nineteenth century. Even poor young men on scholarship who worked their way through school no longer dominated campus life, as they had in the beginning. Cornell students who received their degrees in 1900 would return to a very different place if they lived to attend their fiftieth class reunion.

Joseph Benson Foraker
ᴄᴧ CLASS OF 1869

No member of the United States Senate, President William Howard Taft insisted, is "so reactionary, so unscrupulous, and so able, as Joseph Foraker is." One of the last politicians to win office by "waving the bloody shirt," emblematic of his service in the Civil War, Foraker was also one of the first to lose his congressional seat because of the conviction, advanced by the "muckrakers" of the early twentieth century, that politicians who accepted retainers from large corporations had betrayed the public trust.

Joseph Benson Foraker was born on July 5, 1846, near Rainsford, Ohio. His father, Henry Stacey Foraker, was a prosperous farmer and miller. A member of the Methodist Episcopal Church, Margaret Reece Foraker taught her son to read the Bible and took him with her to antisaloon rallies. One summer, "Ben" memorized 1,396 verses of the Bible. With both parents staunch antislavery Republicans, the fourteen-year-old Foraker attended all the Lincoln rallies in the region in 1860. Two years later he was the first to enlist in the Eighty-ninth Ohio Volunteers. Foraker's unit saw considerable action throughout the Civil War, especially as part of Sherman's march through Georgia to the sea. The last to muster out of the Eighty-ninth, he left the army as a captain.

Foraker entered Ohio Wesleyan University in 1866, and was elected president of his class. But when Cornell commenced instruction in October 1868, and informed "advanced students" they might graduate in one year, he transferred along with two of his friends. At Cornell, he founded Phi Kappa Psi, the fraternity into which he had been initiated at Ohio Wesleyan. One of eight seniors in Cornell's first graduating class, Foraker gave the commencement address. "Three Hundred Lawyers" analyzed the legal profession in Cincinnati, which he planned to join.

After a brief apprenticeship, Foraker passed the bar in 1869. A year later he married Julia Bundy, daughter of a congressman from Ohio. They had five children. Over the next decade, Foraker established a lucrative law practice and entered politics, winning election as superior court judge in Cincinnati in 1879. Although a relative unknown, the Republicans nominated him for governor in 1883, in part because party leaders believed a Cincinnati resident might attract the city's numerous German-American voters, who were unhappy with the saloon tax Republicans had sponsored. Foraker lost, but Republican politicians took note of his political skills. A handsome man with a booming voice, who earned the nicknames "Fire Alarm Joe" and "Boomtara," Foraker on the stump, wrote one journalist, was "a wizard and a hypnotist who can make men forsake their families and their homes and their political principles and their bank accounts." In 1884, at the GOP National Convention, after his featured speech nominating fellow Ohioan John Sherman for presi-

dent, he received a few votes for vice president, including one from Andrew D. White, president of Cornell and a delegate from New York. In 1885 Foraker was elected governor of Ohio.

Foraker was a moderate reformer in his two terms as governor. He advocated taxes on liquor, paid the state debt, endorsed registration of voters, and created a state board of health and a commission to inspect food and drink. Although many Republicans now sought sectional reconciliation, Foraker denounced the South and endorsed equal rights for Negroes. His campaign rallies always ended with the song "Marching through Georgia." Governor Foraker pushed through the Ohio Legislature a repeal of laws that mandated segregated schools for black children. And he won national attention for refusing to return Confederate flags captured during the Civil War to the Southern states, as President Cleveland had directed, saying, "No rebel flags will be surrendered while I am governor."

Eager for a place on the Republican national ticket, Foraker jostled for position with the equally ambitious Ohioans John Sherman, Marcus Hanna, and William McKinley. When he abandoned Sherman during the balloting for president at the 1888 Republican Convention, factionalism and squabbles over patronage intensified and worked against Foraker. He failed to win a third term as governor.

Foraker remained active in politics. At the Republican Convention in 1896 he chaired the platform committee that endorsed the gold standard and delivered the speech nominating William McKinley for president. The party, which controlled the state legislature, rewarded him with a seat in the U.S. Senate, where he served for two terms. Foraker was a reliable supporter of the economic program of the McKinley administration. As a member of the Foreign Relations Committee, he advocated American intervention in Cuba. When the United States declared war against Spain in 1898, his appetite for expansion increased. He urged annexation of Hawaii, re-tention of the Philippines, and the use of force against the Filipino rebels. The Foraker Act of 1900 established a colonial government for Puerto Rico, but, in the face of opposition in the Senate, he withdrew a provision making the islanders citizens of the United States.

Theodore Roosevelt, the Republican vice president thrust into higher office by McKinley's assassination and then elected to his own term as president, found Foraker unsympathetic to progressive reform. Foraker voted against agreements to submit international disputes to arbitration. Although he defended acquisition of the Panama Canal Zone, he opposed the Roosevelt corollary to the Monroe Doctrine, under which the United States forced countries throughout Latin America and the Caribbean to honor their contracts with U.S. citizens and corporations. On the domestic front, Foraker believed it unwise and unconstitutional for the national government to regulate the economy. Dubbed by his critics "the railroad senator" because he had advanced the interests of the railroads while in office, he was one of only three senators (the other two were Democrats from Alabama) to oppose the Hepburn Act, which gave the Interstate Commerce Commission the power to set rates for railroads.

With the Brownsville affair of 1906, Foraker broke completely with the president, but this time in a way that history has vindicated. When Roosevelt approved of the dismissal "without honor" of all 167 Negroes in three battalions because a few allegedly shot up the Texas town, Foraker denounced the decision. He insisted there was no proof that any of the soldiers had participated in the shooting or that there had been a "conspiracy of silence" about it. The soldiers were the "direct and worthy" successors of Civil War veterans, Foraker claimed, who "ask no favors because they are Negroes, but only for justice because they are men." Congress authorized

Secretary of War William Howard Taft to appoint a court of inquiry to hear claims, which resulted in the reinstatement of fourteen men. Foraker remained unhappy, but Roosevelt was enraged—after Brownsville, the senator from Ohio was never invited to the White House. To Republicans who worried that the dispute would split the party, the president replied, "If they split off Foraker, they split off a splinter."

The affair destroyed the slim chance Foraker had to succeed Roosevelt as president in 1908. When he made a quixotic run for the nomination anyway, Taft crushed him. He lost his seat in the Senate as well. In September 1908, in a speech in Columbus, Ohio, William Randolph Hearst read the text of letters to Foraker from John D. Archbold, vice president of Standard Oil Company. The instruction—"Here is still another objectionable bill. . . . I hope there will be no difficulty in killing it"—followed by payments for services as "special counsel" invited the conclusion that the senator was in the employ of the monopolistic Standard Oil Company. Foraker, who had represented railroad companies, including the Cincinnati Traction Company, for which he was a lobbyist during his tenure in the Senate, denied that he had done anything wrong. Employment of this sort, engaged in by many officeholders, did not, he maintained, have "any relation whatever to any public duty." But times had changed. Roosevelt advised Republicans to "throw Foraker over with a bump." The senator withdrew his bid for reelection.

Foraker returned to Cincinnati and resumed his law practice. He tried to regain his Senate seat in 1916, but lost to Warren G. Harding. In retirement, he rekindled his interest in religion, expressing the hope, before he died on May 10, 1917, that "we are now nearing the close of the Christian dispensation."

David Starr Jordan
❧ CLASS OF 1872

In his autobiography David Starr Jordan remarked that he had led three more or less independent lives—that of a naturalist and explorer, that of a teacher, and that of a "minor prophet of Democracy." He failed to mention a fourth life for which he is best remembered, that of university president. That last life, which he did not choose, won him the most accolades but probably brought him the least pleasure.

Jordan was born on January 19, 1851, into a family of five children in Gainesville, New York. His father, Hiram Jordan, and his mother, the former Hulda Hawley, traced a proud ancestry back to English and New England stock and expected their children to achieve something. Jordan acquired much of his early education at home, though when he was fourteen his parents enrolled him in the Gainesville Female Academy because of its excellent reputation. He and the one other boy permitted to register were in a distinct minority. He learned enough to win a scholarship through competitive examination to enter Cornell University. He intended to become either a botanist or a breeder of fine sheep.

Jordan arrived in Ithaca in March 1869, the second year of Cornell's existence. In those days, he recalled, the university had only a "crude and cramped" physical plant, but the years were "enriched by an enthusiasm hard to maintain in days of prosperity." Jordan always relished the role of pioneer. To pay for his education, he worked, like most of his classmates, at various tasks, including digging the hole to lay the foundation for McGraw Hall. He played baseball, wrote for the *Cornell Era,* and in addition to his primary studies in botany and zoology, elected courses in history, English literature, and a variety of modern languages. Even before he entered Cornell, Jordan had amassed such an extensive knowledge of the flora of western New York that Cornell made him an instructor of botany when he was a

junior. In his courses he taught boys who later became distinguished natural scientists, including the equally precocious John Henry Comstock. In 1872, after three and a half years of study, Jordan received not the conventional bachelor's degree awarded to his classmates but Cornell's first master of science degree.

Jordan credited Cornell with exerting a "controlling interest over my whole subsequent career." He also concluded that a degree from Cornell, "a fountainhead of educational and other heresies," made it difficult for him to find a proper academic job. Passed over for positions at the University of Wisconsin, Princeton, Vassar, the University of Michigan, and the University of Cincinnati, he instead was bounced around from Lombard University in Galesburg, Illinois (where he taught all the sciences plus political economy, German, Spanish, and the evidences of Christianity), to high schools in Wisconsin and Indiana, and to Northwestern Christian University (now Butler University), where he received a Ph.D.

Dissatisfied with these academic environments, Jordan used his summers to build his scientific reputation. In 1873 and 1874 he attended a summer school in science established by Harvard's distinguished zoologist Louis Agassiz on Penikese Island in Buzzards Bay, Massachusetts. Agassiz told him to study the fishes of the region, and Jordan apparently liked the work. Although his first notable publication was the *Manual of the Vertebrates of the Northern United States* (1876), most of his subsequent, extensive scientific publications were in ichthyology. These included, with E. W. Evermann, *The Fishes of North and Middle America* (four volumes, 1896–1900) and *American Food and Game Fishes* (1902). An observer, explorer, and taxonomist rather than a theorist, Jordan over his lifetime led expeditions through rivers and coastlands all over the United States as well as in Mexico, Japan, Hawaii, and Samoa. He headed the U.S. Fur Seal Commission (1896–98) and the Salmon Commission (1880–1903) and was a member of the nation's Fish Commission (1877–91, 1894–1909). With these enthusiasms, Jordan quite naturally became one of the founding members of the Sierra Club.

In 1879, with most of these achievements in the future, Jordan received his first appropriate academic post. He was named professor of natural sciences at Indiana University. In 1885, two events abruptly changed his life. Susan Bowen, whom he had married in 1875, died, leaving him with three children. And, without seeking the job, he became president of Indiana University. His domestic life recovered in 1887 when he married Jessie Knight who added three more children to Jordan's family (only three of his six children—two of Susan's and one of Jessie's—survived their infancy). But he carried the burdens of university administration for most of the next three decades.

At age thirty-four, Jordan took up his duties as America's youngest university president. He was extremely successful and guided Indiana from a college with only 135 students toward the front ranks of America's land grant institutions. In 1887 Cornell University took sufficient pride in his accomplishments to break with tradition and award him an honorary degree. Only Andrew Dickson White has been similarly honored. White helped to alter Jordan's career in a crucial way in the late 1880s when Leland Stanford arrived in Ithaca looking for someone to lead a new university he was founding. White turned down the job but recommended Jordan. Jordan, offered the position, accepted and within six months recruited a faculty to teach the first 559 students to arrive in Palo Alto in 1891. It was a Cornell colony. Of Stanford's original fifteen faculty members, two

had been Jordan's classmates at Cornell, five were Cornell graduates, two were lured away from Cornell's faculty, and one was completing a Ph.D. at Cornell.

Jordan had two heady years. Stanford proposed an endowment that made his institution one of the richest in the country. But the bottom fell out in 1893 when Stanford died and his estate was frozen for six years in a probate dispute. Jordan refused to give up and kept the institution afloat, barely. Money started to pour in again after a favorable decision by the U.S. Supreme Court, but Jordan had other problems. Jane Stanford, Leland's widow and the institution's sole trustee, decided to fire one of Stanford's few distinguished faculty members, the sociologist E. A. Ross. She judged him a labor agitator and a radical. To his credit, Jordan tried hard to change her mind, but when he finally caved in, he caved in badly, calling Ross "a dangerous man." This failure to defend academic freedom has dogged his reputation ever since.

Even so, Jordan, who borrowed heavily from Cornell's academic patterns, turned Stanford into an important institution. In 1906, when an earthquake leveled many buildings in the San Francisco Bay Area, Jordan turned down an attractive offer from the Smithsonian Institution in Washington and stayed at Stanford to rebuild the university's physical plant. Not everyone loved him. Students resented his antialcohol policies, and some of the faculty found him authoritarian. In 1913 it was time for a change. Herbert Hoover, Stanford's new board chairman and one of Jordan's first students at Stanford, supported an effort that shifted Jordan from the office of president into the largely ceremonial position of university chancellor. Jordan's accomplishments far outweighed his mistakes. However, at sixty-two, Jordan, once among the most innovative of American educators, was prepared to leave further changes to others.

For most of the rest of his life, Jordan devoted himself to world peace, a cause he had adopted in the aftermath of the Spanish-American War. He proclaimed that "all war is murder, robbery, and trickery." A trustee of the Carnegie Endowment for International Peace and director of the World Peace Foundation, he opposed America's entry into World War I until the very day Woodrow Wilson got his declaration of war from Congress. After that barbaric conflict was over, Jordan resumed his peace crusade and in 1924 won the $25,000 Raphael Herman Peace Award. His antiwar activism was unfortunately linked to his activism in the cause of eugenics. In many books and articles Jordan argued that war destroyed the best blood of a nation. In human wars, the fittest did not survive but were on account of their bravery the

first killed. Jordan defined fitness in racial terms, with blue-eyed Nordics standing at the top of his racial hierarchy.

Jordan was a vigorous, athletic man who loved to climb mountains. In 1881 he was part of a dangerous ascent of the Matterhorn. Like Jordan, many university presidents received honorary degrees. But Jordan, unlike the others, also had a California mountain named for him. His robust health began to fail in the mid-1920s and was shattered in his seventy-eighth year when he suffered the first of a series of strokes that took his life two years later. He died at his home in Stanford on September 19, 1931.

John Henry Comstock
∾ CLASS OF 1874

Thirteen members of the "Struggle for Existence Club" met in the spring of 1872 in a small building in the yard of the campus home of President Andrew D. White. The "Strugs" (who were supporters of Darwinism) voted unanimously to petition the Cornell faculty to authorize a fellow undergraduate, John Henry Comstock, to teach a course in entomology. Appointed as an instructor, Comstock took the initial steps toward developing the first entomology department in the United States.

Comstock was born in Janesville, Wisconsin, on February 24, 1849. When he was an infant his father, Ebenezer Comstock, a farmer and teacher, joined a group of "forty-niners" headed to California in search of gold. He died en route, leaving Susan Allen Comstock with a farm she could not manage and a mortgage she could not pay. Susan took her son to her native state, New York, where she worked as a housekeeper and nurse, depositing "Hanky" with relatives, friends, and, for a time, in an orphanage. When he was a lonely eleven-year-old with a stutter, Comstock

found a permanent and happy home in Oswego County, New York, with Lewis and Rebecca Turner. He applied himself assiduously at school and worked every summer as a cook on vessels sailing the Great Lakes. When an itinerant minister denounced the new "godless institution," Cornell, Comstock's curiosity was aroused. He discovered that Cornell offered a scientific curriculum, and enrolled in 1869. Illness forced him to take the next year off. During that time, searching for a book on lichens and mosses in a shop in Buffalo (he remembered the date—July 2, 1870), he came across Thaddeus Harris's *Insects Injurious to Vegetation*. Its subject matter and beautiful illustrations fascinated him, and he decided, then and there, to make entomology, not botany, his life's work.

Comstock returned to Cornell in the fall of 1870. To pay for his education, he unloaded stones used in the construction of McGraw Hall, earned room and board in Cascadilla Hall as Cornell chimesmaster, and worked in the zoology and physiology laboratories of Professor Burt Wilder. When he had contracted typhoid fever, Wilder had taken him into his home to convalesce. When Comstock graduated in 1874, he began an almost forty-year career on the Cornell faculty, as instructor (1875–77), assistant professor (1877–78), and full professor (1882–1914).

In 1878 Comstock married Anna Botsford, an undergraduate at Cornell. At first she assisted him in his research and agricultural extension work, but soon became a gifted illustrator, a collaborator on many books, author of several of her own, and a leading figure of the "nature study" movement. Anna and "Harry" had no children, but opened their home to an extended Cornell family, including faculty and many of the more than five thousand students Comstock taught during his career.

In the summer of 1878, Comstock worked as a temporary field agent for the U.S. Department of Agriculture. Sent to Alabama to study the cotton leaf "worm," he remembered Andrew White's advice that he use his work to assist the farmers. He became a pioneering advocate of economic entomology, a field that sought to control the population of insects injurious to vegetation. Entomologists must learn, he wrote, "that it is as important to know what insects do as to know their names." In less than a year, he was appointed chief entomologist in the Department of Agriculture. During his two years in Washington, Comstock produced reports on cotton insects and did important research on scale insects.

After a political shuffle that followed the death of President Garfield, Comstock returned to Cornell in 1882 to build the premier entomology department in the United States. Students received training through lectures, in the field (for one class students extracted the honey from a bee tree at night and lured the bees into a box hive), and in laboratories, designed and partially built by Comstock and located first in McGraw Tower and then on the second floor of White Hall. Using funds from the Hatch Act of 1887, Comstock built what may have been the first insectary in the world. When frightened faculty sought guarantees that live insects would not escape the facility, he assured them that insects preferred death to biting a professor. When he retired in 1914, the entomology faculty at Cornell had a staff of thirty-one, including five professors; more than fifty of his graduate students had become professors of entomology or officers in state or federal agencies.

Comstock's *An Introduction to Entomology* (1888), *The Elements of Insect Anatomy* (1889), *A Manual for the Study of Insects* (1895), and *The Spider Book* (1912) became standard texts in the field. To ensure that scientific texts were affordable and available, John Henry and Anna founded the Comstock Publishing Company, whose motto was "Nature through books." Located at first in the Comstock home, then in a chalet on Roberts Place, the firm was bequeathed to the university in 1931 and became the basis of Cornell University Press. During the 1890s, at the request of President David Starr Jordan (one of the Cornell "Strugs" who had helped launch Comstock's career), the entomologist spent winter breaks in Palo Alto setting up the entomology program at Stanford.

Short, energetic, and fidgety, Comstock excused himself in mid-evening from dinner parties and social occasions so that he could arise at 4 A.M. to do research and write. Fascinated by Darwin's *On the Origin of Species,* he sought to understand the evolution of insects and to formulate a system of classification that reflected variation, sequences of character change, and developmental history. His most important work, on the wings of insects, appeared in several articles in the *American Naturalist* in 1898 and twenty years later in a book-length exposition, *Wings of Insects,* on the uniform terminology of insects' wing veins.

While Comstock was working on *An Introduction to Entomology,* Anna told him she knew an artist who would illustrate the book, without cost. Anna supplied drawings and wood engravings for several subsequent works as well. But it was their writing, Anna Comstock recalled, that became "the thread on which our days were strung, despite a thousand interfering activities." The couple collaborated on two popular nature-study books, *Insect Life* (1897) and *How to Know the Butterflies* (1904).

Comstock was a founder of the Entomological Society of America, hosting its organizational meeting at Cornell in 1906 and serving as its first president. He was a fellow of the London Entomological Society, the Société entomologique of France, and the American Society of Naturalists. Comstock remained active long after his retirement from Cornell in 1914 but suffered a debilitating stroke in 1926. He died on Friday, March 20, 1931. On the following Tuesday, in accordance with his wishes, Comstock's ashes were placed next to those of his wife in Lakeview Cemetery on a lovely site overlooking Cayuga Lake.

Edward Leamington Nichols

≈ CLASS OF 1875

"Nearly all really important technical advances," Edward L. Nichols wrote, "have their origin in communities where the great fundamental sciences are most extensively and successfully cultivated." A towering figure in the professionalization of physics in the United States, Nichols insisted that research was a primary function, even duty, of university professors. He founded the *Physical Review,* the first journal in the nation devoted exclusively to physics, and was a founding member and early president of the American Physical Society.

Edward Leamington Nichols was born on September 14, 1854, in Leamington, England, while his parents, Edward Willard Nichols, a music teacher and portrait and landscape painter, and Maria Watkinson Nichols, a former missionary in Smyrna (now Izmir) and Constantinople (Istanbul) in Turkey, were on a two-year sojourn in Europe. Edward received his primary education in the public schools of Orange, New Jersey, and prepared for college at the military academy in Peekskill, New York. He entered Cornell in 1871. A member of the Delta Upsilon fraternity, Nichols also joined the Cornell Musical Association and rowed crew for the Sprague Boat Club. During his first three years he was interested in chemistry, but courses with Professor William Anthony during his senior year changed his career plans. One of the few physics professors in the nation to offer laboratory instruction and to illustrate his lectures with experiments, Anthony built a Gramme dynamo that was exhibited at the Centennial Exposition in Philadelphia in 1876 and then supplied electric current for his lab for many years as well as a small lighting system for the campus. He got Nichols hooked on physics.

Following graduation in 1875, Nichols

spent four years in Germany, studying with prominent physicists in Leipzig, Berlin, and Göttingen before receiving his Ph.D. in 1879. Back in the United States, he received a post-doctoral fellowship from Johns Hopkins, and then worked for a year in the Menlo Park laboratory of Thomas Edison, where he helped develop photometric methods for use with the incandescent lamp. In 1881 Nichols received his first professorial appointment, as chair of physics and chemistry at Central University in Richmond, Kentucky. That same year he married Ida Preston, his sweetheart at Cornell. They had two children. Nichols moved on and up to the University of Kansas in 1883, as professor of physics and astronomy. His papers on color impressions on the eye, a spectrophotometric analysis of pigments and the color of the sky, the senses of taste and smell, and the chemical behavior of iron in a magnetic field established his professional reputation. In 1887 he returned to Cornell to head the physics department.

At Cornell Nichols continued his research on the complexities and practical limitations of artificial light. In 1904 he began a collaboration with his colleague and former student Ernest Merritt on optics, phosphorescence, and fluorescence. They observed and measured the luminescence of zinc sulfate, the fluorescence spectra of organic dyes and uranium compounds, the impact of luminescence on exciting wavelength and electrical conduction, energy distribution in fluorescence spectra, and the rate of decay of phosphorescence. Seventeen of their papers were published under the general title "Studies in Luminescence," the last one appearing in 1917.

As important as his research was Nichols's vision and leadership in promoting research and establishing physics as an academic discipline. At a time when most professors thought their primary role was to be custodians of culture and disseminators of knowledge, he insisted that faculty search for truth. To establish a community of research scholars, he founded *Physical Review* in 1893 with financial help from Cornell, edited it for

twenty years, and contributed book reviews and biographical sketches. It would become the most prestigious journal in the field. To give researchers opportunities to meet one another and to present papers and discuss them, Nichols helped found the American Physical Society in 1899, serving as president from 1908 to 1909. The second honorary member of the Illumination Engineering Society (the first was Edison), he also served as secretary, vice president, and president of the American Association for the Advancement of Science, and as vice president of the American Institute of Electrical Engineers. He served as president as well of the honor society Sigma Xi, first established at Cornell in 1886, which distinguished itself from Phi Beta Kappa in its requirement that members, be they undergraduates, graduate students, or faculty, be selected for their promise and performance in research rather than for their grades. "A country that has many investigators will have many inventors also," Nichols said. "People who get their knowledge at second-hand must be content to follow."

Nichols remained convinced, however, that teaching and research were closely related. He wrote the two-volume *Lab Manual of Physics and Applied Electricity* in 1894, and a three-volume textbook, *The Elements of Physics* (1896–97). Every Thursday night during the spring and fall terms, Nichols held a meeting of his seminar for advanced students in his home. Calm and dignified, ramrod straight in a black frock coat when lecturing, he was, by all estimates, an inspiring teacher, especially supportive of women scientists. When he retired in 1919, he had trained the heads of departments of physics at thirty-five colleges as well as many other faculty members and men and women who held important positions in government and industry.

Nichols disdained administrative work. When a professor "distinguished himself by productive work," he noted, he "is frequently made a dean, director or even president, and is thus retired from what might have been a great career as an investigator. . . . It is as though the authorities were to say: 'X has written an admirable book; we must appoint him bookkeeper—or Y is developing a decided genius for landscape; we will increase his salary and ask him to devote all his time to painting the woodwork of the university buildings.'" And yet, perhaps because he saw opportunities to advance research in the university, he agreed to serve as dean of the College of Arts and Sciences (he was the first dean elected by the faculty under an arrangement that limited the term to two years and provided a permanent staff to handle administrative details, leaving the dean, it was hoped, to focus exclusively on broad questions of policy). He also was one of the first faculty-elected members of the Cornell Board of Trustees.

During his long career Nichols received many awards and honors. He was a fellow of the American Academy of Arts and Sciences, a member of the National Academy of Sciences, and the recipient of the Elliott Cresson Medal of the Franklin Institute, the Ives Medal of the Optical Society of America, the Rumford Medal of the American Academy of Arts and Sciences, and honorary degrees from the University of Pennsylvania and Dartmouth College.

Nichols was not a "laboratory hermit." His interests and activities ranged far beyond physics. An amateur violinist, an avid fisherman, and an ardent traveler who visited all six continents, he helped edit Johnson's Encyclopedia and Webster's Dictionary. A devout Episcopalian and vestryman at St. John's Church in Ithaca, who, according to the *Cornell Alumni News,* combined "perseverance in seeking new knowledge with a conservative regard for old ideals and approved traditions," Nichols had no difficulty reconciling scientific discovery with religious faith. "Thoughtful contemplation of the material universe," he wrote, "leads inevitably to belief in an intelligent creator."

Long after he retired from Cornell, Nichols continued to do research, publishing dozens of papers, most of them on luminescence. He died in West Palm Beach, Florida, on November 10, 1937.

Martha Carey Thomas

CLASS OF 1877

In 1923 the League of Women Voters published a list of twelve outstanding living American women. Of the three Cornell graduates who made the list, M. Carey Thomas had the biggest national reputation. Just retired from her career as dean and then president of Bryn Mawr College, she had been since her student days a prominent figure in the sometimes lonely fight for women's rights. Though never married herself, she hoped to erase the reality facing a woman of her generation that marriage and a career were incompatible.

"Minnie," as she was known in childhood, was born on January 2, 1857, in Baltimore. Her father, James Carey Thomas, was a prominent physician and civic leader, and her mother, Mary Whitall Carey, a reform activist, served as the first president of Baltimore's Woman's Christian Temperance Union. The immediate family was large (Thomas was the oldest of ten children), and the extended family of deeply religious Quakers even larger. One of her aunts, Hannah Whitall Smith, once a writer of popular religious tracts, expatriated to England where her younger daughter married Bertrand Russell and two of her granddaughters married, respectively, Oliver Strachey and Adrian Stephen, the brother of Virginia Woolf. She instructed Carey to refuse the social conventions that kept women subordinate: "Girls have a right to College education. They ought to be made to get it, even at the point of a bayonet."

At age seven Minnie suffered a life-threatening burn on her right leg that left her in severe pain and unable to walk for eighteen months; it did not fully heal for eight years. Becoming a voracious reader to compensate for her lameness, she decided to study Greek, a generally masculine pursuit considered too taxing for women's delicate nervous systems. While a student at the Howland Institute in western New York, she began to chafe at the intellectual narrowness of her Quaker environment and the endless conversations about the schisms of the Friends. The forbidden subjects of music, theater, and novels drew her passionate interest. Thomas eventually decided that the religious fanaticism of some of her ancestors was a form of mental illness.

When her father pushed her to attend Vassar College, she rebelled. Vassar lacked a curriculum comparable in rigor to the elite men's colleges and some of the new coeducational schools. She spent a year honing her skills in Latin and Greek and passed with distinction the exams necessary to enter the classical curriculum of Cornell University. She arrived in Ithaca in 1875 just as Cornell opened Sage College, its first dormitory for women, and discovered that her preparation qualified her to begin study as a junior. Among her first actions was to write her family and insist that she henceforth be called by her middle name, Carey. Two years later she graduated, having won election to Cornell's newly formed chapter of Phi Beta Kappa.

Carey Thomas's memories of Cornell were mixed. She admired Andrew Dickson White, who took a personal interest in her, and found classes up to her ideals. Yet Quaker rules against dancing, which she still obeyed, restricted her mixing with the largely male student body, and she had only one close female friend. At her graduation she wrote in her journal: "Half the men here are uncultivated and Cornell misses all that glorious culture that one reads about in college books." Even so, Cornell offered her the full use of its educational resources, unlike Johns Hopkins, which admitted her as a graduate student in Greek only because her father was on the board of trustees and only on condition that her instruction be carried out in private tutorials rather than in seminars or lectures.

Seeking a more tolerant attitude in Europe, she again challenged her father and left the Unites States for Germany to study at the University of Leipzig. Her close friend Mamie Gwinn accompanied her. In her three years at Leipzig Thomas was allowed to attend classes and write a thesis—but not to stand for a degree. The University of Göttingen made the same refusal. Finally, in 1882 the faculty of the University of Zürich conferred on her a Ph.D. degree, summa cum laude. To underscore this exceptional occasion, Thomas sat for her three-hour oral examination clad in an evening gown and white gloves.

After a year in Paris Thomas returned to the United States hoping to become the president of Bryn Mawr, a Quaker institution scheduled to open in 1885. Although Bryn Mawr's founder was a family friend, the trustees were not ready to entrust a woman, particularly one in her mid-twenties, with the office. Instead, they named Thomas the dean. In that capacity she worked closely with James Rhoads, Bryn Mawr's first president, to set extremely high standards of admission, to establish the first graduate program in any woman's college, and to recruit a largely male faculty committed to both teaching and scholarship. Thomas herself was a professor of English. In 1894, she became president of Bryn Mawr, a post she held until 1922, almost thirty years.

Thomas was determined that Bryn Mawr not be simply another college for women, with special protections and a special curriculum ("There is no sex in intellect," she said). Under her leadership, Bryn Mawr provided a rigorous education in a physical setting that Thomas hoped would resemble Oxford and Cambridge. Her tenure was not without controversy. The original male trustees, all Quakers, objected to her efforts to give Bryn Mawr a non-Quaker identity. Some of them failed to appreciate her leadership role in becoming virtually the first college president to work for women's suffrage. Faculty members complained about her authoritarian style. To a later generation what is perhaps most disturbing about Thomas is the racism and anti-Semitism that underlay her enthusiasm for the eugenics movement. In 1916 she boasted that Bryn Mawr's student body was "overwhelmingly English, Scotch, Irish, Welsh and other admixtures of French, German, Dutch. . . . All other strains are negligible." To her credit, her attitude, which was shared by virtually all other American university administrators, did not stand in the way of one of her major innovations, a Summer School for Women Workers of Industry.

In her novella *Fernhurst,* Gertrude Stein—who knew both women—suggested that there was a lesbian relationship between Thomas and Mamie Gwinn (Gwinn was Thomas's European traveling companion who lived with Thomas in Bryn Mawr's "Deanery" until 1904). Similar speculation surrounded Thomas's longer relationship with Mary Elizabeth Garrett, the wealthy daughter of the president of the Baltimore and Ohio Railroad who left her estate to Thomas when she died in 1915. Surely, however, Thomas's sexual preferences matter less than the results of her collaborations with men and women. In the early 1890s, for example, she and Garrett played a major role in endowing a medical school at Johns Hopkins, one that was explicitly a graduate program and one that was open to women. This last provision represented Thomas's constructive revenge for the discrimination she had experienced at the Baltimore school. Fittingly, Johns Hopkins conferred on Thomas an honorary doctorate, the first it had given to a woman.

Thomas's life recorded many firsts for women, including her selection as the first woman to serve on the Cornell Board of Trustees. Thomas remained active after her retirement. She called upon her not totally extinguished Quaker heritage to become a leader in the world peace movement and was a finalist for the American Peace Award established by Edward Bok. She traveled widely, finding ways to enter places, such as the Taj Mahal, that were formally forbidden to women; took up smoking; and used her wealth to promote equal opportunities for women. She was an ardent supporter of the Equal Rights Amendment, which was first proposed in 1923. In her last public address, at the celebration marking Bryn Mawr's fiftieth anniversary, Thomas singled out a congratulatory telegram she most cherished. From an alumna, it read: "I have forgotten everything I learned at Bryn Mawr, but I still see you standing in chapel and telling us to believe in women." One month later, on December 2, 1935, Thomas died suddenly at her home in Philadelphia.

Hermann Michael Biggs
❧ CLASS OF 1882

"And Biggs, we are all looking to you," Robert Koch, the German doctor who discovered the tubercle bacillus, proclaimed at an international conference on infectious diseases. "What are you going to do next?" Hailed as the "original antitoxin doctor in America," Hermann Biggs responded with a campaign against tuberculosis that enhanced his reputation as a pioneer in public health.

Hermann Michael Biggs was born on September 29, 1859, in Trumansburg, New York, the son of Joseph Biggs, a hardware and dry goods merchant, and the former Melissa Pratt. Inventive and entrepreneurial, at age fifteen Hermann built and operated a telegraph line between Trumansburg and Taughannock Falls, selling shares in the company he and his friends established. When his father died in 1877, Hermann ran and then liquidated the family business.

Two years later he entered Cornell University in nearby Ithaca. Biggs was so eager to become a doctor that he completed his degree in two and a half years, enrolling in as many as twenty-five credits a semester to make it possible for him to take a leave of absence in the fall of 1881 to study at the Bellevue Hospital Medical College in New York City. Biggs's grades were not always outstanding, perhaps because in addition to his heavy course load he was also an active member of Psi Upsilon fraternity, the organist at his church, a singer in the choir, and an editor of the *Cornell Sun*. His senior thesis, "Sanitary Regulations and the Duty of the State in Regard to Public Hygiene," indicated that he already understood the direction his career would take. Conversant with the contributions of Louis Pasteur and Robert Koch to the bacteriological revolution in medicine, which established germs as the cause of many infectious diseases, Biggs was ready to apply this knowledge in the public administration of the science of hygiene. He received his M.D. in 1883 from Bellevue Hospital

Medical College (New York University), where he was first in a class of 167; spent eighteen months as an intern and resident physician; and then studied bacteriology and microscopic pathology for two years in Germany.

Biggs became director of the newly opened Carnegie Bacteriological Laboratory at Bellevue in 1886, establishing himself as a leader in the application of germ theory to public health and preventive medicine. Asked to investigate an outbreak of typhoid fever in Plymouth, Pennsylvania, Biggs became one of the first physicians in the world to analyze a local water supply for bacterial contamination. He insisted that doctors take cultures to confirm diagnoses of cholera and worked with the New York Quarantine Station to administer tests to incoming immigrants. In 1892, amid fear of a cholera epidemic, Biggs was asked to organize and direct the Division of Pathology, Bacteriology, and Disinfection in the New York City Department of Health. Historians disagree about which city in the United States was the first to develop a bacteriological laboratory, but Biggs's lab was almost certainly the first to test the purity of food and water and use the latest scientific techniques in diagnosing disease.

Biggs maintained his professorial appointment at Bellevue throughout his career, but after 1893 he gave most of his attention to health administration. In 1894, with his colleague William Park, he introduced a vaccine to prevent diphtheria, then a scourge of children, and a year later directed the production of the first serum. Biggs had the foresight to license and sell the antitoxin, and other products, to departments of health, doctors, and hospitals throughout the United States.

In 1901, reform Mayor Seth Low asked Biggs to become health commissioner of New York City. Married for only three years (to Frances Richardson of Hornellsville, New York), with two small children, and already suffering from fatigue and poor health, Biggs declined. But he agreed to serve as "General Medical Officer" for the Department of Health. From 1901 to 1914, arguing that health authorities should resort to any measure that was "designed for the public good" and "beneficent in its effects," Biggs set an example in the administration of public health in New York City that was copied throughout the United States. He engineered the passage of reform legislation through Democratic and Republican administrations, shrugging off charges that regulations were "aggressive tyrannies of the Health Board." When he needed it, Biggs received assistance from Tammany Hall boss Charles F. Murphy, whom he had treated for typhoid fever. With Biggs's leadership, the Department of Health increased its staff from 1,000 to 2,466 between 1902 and 1910. It created new laboratories and hospitals, set standards for the reporting of diseases, disinfection, and milk pasteurization, created a Division of Child Hygiene, offered classes for mothers with babies throughout the city, advanced public awareness with pamphlets and publicity campaigns, provided nurses in schools, and arranged for home visits by doctors and nurses to those unable to afford private care.

Even before he became General Medical Officer, Biggs had devoted considerable attention to eradicating tuberculosis, a major killer of Americans between the ages of twenty and forty. To "rob consumption of its terrors," Biggs pushed for ordinances segregating "recalcitrant" TB patients in hospitals and mandatory notification by doctors of diagnoses of the disease. Since germs were spread through dust and sputum, he advocated factory inspection and antispitting ordinances. Biggs encouraged the use of the acid-fast bacillus smear, which allowed physicians to confirm a TB diagnosis quickly and monitor the progress of the disease. In congratulating Biggs on the smear and the provision of sputum microscopy, Robert Koch observed that in New York "a physician could leave a throat culture at a drug store at his neighborhood at 5 P.M. and be sure of receiving a result at 10 o'clock the next morning." With his associates in the health department, Biggs worked to establish TB clinics and to build facilities for those stricken with the disease where staff would monitor nutrition, rest, cough etiquette, and physical isolation to stop the chain of transmission. Their efforts resulted in the construction of the Otisville Sanitarium for Incipient Cases and the Riverside Hospital for Advanced Cases.

In 1914, after declining appointment three times, Biggs agreed to become commissioner of the New York State Department of Health, which had recently been re-created in accordance with recommendations he had made as chairman of an advisory board. In lobbying the legislature for increased funding, he set as his goal saving twenty-five thousand lives in the state and maintained that "public health is purchasable. Within natural limitations a community can determine its own death rate." In his nine years as commissioner, Biggs led efforts to combat epidemics of infantile paralysis, venereal disease, and influenza. He focused as well on maternal and infant health, the chronic shortage of medical care in rural areas, and the training of public health officials.

During World War I, Biggs took a leave of absence to join the War Relief Commission of the Rockefeller Foundation. He helped the French government develop a public health policy that resulted, after the war, in the creation of the Bureau of Social Hygiene, and he was also a key proponent of the League of Red Cross Societies.

Biggs died of bronchial pneumonia in New York City on June 28, 1923. A year later, he was named the university's "greatest graduate" by a group of Cornellians. "If Cornell had nothing more to show for the millions that have been spent on it than Dr. Biggs," declared Professor Walter F. Willcox, "the money would have been well spent."

Florence Kelley
⟶ CLASS OF 1882

When the social reformer Florence Kelley arrived in Ithaca in the fall of 1876 she was one of the university's first women students. Frail and sickly, she took six years to graduate, a prelude, however, to a career of inestimable power and influence. Years later, U.S. Supreme Court Justice Felix Frankfurter described her as the "woman who had probably the largest single share in shaping the social history of the United States during the first thirty years of this [twentieth] century."

Kelley grew up in an influential Quaker family in Philadelphia. Her father, William, one of the founders of the Republican Party in the 1850s, served fifteen consecutive terms in Congress from 1860 to 1890. She chose Cornell because it was then the only eastern university to accept women. Ezra Cornell and A. D. White wanted a university where anybody could study any subject, but not until 1870, two years before Henry Sage had endowed a college for women, did Cornell enroll its first woman student. When Kelley arrived four years later she was proud, she wrote, to join this "serious self-conscious body of pioneers," which by 1876 totaled seventy-six women. At Cornell she founded the university's first sociopolitical club, the Social Science Club, but even more anticipatory of her life's calling, her senior thesis, written after a two-year leave when she was ill with diphtheria, was titled "Some

Changes in the Legal Status of the Child since Blackstone."

Even though that thesis was published immediately, Kelley's application to the law school of the University of Pennsylvania was rejected because, as an official wrote, he found "abhorrent the thought of young men and women meeting in the classroom." For a while after graduation she taught in a night school for working women in Philadelphia that she had helped start. Then she went to Europe, joining her Cornell friend, M. Carey Thomas, future president of Bryn Mawr, as a graduate student at the University of Zurich, the first European university open to women.

Kelley became an ardent socialist while studying in Zurich where she also married Lazare Wischnewetzky, a Polish-Russian, Jewish medical student. With her husband and a year-old infant, Kelley returned to America in 1886 and the three of them settled in New York City, where Kelley became deeply involved in socialist politics. She had met Friedrich Engels in Europe, and her continued correspondence with him led in 1887 to her translating into English and publishing his *Condition of the Working Class in England in 1844*. Until the 1950s it remained the only English translation of this classic text.

Life in New York was difficult. Two more children came in the late 1880s followed by difficulties with her husband, who became physically abusive as his medical career foundered. Her political comrades kicked Kelley out of the Socialist Labor Party for doctrinal errors detected in the introduction to the Engels book. Kelley, in turn, left her husband and abandoned the theoretical abstractions of European socialism. She resumed her maiden name and moved in 1891 with her three children to Chicago, where she took up residence in Hull-House, the innovative settlement house presided over by Jane Addams. Kelley almost single-handedly changed Hull-House's direction from general philanthropy to, as Addams put it, "interest in the industrial conditions all about us."

In Chicago Kelley turned from the grand theories of socialism to the concrete realities of industrial workers' lives, and in particular to a life-long effort to improve the conditions of the women and children who worked in factories and sweatshops. Her strategy was to master the factual and statistical evidence of industrial exploitation. Emotional revulsion against the harsh inhumanity of factory life was not enough, she believed. Accumulating the factual details, the objective data, was the essential first step in changing society. "Investigate, educate, legislate" was how social reform worked in a democratic society, she

never tired of preaching throughout her long career as a social activist.

Kelly practiced her creed. As a special agent of the Illinois Bureau of Labor Statistics, she visited and interviewed, first at work and then at home, over a thousand Chicago women making sweaters for the garment industry in the early 1890s. She spoke frequently at huge rallies protesting sweatshop conditions, and her report and recommendations were embodied in a bill passed by the Illinois Legislature in 1893 that limited the working hours of women and children to eight a day and prohibited commercial production in tenement houses. For the next several years she served as chief factory inspector for the state of Illinois with a staff of twelve (six of them women, as required by law) that supervised the enforcement of the law.

Kelley headed the Chicago team working for the U.S. Department of Labor in its "Special Investigation of the Slums of Great Cities." She and her investigators visited and collected data from every house, tenement building, and room in Chicago's nineteenth ward, where Hull-House was located. The result was a pathbreaking sociological study, *The Hull-House Maps and Papers* (1895), one of the earliest urban occupational and nationality studies in America.

In Chicago Kelley also found time to study law at Northwestern University. Although she never practiced law, she earned a place in American legal history by working closely with Louis Brandeis, the future Supreme Court justice, then a Boston lawyer, in preparing the famous "Brandeis brief," which established the legal right to use sociological data as evidence in court, most importantly in the case of *Muller v. Oregon* (1908) in which the Supreme Court upheld the constitutionality of state legislation limiting the working hours of women.

Kelley moved to New York City in 1899, accepting the position of general secretary in the New York–based National Consumers League, committed then to seeing that consumer goods were made and sold under proper working conditions. Kelley made the League, which had sixty-four chapters in twenty states, into the country's leading promoter of protective labor legislation for women and children, remaining as its head until her death. From her New York home in Lillian Wald's famous Henry Street Settlement House the hot-tempered Kelley—always dressed in black, with a "flute-like" voice—went out and stumped across America, speaking to governors, congressmen, and trade union women, in lecture halls, factories, and universities, tirelessly advocating the elimination of child labor and the creation of a minimum wage. Her greatest achievement was the passage of the Sheppard-Towner Maternity and Infancy Protection Act in 1921, the first-ever allocation of federal funds to health care, in a program administered by the Children's Bureau to combat infant and maternal mortality.

In the Red Scare that swept across America after the Russian Revolution, Kelley was denounced and dismissed as a socialist. Her tireless and ultimately unsuccessful work for an anti-child-labor amendment to the Constitution led one U.S. senator to smear the proposal as "part of the Engels-Kelley program derived straight from the fundamental *Communist Manifesto* of 1848." Kelley was not silenced. When the conservative Supreme Court ruled unconstitutional one after another of the legislative reforms she had championed, she shot back: "No woman participated in the recent decision. Sooner or later women must be added to the Court. The monopoly of the interpretation and administration of the law by men alone can never again be accepted without protest."

It can be no surprise, then, that Kelley was an ardent champion of women's suffrage. She was also one of the founders in 1909 of the National Association for the Advancement of Colored People (NAACP) and a lifelong friend of W. E. B. DuBois. A pacifist opponent of U.S. entrance into World War I, Kelley was a founder of the Women's International League for Peace and Freedom. In the constant political involvement that was her life, Kelley still raised three children, wrote countless pamphlets and several books, while often giving talks three or four times a day, even as her energy waned in her 70s. She died in 1932, before the New Deal's social legislation enacted the reforms she had fought for all her life. The frail Quaker girl who had come to Cornell because it took women, would be remembered, as one of her mourners put it, as a "guerrilla warrior in the wilderness of industrial wrongs."

Anna Botsford Comstock

❧ CLASS OF 1885

Anna Botsford Comstock followed two careers in her life, one as an assistant to her husband, the distinguished entomologist John Henry Comstock, and one on her own as a woodcut engraver and leader in the field of nature study. The first woman appointed to Cornell's faculty, she was made a full professor only on the eve of her retirement.

Comstock grew up in rural Cattaraugus County, New York, where she was born in

the small town of Otto on September 1, 1854. Her father, Marvin S. Botsford, was a prosperous farmer who eagerly supported his daughter's desire for an education. But Comstock attributed her love of learning to her mother, Phebe Irish Botsford, a woman descended from a long line of Quakers. Because there was no high school in Otto, Anna followed the classical curriculum necessary for university admission at the nearby Chamberlain Institute and Female College, a Methodist school. She was happy with her classes, though she resented efforts to convert her to Methodism. An outstanding student, Anna delivered the salutatorian address to her class in Latin, as was customary.

Anna Botsford was advised to attend the University of Michigan, one of the few coeducational universities in the country and the one closest to home. However, in the spring of 1873, Cornell laid the cornerstone for Sage College, its first women's dormitory, and redeemed Ezra Cornell's pledge to his granddaughter to open his university to both women and men. In 1874, Anna Botsford joined thirty-six other women at Cornell who were housed off campus until Sage opened in 1875. Male students numbered 484 and did little to make the women part of their company.

Miss Botsford, a tall brunette, managed to attract male admirers and was briefly engaged to a classmate in 1875. The "affair," she recalled, "fell by its own weight. It was too emotional to meet the realities of life." Although she majored in modern literature, she took a course in zoology with John Comstock, a man six years older who had graduated from Cornell in 1873 and was made an instructor in entomology with only a bachelor of science degree. They became friends, a relationship that continued when she left Cornell after two years of study. After an engagement of his own unraveled, he came courting at her family home in Otto, and started her interest in illustrating the anatomy of insects. They married in 1878, and the now Anna Comstock found herself back in Ithaca, living in a house on the Cornell campus and providing hospitality for her husband's students and colleagues. She returned to school and received her bachelor of science degree in natural history in 1885.

The Comstocks had no children, and she began to spend time in her husband's laboratory drawing illustrations for his lectures. Her self-taught techniques produced drawings that the French scientist V. A. Signoret described as "magnificent . . . by the hand of a master." Comstock spent many hours looking at insects through a microscope. So that she could illustrate her husband's books, Anna Comstock received instruction in wood engraving from John P. Davis at the Cooper Union in New York. The "superlative accuracy" of her work helped establish the success of John Comstock's books (his *A Manual for the Study of Insects* aptly acknowledged her as "junior author"), but it also established for her an independent reputation. In 1888 she became one of the first four women to be initiated into Sigma Xi, a new national honor society for the sciences. Her work was exhibited at expositions in New Orleans, Chicago, Paris, and Buffalo and won her election to the American Society of Wood-Engravers, the third woman so honored.

Anna Comstock never earned an advanced degree, but then neither did her husband, who became a full professor at Cornell in 1882. An academic opportunity arose for her in 1895 when she was named to the New York Committee for the Promotion of Agriculture. Charged to think of ways to arrest the migration from country to city, the committee recommended that rural children be taught through nature study to appreciate farming. The state legislature appropriated funds for Cornell's College of Agriculture to implement a pilot project. Liberty Hyde Bailey, Cornell's distinguished horticulturist, was named head of the "nature study" movement, but Anna Comstock did much of the work. She prepared leaflets for classroom use, taught nature study during Cornell's summer sessions, and lectured to teachers' institutes on the importance of nature study. She also brought Martha Van Rensselaer to Cornell to start a program to aid women farmers. Thus began Cornell's College of Home Economics.

In 1899 Cornell named Anna Comstock an assistant professor of nature study in the University Extension Division. In 1900, after several trustees objected to the novelty of a woman professor, she was demoted to lecturer. She remained at that rank until Cornell dared again to make her an assistant professor in 1913, withholding further promotion until 1920, two years before she retired from full-time teaching. Now at least she was able to write her own practical manuals for teachers and young students. These included *Ways of the Six-Footed* (1903), *How to Keep Bees* (1905), and *Trees at Leisure* (1916). She also wrote a novel, *Confessions to a Heathen Idol* (1906), which most people regarded as partly autobiographical. Her central character proclaimed, "I give too much of my life away, and to too many people."

Her greatest contribution to nature study came in 1911 when she published her illustrated *Handbook of Nature Study*. Her husband thought the book would not sell, but the Comstock Publishing Company, which the couple had founded with their friend, Professor Simon H. Gage, printed the 900-page book expecting to lose $5,000. That expectation was happily way off the mark. Eventually translated into eight languages, *The Handbook of Nature Study* went through many editions and became the all-time best-seller among books issued by Comstock Publishing Company and the publishing house of which it became a part, Cornell University Press. It has never gone out of print.

Comstock did not confuse nature study with experimental science. Perhaps for that reason she never complained about her lack of academic advancement or about discrimination. In fact, she never worked actively for any women's cause, including the suffrage movement. Her excuse was lack of time. After retirement she continued her professional work, speaking, teaching occasionally, and editing the *Nature-Study Review.* She made regular appearances as a lecturer at Chautauqua. Her husband suffered a severe stroke in 1926, two years before their fiftieth wedding anniversary. It began a period of great sadness for her ("All that came after was merely existence"). The Comstocks had enjoyed a deeply companionate marriage, and she cared for him until she died of cancer on August 24, 1930. He outlived her by seven months.

Although Cornell's alumni body twice refused to elect Comstock to Cornell's board of trustees, she won many honors. The League of Women Voters in 1923 named her and two other Cornell graduates, M. Carey Thomas and Martha Van Rensselaer, to their list of the twelve outstanding women in America. Nearby Hobart College conferred on her an honorary doctorate in 1930. After her death, Cornell named a student residence for her and in 1934 named the building that housed the Department of Entomology for both Comstocks. But perhaps one honor conferred on her in 1988 would have pleased her the most. The National Wildlife Federation inducted her into its Conservation Hall of Fame, where she joined, among others, Henry David Thoreau, John James Audubon, John Muir, and Rachel Carson (who had been deeply influenced by the nature study movement). Nature study always meant for her what we now call ecology, a hope that with proper training "man shall be enabled to enjoy nature through seeing how creatures live rather than watching them die."

Veranus Alva Moore

CLASS OF 1887

Veranus Alva Moore in many ways embodied the American ideal of the self-made man who overcame hardship to enter a career marked by professional distinction and unstinting public service. For over thirty years Cornell was the primary beneficiary of his dedication as Moore built its College of Veterinary Medicine into an institution respected around the world for its pioneering excellence.

Moore was born on April 13, 1859, in Hounsfield, New York. His father, Alva Moore, farmed and worked on the Lehigh Valley Railroad until he died of malaria when Veranus was thirteen years old. His mother, Antoinette Elizabeth Moore, was not in good health, and Veranus Moore interrupted his schooling to do farmwork in order to keep the family, which included three younger brothers, financially afloat. A farm accident suffered when he was fourteen further complicated matters. He stepped on a nail, which, in an era that was only beginning to apply the germ theory of disease, led to a bone infection that partially crippled him for the next ten years. One fortunate consequence of his illness was that, during a stay at Bellevue Hospital in New York City, Moore developed an interest in medicine as a possible career.

Moore was able to return to school and even received a common school teaching certificate in 1880, three years before he graduated from Mexico Academy in his home county of Oswego. The academy's principal, James Gifford, recognized Moore's potential and encouraged him to continue his education. In the fall of 1883, Moore, still using crutches to walk, entered Cornell to study natural history and biological sciences. He financed his education working as a steward for an eating club and with odd jobs for professors. One of his teachers, Professor Simon H. Gage, recommended Moore for a position in the Bureau of Animal Industry (BAI) of the

Department of Agriculture. The BAI, founded in 1884, established America's first laboratory devoted to the study of infectious diseases in livestock. Having completed his Cornell degree requirements early, Moore was able to begin work in Washington, D.C., during the spring term of his senior year. He returned to Ithaca in June 1887 to receive his bachelor of science degree with honors for general excellence.

Moore worked in Washington with two other Cornell graduates, Daniel E. Salmon, who had helped found the BAI, and Theobald Smith, who made a major breakthrough in livestock treatment by discovering the intermediate host in the transmission of Texas fever to cattle. Moore succeeded Smith as chief of the Division of Animal Pathology in 1895. While building his credentials in animal research, Moore enrolled in night classes in Columbian Medical School (now George Washington Medical School) and earned an M.D. degree in 1890. Although he never practiced medicine, he taught histology for a few years at Columbian in addition to his duties at BAI.

By the time he left Washington, Moore had married Mary Louise Slawson and begun with her their family of three children. It was Cornell that drew Moore away from the BAI. The New York State Veterinary College opened at Cornell, and in 1896 its first dean, James Law, invited Moore to join the faculty as professor of comparative pathology, bacteriology, and meat inspection. Moore published a number of important papers and books on the diagnosis of infectious diseases in animals and was especially recognized as an authority on bovine tuberculosis. When Upton Sinclair's novel *The Jungle* created a furor over the unwholesome practices of America's meatpacking industry, President Theodore Roosevelt appointed Moore to a commission that evaluated the effectiveness of new meat inspection laws passed in 1907.

In 1908 Law retired and Moore was named dean of the veterinary college, a post he held for the next twenty-one years. When Moore finally stepped down from his administrative duties in 1929, he had increased the faculty from thirteen to thirty and the number of students per class from 80 to 135. During his tenure as dean, Cornell graduated 550 veterinarians, a substantial proportion of the scientifically trained animal doctors in the country. The college created an experiment station where tests were conducted to find out the cause and cure of disease among animals living under normal farm conditions. Moore also established an ambulatory clinic, which brought large animals to Cornell's hospital for treatment, and a small animal clinic. These were all innovations of immense practical importance. To improve research, Moore added a graduate program to what previously had been an undergraduate major, and also organized departments devoted to specialized areas.

Moore's work on infectious diseases led to his many consulting posts for state and national governments and for the livestock industry. He served as president of the Society of American Bacteriologists in 1910, and during World War I he organized the Veterinary Corps of the U.S. Army. He maintained active membership in many professional associations and was a delegate to the International Veterinary Congress meetings in 1905 and 1930. He was a corresponding member of the Central Veterinary Society of France, and in 1930 became the second American to be elected a fellow of England's Royal College of Veterinary Surgeons.

Moore worked in the first generation of men who organized the science of veterinary medicine, and no one played a more important role in shaping how veterinarians in America were trained. He won many honors, including honorary degrees from the University of Pennsylvania and Syracuse University. However, the outpouring of tributes that followed his death on February 11, 1931, after an abdominal operation, were the result of something more than his professional eminence and his role as a classroom teacher, a role he never abandoned during his long term as dean. Moore was a passionate believer in community service. For twelve years he sat on both Ithaca's board of education and its board of health. As a result, the residents of Ithaca consumed unusually pure milk and safe meat. Moore spent the last two years of his life solving a financial crisis for the Ithaca Memorial Hospital, where he had been a trustee since 1918. He was an officer of Ithaca's First Methodist Church, a director of the Ithaca Savings and Loan Association, and a loyal member of Ithaca's Rotary Club, American Legion, and Masonic lodge. He belonged to a generation that, whatever their national or international fame, put their local reputation first and joined clubs committed to community pride and betterment. His friends and colleagues, in remembering what Moore had accomplished, uniformly stressed what would have mattered most to him: he was a decent and caring human being.

Mario Garcia Menocal

❧ CLASS OF 1888

Mario Garcia Menocal is the only Cornell undergraduate who later became a head of state. Depending on who is telling the story, he was either a national hero of Cuba, a leader who abandoned reform to enrich himself, a republican defender of Cuban autonomy, or an authoritarian toady of American dollar diplomacy. The tumultuous history of Cuba in the twentieth century lends each of these reputations a plausible foundation in fact.

Menocal spent his formative years outside of Cuba. Two years after his birth on December 17, 1866, Cuba's Ten Years War against Spain broke out. His father, Don Gabriel Menocal, had to flee Cuba because of his revolutionary activities. He took his wife and four sons to Mexico, where he settled as a sugar planter. When Mario turned thirteen, he went to the United States for his education, first to the Institute of Chappaqua, New York, then to the Maryland College of Agriculture, and finally, in 1884, to Cornell.

At Cornell Menocal studied civil engineering. He was a member of Bench and Board and Delta Kappa Epsilon. He remained a loyal DEKE throughout his life and once arranged to have its national convention meet in Havana. After receiving his bachelor of science degree from Cornell in 1888, the same year that one of his brothers graduated from the university, Menocal used his engineering skills to help his uncle with a U.S. government study of the feasibility of a canal route through Nicaragua. Three years later he returned to his native country, still under Spanish rule, and worked for a French company and a railroad construction firm.

When Cuba renewed its fight for independence in 1895, Menocal joined the struggle as a lieutenant and gained a reputation as a brilliant strategist. After the United States declared war on Spain in 1898, Menocal rose to the rank of major general in charge of Havana and Matanzas Provinces. He was credited

with heroism in several important battles, including ones at Victoria de las Tunas, with which he was associated all his life, and at Guáimaro, where he braved enemy fire to place a bomb against a cathedral where the Spaniards were garrisoned. One reporter who met him on the battlefield recalled that Menocal interrupted his firing long enough to ask what shows were playing on Broadway—while at Cornell, he had learned to love New York City.

During the American occupation of Cuba, which lasted until 1902, Menocal served the American military government as chief of the Havana police, as inspector of public works, and as chief of the Lighthouse Board. He also made himself a wealthy man by managing the Chaparra sugar plantation for the Cuban American Sugar Company. Under his direction, Chaparra became one of the largest sugar-producing estates in the world. Chaparra also allied Menocal with American capitalists who were pushing aside Europeans as well as Cubans to achieve dominant economic power in Cuba.

The United States granted independence to Cuba in 1902, but under the provisions of the Platt Amendment, which gave the United States the right to intervene in Cuba to assure a stable government that could guarantee life, property, and individual liberty. Predictably, property mattered most to the Americans. Leonard Wood, the American military governor of Santiago during the occupation, defined stability for Cuba as a period when "capital is willing to invest in the island." Menocal, and all other Cubans who entered politics, had to please Washington as well as their countrymen. That would have seemed proper to Menocal's mother who had extracted from her son a promise to put the republic of Cuba firmly under the protection of the United States.

In 1908 Menocal ran unsuccessfully for the presidency on the Conservative Party ticket. In 1912, he ran again, this time on the slogan "Honesty, Peace, and Work," and was elected Cuba's third president. For several years, his administration instituted reforms and could justly claim credit for improvements in education, public health, and agriculture. Menocal established a Cuban monetary system that introduced the Cuban peso. However, when Menocal announced his intention to seek a second term in 1915, things turned sour. He faced accusations of corruption similar to the ones he had used successfully against the previous administration. One critic said that Menocal "had virtually enthroned the greed for money." The 1916 election threw Cuba into crisis, and the opposition Liberals began an armed revolt to protest Menocal's strong-arm tactics to "steal" the election from them. In the end the United States threw its weight behind Menocal's dubious claim of victory at the polls because, in the judgment of the assistant secretary of the navy, Franklin D. Roosevelt, he represented a "continuation of orderly progress." The United States also feared that Menocal's opponents were flirting with Germany. When he was safely settled into his second term in 1917, Menocal repaid his debt to the United States by having Cuba declare war on Germany within twenty-four hours of America's entry into World War I.

Menocal's second term was marked by economic prosperity for Cuba (as well as for American investors whose holdings in Cuba soared between 1910 and 1920) because the price of sugar reached giddy heights. Cuba entered a brief era dubbed "the Dance of the Millions," a dance that abruptly ended in 1920 when sugar prices collapsed and Cuba faced another presidential election. By manipulating the Americans again, Menocal managed to see power handed over to Alfredo Zayas, a

former opponent turned ally. It was a bittersweet victory, however, since Menocal's political circle had in their opportunism largely destroyed the reputation of his Conservative Party. A Conservative would never again sit in the presidential palace. Personally, Menocal had done quite well. His estimated wealth when he left office was $40 million, forty times greater than when he took office, although the collapse of sugar prices reduced a proposed major gift to Cornell to the small sum of $150.

Menocal ran twice more for the presidency—in 1924 and in 1936—but each time he was soundly defeated. He also led an unsuccessful uprising in 1931 to unseat the president, Gerardo Machado. For his part in that affair, Menocal spent six months in jail and then two years in exile in Miami. Despite these setbacks, he remained an influential and respected public figure. He returned to Cuba to found the Democratic Republic Party. On several occasions he was Cornell's delegate to academic ceremonies held at the University of Havana. In 1940 Menocal did two things of considerable importance: He was a delegate to the convention that drafted a new, more democratic constitution for Cuba. And, by joining a political coalition that overwhelmingly elected Fulgencio Batista to the presidency, he became a close advisor to Cuba's new strongman.

Menocal died on September 7, 1941, of liver, kidney, and circulatory ailments. His widow, Mariana Seva, and three children survived him. One of his grandchildren had just entered Cornell. Thousands of Cubans visited the Menocal home and crowded the grounds of the national capitol where his body lay in state. President Batista suspended all amusements and ordered all radio broadcasts to focus on Menocal's achievements. Cuban flags flew at half-mast for nine days. It was a proud time for a remarkable man and his remarkable family. However, Menocal's close association with Batista came back to cloud his reputation. In 1952 Batista, who lost the presidency in the 1944 election, returned to power not in an election but in a coup that suspended the 1940 Constitution that Menocal helped draft. In 1956, Fidel Castro's revolution began in the Sierra Maestra Mountains, and within a few years many men and women who had honored Menocal found themselves living as he once had done, exiled in Miami.

John R. Mott
∾ CLASS OF 1888

The Nobel Peace Prize has been conferred on only one Cornell graduate, John R. Mott, class of 1888. Somewhat ironically, given Cornell's early reputation as a godless institution, Mott won the coveted prize for lifelong dedication to a religious mission that started in Ithaca.

John R. Mott (the middle initial does not stand for anything) was born in Livingston Manor, New York, on May 25, 1865, but the family (John had three sisters) moved to Postville, Iowa, when John was four months old. Mott's father, for whom John was named, prospered in farming and in the retail lumber trade, but it was John's mother, Elmira Dodge Mott, who had the greater influence. She instilled in her son a passion for reading and for Methodism. When John was thirteen, he had his first powerful religious experience at a local revival led by a YMCA agent, evangelist J. W. Dean. Christ stayed with him, as did the YMCA.

After studies at Upper Iowa University, a small Methodist school, Mott arrived in Ithaca at age twenty to pursue his studies at Cornell. Entering as a sophomore, he was greeted by members of the Cornell University Christian Association (CUCA, Cornell's YMCA-affiliated organization) who found him rooms with a "Methodist lady" on Buffalo Street. With majors in history and philosophy Mott excelled as a student and graduated with a Phi Beta Kappa key that he wore for the rest of his life. George Lincoln Burr, Cornell's librarian and a distinguished historian, pushed Mott toward an academic career.

However, Mott's main extracurricular commitment took him in a different direction. He became president of CUCA and led a successful financial campaign for a building to house Cornell's campus YMCA activities. Alfred S. Barnes, a New York publisher, philanthropist, and Cornell trustee, pledged $50,000 to add to the $10,000 already collected on campus. Thus Barnes Hall was constructed, the second building at Cornell after Sage Chapel dedicated to religious work.

Following his sophomore year, Mott attended the first college students' summer school at Mount Hermon organized by the famous revivalist Dwight Moody. There, Mott pledged himself with one hundred other young men to a life of "soul saving" work in foreign missions. Upon his graduation from Cornell he accepted a job as national secretary of the Intercollegiate YMCA. From that moment he held a paid position with the American YMCA until his retirement in 1928. He spent several years crisscrossing the United States promoting "Y" work at American colleges and universities, but he soon returned to the pledge that he had made at Mount Hermon to the field of foreign missions. In the next decades he led, helped found, or otherwise played crucial roles not only in "Y"-sponsored mission programs but also in a myriad of related organizations, including the Student Volunteer Movement for Foreign Missions and the World Student Christian Federation.

Mott titled a book he published in 1900 *The Evangelization of the World in This Generation.* That energetic and optimistic slogan reflected a crest of American Protestant confidence. Mott loved to travel, especially by rail, and logged an average of thirty to forty thousand miles annually by train and ship for more than forty years. By the time he was done, he has crossed the Atlantic over one hundred times and the Pacific fourteen times. His first trip to Europe was in 1891, the same year he married Leila Ada White, his partner in religious work for the next sixty-two years. In 1895 he began his first trip around the world, a journey that kept him abroad until the beginning of 1897. His many subsequent visits to the Holy Land, India, China, the Philippines, Australia, and Japan often made him a stranger to his homes in the United States, first in Oak Park, Illinois, where he lived near but never met Frank Lloyd Wright, and then in Montclair, New Jersey, close to the YMCA national headquarters in New York City. Nonetheless, he and Leila reared four children.

Mott's goal was to extend the kingdom of Christ around the world, but part of his success in building organizations in Europe, Asia, Africa, and South America stemmed from his respect for other religions and a rare "color" blindness in his social relations. In his career, Mott proved himself a genius at rais-

ing money, making lifelong friends of John Rockefeller Jr., Cyrus McCormick, and John Wanamaker. Perhaps his most important backer was Woodrow Wilson, whom Mott met when the future president briefly and unhappily taught at Cornell during Mott's undergraduate days. In 1910, Wilson, then president of Princeton, conferred on Mott an honorary degree as "a new Crusader bent on the Christian conquest of the world." In 1914 President Wilson helped Mott when the newly named general secretary of the YMCA of the United States guided his organization through an extraordinarily ambitious wartime relief program that aided troops on both sides of the conflict until the United States entered the Great War. When war was declared, as chairman of the National War Work Council, Mott offered Wilson the Y's resources for the support of soldiers. Wilson tapped Mott to be part of a diplomatic mission to Mexico in 1916 and also one to Russia led by former Secretary of State Elihu Root in the summer of 1917. The purpose of the latter was to promote democratic leanings in Russia's new Provisional government. Both missions failed.

Mott felt the disappointment that many others shared about the inadequate Treaty of Versailles. His spirits also sagged when the Interchurch World Movement, which had been grandly conceived with Mott's help in 1918, collapsed in 1920. Nonetheless, Mott continued to travel the world and to meet the great leaders of his time. Domestically, and despite his friendship with Wilson, his political tastes ran toward Republicans. He knew Harding, was close to Coolidge, and much preferred Hoover to the Catholic Al Smith and the "wet" Franklin Roosevelt. He was a nonsalaried officer for many ecumenical organizations, and received honors in many countries. He demonstrated his single-minded dedication to missions on more than one occasion when he turned down opportunities that other ambitious men would have seized—for example, the presidency of several colleges, including Oberlin; the deanship of the Yale Divinity School; and the post of American ambassador to China.

In 1946, he shared the Nobel Peace Prize with the Quaker peace activist Emily Green Balch. He was awarded the prize less for his mission to turn the world to Christ than for his efforts to bring all nations together in dialogue, or, as the Nobel committee said of him in Oslo, "his earnest and undiscourageable effort to weave together all nations, all races and all religious communions in friendliness, in fellowship, and in cooperation." At the very least he had helped bring medical care and education to places where it was much needed.

Although Mott was eighty-one when he received the Nobel Peace Prize, he was not yet ready to retire. He went to Germany after World War II to begin a program of reconciliation. In 1948 in Amsterdam he was chosen as the first president of the World Council of Churches. His wife, Leila, died in 1952 and Mott went to India to recover. When he returned to the United States, he married a family friend, Agnes Peter, who had never

married. She traveled with Mott until he died on January 31, 1955. The Swiss theologian Karl Barth had heard Mott speak early in his career and had heard in his impressive oratory "a univeralism quite American." That universalism had in fact left out many things, and Mott, despite his cosmopolitan travels and his willingness to stretch the idea of religious ecumenicalism along lines suggested by the World's Parliament of Religions (which he addressed in Chicago in 1893), never quite overcame the need to measure the progress of the world by American Protestant standards. The mission to convert the world to Christ not only failed but was also discredited. Nonetheless, his energy, his efficiency, his infectious good spirits, and his amazing ability to charm almost anyone left a legacy of an international network of charitable missions. His home institution, the YMCA of the United States, moved in secular directions that Mott detected during his life and tried unsuccessfully to reverse. Even so, the prominence he gave to that organization remains his finest achievement.

William Alanson White

๙ CLASS OF 1889

William Alanson White did not complete high school. Nor did he quite receive his undergraduate degree. But his four years at Cornell prepared him well for a career as an expert on mental health and one of the leading disseminators of psychoanalysis in the United States.

Born in Brooklyn, New York, on January 24, 1870, White was such an inquisitive youngster that his parents, Harriet Augusta Hawley White and Alanson White, dubbed him "the Question Mark." William attended private schools until difficulties in his father's business reduced the family's income. Intent on a college education and a career in medi-

cine, he added two years to his age to be eligible to take an examination for a scholarship to Cornell. White did not do especially well on the exam—he located New York City farther up the Hudson River in the section on geography—but because there were fewer applicants than scholarship spaces allotted to Brooklyn by the New York State legislature, he entered Cornell in the fall of 1885.

White lived in Ithaca on about $5 a week, renting an unheated apartment and often foregoing a meal. During one entire year he spent ten cents on amusement—for a seat in the gallery of a local theater. With his tuition paid by New York State, White earned money to buy books by working in the physiology laboratory of Professor Burt Wilder. A voracious reader, especially in the natural and social sciences and the evolutionary philosophy of Herbert Spencer, White was fascinated by his courses and his teachers. He completed the premedical requirements, and discovered psychology in a course on physiological psychology, one of the first offered in the nation. Jacob Gould Schurman's lectures on Christian ethics and mental philosophy strongly impressed him as well. White's four years at Cornell were "as happy as any period in my life." He took only what interested him and registered for "all the hours they would permit me to." Yet because he never passed a required course in trigonometry, he left Cornell with a rich undergraduate education but without a degree.

In 1889 White entered the Medical School of Long Island College Hospital. He graduated in two years, worked as a house and ambulance surgeon in the Eastern District Hospital in Brooklyn, at the Alms and Workhouse Hospital on Blackwell's Island, and then briefly back at Long Island Hospital. In 1892, at Binghamton State Hospital, an institution housing patients with mania, melancholia, paresis, and paranoia, White found his life's work. A constant presence in the wards as observer, physician, and director of the choir, band, and orchestra, he grew to appreciate the patients as people, concluding that they were "much more like the rest of us than they are different from us." White began to publish, first with papers on the physical basis of insanity (every mental fact, he asserted, has causal antecedents) and the reformation of criminals, and then, with research psychologist Boris Sidis, on the "subconscious"—multiple personality, amnesia, and hypnosis—as well as the language and behavior of patients. With a growing reputation as a scholar and

practitioner, White was appointed by President Theodore Roosevelt in 1903 as superintendent of the Government Hospital for the Insane (later Saint Elizabeth's Hospital) in Washington, D.C.

During White's thirty-four years there, St. Elizabeth's emerged as a leading center for research and training, and for the treatment of mental illness. He established a psychological laboratory in 1907, one of the first of its kind in a mental hospital in this country, and used it to train a generation of psychologists and pathologists, including the later prominent psychologists and psychiatrists Grace Kent, Edward Boring, and Harry Stack Sullivan. Convinced that physical and chemical restraints, in almost all cases, served the interests of the staff and not the patients, White abolished them. To further humanize treatment in a large hospital (in 1903 St. Elizabeth's had 2,300 inmates), White inaugurated staff conferences to review regularly the clinical status of every inmate. He increased the proportion of unlocked wards and built recreational facilities, a cafeteria, and a beauty parlor for patients. White also appointed the first woman physician to the hospital staff and began to assign female nurses to male wards.

Saint Elizabeth's became a model for public and private hospitals throughout the nation. White became a missionary for the reforms he implemented. In 1908 the staff of Saint Elizabeth's began training personnel of the Public Health Service and the Marine Hospital Service to detect mentally ill immigrants on Ellis Island. White's advocacy led to the training of U.S. Army and Navy medical officers in psychiatry and, after World War I, of personnel in the Veterans' Administration as well. While he was superintendent, White became Professor of Psychiatry at Georgetown University, George Washington Medical School, and the medical schools of the U.S. Army and Navy.

During a trip to Europe in 1907 White learned about psychoanalysis and became one of its first and most important champions in the United States. *Outlines of Psychiatry* (1907), the first of his nineteen books, became a standard in the field, with fourteen editions published by 1935. All with New York neurologist Smith Ely Jelliffe, White wrote *Diseases of the Nervous System,* which went through six editions between 1915 and 1935; founded the Nervous and Mental Disease Monograph Series, which made available in English translation the works of Freud and other European analysts; and in 1913 launched the *Psychoanalytic Review,* the first English-language journal on psychoanalysis. White served as president of the American Psychiatric Association, the American Psychoanalytical Association, and the American Psychopathological Association; he helped found and was the first president of the International Congress on Mental Hygiene.

White applied psychiatry to social problems in common-sense, jargon-free lectures, essays, and books. His range was breathtaking: substance abuse, sex education, eugenics and heredity, industrial medicine. He became especially well known for his work in forensic psychiatry because of his testimony for the defense in two spectacular cases: the trial of Harry K. Thaw in 1906 for the murder of architect Stanford White, and the 1924 trial of Richard Loeb and Nathan Leopold for the kidnapping and murder of a fourteen-year-old boy, Bobby Franks. White opposed capital punishment, calling it immoral, ineffective,

and "stupid." In 1933, he argued that racial bias affected the application of the death penalty. Skeptical about the ability of juries to assess insanity, he wished to separate their consideration of the guilt or innocence of a defendant from a judgment about mental competence. White played a key role in calling for, and then drafting, a historic set of guidelines, issued jointly in 1930 by the American Bar Association and the American Psychiatric Association, on the use of psychiatry in courts and prisons.

"A slave to his institution and to his professional goals," according to Smith Ely Jelliffe, White did not marry until 1918, when he was forty-eight. His wife, Lora Purman Thurston, was the widow of a United States senator whose social and political contacts proved enormously helpful to her new husband in 1926 when Congress investigated his management of Saint Elizabeth's. The couple had no children, although White became stepfather to Thurston's daughter. White completed two autobiographies, *Forty Years of Psychiatry* (1933) and *William Alanson White: The Autobiography of a Purpose* (1938), while continuing his work as superintendent, and his advocacy, unconventional at the time, of treating "the organism-as-a-whole," now called holistic medicine. He died, after a short illness, in Washington, D.C., on March 7, 1937.

Ida Henrietta Hyde

⚶ CLASS OF 1891

Ida Henrietta Hyde was almost thirty-four when she received her undergraduate degree from Cornell. By that time she already had encountered many of the obstacles that dog women who wish to pursue a career. Later, when she was a successful physiologist, she remembered her struggles and did what she could to make life easier for future generations of women scientists.

Hyde, born on September 8, 1857, in Davenport, Iowa, was the second daughter of German immigrant parents. Her father, originally named Meyer Heidenheimer, left the family when she was very young. Her mother, Babette Lowenthal Hyde, moved with her children to Chicago, where Ida attended public schools. At age sixteen, she was apprenticed to a millinery establishment and spent seven years as a buyer and sales clerk. The work did not stifle her desire to learn. Seizing every opportunity to read, she credited Alexander von Humboldt's *Views of Nature* with awakening "a longing to learn about the plants, animals, minerals, and stars." She attended night classes at the Chicago Athenaeum, a school for working people, and in 1880 abruptly quit her job to study at Illinois Industrial University, a school her younger brother had attended.

This first attempt at higher education collapsed after one year when the money ran out. No one was encouraging her efforts. She worked for another seven years, this time teaching elementary school in Chicago. Finally, in 1888 she had sufficient savings to enter Cornell. She received her bachelor's degree in 1891 in biological sciences. For her graduate work, she chose Bryn Mawr, a newly founded college for women whose first dean and future president was the notable Cornell graduate, M. Carey Thomas. At Bryn Mawr, Hyde worked with the physiologist Jacques Loeb and the zoologist Thomas Hunt Morgan. Spending summers at the Marine Biological Laboratory at Woods Hole, she pursued research on the embryonic development of jellyfish.

Her research came to the attention of Alexander Goette at the University of Strasbourg. He invited Hyde to come to Germany (Alsace was not then part of France) to work in his lab and finish her doctoral studies. Financed by a fellowship awarded by the Association of Collegiate Alumnae (later renamed the American Association of University Women), she arrived in Strasbourg in 1893 only to find that women could not enroll as students in German universities. In an essay, "Before Women Were Human Beings," she recalled what it was like to be treated as a "cu-

riosity" by German professors and students. Determined to find a German university that would accept her, Hyde entered into complicated negotiations with the University of Heidelberg. She finally gained entrance there as its first woman student. Her troubles were not completely over, because the medical school would not let her take courses in her major field of physiology. Nonetheless, she was awarded a Ph.D. with honors in 1896.

Proud of its graduate, Heidelberg University awarded Hyde support to study the salivary glands of the octopus at its "table" at the Naples Zoological Station. This unusual facility in Italy was founded by Anton Dohrn, a German marine biologist who invited subscribing institutions to pay $500 a year for a "table," actually a small, fully equipped laboratory that they could staff with people of their choosing. So grateful was Hyde for the "generous spirit" and the absence of sex discrimination at the station that she was determined to establish a "table" there for American women scientists. Finding donors to raise the necessary annual fee of $500 was not easy, but Hyde worked with a fund-raising committee and convinced ten universities with large numbers of women students, Cornell among them, to each contribute $50. The Naples Table Association for Promoting Scientific Research for Women existed until 1933 and over the years served as an important research base for nearly forty women.

Professor Dohrn supported Hyde's women's table, partly because he respected her scientific work and partly because he wanted to offer a useful role for women "who do not win in the lottery of life and cannot partake in . . . the highest functions of a woman." Dohrn had in mind the female roles of wife and mother. Hyde, in fact, never married, but she did not share Dohrn's opinion that she had thereby missed something. From 1896 to 1898 she held a fellowship at Radcliffe College. Recommended by the distinguished American physician Henry P.

Bowditch, she became the first female researcher at Harvard Medical School. In 1898 she accepted a position as assistant professor of physiology at the University of Kansas. In 1905, after having become, in 1902, the first woman member of the American Physiological Society, she was made a full professor in Kansas's Department of Physiology and also held an appointment in the university's medical school. She stayed at Kansas until she retired in 1920.

Hyde's work as a scientist took both theoretical and practical directions. She conducted research on circulation, respiration, embryology, and sense organs. She was especially interested in the effects of the environment and nutrition on the nervous system. This interest led to experiments that assessed how drugs, alcohol, and caffeine affected humans. She lectured on public health, including the dangers of sexually transmitted diseases, and set up a program to provide health examinations for Kansas school children. A dedicated teacher, she wrote two widely used textbooks, *Outlines of Experimental Physiology* (1905) and *Laboratory Outlines of Physiology* (1910).

A resolution passed in 1946 by the Federation of Cornell Women's Clubs cited Hyde for the work she did "to open the doors of opportunity for women in the fields of scientific research and science teaching." In addition to the American women's table she promoted in Naples, she also helped set up a research facility for women at the Marine Biological Laboratory at Woods Hole. Out of her own funds, she established a number of scholarships to help women science students. Cornell was a beneficiary of this generosity as were the University of Kansas, Bryn Mawr, and Johns Hopkins. Remembering the important help she had received when she first went to Germany, she endowed the Ida H. Hyde Woman's International Fellowship of the American Association of University Women.

Hyde moved to California in the mid-1920s, first to San Diego and then to Berkeley. She lived quietly for the last twenty years of her life and died on August 22, 1945, just short of her eighty-eighth birthday. Born before the beginning of the Civil War, she lived until the end of World War II. She had been part of many progressive changes in the lives of American women, but at the end of her life an American woman scientist was still a rare thing. Exceptional at the beginning, exceptional at the end, Hyde in her achievements was not typical of the women who went to Cornell in the nineteenth century. But few other American institutions of higher learning could have provided her with the opportunities that made her career possible.

Myron Charles Taylor
❧ CLASS OF 1894

Although Myron Charles Taylor needed only one academic year to get his undergraduate degree at Cornell, he never in his subsequent career as industrialist, banker, and diplomat forgot his alma mater. A generous benefactor of the university, he also served on the Cornell Board of Trustees for twenty-five years.

From his birth on January 18, 1874, until his death eighty-five years later, Taylor was accustomed to great wealth. His father, William Delling Taylor, amassed a fortune in the textile and leather industry and lived with his wife and son in a mansion in Lyons, New York. Taylor's mother, the former Mary Morgan Underhill, and father both traced their families back to colonial America. The son would appropriately become the president of the New York State Genealogical Society from 1931 to 1936 and maintain the family's country home in Locust Valley, Long Island, which had been the site of a farm run by a seventeenth-century forebear. However, if the young Taylor grew up to enjoy the leisured pursuits of the rich—tennis, golf, yachting, world travel—he also led a disciplined, sober life of work and achievement. The family tree was weighted down with Quakers, and their values framed Myron's childhood.

Myron Taylor graduated from Lyons Union School, attended the National Law School in Washington, D.C., for one year, and then transferred to Cornell to complete what was then a two-year undergraduate program in law. He received a bachelor of laws degree in 1894, having studied at Cornell with Charles Evans Hughes, the future Supreme Court justice. When not studying, Taylor sang with the Glee Club. On his twenty-first birthday he was admitted to the New York bar and joined a Manhattan law firm. He married Anabel Stuart Mack in 1906. For over fifty years they enjoyed a close, companionate marriage. They had no children.

Taylor's career in law was brief, for he quickly used his family connections to enter the textile business. He took control of a troubled company, Consolidated Cotton Duck Co., simplified its finances, installed modern equipment, and reorganized it into the highly profitable International Cotton Mills. Taylor's management style exemplified the scientific management principles of another famous but unrelated Taylor of that period, Frederick Winslow Taylor, the industrial efficiency engineer. His next successful venture was the creation of Taylor, Armitage, and Eagles, a company that produced cotton tire cord for automobiles. It earned large profits during the Great War and when Taylor left the business in 1923 he was worth $20 million.

Most of Taylor's enterprises during the 1920s revolved around banking. He served on a number of corporate boards, and in the late 1920s, just before the 1929 stock market crash, he engineered the merger of Guaranty Trust and the National Bank of Commerce to create the largest bank in the United States. Semiretired and on a world cruise with his wife, Taylor could have weathered the Depression in luxurious ease. Instead he was drawn into his most famous business role, as the savior of U.S. Steel. In 1932, with the backing of J. P. Morgan and his close friend George F. Baker (another Cornell benefactor), Taylor, who had become chair of U.S. Steel's finance committee in 1927, was named chairman of the board and chief executive officer. He succeeded Elbert Gary, whose mismanagement of the firm had put it in bad shape even without the Depression. In 1932 U.S. Steel had a shrinking share of a shrinking market and was operating at less than 20 percent capacity.

Taylor, who eschewed publicity and rarely gave interviews, was tagged by the press as "the man nobody knows." But Wall Street noticed his actions. With little fanfare, he wiped out U.S. Steel's $350 million funded debt, spent $500 million on plant improvements, and in the middle of the Depression restored the company to its place at the head of the industry. By 1938, U.S. Steel was operating at 85 percent capacity. Perhaps even more remarkably, Taylor supported the New Deal and broke with the steel industry's historic opposition to trade unionism. No radical, Taylor issued dire warnings about high taxes, but he understood the need for government relief programs during the Depression. He accepted Franklin Roosevelt's request to serve on the Industrial Advisory Committee of the National Recovery Administration and to draw up the NRA's steel industry code. When the Supreme Court struck down that initiative Taylor decided to carry through a key proviso of the code and negotiate with the Steel Workers Organizing Committee. Taylor was a reserved man who was variously described as pompous or aloof. His colleagues remembered him as a poor mixer who wore high, stiff collars and dark suits. Yet none of these traits prevented him from sitting down with John L. Lewis and reaching a collective bargaining agreement with the fiery leader of the Congress of Industrial Organizations (CIO). Taylor pushed a reluctant steel industry into compliance with the Wagner

Act, which ensured the right of workers to bargain collectively.

Taylor's characteristic move was to step down from any venture once he had succeeded. Thus, in 1938 he resigned as chief executive officer of U.S. Steel, retaining only a post on the board. Wall Street pundits thought it likely that Roosevelt would name him ambassador to Great Britain. Instead, in 1939, the president asked him to serve as his personal representative to the Vatican, with the charge of keeping it neutral during the impending war. The United States had had no diplomatic ties to the Vatican since 1867; and Protestant groups, liberal and conservative, predictably attacked the initiative as a violation of the separation of church and state. Roosevelt kept the position a non-ambassadorial one, hence removing the need for Senate confirmation, and deliberately looked for a Protestant. Taylor was now an Episcopalian, having left the Quaker ranks, and knew Italy well. He often vacationed at Schifanoia, his villa in Florence that had belonged to the Medici family, and knew Pope Pius XII. He also knew Mussolini, whose autographed portrait had once adorned his office wall alongside one of Roosevelt. Although Taylor was not allowed entry into Italy from 1942 to 1944, he kept his title and returned to Rome as soon as it fell under the control of the Allies. When Roosevelt died, Truman continued Taylor as a presidential envoy to the Vatican until Taylor stepped down in 1949. American Protestant leaders of the Federal Council of Churches, although recognizing Taylor's effectiveness during the war years, made sure that there was no replacement.

Through these active years Taylor was a patron of the arts, serving as a trustee of the Metropolitan Opera and the Metropolitan Museum of Art, and he made substantial charitable gifts. Cornell's law school became a graduate program in 1925, and Taylor wanted it to have a better home than Boardman Hall. Constructed largely with his money, the Myron Taylor Law School building was dedicated in 1932. Taylor was also interested in promoting interfaith cooperation. He served as chair of Roosevelt's Intergovernmental Committee on Political Refugees, which played a notable, however insufficient, role in helping Jews flee Nazi Germany. For that he received a medal from the *American Hebrew* magazine in 1939. Ties to Jewish and Catholic groups made it natural for him to give Cornell money to build Anabel Taylor Hall, a center for interfaith religious activity completed in 1952 in complementary Gothic style to the adjacent law school building. Taylor also endowed the Cornell Lectureships in International Affairs and in a final bequest gave money to add a residential hall to the law school named for Charles Evans Hughes.

Taylor died at his Manhattan home on May 6, 1959. His wife had died a few months earlier. The obituary in the *New York Times* remarked that "his had been a useful life." It was perhaps a modest tribute but one that would have struck Taylor, who detested hyperbole, as sufficient.

Glenn Scobey Warner

❧ CLASS OF 1894

During the 1920s two coaches and their different game styles dominated American college football—Knute Rockne of Notre Dame and the older Glenn Scobey Warner, better known as Pop. Pop Warner graduated from Cornell's School of Law in 1894 when it was still an undergraduate program. Many years later, during a visit to Cornell, he was introduced as "the inventor of the single wing, the double wing, and Jim Thorpe." It was almost true.

Warner was born in Springville, New York, on April 5, 1871, the son of William Henry Warner and Adeline Scobey Warner. His hometown is now appropriately the site of the Pop Warner Museum, but Warner spent much of his youth on a cattle ranch near Wichita Falls, Texas. That fact perhaps explained Warner's physical bulk, which impressed everyone when he arrived at Cornell in 1892 after graduating from Griffith Institute in Springville. Cornell's football coach noticed the 200-pound six-footer as Warner stood on the sidelines watching a practice session. The coach asked him whether he had ever played football. Warner not only had not played the game but he had never seen it played. No matter. The same inexperience characterized

the players already on the team. Warner was suited up, placed at left guard, and thrust into action on the winning side in a football game against Syracuse the next day.

From his teammates, Warner acquired the nickname "Pop" because at twenty-one he was older than the others. Cornell's newly founded School of Law required only one year of high school and granted degrees after two years of study. Although Warner received his bachelor of laws degree in 1894, he played a third year of Cornell football while enrolled as a graduate student in law during the academic year 1894–95. American college football in those early years was a slow and brutal game. The offensive side massed its players behind the line of scrimmage and charged its opponents with the intention of inflicting as much injury as possible while moving the ball a few yards toward the goal line. It was a game that Warner helped to transform, though not yet. At Cornell, Warner also played baseball, participated in the hammer throw and the shot put, wrestled, and earned heavyweight boxing honors. On graduation, he gained entrance to the New York Bar and for a few brief months hung out a shingle in Buffalo.

Whatever drew him to football coaching, it was not the money. He coached for one summer at Iowa State Agricultural College for $150 and then at the University of Georgia for a weekly salary of $34. Cornell hired him as coach in 1897 for $600 per year. He roomed with Frank Gannett, then writing for the Cornell *Sun,* who later recalled that Warner thought about football twenty-four hours a day. In 1899, when he married Tibb Loraine Smith, his partner until he died, he had scant prospect of being either rich or famous.

The prospect, in fact, diminished in 1899 when Warner became the athletic director and the coach of football, baseball, track, and boxing at Carlisle Indian School in Carlisle, Pennsylvania. Financed by the Bureau of Indian Affairs, Carlisle was a coeducational school with one thousand students and little money to spend on athletic programs. Yet in his years at Carlisle, from 1899 to 1914 (he returned to Cornell in 1904 for two seasons), Warner gained a reputation for innovation that marked the rest of his career. In 1906 the rules of football changed, in part because of President Theodore Roosevelt's criticism of the large number of injuries associated with the sport. Among other things these changes legalized the forward pass and required seven members of the offensive team to be on the line of scrimmage at the beginning of a play.

Warner's inventive mind saw endless possibilities in the new rules, and he had swift, nimble players who moved the game into a new era of faster competition. His teams regularly destroyed the eastern powerhouse teams of Harvard and Yale and in 1907 beat Amos Stagg's strong University of Chicago eleven. The most famous of Warner's players was the twice all-American halfback Jim Thorpe, whose pentathlon and decathlon gold medals in the 1912 Olympics Games in Sweden won him the title "greatest athlete in the world."

Warner was one of the first coaches to use the single-wing attack, although he later became more closely identified with his double-wing formation. The offensive maneuvers he created included the mousetrap play, the screen pass, the reverse play (single and double), fake passes and runs, rolling blocks, and unbalanced lines. He introduced to the game numbered jerseys, dummy scrimmaging, and the three-point "crouch" for linesmen. Not all of Warner's strategies lasted. When he had his players stuff the ball under the jersey of one of their teammates who then carried the ball undetected across the goal line, rule makers saw fit to make the "hidden ball" play illegal. Nor were rule makers happy when Warner tried to confuse his opponents by sewing images of footballs on the jerseys of all his Carlisle players. One way or the other what Warner did set the boundaries for how the game of football came to be played.

At Carlisle, Warner won 109 games, lost 42, and tied 8. However, with the government planning to close the school, Warner decided in 1915 to move to the University of Pittsburgh. His Panthers were undefeated in three consecutive seasons and won thirty-one straight games. In 1923, Warner moved again, this time to Stanford where he coached the all-American fullback Ernie Nevers, the only player Warner placed in the same category of greatness as Thorpe. Beginning in 1925, Warner took Stanford to three consecutive Rose Bowls, although in the first of those contests, Stanford suffered a resounding loss (27–0) to Knute Rockne and his famous backfield, which was dubbed the Notre Dame Four Horsemen.

By the early 1930s, Warner's Stanford teams had won 71 games, lost 17, and tied 8. But the 1932 season was disappointing, and Warner, in a move he later called his worst mistake, accepted the job of head football coach at Temple University. His 1934 Temple team won the Sugar Bowl, but the spotlight had shifted to other football coaches. Warner retired in 1939, after forty-four years as a head football coach, with a career record of 312 wins, 104 losses, and 32 ties. Only Stagg had more victories.

Warner returned to Palo Alto where in retirement he served as an advisory coach to San Jose State College. He had time to paint, one of his lifetime avocations. Warner had never been a flashy man, although the force of his personality struck everyone he influenced.

His personal life was marked by steadiness. He was a staunch Republican and a staunch Methodist. He died of throat cancer on September 7, 1954, having played an enormous role in turning football into a major spectator sport. Pop Warner Football, locally organized in Philadelphia in 1929, is today a national youth organization sponsoring football and cheerleader training for 300,000 kids ranging in age from eight to thirteen.

Warner's male-centered view of athletics recalled the American philosopher William James's call for a moral equivalent of war. "Love of sports" is normal, he said; distaste for athletic competition is abnormal. "The youth who doesn't thrill to the strain of struggle and the joy of victory isn't much of a lad." Football for Warner was quite simply a ritualized expression of the American Creed.

Emily Dunning Barringer

⌘ CLASS OF 1897

Determined that there would be no "free and easy pajama lounging around the house's quarters," doctors and hospital staff petitioned for the revocation of Emily Barringer's appointment as intern. She outlasted and outworked them, becoming the first female ambulance surgeon in the United States.

Emily Dunning Barringer was born on September 27, 1876, in Scarsdale, New York. With a home in the suburbs, and another on East Eighteenth Street, and summer excursions to the family hunting lodge in Saranac Lake, Emily's early years were idyllic. But while she was in her teens her father, John Dunning, a broker, suffered substantial losses that forced him to spend most of his time in Europe recouping the family fortune. Left behind to fend for herself, Frances Gore Lang Dunning took in boarders, while vowing to prepare all of her six children to make a living, if they had to. After witnessing the diffi-

cult birth of her youngest brother, Emily announced that she would be a nurse. Her mother and Mary Putnam Jacobi, a family friend and a prominent physician in New

York City, encouraged her to set her sights on a medical career. "If I had been backed by the U.S. Marines with the Red Cross thrown in for good measure," Emily wrote, "I couldn't have felt more secure in my rear guard."

Having drawn on savings to send her daughter to Miss Brackett's School in Manhattan, Frances Dunning now called on Henry Sage, the founder of the Sage College for Women at Cornell and Emily's heretofore absent great-uncle, to provide financial assistance to send her to Ithaca. Uncle Henry quizzed Emily, determined that she was bright and earnest enough, and offered to pay her tuition. She entered Cornell in 1894.

Though Dunning hustled to graduation in three years, Cornell was a "bubbly champagne-like interval between the difficulties of my childhood and the cares of my professional life." She worked hard, learning microscopy from Professor Simon Gage and bacteriology in the Veterinary College, dissecting pickled embryonic pigs shoulder to shoulder with the boys in introductory biology, and then cutting open animals secured from Professor Burt G. Wilder's "Cat House." She was also a popular and outgoing undergraduate, a member of Kappa Kappa Gamma sorority, and rowed with the first women's crew to venture out in the inlet of Cayuga Lake. She joined the Dramatic and Lyric Clubs, the Sports and Pastimes Association, and served as vice president of her class.

In 1897, Dunning entered the medical college of the New York Infirmary for Women and Children. When Cornell Medical School opened its doors in 1899, she transferred to it along with the rest of the student body. When she graduated, she discovered that public examinations for internships in general hospitals were not open to women, who were expected to take posts in the few institutions willing to reserve spaces for them. Dr. Jacobi's lobbying persuaded the trustees of Mount Sinai to allow Dunning to take "the Hospital Quiz," but on the day of the examination they reneged. Emily took the test, knowing it would do her no good (in 1939 she found out she had

won first place). Then Gouverneur Hospital, a downtown branch of Bellevue and Allied Hospitals, gave her permission to compete for one of four internships, with responsibilities in general medicine, general surgery, and ambulance (emergency) duty. Again she outperformed everyone, and again the position was denied to her, this time by Commissioner of Health John W. Keller, a Tammany appointee, who refused to be responsible "for having a young woman doctor out on that ambulance service break her neck."

Discouraged, Dunning accepted a position in Dr. Jacobi's office. In 1902, however, the reform mayor, Seth Low, pressed by Jacobi and others, persuaded Gouverneur to open the exam to women. Dunning prepared in haste and took the test. Placing fifth on the written exam but with a near perfect score on the oral examination, on January 1, 1903, she became the first female doctor to intern at a New York City hospital.

She prepared meticulously for her work. She installed a portable bathtub in her room when she learned no provision had been made for her to bathe. In an age when stylish women wore full-length dresses that touched the ground, she accepted an offer from V. Ballard and Sons to design a suit for the first woman ambulance surgeon that would attract as little attention as possible. They produced a practical, durable, good-looking outfit: a jacket cut with military simplicity and a simple red cross on the sleeve, and a feminine skirt, as comfortable as bloomers, each with numerous and ample pockets.

The doctors and interns at Gouverneur hazed her mercilessly. On her first night, Dunning was assigned catheterizations on the male surgical ward in the hope that patient protests would end her tenure at the hospital. Then a doctor interrupted her dinner to send her to fix the dressing on a varicose ulcer filled with maggots. Again and again, her "colleagues" conspired to extend her first-call rounds, sometimes to sixty hours, by dispatching her to emergencies. She often had to listen to tenement children from the East Side yelling "Lady Doctor, get a man" as they clung to the back of the horse-drawn carriage. Nonetheless, the grueling ambulance work was an escape. Dunning became a favorite of ambulance drivers, who respected her grit and her skill with patients. She rose through the ranks of the hospital as well, becoming house surgeon in July 1905, six months before she received her diploma. Only then could she contemplate a honeymoon, with Ben Barringer, a urologist, whom she married in 1904, and with whom she would have two children. The couple went to Vienna—where they attended classes in medicine!

When Dr. Barringer returned to New York, she began what would be a long and distinguished career as a gynecologist, specializing in the study of venereal diseases. A member of the gynecological staff at New York Polyclinic Hospital, she also served as attending surgeon at the New York Infirmary for Women and Children. During World War I, Barringer led a fund-raising effort to purchase ambulances for the battle zones of Europe.

After the war, Barringer joined the staff of Kingston Avenue Hospital, where she later became director of gynecology. In 1941 she was elected president of the American Medical Women's Association.

World War II roused Emily Barringer to lead another crusade to extend the rights of women physicians. The armed forces at this time refused to commission female doctors or send them into battle zones, hiring them only as contract surgeons attached to the Women's Army Auxiliary Corps, with no military benefits. As chair of a special committee of the American Medical Women's Association, Barringer lobbied Congress and President Franklin D. Roosevelt to pass legislation giving women the right to obtain appointments in the Army and Navy Medical Corps. She succeeded: In 1943 Roosevelt signed the Sparkman Act, authorizing the U.S. Army and Navy to commission women physicians and surgeons. They were to receive the same benefits as members of the Reserve Officers Corps that had an equivalent grade and length of service.

On April 8, 1961, the physician whom patients called "Dr. Emilee," who had fought prejudice to earn the right to sew up scalps cracked in gang fights in the Bowery and to revive firemen prostrated by smoke inhalation, died in New Milford, Connecticut.

Louis Agassiz Fuertes
∾ CLASS OF 1897

"If the birds of the world were made to select a human being who could best express to mankind the beauty and charm of their forms, their songs, their rhythmic flight, their manners for the heart's delight," said Frank Chapman, curator at the American Museum of Natural History, "they would unquestionably have chosen Louis Fuertes." A first-rate ornithologist, Fuertes was second to none as a painter of birds and small animals.

Louis Agassiz Fuertes was born in Ithaca, New York, on February 7, 1874, the son of Estevan Antonio Fuertes, a native of Puerto

Rico who had recently been appointed professor of civil engineering at Cornell. Before settling on the name of the distinguished Swiss-born, Harvard-based naturalist for his son, Fuertes considered naming him Ezra Cornell. Louis's mother, Mary Stone Perry Fuertes of Troy, New York, was an accomplished pianist who imbued a love of music in her son. By the age of eight, Louis was drawing birds. An original edition of John James Audubon's *Birds of America* that he found in the Ithaca Library was an integral part of his self-styled program of ornithological and artistic education. He described the book as "my daily bread"; his study left him determined to "do justice to the singular beauty of birds."

Educated in the public schools of Ithaca and at a preparatory academy in Switzerland, Fuertes entered the College of Architecture at Cornell in 1893, in accord with his father's wishes that he become an engineer. Drawing and a dizzying array of extracurricular activities, however, engaged him far more than his course work. His grades ranged from 35, 44, and 53 in philosophy, mathematics, and chemistry to 93 in vertebrate zoology and 100 in drawing. A devoted member of Alpha Delta Phi fraternity and a mainstay of the Glee Club, Fuertes was a charter member and president of the Savage Club, and a writer and illustrator for the *Cornellian*, the *Cornell Widow*, and the senior class *Souvenir Book*. He belonged to Sphinx Head, Aleph Samach, Skull and Coffin, Gannonsi, Bench and Board, and Mermaid, and served as chairman of the Junior Promenade Committee. Gregarious and witty, Fuertes won the nickname "Monk" as a tribute to his uncanny imitation of an organ-grinder monkey. On a trip to Washington with the Glee Club, he met the ornithologist Elliott Coues, who told him he had enough talent for a career as a painter of birds. After that first conversation, he "never thought of adopting any other profession."

Fuertes enlisted Professor Liberty Hyde Bailey to persuade his father to allow him to follow his calling as an artist. "Let him go," Bailey told Estevan Fuertes. But it was prob-ably Coues's patronage that did the trick. In 1895, Coues arranged for Fuertes to exhibit fifty of his paintings at the American Ornithologists' Union. Next came a contract from Macmillan to provide 111 illustrations for *Citizen Bird,* a children's book that Coues coauthored with Mabel O. Wright, and a commission to supply four plates for the *Osprey,* a new ornithology magazine. "Never mind your schoolwork," Coues told Fuertes. "What matters is what you are doing for me." Fuertes completed his degree in 1897, with a thesis on the coloration of birds, illustrated with watercolor paintings and with feathers attached to some pages. Professor J. M. Hart gave him a grade of 80.

With his career already launched (he was perhaps the first person without an independent income to make a living painting birds), Fuertes studied with the artist Abbott Thayer, an expert on the optical properties of color and light, at Thayer's summer home in Dublin, New Hampshire. The congenial Fuertes was soon accepted as a beloved and much-admired member of the Thayer family. "It shall come by slow degrees into the irregularly and imperfectly working and fashion-swayed mind of the populace," Abbott's son Gerald, a fine painter in his own right, predicted in 1903, "that you are not only the single living bird painter worthy of the name, but by long odds the greatest that has ever lived."

To see more bird species, Fuertes made a number of forays into the field: a trip to Florida with Thayer in 1898, an expedition to Alaska with the railroad magnate E. H. Harriman in 1899, and research field trips to the Bahamas in 1902, Saskatchewan and Alberta in 1907, the Magdalen Islands off Quebec in 1909, Mexico in 1910, Colombia in 1911 and 1913, and Abyssinia (now Ethiopia) in 1926 and 1927. The copious notes and sketches he made on these expeditions continue to fascinate ornithologists. In 1904, Fuertes married Margaret Sumner of Ithaca. Their honeymoon trip to Jamaica, the bride should have known, became an ornithological expedition, Mrs. Fuertes's first and last.

The couple returned to Ithaca to take up residence in a three-story shingle and clapboard house on the corner of Thurston and Wyckoff avenues, north of Fall Creek gorge and the Cornell campus. There they reared their two children, and Fuertes presided over what Professor William Strunk Jr. called "the best club in town," a mecca to students, Boy Scouts (Fuertes enjoyed leading Troop 4 on field trips), neighborhood kids, professors, aspiring artists, Rotarians, farmers, and friends. Fuertes, his daughter remembered, could paint and talk, paint and listen, or paint and not listen. By this time, Fuertes had won acclaim for illustrations in several bird books, in *The Auk* (the professional journal of the American Ornithologists' Union), and numerous publications of the federal government. The commissions kept coming—for educational leaflets published by the National Audubon Society; for three of Frank Chapman's books: *The Warblers of North America* (1907), *Handbook of Birds of Eastern North America* (1912), and *The Distribution of Bird Life in Colombia* (1917); for illustrations in *National Geographic* to accompany the articles Fuertes wrote; for *The American Museum Journal* and *The Country Gentleman;* for almost every major bird book of the time, whether written for adults or for children, as well as a few books devoted to small animals. Anna Botsford Comstock, whose fame was partly based on her drawings of insects, asked Fuertes to help with numerous nature studies published by the Comstock Publishing Company (later Cornell University Press). A series of collecting cards on the birds of North America sponsored by Arm & Hammer (the baking soda company) helped popularize birdwatching and win public support for conservation.

A painstaking ornithologist, who at his death left a collection of thirty-five hundred exquisitely prepared bird skins and over one thousand field and studio sketches of more than four hundred species of birds, Fuertes also had a remarkable ability to re-create from memory birds he had observed. "His pictures are instinct with life," a contemporary wrote, "and differ from the work of the inexperienced or unsympathetic artist as a living bird differs from a stuffed one." Scientists testified to Fuertes's accurate depiction of anatomy and pose, while artists praised his composition, use of color and light, and attention to background and environment.

On August 22, 1927, as the Fuerteses returned from a trip to Tannersville, New York, to show pictures of Abyssinia to their friends, their car was struck by a southbound Delaware and Hudson express train at a grade crossing. Mrs. Fuertes suffered shock and burns on her left leg. Her husband, who was driving, was killed. An exhibition and sale of his pictures and a memorial service was arranged at Cornell for October. Was there precedent for scheduling a service for someone who was not a member of the faculty (Fuertes turned down an offer of a professorship but lectured in ornithology at Cornell from 1922 until 1927), someone asked Cornell's president, Livingston Farrand. "There is no precedent for Fuertes," Farrand replied.

Isadore G. Mudge

❧ CLASS OF 1897

According to John Waddell, her biographer, Isadore Mudge was "the best known and most influential reference librarian in the history of American librarianship." No person did more than she did to raise the standards of reference collections and reference services.

Isadore Gilbert Mudge was born in Brooklyn, New York, on March 14, 1875, the daughter of Alfred Mudge, a lawyer, and Mary Gilbert Ten Brook Mudge, whose father had been a librarian at the University of Michigan. Unusual for their time in their commitment to an education for all their children, the Mudges sent their two daughters and two sons to college—and into professional careers. Isadore graduated from Adelphi Academy in Brooklyn in 1893. That fall she entered Cornell University, the institution her step-grandfather, Charles K. Adams, had served as president. Serious and studious (she engaged in few extracurricular activities outside of her sorority, Kappa Alpha Theta), Mudge majored in philosophy and was one of three undergraduates elected to Phi Beta Kappa in their junior year. Strongly influenced by George Lincoln Burr, a professor of medieval history, archivist, and rigorous teacher of research methods who was also the Cornell librarian, Mudge decided to become a reference librarian. In 1898 she entered the New York State Library School at Albany, which, under Melvil Dewey, had become the leading institution for library education in the United States. Mudge compiled an outstanding record, including a grade of 100 in reference, and received a bachelor of library science degree, first in her class, in 1900.

With libraries proliferating, librarianship becoming more professionalized, and important positions open to women, it was a good time to enter the field. Mudge was hired immediately by the University of Illinois at Urbana as head reference librarian and instructor in the library school, then under the director-

ship of the "demanding" Katherine Lucinda Sharp, who also had been a stellar student of Dewey's. In three years at Illinois, Mudge did much to develop a comprehensive reference collection, located "where it can be most easily and conveniently consulted," and to train librarians to guide students to make "independent and intelligent" use of it. A confirmed easterner, Mudge became head librarian at Bryn Mawr in 1903. She resigned in 1908, and for the next three years, while teaching part time at the Simmons Library School in Boston, published the first of nearly thirty articles and reviews of reference books in the *Library Journal.* She also worked with William Dawson Johnston, librarian at Columbia University, on a directory of special collections in American libraries; and, with Minnie Earle Sears, her close friend and companion, she completed a *Thackeray Dictionary.* Most important, after the death of Alice Bertha Kroeger in 1909, the American Library Association appointed her editor of the *Guide to the Study and Use of Reference Books,* then the most comprehensive bibliography of reference tools in the field. Mudge had, in fact, conceived of a reference text much earlier. But when, at an American Library Association conference, Alice Kroeger showed Mudge a draft of her proposal for a book, she deferred to her colleague. Mudge completed a supplement to Kroeger's second edition and four editions of her own, published in 1917, 1923, 1929, and 1936 (her last edition contained 3,873 titles in 504 pages). Each one was hailed as a landmark achievement, prompting generations of librarians and library school students to refer to their work with bibliographies and indexes as "mudging."

Mudge had set her "mind on wanting Columbia from the days that I was at Cornell." In 1911 she joined Columbia University's library staff, and her wish was granted. When Nicholas Murray Butler, president of Columbia, found the institution's new librarian "incredibly resourceful" in meeting his bibliographic needs, he became an avid supporter. For her part, Mudge adopted as mottoes for the reference department two of the quotations she had located for Butler: "Verify our title" and "God Almighty hates a quitter." Creating a reference department almost from nothing, Mudge persuaded the president to augment the budget for books and staff. A first-rate reference library, she believed, must have dictionaries, encyclopedias, atlases, biographical dictionaries, books of quotations, statistical abstracts, and manuals from state and national governments. Her philosophy that reference service for every patron was an essential library responsibility—a commonplace idea now but a significant departure from common practice in the early twentieth century—became the norm at Columbia, and in time, throughout the nation. With an almost uncanny ability to assess the needs of students and professors, Mudge coined the phrase "material, mind, and method" to encapsulate the components of effective reference: librarians must know the bibliographical sources (her own pamphlet, *Bibliography,* published in 1915, became a standard work), have intelligence and a good memory, know how to analyze the problem, respond to the questioner, be "approachable," and identify alternative methods if the first suggestion proves inadequate.

In 1927 Mudge added to her duties an associate professorship at the School of Library Service at Columbia. As graduates of the school assumed important positions throughout the country the Mudge Method, articulated in her course "Bibliography and Bibliographical Methods," won national renown. (Margaret Hutchins, one of her protégés, published an article in the *Library Journal* about Mudge's reference methodology.) Mudge also exerted her influence as a member and officer of the American Library Association. She proved to be an articulate supporter of practices such as depository sets of Library of Congress cards, the Union List of Serials, the expansion and refinement of Wilson Services (a publisher of reference annuals), and standardized interlibrary loan policies.

Mudge retired from the Columbia University Library Reference Department in 1941 and from the School of Library Service in 1942. With Minnie Sears she worked to restore a pre-American Revolution carriage house she had purchased in Westchester County, New York. During World War II, she sold the daffodils she set out on the hillside near her beautiful peach orchard to raise money for war relief. Picked with the help of Columbia faculty wives, the daffodils were brought to the campus and sold for twenty-five cents a dozen. One spring fifteen thousand blossoms were sold.

When physical infirmities made it impossible for her to remain in the house in Westchester, she moved to the College Manor Nursing Home in Lutherville, Maryland, where she died on May 16, 1957. The next year the American Library Association established the Isadore Gilbert Mudge Citation, to be bestowed annually on a person who, in the image of Mudge, had made "a distinguished contribution to reference librarianship."

Frank Ernest Gannett

❧ CLASS OF 1898

The newspapers he owned, Frank Gannett insisted, were a "group," not a "chain." Accounting and purchases of large equipment were centralized, and no Gannett paper accepted advertisements for alcohol. But each newspaper developed its own editorial policy and remained responsive to local community concerns. This policy helped Gannett become the largest multiple-newspaper owner in the United States, exceeded in circulation only by Scripps-Howard and Hearst.

Frank Ernest Gannett was born on September 15, 1876, in Bristol, New York, near Rochester. His parents, Joseph Charles Gannett and Maria Brooks Gannett, were farmers and subsequently itinerant hoteliers. Young Frank hustled for a buck, selling newspapers, hawking pictures of the Johnstown Flood to Steuben County farmers, and working as a bookkeeper and assistant bartender. He enjoyed selling newspapers so much that by the time he won a scholarship to Cornell in 1894 he had decided on a career as an editor and publisher.

Gannett brought unusual ambition and enterprise to Ithaca. He waited on tables at Cascadilla, collected clothes for a laundry and pants for a presser, pocketed two dollars each Sunday as an usher at Sage Chapel, and found time to be president of the Debate Club and chief trumpeter for the Cornell Corps of Cadets. During the summers he sold a medical compendium, *The College Physician,* door-to-door. When he graduated in 1898, Gannett had $1,000 in his pocket. Except for Greek, he was also a fine student, specializing in economics, with a senior thesis on the history of insurance legislation in New York State.

A writer and editor for the Cornell *Sun,* Gannett covered President Jacob Gould Schurman, who took long walks with the young man, invited him to his home for hot cocoa, and encouraged him to pursue a career in journalism. Gannett began immediately. He worked as business manager for the *Cornell Era* and the *Cornell Magazine.* In his junior year he became a reporter for the *Ithaca Journal* and the *Syracuse Herald,* covering the campus for $3 a week. He peddled stories to other newspapers as well. Written by him or by Cornell undergraduates whom he hired, they covered everything from Pop Warner's football team to the agricultural experiment station.

After graduating, Gannett took a job with the *Herald* but soon was named chairman of the first Philippine Commission, led by Schurman, which was charged with recommending to President McKinley an appropriate form of government for the territory ceded to the United States at the end of the Spanish-American War. In Manila, the commissioners dubbed the eager Gannett "Can Do." Offered a position with a second Philippine Commission, led by William Howard Taft, at the princely sum of $3,000 a year, Gannett, by this time a staunch antiimperialist, declined. In 1900 he returned to the United States, where a chance encounter on the Cornell campus returned him to newspaper work. Professor Duncan Campbell Lee needed a city editor for the *Ithaca Daily News,* which he had recently purchased. At the *News* Gannett did just about everything: he experimented with type and column heads; he served as managing editor and business manager; and he broke the story on the typhoid epidemic of 1903 when the rival *Ithaca Journal,* afraid of the impact on the community of adverse publicity, downplayed the seriousness of the outbreak. Following a dispute with Lee, Gannett resigned in 1905, working briefly for *Frank Leslie's Illustrated Weekly* and the *Pittsburgh Index.*

In 1906 Gannett realized his dream of owning a newspaper. With Erwin Davenport he acquired the *Elmira Gazette* for $20,000. Within a year the partners engineered a merger with the *Elmira Evening Star* to create the *Elmira Star-Gazette.* In 1912, Gannett became part owner of the *Ithaca Journal.* Although at this time a Democrat, he maintained the *Journal*'s editorial support for the Republican Party. In 1919, the *Journal* and the *Ithaca News* merged to form the *Journal-News.*

With financial support from auto manufacturer John Willys, Gannett and Davenport acquired two Rochester papers in 1918, the *Evening Times* and the *Union and Advertiser.* They merged them into the politically independent *Rochester Times-Union,* and Gannett moved to Rochester as editor. There he met Caroline Werner, daughter of a deceased judge of the New York State Court of Appeals. The couple married in 1920. They had two children. In 1921, Gannett and Davenport gobbled up two afternoon papers in Utica, combining them into the *Utica Observer-Dispatch.* Two years later they established a monopoly in Elmira, with the purchase of the *Elmira Advertiser* and a Sunday paper, the *Elmira Telegram.* For all of their holdings, they formed the Empire State Group, but Gannett soon bought out his partners, establishing the Gannett Company, Inc.

During his career Gannett acquired twenty-seven newspapers but never founded one. His most successful purchases came in New York State. He paid $2 million for the *Albany Knickerbocker Press,* a daily, and the *Albany Evening News;* $4 million for the *Brooklyn Daily Eagle;* and $3.5 million for the *Rochester Democrat and Chronicle,* which also gave him membership in the Associated Press. In 1928, he branched out into Connecticut, paying $5.5 million for the venerable *Hartford Times.* By now a Republican, he permitted the *Times* to continue its support of the Democrats. On two occasions Gannett failed to acquire the *Chicago Daily News,* and his bid for the *Kansas City Star* was also not accepted. In 1927 he bought the *Winston-Salem Sentinal,* but within six months changed his mind and sold the paper. Gannett was also cautious when acquiring other media properties, but did purchase four radio and two television stations during his career. Proud of the independence he granted his papers, he was stung in 1929 by accusations that a creditor, International Paper Company, had sought editorial support for private power companies. Although he denied the allegations, Gannett ended his connection with IPC.

In the 1930s Gannett spent much of his time and some of his money fighting Franklin D. Roosevelt. To oppose the president's plan to add justices to the U.S. Supreme Court in 1937, he founded the Committee to Uphold Constitutional Government. Denounced by Secretary of the Interior Harold Ickes as "mail-order government" (a reference to letters sent to millions of Americans), the committee helped defeat FDR's government reorganization plan in 1938. These activities stoked Gannett's political ambitions. He unsuccessfully sought the Republican nomination for governor of New York in 1938. Two years later he threw his hat in the ring in a quixotic bid for the GOP nomination for president, taking to the air (a promoter of commercial aviation, he wrote *Winging Round the World* in 1947) and the airwaves to make 150 speeches in thirty-eight states. Defeated as well in his bid for the chairmanship of the Republican National Committee in the 1940s, Gannett remained active as an opponent of New Deal and Fair Deal legislation and as a fervent anticommunist and a supporter of the presidential aspirations of Douglas MacArthur and Robert A. Taft. He was also a member of the policy committee of For America, an organization established to combat "super-internationalism and internationalism" and to work for states' rights and "enlightened nationalism."

Gannett turned to philanthropy as well, largely through the Gannett Foundation that he established in 1935. Appointed to the Cornell Board of Trustees in 1926, he never forgot the typhoid epidemic of 1903, when one of every ten Cornell students was taken ill. In 1955 he donated $450,000 to build a student health clinic, which offered "screening" services and treatment for colds, allergies, and athletic injuries. For their work promoting health, higher education, and opportunities for youth in Rochester, Frank and Caroline Gannett received the city's Civic Medal in 1955.

After fracturing his spine in a fall and subsequently suffering a stroke in 1955, Gannett was confined to his bed. He retired as president of his company in 1957 and died in his home on December 3 of that year.

Cornell Comes of Age, 1900–1945

I N APRIL 1940, Carl Becker, a distinguished member of Cornell's history faculty, delivered an address at the celebratory occasion marking the seventy-fifth anniversary of the signing of the university's charter. Becker's lecture, "The Cornell Tradition: Freedom and Responsibility," recalled the moment in 1917 when he first arrived on campus: "There was about the place a refreshing sense of liberation from the prescribed and the insistent, an atmosphere of casual urbanity, a sense of leisurely activity going on, with time enough to admire the view, and another day coming." If there were rules governing what he was supposed to do to earn his meager teacher's salary, no president or dean or department head bothered to enunciate them.

Cornell, on the eve of America's entry into World War I, was not as unstructured as Becker supposed. But it was an astonishingly egalitarian institution where professors and administrators rarely pulled rank and where students who showed the slightest desire to learn found an easy welcome in the offices and the homes of the men and two women who constituted the faculty. Jacob Gould Schurman had been president since 1892 (and would not step down until 1920, after twenty-eight years of service). The number of undergraduate students had passed the five thousand mark, making Cornell the eighth largest university in the United States. Seven years earlier it had been the second largest, but increasing the student population was not Schurman's aim.

More important to him was fulfilling Cornell's commitment to agriculture. When Schurman assumed office, the College of Agriculture enrolled fewer students than any other school or college. Now it enrolled the most. Astutely aided by horticulturist Liberty Hyde Bailey, Schurman had persuaded the New York State legislature to take over its funding. It was rechristened as a state college in 1904 and saw its first three buildings, Stone, Roberts, and East Roberts, open on the north side of what became the Ag Quad. A large auditorium for agriculture, finished with state funds in 1913, bore the name of Professor Bailey who became dean of the college in 1903 and, in ten years time, raised the number of full professors in the college from six to forty-six. From that time until the present, the College of Agriculture has been Cornell's most internationally recognized school.

The Ag Quad early in the twentieth century. (From *Cornell in Pictures,* courtesy Kroch Rare and Manuscript Collections, Cornell University.)

Another development within the College of Agriculture had important consequences for women at Cornell. Martha Van Rensselaer organized some courses in home economics for the wives of farmers. In 1907, despite Schurman's famous outburst that he would have no cooks at Cornell, home economics became a department headed by two women, Van Rensselaer and her colleague Flora Rose, who in 1911 became the first two women at Cornell to be named full professors. The faculty in 1911 solemnly declared itself as "in general" opposed to women professors and then made an exception for home economics. The department, specializing in food and nutrition, gained its own building in 1913, Comstock Hall, complete with a cafeteria that was the most popular eatery on campus. In 1922 a few courses taught in cooperation with Home Economics resulted in a department of hotel management. With generous gifts from Ellsworth M. Statler, who attended the second Hotel Ezra Cornell in 1927, it eventually became independent, the Statler School of Hotel Management. But home economics got that status much faster. In 1925, the College of Home Economics separated from the College of Agriculture and in 1933 moved into Martha Van Rensselaer Hall.

After agriculture, the most numerous group of Cornell students in 1917 were in the College of Arts and Sciences, a new name that had been given to the old Academic Department in 1903. Under Schurman's administration, the elective system inaugurated by President White was reorganized according to a framework that, despite modifications, still exists. All students in the College of Arts and Sciences had to choose courses to meet distributional requirements in mathematics, science, language, philosophy, history, and English and to select in their last two years of study a concentration subject or major. On the east side of the Arts Quad, a small animal husbandry building was incorporated into the much larger Hall of Humanities (later Goldwin Smith Hall), which opened in 1906. In the same year, money given to Cornell by John D. Rockefeller, who was born in the small town of Richford near Ithaca, made possible Rockefeller Hall, which housed the largest and best-equipped physics labs in the United States.

A final bit of institutional rearrangement under Schurman was meant to save the engineering schools from a declining number of students. In 1919 the College of Civil Engineering and the Sibley School of Mechanical Engineering were combined into the College of Engineering. The name had changed but the inadequate facilities of the new college were still crowded into Lincoln, Franklin, and Sibley Halls, whose dome was completed in 1902. In 1921, with new engineering fields being added, Dexter Kimball was named dean and told to restore Cornell's reputation as an engineering school.

Students got used to going to classes on what appeared to be a permanent construction site. Anyone who walked over the suspension bridge and looked down on the power plant hundreds of feet below (a possibility after 1900) knew that they had come to an exceptionally beautiful campus. It was a place for pedestrians even though Cornell posted its first speed limit (ten miles an hour) for automobile traffic in 1911. No one discussed parking. Most students lived off campus, moving in increasing numbers up from the "flats" (despite the activities of Ithaca's prewar movie industry centered there) to find rooms on Eddy Street and College Avenue. Cornell's male social elite lived in grand fraternity buildings, and a smaller number of women resided in the few and much less imposing sorority houses that had come into being. Cornell continued its policy of building student housing for women, adding Prudence Risley Hall to the existing Sage Hall in 1913. It cared less about dormitories for male students although a gift from George Baker in 1914 made possible the construction of the Gothic-inspired Baker Court and Founder's Hall at the foot of the hill that sloped west from the Arts Quad. A special sort of student housing was provided when Lucien L. Nunn donated a residence for the Telluride Association in 1911. Telluride House residents, who include undergraduate and graduate students and a few professors, get free room and board and run the house cooperatively.

Clubs and publications formed in the nineteenth century were joined by many new organizations that represented the diverse student body. Cornell students developed rituals. Architects, for example, decided to celebrate Ithaca's never-arriving spring on St. Patrick's Day each year by building a one-hundred-foot-long snake that they marched around the campus. One important addition to student life was the Cosmopolitan Club, an organization conceived originally to cater to the special social needs of Cornell's foreign students, but that spread to other colleges in the United States as a forum to champion an ideal of humanity that transcended nations and cultures. Cornell's Cosmopolitan Club was an especially attractive haven to an extraordinary group of Chinese students who graduated from Cornell in the first two decades of the twentieth century, despite the racist federal Chinese Exclusion Act.

Prudence Risley Hall. (From *Cornell in Pictures,* courtesy Kroch Rare and Manuscript Collections, Cornell University.)

The Cornell student body was becoming more diverse, but it was not without the problem of discrimination. Women complained about their exclusion from many clubs and honor societies. Social fraternities that had once admitted Jewish students changed their policies once Jews became numerous on campus. In response, Jewish men formed their own fraternity, Zeta Beta Tau, in 1907. By far the worst situation was that of the few African American students, who were excluded from university housing and virtually all social clubs.

Perhaps the most visible change in male student life came when a greater emphasis was placed on intramural and intercollegiate sports. Winters were cold enough to freeze Beebe Lake and occasionally Cayuga Lake as well. Ice hockey was as natural a winter sport as rowing was the rest of the year. Cornell teams excelled in track (Alumni Field opened in 1915 with a track meet), and a Big Red team that won the national championship in 1915 was the first to play in the university's new football stadium (the gift of Jacob Schoellkopf).

In April 1917, Cornell and the rest of the United States went to war with Germany. Cornell had built a drill hall (Barton Hall) in 1914 to accommodate the military training required at land grant schools. But the declaration of war transformed Cornell into a military camp. The faculty in April voted leaves for all students taken into service and degrees for seniors who disappeared before the end of their final term. The university began the fall term in 1917 with 3,859 students in contrast to the 5,264 the previous year. Student life was dormant and

Cornellians practice Manual of Arms in front of Kappa Alpha house in 1917. (From *Cornell in Pictures,* courtesy Kroch Rare and Manuscript Collections, Cornell University.)

patriotism obligatory. By 1918 most of Cornell's programs had been retailored to turn out military officers. Male students wore uniforms and did not protest when the town of Ithaca went "dry" in October. Andrew Dickson White died in 1918, saddened by the unhappy fate of Germany, where he had once served as minister and had been a friend of Kaiser Wilhelm. The names of 270 Cornellians who died in the war are carved into an arcade that connects two Gothic memorial towers that were completed on the West Campus in 1931.

The armistice quickly returned the academic routine to normal and in June 1919 the university celebrated its fiftieth anniversary, a ceremony delayed one year because of the conflict in Europe. A statue of Ezra Cornell, the work of Herman Atkins MacNeil, was unveiled on that occasion. It stood across the Arts Quad from Karl Bitter's statue of White, which was erected in 1915. In 1936 mysterious painted footprints appeared on the path between them, suggesting that the two men met each night in the center of the Quad to discuss Cornell's future. The footprints are still there.

In 1921 Cornell acquired a new president. Livingston Farrand, a medical doctor and anthropologist, former president of the University of Colorado, and most recently head of the American Red Cross, remained a popular campus figure during a term that lasted through 1936. In the 1920s he oversaw the continuous expansion of Cornell's physical plant. A gift from George F. Baker allowed the chemistry department in 1923 to move out of fire-damaged Morse Hall into splendid new facilities just north of Rockefeller Hall. Also in the early 1920s, Leonard Elmhirst, class of 1921, went to the widow of Willard Straight (her notable Cornell husband was a victim of the 1919 flu epidemic) and begged her to make a gift to improve undergraduate life. Dorothy Straight liked Elmhirst and made a substantial donation. They married and she traveled to Ithaca as his wife to attend the opening of Willard Straight Hall in 1925. It was the grandest student center in the United States. A large gift from Allen Balch and his wife, the former Janet Jacks, created a third dormitory for women, the posh Balch Hall, which opened in 1929 on the eve of the stock market crash.

The 1929 crash began a decade of hard times. With one exception, the major buildings erected during the 1930s, and there were not many, were state funded. The exception was the law school, which in 1925 reorganized its curriculum as a three-year graduate program. Myron Taylor, a graduate of the old undergraduate program, provided the university with money to build the hall that bears his name. It opened in 1932.

The natural beauty of the Ithaca area was enhanced during the Depression years by FDR's public works projects, which constructed trails through nearby parks, much of the land the gift of Robert H. Treman, class of 1878. Students had new majors to choose from in music (there had been a university orchestra since 1904), fine arts, speech, drama, and city planning. The Greek system remained strong, although during the 1930s Cornell, like other U.S. colleges, generated a number of radical political clubs. They protested compulsory military drill at Cornell until the end of the 1930s when a new war in Europe abruptly changed world politics. In 1929 the Cornell University Christian Association changed its name to Cornell United Religious Work and admitted Catholics and Jews. And, in another noteworthy change in campus life in the 1930s, James Lynah, the director of Athletics and Physical Education, took the university out of the business of recruiting athletes. This departure from policies that elsewhere lowered admission requirements for athletes paved the way for the creation of the Ivy League after the war.

In 1937, Farrand retired and Edmund Ezra Day became the fifth president of Cornell. With a Ph.D. in economics from Harvard, Day had been a professor and dean of the University of Michigan before becoming director of the social sciences at the Rockefeller Foundation. He brought Cornell a wealth of administrative experience, and he needed all of it. Some critical parts of the university were in bad need of repair. The university library, once among the finest in the country, had fallen far behind in acquisitions. In the 1940s the trustees voted, in an effort to arrest the declining reputation of the College of Engineering, to relocate it to a new quad on the south end of campus. Day had to find money for the huge project. The New York architectural firm of Shreve, Lamb and Harmon (Shreve was a Cornell graduate) prepared plans, but the only building completed during the 1940s was Olin Hall, a radically modern departure from Cornell's other buildings. The attack on Pearl Harbor in December 1941 put a lot of university plans on hold.

Willard Straight Hall is devoted to all student activities other than athletics. (From *Cornell in Pictures,* courtesy Kroch Rare and Manuscript Collections, Cornell University.)

Cornell enrolled over seven thousand students in the 1940–41 academic year. The next year enrollment fell to fewer than five thousand. As had happened in 1917, military courses took over the curriculum. Programs in all of Cornell's colleges, including Home Economics, were redirected to support the war effort. Government money loosened by the war brought some academic benefits to Cornell—funds to encourage certain kinds of scientific research, to improve language training, to build area studies programs. Women students improved their standing simply because they formed a larger percentage of the student body than in the past. In most ways, however, the war disrupted normal student life and Cornell's ability to plot its future.

One thing about Cornell, something noted by Carl Becker in his 1940 address, had not yet changed. "In no other university that I am acquainted with," he said, "does formal authority count for so little in deciding what shall or shall not be done." Cornell did not even have a building to house a central administration until the end of World War II, and when that building (named later for President Day) opened in 1947, it was a drab, graceless structure that was—and is—the least inviting place on campus to enter and to work in. Under Cornell's canopy of democratic informality, students learned that they enjoyed considerable freedom but also that they had an immense responsibility for putting that freedom to good use.

Walter Clark Teagle
CLASS OF 1900

Even as a student Walter Teagle knew a lot about petroleum. He received a grade of 100 in industrial chemistry at Cornell, graduated with a major in chemical engineering in three years, and was asked to stay on as an instructor in petroleum chemistry. His father's advice was emphatic: "Come home at once." Teagle did—to become "the Oil Czar of the World."

Walter Clark Teagle was born into an oil family in Cleveland, Ohio, on May 1, 1878. His father, John Teagle, was one of the independent oilmen John D. Rockefeller disdained as "a lot of pirates." When her husband was not around, Amelia Belle Clark Teagle boasted that her father had been one of Rockefeller's original partners. John Teagle expected his son to enter the family business, dispatching him to Cornell in 1896 to study chemical engineering and requiring him to do manual work at the refinery each summer. Walter read trade journals with intense interest and did brilliant work in classes related to the petroleum industry. But he preferred socializing to studying for his other courses. At Alpha Delta Phi fraternity, the handsome six-foot-two Teagle was known as "Bootie" or "Boots." He was chairman of the Sophomore Cotillion and the Junior Promenade Committees; assistant manager of the baseball and football teams; business manager of the *Cornell Widow;* a member of the banqueting societies, Undine and Bench and Board; and a member of the honor societies Aleph Samach and Quill and Dagger.

Teagle returned to Cleveland in 1899 to work for his father, first as a company chemist and then as a salesman. Within two years Rockefeller's Standard Oil Company judged him an essential asset of his father's company, Scofield, Shurmer & Teagle, which they purchased in a transaction that remained a secret to the public and many SS&T employees. Teagle managed the marketing division of the newly named Republic Oil Company before

the leaders of Standard Oil brought him to New York to work in the export trade department. In 1903 Teagle married Edith Castle Murray, the daughter of a steel manufacturer from Cleveland. She died, apparently of tuberculosis, in 1908. Three years later, he married Rowena Bayliss Lee.

A workaholic with an encyclopedic knowledge of the industry, Teagle had a breathtaking rise to power at Standard Oil. In 1909 he was named to the board of directors. After a 1911 Supreme Court decision declared the company in violation of antitrust law and split it into thirty-four competing companies, Teagle became a vice president and manager of foreign business of Standard Oil of New Jersey as well as president of Standard Oil of Ohio and the West India Oil Company. In 1914 he became president as well of Imperial Oil Company Ltd. and the International Petroleum Company Ltd. (the Canadian affiliates of Jersey Standard). Between 1913 and 1917 refinery production at Imperial rose from four to twenty million barrels. In November 1917 Teagle became president and chief executive officer of Standard Oil of New

Jersey (later known as Jersey Standard). According to his biographer, he was to have a more substantial impact on it than anyone but the senior Rockefeller.

Faced with a series of bitter strikes as he assumed power, Teagle, a master of public relations, became a pioneer in sponsoring the idea of welfare capitalism. In a series of moves designed to head off unionization, Jersey Standard increased wages 10 percent, allowed employee-elected representatives to discuss working conditions with management over dinner, and in 1918 announced a policy of annuities and benefits for employees. In 1925 he instituted an eight-hour day for refinery workers.

As World War I ended, Teagle acted on his conviction that "the real source of power in the oil business is control of production." In 1919 he overruled company lawyers, who predicted that acquiring oil in another state would trigger antitrust action, and purchased a 50 percent stake in Humble Oil and Refining Company of Texas, which owned vast reserves of crude. In the 1920s and 1930s he expanded Jersey Standard's holdings overseas to Sumatra, Colombia, Peru, and Venezuela. With the help of the U.S. State Department, and in a consortium with six other oil companies, Teagle opened Iraq (then known as Mesopotamia) to American development in 1922, the first such venture in the Middle East. In 1934 Jersey and Standard of New York (Socony) ceased competing by creating the Standard-Vacuum Oil Company, and turning over to it all assets east and south of the Suez Canal.

Teagle was not always successful. In failing to secure oil rights in Bahrain, he made what some called a billion-dollar error. He lost an additional $9 million when Jersey Standard purchased the rights to oil fields that had been confiscated by the newly formed Soviet Union. In twenty years as president, however, Teagle increased the company's crude oil production from 128,000 to one million barrels a day, its tanker fleet from 55 to 190, and its assets from $475 million to $1.8 billion. The company's share of world oil production shot up from 2 percent to 11.5 percent.

Teagle also made far-reaching reforms in the administrative structure of Jersey Standard. To ensure the parent company made policy but did not manage, he convinced board members in 1927 to divest Jersey Standard of all operating functions and become solely a holding company. With separate affiliates for manufacturing, marketing, and research, and a coordination and budget department to plan and assess their work, Jersey Standard became a modern multidivisional corporation.

Research, especially in the field of petrochemistry—the development of the by-products and derivatives of petroleum refining—was also high on Teagle's agenda. During the 1920s Jersey Standard and I. G. Farbenindustrie A.G. in Germany agreed to finance joint research in fuel efficiency and quality and in the synthetic production of mineral oils and antiknock agents. In 1930 Jasco Incorporated, of Baton Rouge, Louisiana, was set up as a development corporation for petrochemical products, including synthetic rubber. It was staffed and funded by the two corporations.

A staunch Republican, Teagle played poker with President Harding and was a close friend of President Coolidge. In 1932 Herbert Hoover appointed him to the Federal Reserve Board and as head of the national Share-the-Work movement, an effort to persuade businessmen to stabilize employment by reducing the workweek to forty hours. Teagle answered the call of Franklin D. Roosevelt, a Democrat, as well, serving on the National Industrial Recovery Review Board; the National Labor Relations Board; the Commerce Department's Business Advisory Council; a committee to establish a framework for the Social Security Act, the Advisory Council on Economic Security; and the War Labor Board.

In 1937 Teagle stepped down as president of Jersey Standard, though he remained chairman of the board. In 1942 he was named in two antitrust suits brought against the corporation by the government. Justice Department lawyers had watched him closely since

1928, when, at a conclave in Scotland, he had agreed with Sir John Cadman of Anglo-Persian and Sir Henry W. A. Deterding of Royal Dutch Shell to divide foreign business on the basis of the portion currently held by each company and regulate petroleum output "to conform more closely to requirements of the consuming market." Although Jersey Standard did not implement the agreement out of fear that doing so might trigger government action, Teagle continued to search for ways to limit unbridled competition. According to the Justice Department, the Jersey Standard agreement with I. G. Farben, which remained intact after the German invasion of Poland, enabled Nazi Germany to develop and produce tetraethyl lead (a component of aviation fuel), 100-octane gasoline, toluene, and artificial rubber. Over Teagle's objections, Jersey Standard settled the suits, agreeing to pay $50,000 and release its patents. A Senate committee chaired by Harry Truman refused to let the controversy die, charging the company, and by implication its president, with something approaching treason. In 1942 Teagle retired as board chairman of Jersey Standard and resigned from the government posts to which he had been appointed.

Retirement gave Teagle more time to indulge his passions—hunting on his Georgia plantation, fishing in Canada, and breeding dogs. He turned as well to philanthropy. Through the Walter Clark Teagle Foundation, established in 1944, he supported medical research, religious institutions, and college scholarships for Jersey Standard employees and their children. Teagle maintained strong connections with Cornell. In 1924 he began a thirty-year run as a member of the university's board of trustees. His financial support continued after Walter Jr., his only child, was not admitted as an undergraduate. In 1954 Teagle Hall, a men's sports building with two swimming pools, was dedicated, funded by a $1.5 million gift by Teagle. At the ceremony, he made a brief speech, underscoring his interest in physical exercise and intercollegiate and intramural athletics. As the festivities ended, Teagle rose and with his black cane conducted the band while it played the Alma Mater. Walter Teagle died at his home in Byram, Connecticut, on January 9, 1962.

Willis Haviland Carrier

CLASS OF 1901

Willis Carrier left a legacy that includes the wasting of energy, indoor air pollution, and perhaps the depletion of the ozone layer. But, as historian Marsha Ackerman has noted, few people in the United States choose to forego the comforts made possible by "the father of air-conditioning."

Willis Haviland Carrier was born in Angola, New York, on November 26, 1876. An only child living on a fruit and dairy farm, Carrier amused himself by making up games, which often revolved around mechanics. He learned fractions when his mother, a schoolteacher, cut apples into halves, quarters, and

eighths; listened as an aunt explained atmospheric pressure; and, on more than one occasion, tried to build a perpetual-motion machine. After graduating from Angola Academy in 1894, in the midst of a nationwide depression, Carrier taught at a local school for two years, then completed college entrance requirements at Central High School in Buffalo before entering Cornell as a scholarship student in 1897.

To cover the cost of his room, board, books, and clothing Carrier mowed lawns, tended furnaces, and waited on tables. In his senior year, Carrier and a friend formed a co-operative student laundry agency, one of the first "co-ops" on a university campus, with each entrepreneur pocketing close to a thousand dollars. Carrier also found time to box, run cross-country, and row on the senior class crew team. In 1901, he submitted his senior thesis, "Design and Construction of an Alternating Current Wave-Tracer," and received his degree in electrical engineering. He took a job close to home with the Buffalo Forge Company, a manufacturer of industrial heating equipment.

At Buffalo Forge, Carrier designed draft fans to maximize boiler efficiency as well as equipment for drying lumber and coffee. Recognizing that inaccurate measurements of air pressure, humidity, and heat hampered the efficiency of his firm's products, he persuaded Buffalo Forge to allow him to start an industrial research laboratory. After the company doubled his salary to $20 a week in 1902, Carrier married a Cornell classmate, Edith Claire Seymour. The couple had no children. Edith died in 1912, and a year later, Carrier married Jennie Tifft Martin, with whom he adopted two sons.

Meanwhile, Buffalo Forge had been approached by the Sackett-Wilhelm Lithography and Publishing Company of Brooklyn, which printed *Judge* magazine. Hot or cold weather and high humidity, the publishers complained, caused paper to expand or contract and affected the flow of ink and the rate of drying. Sometimes they had to discard an entire run of the magazine. Using U.S. Weather Bureau

data, Carrier set about designing a system that controlled temperature, humidity, air circulation, and ventilation, while also cleansing the air. In July 1902 he presented his plan for what later would be called "manufactured weather." Two sections of coil were installed in the print shop, one circulating cold artesian well water, the other connected to an ammonia refrigerating compressor. The effect was the equivalent of melting 108,000 pounds of ice in a twenty-four hour day. To maintain 55 percent humidity during the winter months, Carrier added a humidifier, consisting of perforated pipes that circulated low-pressure steam from boilers. On a 0 degree day, eighty-six gallons of moisture would be added every hour to the 20,000 cubic feet of ventilation air brought into the building.

The system worked, but Carrier realized that since air holds less moisture as it gets colder, he could control humidity by saturating air while controlling its temperature. But he needed a mechanism that could handle large quantities of water while producing a fine mist, a fog of chilled water, to cool the air around the mechanism. When W. N. Barnard, one of his engineering professors at Cornell, told him about a nozzle for spraying insecticides, Carrier held the last piece of the puzzle. In 1904, he applied for a patent for an "Apparatus for Treating Air."

Although Stuart Cramer, a North Carolina textile engineer, coined the term "air-conditioning" in 1906, Carrier, with his revolutionary approach to cooling, became, as writer Robert Friedman put it, "the Johnny Icicle planting the seeds of climate control across America": a paper mill in New York in 1906, a pharmaceutical plant in Detroit in 1907, a celluloid-film plant in New Jersey in 1908, a tobacco warehouse in Kentucky in 1909, a candy factory in Milwaukee in 1909, a bakery in Buffalo in 1911.

In 1911, Carrier read a paper at the annual meeting of the American Society of Mechanical Engineers that marked his most important theoretical contribution to the field. His formula for determining the evaporation of moisture was dubbed "the Magna Carta of Psychrometrics," and became the standard for calculations in the air-conditioning industry.

With the onset of World War I, Buffalo Forge decided to concentrate on manufacturing. On July 1, 1915, Carrier and six employees, with capital of $32,600, formed the Carrier Engineering Corporation. By the end of the year, the new company had secured forty contracts.

In the 1920s, with a roaring economy and another invention, Carrier began to promote "air-conditioning for comfort" in hotels, movie theaters, and even private homes. His refrigerating machine, using centrifugal compression and the safe refrigerant dielene, instead of toxic ammonia, marked the first major advance in refrigeration in fifty years. Carrier cooled Grauman's Metropolitan Theatre in Los Angeles, then "stopped them cold" in the Rivoli Theatre in Manhattan, where ticket sales rose more than $100,000 over the previous summer. By 1930, the Carrier Corporation had air-conditioned over three hundred theaters.

As the preeminent air-conditioning company in the country, Carrier was tapped to cool Madison Square Garden, where the ice-skating rink constituted quite a challenge; the engine room of the USS *Wyoming;* and both chambers of Congress, where one wag said there was as much hot air in winter as in summer. In 1939, another Carrier invention, the Conduit Weathermaster System, made it possible to air-condition skyscrapers. With space at a premium, Carrier realized he could use smaller pipes if he sent moisture-controlled air at high speed through narrow ducts. The temperature of the air was regulated through units, placed under the window in each office, that had chilled or warmed water, depending on the season, circulating in their coils. The Conduit Weathermaster allowed architects to seal windows and eliminate air shafts for lighting or ventilation.

Penetrating the residential market proved to be more difficult. In the 1930s few Americans had $1,500 to air-condition their homes, and Carrier's units, such as the "Atmospheric Cabinet," were bulky and balky. Carrier returned to the industrial and commercial market, leaving it to others in the 1950s to introduce a "Model T" air conditioner for the home. But that did not prevent Carrier from describing the air-conditioned life of the future. At any time of year, he predicted in a radio interview in 1936, "the average businessman will rise, pleasantly refreshed, having slept in an air-conditioned room. . . . In fact, the only time he will know anything about heat waves or Arctic blasts will be when he exposes himself to the natural discomforts of [the] out-of-doors."

During World War II, in what he called his greatest engineering achievement, "the chief" designed and installed a wind tunnel to simulate freezing high-altitude conditions for the testing of fighter planes. His system cooled ten million cubic feet of air per minute to minus sixty-seven degrees. Carrier told colleagues and friends that his wind tunnel had shortened the war.

A talented engineer who published 109 articles, mostly on technical subjects, Carrier was also an enthusiastic missionary for air-conditioning who contributed essays to *Good Housekeeping, Popular Mechanics,* and *Scientific American.* A pragmatist—"I fish only for edible fish, and hunt only for edible game, even in the laboratory"—Willis Carrier built a giant corporation, with clients on several continents. He died on October 7, 1950, survived by his third wife, Elizabeth Marsh Wise, whom he had married two years after Jennie Martin died in 1939. In 1999 *U.S. News & World Report* named him one of twenty-five Americans who "shaped the modern era."

Willard Dickerman Straight

❧ CLASS OF 1901

"After designing the marble palaces which will make Cornell a university after his own heart," the prophet for the class of 1901 predicted, "Willard Dickerman Straight will build the most stupendous skyscraper in the New York City, the home of the *Twentieth Century,* the first newspaper to be issued by the Harmsworth Journalism Trust Company. Straight will be appointed editor and artistic director of the new paper; and he will immediately cause the abolition of the old clothes lines which now disgrace the back verandas of the city's tenements." It was an inspired—and not entirely inaccurate—prophecy.

Willard Straight was born in Oswego, New York, on January 31, 1880. When he was six, he lost his father, Henry Straight, an instructor in natural science at Oswego Normal School, to tuberculosis. Emma May Dickerman then took her son to Tokyo, where she taught at a school for girls. There, Willard began his life-long fascination with Asia. When, in 1890, Emma also succumbed to tuberculosis, Willard and his sister Hazel were adopted by Dr. Elvire Rainier and Laura Newkirk, who shared quarters in a "Boston marriage" in Oswego. Dr. Rainier encouraged Willard's artistic inclinations, but when she found the boy stubborn and willful, she sent him to the Bordentown (New Jersey) Military Institute, which delivered on its promise to inculcate in students discipline and a "strong manly character." Straight narrowly missed acceptance by West Point and in 1897 entered Cornell to study architecture.

Devoted to his work, Straight joined all the teams, boards, and clubs open to a poor but socially ambitious young man. A member of Delta Tau Delta fraternity, he lived at the chapter house, where his brothers called him "Izzy"—as in "Is he straight?" Since he showed Victorian restraint in all things, especially sexual, he most certainly was. Straight contributed articles and drawings to the *Cor-*

nell Widow, the student humor magazine, and served as its editor. He also was editor of the *Cornell Era,* the school literary review. He was art editor and editor in chief of the *Cornellian;* member and president of the Savage Club, a town-and-gown dramatic and entertainment society; officer of the senior ball committee; and member of the honor societies, Aleph Samach, Bench and Board, and Sphinx Head. As he gained confidence and social standing at Cornell, Straight was introduced to the world of ideas by history professor H. Morse Stephens, an Englishman and author of a book on the French Revolution. He came to call him "Foster Father." Devoted to Rudyard Kipling, Stephens supported colonialism, British Empire-style. Under his tutelage, Straight became a self-professed "imperialist, confirmed and deep-dyed," though one who desired and worked to prepare each colony for economic and political independence.

After graduation in 1901, Straight returned to Asia, where he remained for most of the next eleven years. He worked first for the Chinese Imperial Maritime Customs Service in Nanking and Peking, as personal aide to its chief, Sir Robert Hart. In 1904, Straight reported on the Russo-Japanese War for Reuters and the Associated Press, and then secured an appointment as American vice-consul in Seoul, Korea. Persuaded that the United States should oppose Japanese expansionism in Asia, he found himself a lonely voice in a government tilting toward Japan. After a short stint as vice-consul in Havana, Straight returned to Asia as consul general in Mukden, Manchuria, where he built a network of contacts among young diplomats and members of the Chinese government, designed to call attention to Japanese violations of Chinese sovereignty. After an incident in which Straight brandished a (unloaded) revolver to throw riotous Japanese soldiers off the property of the consulate, the State Department recalled him to the United States, where he served as chief of the Division of Far Eastern Affairs. There, he saw the deal he had negotiated to establish a U.S.-funded Chinese bank committed to building a Chinese-owned railroad torpedoed by Theodore Roosevelt's administration. Straight tried again to establish such a bank, first as representative of a consortium of interests known as the American Group, whose principal member was J. P. Morgan and Company, and then in 1915 as representative of the American International Corporation of the National City Bank. After the Chinese revolution of 1911 had overthrown the Ch'ing dynasty, Straight urged the United States to deal with military ruler Yuan Shih-kai and then, once Yuan was gone, with the Republic of China. Straight also promoted interest in Asia as president of the American Asiatic Association and by helping to found *Asia* magazine, a popular monthly that grew out of the business-oriented *Journal of the American Asiatic Association*.

Straight believed that American influence in Asia would be strengthened if policy makers viewed politics and business as inseparable. Committed to an Open Door policy—which would give all nations equal commercial rights—in China, he pushed for a U.S. sphere of influence there, and in Manchuria as well. Some historians now view Straight's vision of and advocacy for a systematic program of worldwide investment and market expansion, and his conviction that Japan constituted a threat to U.S. interests in China, as prescient.

In 1911 Straight married Dorothy Whitney, daughter of deceased Wall Street financier William C. Whitney. With the exchange of vows he acquired wealth and power, as well as a wife. The couple had three children. In 1914 the Straights provided the inspiration, much of the planning, and the financial backing for a new political and cultural journal, *The New Republic*. Along with Herbert Croly, who became editor, Willard Straight played an important role in making *The New Republic* a lively and influential journal of liberal thought and opinion. The Straights played a similar, if somewhat less essential, role in establishing the New School for Social Research in New York City, an institution, in Willard's words, "for folks who do things," and, as Dorothy put it, "a sort of N. R. [New Republic] experiment in the educational world."

When the United States entered World War I, Straight joined the American Expeditionary Force as a major. For his work in organizing the War Risk Insurance Bureau, he received the Distinguished Service Medal. From Paris, where he had been assigned to the American peace mission as the war ended, Straight cabled Croly that *The New Republic* must support the League of Nations and press for ongoing support by the United States for the reconstruction of Europe. He died on December 1, 1918, two weeks after the armistice, one of millions of victims of a worldwide influenza epidemic.

A member of the Cornell Board of Trustees for the last five years of his life, Straight stipulated in his will that a portion of his estate be devoted to "the enrichment of human contacts of student life." In 1925, thanks to Dorothy Straight (by then Mrs. Leonard Elmhirst), Willard Straight Hall opened its doors as the Cornell student union. Equipped with a theater, perhaps in homage to Straight's participation in the Savage Club, the building, "to be guided and governed by the students," was designed as a physical environment conducive to the cultivation of friendships between young men and women, students and faculty, and people of all groups, races, and nationalities. "Perhaps it will be possible," Dorothy concluded, speaking for her late husband, "for the students here to hammer out together their social faiths, their religious creeds, their philosophies, their political beliefs, their own roads to freedom. We trust those faiths and fears, those hopes and doubts, may be built into the very bone and structure of this building."

Richmond Harold Shreve

❧ CLASS OF 1902

What do Cornell's Olin Hall, New York's first government-assisted housing projects, and the Empire State Building have in common? The answer is Richmond Harold Shreve, who graduated from Cornell's College of Architecture in 1902 and rose to national prominence as an architect whose firm combined elegant design with an unmatched reputation for efficiency.

Shreve was born in Cornwallis, Nova Scotia, on June 25, 1877. His father, also named Richmond, became dean of the Cathedral of Quebec, Church of England, but in 1885 moved his family (Shreve's mother was the former Mary Catherine Hocken) to Albany, New York. When Shreve became a naturalized U.S. citizen in 1906, after his graduation from Cornell, he quite naturally shifted his religious affiliation to the Episcopal Church. Like his religious identification, his politics never wavered throughout his adult life. He was a Republican, even if some of his most famous projects grew from public funding provided by the New Deal.

At Cornell Shreve won election to the honor societies Aleph Samach and Sphinx Head. He also was president of his sophomore class, managing editor of the *Cornell Widow*, and chairman of the senior ball committee. Following his graduation in 1902, he served on the faculty of the College of Architecture for four years while pursuing graduate studies in structural engineering. In that interval he became a local associate of the New York firm of Carrère and Hastings, which designed both Goldwin Smith Hall and Rockefeller Hall on the Cornell campus. Shreve's supervision of the construction of Goldwin Smith won high praise and also a job with Carrère and Hastings. In 1906, when he left Ithaca for New York City, he married Ruth Bentley, a Cornell classmate. In their long marriage, they had three sons, all of whom graduated from Cornell.

Both Carrère and Hastings had trained at the École des Beaux Arts in Paris, and their designs, most notably the New York Public Library, reflected that background. Carrère died in an automobile accident in 1911, and Hastings retired in 1920. Shreve and William Frederick Lamb, who had joined Carrère and Hastings a few years after Shreve, remained the senior architects in the firm until 1924 when they formed an independent partnership. In 1929 they gained a third partner, Loomis Harmon. Shreve, Lamb, and Harmon divided responsibilities. Lamb and Harmon did the design work, and Shreve managed the business and the production schedules for the firm's projects.

Shreve (or R. H.) was also the most publicly visible of the three partners. From 1927 until 1929, he was president of the New York Building Congress, an organization of all members of the building trades. Shreve's understanding of all the things that determined a successful building project—real estate, labor, engineering, cost—made him uniquely suited to supervise large construction. His firm's work on the General Motors building at Columbus Circle won the admiration of John J. Raskob, who had been a vice president of General Motors. In 1929 he was working with Al Smith, New York's former governor and presidential candidate who had lost to Herbert Hoover in 1928, to build the world's tallest office building. Raskob had the money connections and Smith the political connections. Both were Irish Catholic.

Shreve, Lamb & Harmon were retained as architects for the Empire State Building on September 9, 1929. One of their charges was to build something higher than Walter Chrysler's building, which was under construction and had already reached sixty-eight out of an eventual seventy-seven floors above Forty-second Street. Demolition of the Waldorf-Astoria Hotel located on the Fifth Avenue site of the Raskob/Smith venture began almost immediately, and excavation for the foundation of the Empire State Building was set for January 1930. Construction upward began in March 1930 at the unprecedented rate of four and a half stories a week, and the building opened on May 1, 1931. It was a feat of construction efficiency that would have astonished the most optimistic exponent of Frederick Winslow Taylor's principles of scientific management. Shreve thought of the project as a "great assembly line—only the assembly line did the moving; the finished product stayed in place." Quite aside from the speed of its construction, the Empire State Building redefined the aesthetics of skyscraper design and became for a long time the most famous construction of the twentieth century. Neither neo-Gothic nor neoclassical, utterly non-Bauhaus and only partly Art Deco, the building defied categories. Originally projected for eighty, then eighty-five, stories, the architects added a dirigible-mooring tower that pushed the final structure up another sixteen floors. From a practical standpoint the never-used mooring tower was a terrible mistake, but it nonetheless proved to be an aesthetic triumph.

Shreve always said that he left the design of buildings to Lamb, but in fact some of his specifications for the Empire State Building—for example, the narrow-silled windows and the use of limestone on the façade—were responsible for the startling visual success of the project. It made little difference that his suggestions were meant to lower costs and increase the speed of construction. The structural engineer was H. G. Balcom, an 1897 graduate of Cornell. Starrett Brothers and Elken were the general contractors. Everyone associated with the project praised Shreve's ability to organize them as a team. The Empire State Building won universal acclaim even though its managers now had to lease a huge building that was conceived just before the stock market crash of 1929 and finished as the Great Depression took hold. Many of the construction workers on the Empire State Building, who were so memorably recorded by the camera of Lewis Hine, left the project to join breadlines.

For the rest of the 1930s, American architects, if they worked at all, worked mostly on small projects. The exceptions were the projects backed by government money. In 1933, Mayor Fiorello La Guardia appointed Shreve director of the slum clearance committee of New York, which drafted the legislation for the New York City Housing Authority. Despite his Republican Party affiliation, Shreve called on the national government to subsidize the construction of new housing designed by private architectural firms. He acted as chief architect for the design and construction of the Williamsburg housing project in Brooklyn and the Vladeck housing project in Manhattan, both for low-income families. He also placed his stamp on the massive, privately funded Parkchester project in the Bronx, an apartment complex for 40,000 people on a landscaped site of 130 acres. Buildings covered less than a third of the land. The rest was devoted to recreational areas, gardens, sports facilities, and roads. These projects set the standards for urban renewal programs for the next generation.

By the end of the 1930s Shreve had received the highest awards of his profession, including election to the American Institute of Architects and a Gold Medal from the New York chapter. He was one of seven architects and engineers named to the Board of Design responsible for the plan of New York's World's Fair of 1939. From 1941 to 1943 he was president of the American Institute of Architects.

In 1937 Shreve's alma mater asked his firm to plan a new set of buildings to house its engineering facilities in Ithaca. In 1941 Shreve, Lamb & Harmon designed Olin Hall and subsequently Kimball and Thurston Halls. Shreve, however, was nearing the end of his life. He became seriously ill in 1945 and died in Hastings-on-Hudson, New York, on September 10, 1946. Shreve, Lamb & Harmon continued as an architectural firm into the 1970s and then dissolved. During the firm's existence, it provided a fellowship for an outstanding graduate of Cornell's College of Architecture to work there for one year. Shreve established the fellowship in 1929 to ensure that future generations of architects would understand architectural design not merely as something that struck other architects as beautiful but that would please their clients and the countless numbers of people who would live and work in the gigantic constructions of modern urban America.

Arthur Garfield Dove

CLASS OF 1903

Born in Canandaigua, New York, on August 2, 1880, Arthur Garfield Dove was named by his father, William George Dove, an affluent brick maker and building contractor, after the Republican presidential and vice presidential candidates in that election year, James Garfield and Chester A. Arthur. Thirty years later this scion of bourgeois, rural America emerged as the boldest American exemplar of nonrepresentational painting. The trajectory from small-town boy to artistic radical was not an obvious one, although Dove's art,

along with everything else about his life, reflected a responsiveness to nature rooted in his youth.

In 1882 Dove's family (his mother's maiden name was Anna Elizabeth Chipps) moved to the town of Geneva on the shores of Seneca Lake. A sister died in infancy, and Dove remained an only child until he was twelve. In 1892, the year his brother was born, Arthur resigned from the Presbyterian Church because of a dispute with the minister over whether the agnostic views of Robert Ingersoll deserved a hearing. This rebellious act perhaps reflected the influence of Newton Weatherly, an eccentric neighbor with a passionate interest in natural history. Weatherly took Dove on hikes, taught him to hunt and fish, and educated him in the ways of farming. He also brought Dove his first canvases for painting. Later, Dove said of his talent, "I can claim no background except perhaps the woods, running streams, hunting, fishing, camping, the sky."

After Dove graduated from Auburn High School, he spent two years at Hobart, the local college, and then transferred to Cornell, where he graduated in 1903. His father insisted that he study law, but Dove was more interested in the art lessons he took from Charles Wellington Furlong, a magazine illustrator and an instructor in industrial drawing in Cornell's School of Mechanical Engineering. Dove did illustrations for the 1902 *Cornell Yearbook,* although, when he graduated a year later, the only notation by his name was membership in the Sigma Phi fraternity. Dove carried his portfolio to New York City and found lucrative employment doing illustrations for America's leading magazines. In 1904 he married Florence Dorsey, his hometown sweetheart. She tolerantly accepted Dove's decision to renounce commercial drawing for serious painting. Early in 1908, with a small amount of savings, the couple headed for France.

In Paris Dove met a group of young American artists who, like Gertrude Stein, had fled the United States in search of creative inspiration. The group included Jo Davidson, Max Weber, Arthur B. Carles Jr., and Alfred Maurer. Maurer, who was studying with Matisse, became Dove's best friend and guide in the revolutionary art world of early twentieth-century Paris. Picasso had just exhibited "Les Demoiselles d'Avignon," and Dove absorbed influences from the French impressionists,

Cézanne, cubism, and the Fauves. His work was good enough to be exhibited at the Salon d'automne in 1908 and 1909. Dove actually spent little time in Paris, preferring to paint in a small village in the south of France, Cagnes-sur-mer.

In the latter part of 1909 Dove and his wife returned to New York City where he reluctantly resumed work as an illustrator. Except for the opportunity it provided for him to visit the Museum of Natural History where he could examine the structure and coloring of butterfly wings, leaves, and tree bark, Dove hated Manhattan. However, in the city he transformed his approach to painting. Carrying a letter of introduction from Maurer, Dove met Alfred Stieglitz, the great photographer and America's leading exponent of artistic modernism. Stieglitz presided over New York's best-known salon of experimental art, Gallery 291 in Greenwich Village. He instantly saw genius in Dove's work and became his lifelong friend and sponsor. Only two other American painters received such a sustained blessing from Stieglitz, John Marin and Stieglitz's second wife, Georgia O'Keeffe. In 1910, Stieglitz included Dove's still life *The Lobster* in a show of "Younger American Artists." More importantly, in the same year Dove painted six small oils that he called "Abstractions 1 through 6." In so doing, he became the first American to paint nonrepresentational canvases. He never retreated from that style, even with the resurgence of realism in the 1920s and 1930s.

Dove's turn toward abstraction drew comparison with a similar and almost simultaneous turn in the work of Wassily Kandinsky, the Russian born-artist then living in Germany. However, the differences were marked. Kandinsky sought to paint the inner feelings of the artist, whereas Dove's canvases grew from the painter's experience with nature. Though abstract, they usually had some recognizable reference to the visual world. Over the years, Dove's manner of nonrepresentation changed but not his underlying philosophy. He used color and form to reveal the "shy" interior life of things, from cows to pastures to sunrises to ships. His paintings went beyond French modernism but also referred back to the landscapes of the American Hudson River School.

Dove's wife gave birth to a son in 1910, and Dove moved his family from New York to Westport, Connecticut. To make his living he turned to chicken farming and lobster fishing. Stieglitz continued as his sponsor, giving him his first one-man show at Gallery 291 in 1912. But for the next ten years the hard work of feeding his family left Dove with little time to paint. His father refused to help him, telling Stieglitz, "I won't encourage this madness."

Dove never solved the problem of financial security, but in 1920 he met a soul mate, Helen Torr, a painter and who lived in Westport with her husband. Leaving their spouses, he and "Reds" (Torr's nickname because of the color of her hair) took up residence on a houseboat on the Harlem River next to Manhattan Island. In 1923 they bought a forty-two-foot yawl, the *Mona,* where they lived for seven years, cruising Long Island Sound and docking at Halesite. The five-foot six-inch ceiling on the *Mona* made standing at an easel difficult, but Dove's love of the sea compensated for the cramped living conditions. During the 1920s, Dove reenergized his career, painting oils as well as pastels and watercolors. He also created some marvelously witty collages.

Stieglitz closed Gallery 291 during World War I but opened the Intimate Gallery in 1925 and An American Place in 1929. Every year until his death Dove exhibited with Stieglitz. Dove found another important sponsor in Duncan Phillips, who in 1921 opened in Washington, D.C. the first contemporary art museum in America. Phillips bought his first Dove painting in 1926 and after 1930 paid Dove a small yearly stipend, never more than $1,000, in exchange for his choice of paintings in Dove's exhibitions. It wasn't much, but it allowed Dove to refuse an offer to work for the Federal Art Project in the mid-1930s.

Florence Dorsey had refused to divorce Dove, but her death in 1929 permitted Dove to marry Torr in 1932. In 1933, his mother's death forced Dove back to Geneva where he worked with his brother to settle the estate. He disliked Geneva ("Everyone in Geneva is dead or dying or just walking around"), but stayed there until 1938 because no one wanted to buy the family's property during the Depression. Finally, he and Helen moved back to Long Island, to Centerport, where they lived in what had once been a one-room post office. Dove liked it because the land jutted out into Long Island Sound.

After 1940, Dove's health failed. He suffered through pneumonia, a heart attack, and a kidney malfunction. Though a semi-invalid, his art entered a new and final period of creativity. Stieglitz died in 1946, shortly after exhibiting Dove for the last time, and Dove suffered a fatal stroke only a few months later, on November 23. Georgia O'Keeffe said simply of his work: "Dove is the only American painter who is of the earth." A Long Island fisherman who often sailed with Dove best summed up the character of this quiet, unpretentious, and luminous painter: "For with Dove people come into more contact with the reality of the water beneath and the wind around . . . not through anything he said, simply through his presence."

Willis Ray Gregg

⚓ CLASS OF 1903

"Weather is bad," Willis Gregg insisted, "only when it catches you unaware and unprepared." With accurate forecasting, "tomorrow will be always fair—and you'll live longer to enjoy it." As America's "Number One Weather Man," Gregg brought scientific meteorology to farmers and fliers.

The son of Willis Perry Gregg and Jennie Ray Gregg, Willis Ray Gregg was born on a farm on January 4, 1880, in Phoenix, New York, the "lake effect" snow capital of the United States. When he entered Cornell's College of Arts and Sciences, Willis was already interested in a career as a scientist. A member of the Geological Society at the university, he also joined the Jacob Gould Schurman Debate Club. Soon after his graduation in 1903, Gregg got a job with the United States Weather Bureau in Grand Rapids, Michigan, as assistant observer. He moved slowly up the ranks, with service at Cheyenne, Wyoming, and Mount Weather Observatory in Virginia, which was then the Weather Bureau's research headquarters. Under the supervision of physicist William R. Blair, Gregg designed experiments, using kites and balloons to examine the upper atmosphere. He charted air masses as they brushed and collided or, as "fronts," moved their quarrels to the next county. By compiling the only continuous survey of aerological data in the Weather Bureau, Gregg gained a reputation for "knowing his weather from the ground up," particularly way up. When the Bureau established an aerology section in 1914, Gregg came to Washington, D.C., as assistant chief under Blair. That same year he married Mary Chamberlayne Wall. The couple later adopted a daughter.

Gregg became head of the Aerological Division in 1917, remaining there until 1934. Assuming leadership at a critical moment in the history of aviation, Gregg established meteorology as an essential tool for military and commercial pilots. When the United States entered World War I in 1917, the U.S. Army provided funds to the Aerological Division for upper atmosphere research but not for additional kite and balloon stations. Gregg helped the Army design searchlights for antiaircraft defense. He assisted pilots on several historic flights. He served as special meteorological advisor at Trepassey, Newfoundland, for the transatlantic flight of three U.S. Navy seaplanes, one of which reached Portugal in 1919. He worked in a similar capacity in Mineola, New York, when the British dirigible R-34 crossed the ocean in the other direction.

Gregg became a skilled bureaucrat, lobbying his colleagues at the Weather Bureau and members of Congress to increase appropriations for research and additional weather stations. By the mid-1920s the Aerological Division provided weather forecasts for airmail flights every night. Gregg's publications established him as an expert on meteorology and aviation. He contributed chapters on atmospheric temperature and pressure to *Introductory Meteorology* (1918), an instructional manual for the Army Training Corps. *An Aerological Survey of the United States* (part 1, 1922; part 2, 1926) and *Aeronautical Meteorology* (1925) became classics in the field. In 1926, with the Air Commerce Act, Congress made the U.S. Weather Bureau officially responsible for providing meteorological information to civil and military aviators. By 1934 the Aerological Division was the largest department in the Bureau.

In 1934, following the retirement of Charles Marvin, Gregg was appointed chief of the Weather Bureau. Although the agency's budget had been cut significantly because of the Depression, he vastly improved weather warning systems. Agreeing with a presidential science advisory board that the hurricane program was "sadly sketchy," Gregg secured congressional funding to increase the number of daily observations from two to four; to install a teletype network connected to fifteen coastal cities to ensure twenty-four hour operation; and to establish warning centers in Jacksonville, New Orleans, and San Juan, Puerto Rico, to supplement the center in Washington, D.C. Acknowledging that the flood predictions supplied by the Bureau were "woeful," Gregg used the meteorological research division, which he created in 1936, to study rainfall in headwaters areas, purchase rain gauges, and utilize evaporation data and mountain snowfall studies. Each year the Bureau made water-supply forecasts for arid and semiarid regions, based on snow surveys. Limited funds prevented Gregg from issuing hourly rainfall measurements, which would have helped assess the risk of floods.

Although eager to increase information for pilots, Gregg found it difficult to maintain the services he had painstakingly put in place as head of the Aerological Division. The airway service appropriation for fiscal year 1937, for example, was 13 percent less than it had been for fiscal year 1932, even though the miles flown had increased 50 percent during the intervening five years. Nonetheless, during Gregg's tenure the Bureau continued to provide dew point readings, which were useful in predicting fog formation and icing, and hourly teletype reports on temperature, barometric pressure, wind, and the condition of landing fields affected by rain or snow. Upper-air maps, showing wind velocity and direction at various levels up to 13,000 feet, a service begun in July 1933, continued as well. In 1935 Gregg found enough funds to issue

aviation weather maps every six hours, each with a forecast for the next eight-hour period. He helped institute regular radio broadcasts to pass weather information along to pilots every thirty minutes.

Well placed in professional organizations, Gregg pressed the case for an activist Weather Bureau. He served as chairman of the Subcommittee on Meteorology of the National Advisory Committee on Aeronautics; was treasurer for fifteen years and in 1938 president of the American Meteorological Society; played a leading role in the Daniel Guggenheim Committee on Aeronautical Meteorology and the Interdepartmental Committee on the Coordination of Meteorological Service for Aeronautics; and was a member of the American Association for the Advancement of Science, the American Geophysical Union, the International Meteorological Organization, and the Royal Meteorological Society.

In speeches and essays for the general public, Gregg claimed that with "comparatively small increases for weather research," crop failures could be reduced, nutritional standards raised, death, injury, and property loss from storms and droughts diminished, and travel by land, sea, and air made safer. At the frontier of science, weather research had practical value "for you and me in everyday life."

On September 14, 1938, while attending an aviation conference called by the Air Transport Association of America, Willis Gregg collapsed and died of coronary thrombosis. A talented and visionary civil servant with a farsighted belief that the aviation industry depended on accurate weather forecasting, Gregg disproved the notion that everybody talks about the weather but nobody does anything about it. That the U.S. Weather Bureau played such a vital role in the Allied victory in World War II is only part of his remarkable legacy.

George Jean Nathan
⚓ CLASS OF 1904

Despite his claim that he had not "disturbed in the least the prosperous mediocrity of our theater," George Jean Nathan for decades was the most influential drama critic in the United States. He helped launch Sean O'Casey in America, championed William Saroyan's work, and his encouragement of Eugene O'Neill was especially important. The world's "greatest two-act theater-goer," according to fellow critic Brooks Atkinson, Nathan could destroy a play merely by grabbing his top hat, walking stick, and stylish overcoat (by his own count he owned forty-eight of them) and heading for the exit before the curtain rose on act 3. In the midst of the Depression, a congressional committee, looking for a scapegoat, threatened to subpoena Nathan for causing, with his slashing reviews, a precipitous drop in attendance on Broadway.

George Jean Nathan was born on February 14, 1882, in Fort Wayne, Indiana. His father, Charles Naret Nathan, a wealthy and worldly man, was educated in Heidelberg, spoke eight languages, and owned vineyards in France and coffee plantations in Brazil. Even though the family of his mother, Ella Nirdlinger, had helped found Fort Wayne, George Nathan concluded as a young man that "the country is for yokels and cows. . . . My future is in New York—London, Paris and Rome." In 1888 the Nathans moved to Cleveland, where George studied languages with private tutors, took piano lessons, and read avidly in history and drama. Every other summer he accompanied his father to Europe, enrolling as a special student in universities in Bologna, Heidelberg, and Paris.

In 1900 Nathan entered Cornell. Harvard's "English imitativeness" had offended him, and Cornell, more than any other American university, resembled the German institutions he admired. A "charming and beautiful" place, Cornell attracted him as well because "all the boys from Cleveland" were going there.

Enrolled in the so-called Arts course, where he specialized in literature, drama, history, languages, and psychology, Nathan attained prominence on campus socially as well as intellectually. A member of Kappa Sigma fraternity, he drank with various "bibbing vereins," was elected to the senior honor society Quill and Dagger, wrote and acted in sketches for the Savage Club, the Sunday Night Club, and the drama club Masque, and served as editor of both the *Cornell Sun* and the *Cornell Widow.* Among the special events Nathan planned was Cornell Spring Day, where he created the mysterious "Mzupzi," a campus sensation ultimately revealed—at twenty-five cents a peek—to be the two-year-old son of the black cook at the Cayuga Hotel; and the first-ever Widow Ball, a party that began at 10 p.m. Friday and continued until early morning Tuesday, during which fifty Cornellians landed in the infirmary for drinking too much—some of them, Nathan claimed, to ogle the beautiful nurse in attendance. A superb fencer, who had studied under celebrated foilsmen in Europe, Nathan won the Amsler Gold Medal in the sport, and continued to compete in matches for several years after graduation.

In 1904 Charles Naret Nathan died, putting an end to his son's plans to do graduate work at Oxford. Instead, his uncle, Charles Nirdlinger, who had been drama critic and foreign correspondent for the *New York Herald,* got him a job as a reporter for the newspaper. Assigned to the Sunday section, and permitted to review plays, Nathan chafed at pressure by editors that he say something favorable, and jumped to accept when Lynn Wright, a former *Cornell Sun* editor, offered him the drama critic's chair at *Outing* and *Bohemian* magazines in 1906. Within two years he was contributing essays to *Harper's Weekly* and *Smart Set,* the self-styled "magazine of cleverness," where he became friends with the journalist, critic, and social commentator H. L. Mencken. By 1912 his reviews were syndicated in forty-seven newspapers. In 1914 Nathan and Mencken became coeditors of *Smart Set.* For nine years the "critical Katzenjammer Kids" made the magazine a "succès d'estime," despite its modest circulation. In "Three-Minus One," a poem about Mencken, Nathan, and God, the prolific verse writer Berton Braley genially gibed at their brashness: "And two of the three were always right / And everyone else was wrong. . . . When God objected—they rocked the boat / and dropped him into the sea, / 'for you have no critical facultee' / Said Mencken / And Nathan / to God."

Dubbed by journalist Randolph Bartlett an "exterminator of humbugs," Nathan pilloried provincialism and puritanism, attacking the "corsetted emotion" of "mincing, waspwaisted and furtive" dramatists and insisting that "a trace of brusque vulgarity is essential for first-rate drama." He was prolific, writing forty books as well as thousands of columns in more than thirty prominent periodicals including *Puck, Judge, McClure's, Cosmopolitan, Vanity Fair,* and *Esquire.* In 1924, after *Smart Set* folded, Nathan and Mencken, along with publisher Alfred Knopf, launched the *American Mercury.* In puncturing the pretensions of

"the booboisie" and embracing the "aesthetic happiness of the minority," the magazine reflected the critical tone of the 1920s. But, although Nathan was no less an elitist than Mencken, he did not share his interest in having the magazine cover politics and economics: "I have never voted. I shall never vote. . . . An art gallery is more important to me than Vice President Dawes." Stimulated by "life's music and color, its charm and ease, its humor and loveliness," Nathan's end in life was "the achievement of a large and selfish pleasure." He resigned the editorship of the *Mercury* in 1925, although he continued as drama critic until 1930.

In the 1930s, along with O'Neill, Theodore Dreiser, Ernest Boyd, and James Branch Cabell, Nathan launched the *American Spectator,* a magazine dedicated to the "untrammeled expression of individual opinion," with an emphasis on literature and drama. Nathan left the *Spectator* in 1935, and six years later he rejoined the *Mercury,* then owned by Lawrence Spivak. Although the magazines changed, Nathan's approach to drama did not. With irreverent wit (he included the dogs in the musical *Keep 'Em Flying* on his list of the ten best actors of the season) and verbal dexterity he insisted on a common-sense approach that eschewed any theories that "denuded the arts of their splendid, gypsy gauds." A playwright, Nathan insisted, "may successfully do almost anything he chooses to do, provided only he has the necessary imagination and inventive skill for the doing." A critic who could not enjoy *Hamlet* one night and the Follies the next "seems to me to have something constitutionally wrong with him." The best critic combined "the mind of a gentleman with the emotions of a bum."

Nonetheless, great drama, Nathan believed, had no messages other than its own internal dignity and splendor: "The theater is, above everything else, a pleasure temple: the mind has no place in it." Nathan had little interest in plays that "take on the aspect of so many rush telegrams, delivered by a breathless messenger-boy, which contain information that the recipient has read in the day before yesterday's newspaper." A mixture of iconoclasm, hedonism, and "art for art's sake," Nathan's theater criticism and his social commentary have not worn well. But his work bears rereading, not only for its style but also as, in essence, a history of the American theater over a half a century.

Nathan remained a bachelor for most of his adult life. In the late 1920s and early '30s he squired actress Lillian Gish to play openings, restaurants, concerts, and to the chateau in France owned by Eugene and Carlotta O'Neill. In a rave review of Gish's performance as Helena in *Uncle Vanya,* Nathan praised her smile as "a bit of happi-

ness trembling on a bed of death." Apparently, Gish repeatedly turned down his proposals of marriage. In 1955 Nathan tied the knot with actress Julie Haydon, who he had met a decade earlier at rehearsals in Chicago of Tennessee Williams's *The Glass Menagerie.* Embarrassed by his Jewish lineage, Nathan accepted Roman Catholic communion soon after his marriage. And just before he died, on April 8, 1958, with Haydon at his side at the Royalton Hotel in New York where he had lived for half a century, Nathan, who had exhibited what Mencken called a "high and mighty sniffishness" about many dogmas, including religion, asked for Catholic last rites.

Jessie Redmon Fauset
ᔕ CLASS OF 1905

"Is this colored world that Miss Fauset draws quite true?" Mary White Ovington asked in a skeptical review of the novel *There Is Confusion.* But most others praised Jessie Fauset for describing middle-class African Americans to readers who knew blacks only as domestic servants, "uncles," or criminals. The poet Langston Hughes called her a "midwife" of the Harlem Renaissance of the 1920s.

Jessie Redmon Fauset was born on April 27, 1882, in Camden County, New Jersey. Her mother, Annie Seamon Fauset, and her father, Redmon Fauset, a minister in the African Methodist Episcopal Church, were pillars of the African American community established near Philadelphia. The only black in her class in the Philadelphia High School for Girls, Jessie bristled at classmates who would not return her greeting, channeling her anger into academic achievement so distinguished that school officials honored her by inviting her father to give the graduation invocation. When administrators at Bryn Mawr discouraged her from applying, Fauset accepted a scholarship

from Cornell, which she entered in 1901. As the first black woman at the university, she spent much of her time alone (black males were numerous enough to found their own fraternity, Alpha Phi Alpha). Fauset performed splendidly in a classical curriculum that was heavy on language requirements, with four years of Latin and German and two of Greek and French. In 1905 she was elected to Phi Beta Kappa, the only black student at Cornell to achieve that honor before 1921.

After graduation, Fauset found that no high school in Philadelphia would employ her. She taught briefly in Baltimore, before taking a position teaching French and Latin in the M Street (later Dunbar) High School in Washington, D.C., a prestigious high school for African Americans. While teaching, she worked on an M.A. in French at the University of Pennsylvania, which she completed in 1919.

An aspiring writer, Fauset corresponded with W. E. B. DuBois, the leading black intellectual in the nation, whom she had met through Walter Willcox, dean of Cornell's College of Arts and Sciences. She admired DuBois, she wrote, for teaching "our colored men and women race pride, self-pride, self-sufficiency (the right kind) and the necessity of living our lives, as nearly as possible, absolutely, instead of comparing them always with white standards." In 1912 she began sending essays, poems, book reviews, and short stories to *Crisis,* the official publication of the National Association for the Advancement of Colored People, which DuBois edited. In 1919 DuBois made her literary editor of the magazine, and she moved to New York.

For the next seven years Fauset managed the office when DuBois took extended trips to Europe or Africa and contributed to *Crisis* fiction and articles that ranged from a description of her experiences as a delegate to meetings of the Pan-African Conference in London, Brussels, and Paris, to an analysis of Montessori education. From 1920 to 1921 she edited and contributed scores of stories and poems to a monthly magazine for children, *The Brownies' Book.* Most importantly, Fauset discovered, published, and served as mentor to some of the greatest writers of the Harlem Renaissance, including Jean Toomer, Nella Larson, and Countee Cullen. When an as yet unpublished Langston Hughes submitted a

piece to *The Brownies' Book* she wrote DuBois: "What colored person is there, do you suppose, in the United States who writes like that and is yet unknown to us?" On many evenings these artists transformed the apartment on Seventh Avenue that Fauset shared with her sister into a salon.

While at *Crisis,* Fauset completed *There Is Confusion* (1924). Praised by DuBois as "the novel that the Negro intelligentsia have been clamoring for," *There Is Confusion* told the story of the cultured Marshall family of Philadelphia. Like Fauset herself, the novel's heroes and heroines believed that race prejudice was "an awful nuisance," and in some places "an awful menace," but not so pervasive or powerful as to prevent blacks from making "headway in this awful country." In *There Is Confusion* Joanna Marshall adapts the dances of black children for the stage; Peter Bye shakes off anger at the white branch of his family and becomes a surgeon; and Maggie Ellersley, the daughter of a poor laundress, opens a chain of beauty shops.

Fauset resigned her position at *Crisis* in 1926, perhaps because her relationship with DuBois, a famously prickly man, had cooled. She told friends she would take a job as a publisher's reader (and work at home if her employer was concerned about her race), with a philanthropic foundation, or as a social secretary in a private family. Although she preferred not to teach, she eventually accepted employment teaching French at DeWitt Clinton High School in New York City, where she remained until 1944.

In 1929 Fauset published her most-acclaimed novel, *Plum Bun.* Making ingenious use of nursery rhymes, she told the story of light-skinned Angela Murray, who sees race as a "handicap which if guessed at would have been disabling as a game leg or an atrophied body," and decides to "pass" for white. Alert to racism and sexism, *Plum Bun* demonstrates that "passing" is a mistaken fantasy, not a ticket to paradise. Angela's "Mr. Right" is not rich, white Roger Fielding but poor, black Anthony Cross.

Convinced that "there ain't no such colored people as these," characters who speak decent English, have high ideals, and are self-supporting, several publishers turned down her next novel. Set in the small town of Red Brook, New Jersey, filled with allusions to Greek mythology, *The Chinaberry Tree* appeared in 1931, but only after the white writer Zona Gale agreed to certify in an introduction that "respectable" blacks, like those depicted in the novel, did, indeed, exist. In her own foreword, Fauset reminded readers that there were "breathing spells, in-between spaces where colored men and women work and love and go their ways with no thought of 'the problem.'" Although *The Chinaberry Tree* explored miscegenation, illegitimacy, and their consequences, it concentrated on the home life of blacks who are "not being pressed too hard by the Furies of Prejudice, Ignorance, and Economic Injustice."

In *Comedy: American Style* (1933), Fauset explored black self-hatred. The "race mania" of Olivia Blanchard Cary contributes to the suicide of her dark-skinned son, the disastrous marriage of her light-skinned daughter to a white racist, and the alienation of her family from their own community. Fauset gives to Grandfather Cary her moral: "that greatness knew no race, no color; that real worth was the same the world over; that it was immediately recognizable and that it was a mark of genuine manhood to know no false shame."

Comedy: American Style was the last novel Fauset published. Beginning in the 1930s, a literary appetite grew for fiction that dealt with the masses rather than the middle class. Compared with the work of Richard Wright, Ralph Ellison, and James Baldwin, the novels of Jessie Fauset seemed Victorian, rear guard, and naïve about the capacity of individuals to overcome racial oppression. During the '30s and '40s, Fauset traveled with Herbert Harris, an insurance executive, whom she had married in 1929, or by herself, to deliver lectures on black literature. In 1949 she was a visiting professor at Hampton Institute and also taught French and writing at Tuskegee Institute. She died on April 30, 1961, in relative obscurity, only to be rediscovered in the 1980s and '90s by critics who looked beyond the sentimentalism of her "fastidious and precious" romances to discover sophisticated treatments of the intersection of gender, class, and race, and who anointed her, once again, a pivotal figure of the Harlem Renaissance.

Leo Max Frank

❧ CLASS OF 1906

Leo Frank "is a graduate of Cornell," a police reporter for the *Atlanta Georgian* wrote, "a smooth, swift and convincing speaker. If you have seen any good pictures of him you will understand what I mean when I say that he looks like a pervert." A Northerner, an industrialist who paid low wages to female workers, and a Jew, Frank had three strikes against him in Atlanta, Georgia, in 1913. In one of the most sensational trials of the century, Frank was convicted on flimsy and fabricated evidence of murdering Mary Phagan.

Leo Max Frank was born in Paris, Texas, on April 17, 1884. A few months later, the Frank family moved to Brooklyn. Leo's mother, Rae Frank, was a native New Yorker; Rudolph Frank, his father, received his M.D. in Germany before emigrating to the United States. Educated in the public schools and at Pratt

Institute, Leo Frank entered Cornell to pursue a degree in mechanical engineering. Although he enjoyed playing basketball, Frank spent most of his time outside of class competing for the Debate Club. "His genius found expression in three-phased generators and foundry work," the *Cornell Class Book* joked, "where he soon gained the reputation of being the champion hot-air artist of the University by his happy faculty of talking all day and saying nothing. . . . This proficiency will doubtless win Max success as a gas jet."

Following graduation in 1906, Frank took a job with the B. F. Sturtevant Company of Hyde Park, Massachusetts. In 1908, he moved to Atlanta, as superintendent of the National Pencil Factory, owned by his uncle. Two years later, he married Lucille Selig, daughter of a wealthy Atlanta family. The couple had no children. Frank quickly established himself in the city's Jewish community: in 1912, he was elected president of the Jewish community service organization B'nai B'rith. Frank attracted no public notice until Confederate Memorial Day, April 26, 1913, when thirteen-year-old Mary Phagan, a laborer in the factory that Frank managed, was raped and murdered. Phagan had gone to the office that day to collect her pay, and Frank appeared to be the last person to have seen her alive. After noticing bloodstains (later determined to be drops of paint) outside of Frank's office, the police summoned the superintendent for an interrogation. The *Atlanta Constitution* described Frank as "a small, wiry man wearing eyeglasses of high lens power," and continued that he was "nervous and apparently high strung. He smokes incessantly." With pressure mounting for a solution to the case, the police arrested Frank.

There was another suspect as well. Jim Conley, an African-American janitor at the factory, had been seen washing blood from a shirt shortly after the crime was committed. The police confiscated the shirt but lost it before the blood could be tested. They also failed to test the fingerprints on Mary Phagan's jacket and those on the back door of the

basement where the body had been discovered. After intense questioning, and several illogical and contradictory affidavits, Conley claimed that Frank asked him to "watch out" when Mary Phagan "came to chat" in his office. He further said that he heard Phagan scream, then saw the superintendent emerge from the metal workroom, trembling, with a cord in his hands. Frank, Conley's story concluded, promised the janitor $200 if he would put the body in the basement and write a note to implicate the night watchman, Newt Lee.

Frank hired prominent Atlanta criminal attorneys Luther Rosser and Reuben Arnold to defend him. The prosecution team was led by Georgia Solicitor-General Hugh Dorsey, who would parlay the case into a successful run for governor. In a headline, the *Atlanta Constitution* promised the "Greatest Legal Battle in the History of Dixie." Unfortunately for Frank, Rosser and Arnold mounted an inept defense. They presented an array of witnesses who accounted for all but eighteen minutes of Frank's time, not nearly enough time to kill Mary Phagan, carry the body to the cellar, write the note, and race back to the office. Over one hundred witnesses testified to Frank's good character. But the defense failed to focus the jury's attention on the sloppy police investigation. Even worse, in three days of cross-examination, they did not catch Conley in a major misstatement.

The defense concluded by putting Frank himself on the witness stand. For four hours, according to the *Atlanta Constitution,* his words "carried the ring of truth in every sentence." But his testimony did not help. In his summation, Dorsey focused on the failure of "two of the ablest lawyers in the country" to discredit Jim Conley. He insisted that Conley could not have composed the note because he would have called himself a "nigger," not a "Negro." The jury took less than four hours to convict. When the local baseball team put the verdict on the scoreboard, fans greeted the news with cheers. Crowds outside the courthouse yelled "Hang the Jew." Although he expressed doubts about Frank's guilt,

Judge Roan sentenced him to hang. The trial, Reuben Arnold concluded, was "the most horrible persecution of a Jew since the death of Christ."

Frank made three appeals to the Georgia Supreme Court and two to the U.S. Supreme Court. All were denied on technical grounds. But pressure mounted for a retrial, commutation, or pardon. Petitions containing more than a million signatures poured in to Georgia. Among those who protested the verdict were Cornell students, alumni clubs, and President Jacob Gould Schurman. Several state legislatures passed resolutions urging commutation, and mass meetings were held in Boston, Chicago, Minneapolis, and Rochester, New York. After a thorough review of the case, Governor John Slaton concluded that the absence of blood on the second floor, the sawdust and grime in Mary Phagan's nostrils and mouth, and the use of old order pads, available only in the basement, to write the murder note, suggested strongly that Jim Conley almost certainly lied. In June 1915, in an act that effectively ended his political career, Governor Slaton commuted the death sentence to life imprisonment.

The nation's press and public responded jubilantly, and in letters to philanthropist Julius Rosenwald and U.S. Supreme Court Justice Oliver Wendell Holmes Frank renewed his faith that "Right and Justice" would "hold complete sway." From his prison farm in Milledgeville, he wrote to his wife every day, requesting handkerchiefs and pajamas, writing pads, a can opener, BeechNut gum, and fig bars ("I don't want sweet crackers, too rich"). But some Georgians decided on a different ending for the Leo Frank case. Thousands marched on the governor's mansion. Slaton might have been lynched had a battalion of the National Guard not been on the scene to protect him. On August 15, 1915, the "best citizens" of Marietta, Georgia, Mary Phagan's hometown, kidnapped Frank and lynched him.

The hatred of urbanization, industrialization, and foreigners brought to the surface by the trials of Leo Frank helped convince "Colonel" William J. Simmons that the time had arrived to establish a fraternal organization to revive Southern, rural, Protestant values, and put Negroes, Catholics, and Jews in their place. In the autumn of 1915, Simmons and thirty-three members of the Knights of Mary Phagan met on a mountaintop outside of Atlanta and reestablished the Ku Klux Klan, the secret order that had been the scourge of the South in the years following the Civil War.

The B'nai B'rith drew a different lesson from the conviction of Leo Frank. Less than a month after the trial ended, the Jewish service organization established the Anti-Defamation League. Leo Frank's conviction, wrote Adolph Kraus, president of B'nai B'rith, was part of a pattern of discrimination that demanded "organized and systematic effort on behalf of all right-thinking Americans."

The Leo Frank case has continued to fascinate Americans, with several books, movies, and, in 1998, a Broadway musical, *Parade,* devoted to it. In 1982, Alonzo Mann, who was an office boy in the National Pencil Factory when Mary Phagan was murdered, claimed that he had seen Jim Conley carrying her body. Four years later, the Georgia Board of Pardons granted Frank a posthumous pardon, and Stu Lewengrub, southeastern director of the Anti-Defamation League, announced, "We can now finally close our files on our first case."

Louis Robert Wolheim

CLASS OF 1906

A great deal about Louis Wolheim is clouded by the exaggerated stories he told about himself. Among them is the myth that he owed his distinctive physiognomy to three broken noses he suffered while playing as the star fullback for Cornell's football team. What is true, however, is that Wolheims's face ("I am the ugliest son-of-a-bitch in the world," he declared) became his meal ticket and helped to launch his distinguished career on the Broadway stage and in early American movies.

Wolheim was born in New York City on March 28, 1881, an only son. His parents were Jews with German and Polish backgrounds. Nothing is known of his mother, but his father, Elias Wolheim, who worked in several menial trades, had the ambition to see that his son received not one but two undergraduate degrees. The first was from City College of New York in 1903. The second, conferred in 1906, was a bachelor of science degree in mechanical engineering from Cornell. Wolheim suited up for Cornell's football team in 1904 when Pop Warner was coaching at his alma mater, but he was not a star. He was a second-string back who was put into games, according to one friend, only to scare the other team with his face. Wolheim did break his nose, but probably from boxing rather than football.

At Cornell, Wolheim had a deserved reputation for boisterous conduct, but he was also an excellent student and possessed real genius in mathematics. In the 1906–7 academic year he enrolled at Cornell as a graduate student with the intention of gaining a Ph.D. Because he needed money, he worked briefly in Manhattan for an engineering firm. He may or may not have been fired for walking into the office smoking a cigarette, but he left the job and returned to Ithaca where he seems to have been something of a bum and something of a local sage. He taught math at the Cornell Preparatory School and worked as a

clerk at the cigar stand in the Ithaca Hotel where he made friends with the various people who came to town and drank with them at the Dutch Kitchen, the hotel bar. Here Wolheim tutored Cornell undergraduates and became known to locals as "Wolly."

In 1910, he left for Mexico where he spent almost three years. He almost certainly did not, as he claimed, go in search of a gold mine, nor was he held for ransom by bandits, nor did he carry messages for the Mexican leader Francisco Madero in his struggle against Victoriano Huerta. He learned Spanish, however. He already knew Yiddish and would somewhere learn French. Despite all appearances, Wolheim had a scholar's love of learning. Years later he said that his real ambition had always been to be a professor at a small-town college.

Returning to Ithaca, he resumed work at the Ithaca Hotel and continued to win friends with his charming lies. However, a new enterprise had enlivened life in Ithaca—the movie industry. In 1913 Theodore Wharton joined his brother Leopold in forming a highly profitable motion picture company, Wharton Incorporated, in Ithaca. They were the first directors to establish their own studio as independent producers. And they were the first directors to cast Wolheim in movies—mostly as an extra.

In 1914 Lionel Barrymore arrived in town to work in a Pearl White serial, *The Romance of Elaine*. He stayed at the Ithaca Hotel, took one look at Wolheim's face, and remarked, "What a fortune here, if only he could act." Barrymore returned to New York City and after a few more films with the Whartons, Wolheim followed him. Barrymore set him up in a few movies shot in New Jersey, got him a small role on stage in *The Jest* in which Lionel costarred with his brother John, and saw to it that he took acting lessons. He also introduced him to Eugene O'Neill, who was writing a play about a brutish man who in the first scene appears as a stripped-to-the-waist ship stoker and in the last lies dead in a gorilla cage. Although Wolheim first won attention from New York's stage critics for his role in a 1920 play, *The Broken Wing,* a role that allowed him to use his Mexican accent, it was his 1922 appearance as Yank in O'Neill's sensational *The Hairy Ape* that made him a star. He had one other stage triumph, as Captain Flagg in Maxwell Anderson and Laurence Stallings's 1924 antiwar drama *What Price Glory.*

Wolheim did other stage work, and received writing credits for two plays, one adapted from a French drama and the other from classic Yiddish theater. But he also continued to work steadily in films made on the East Coast. His characters were not exactly romantic leads. In John Barrymore's 1920 version of *Dr. Jekyll and Mr. Hyde* he played the proprietor of a dive that Hyde frequented. In 1921 he was the executioner who strapped Lillian Gish to the guillotine in D. W. Griffith's *Orphans of the Storm.* In 1922 he appeared as a villain who menaced John Barrymore in *Sherlock Holmes.* Barred from romance on screen, he found it in his personal life. In 1923 he married Ethel Dane, an actress, painter, and sculptor. Despite his earlier reputation for carousing, Wolheim settled happily and quietly into a marriage that lasted for the rest of his life.

In 1927 the movie industry on the East Coast had almost entirely disappeared, and Wolheim moved to Los Angeles, where he lived in Beverly Hills. He costarred in one of the first movies produced by Howard Hughes, *Two Arabian Knights,* and made his first semi-talkie in 1928, *The Shady Lady.* In 1930 he found his most memorable role as Militiaman Stanislaus Katczinsky in Lewis Milestone's great Oscar-winning film *All Quiet on the Western Front.* A veteran member of the German army, the character Katczinsky dies of a random bullet after caring for his recruits through four years of the Great War's senseless battles. The role called upon Wolheim to reveal behind his grizzled face a man of humor and of deep sentiment.

Shortly after that triumph, Wolheim signed a contract with RKO that guaranteed him a starring role in all the films in which he appeared. He was also allowed to direct one film, *The Sin Ship.* But by this time Wolheim, only fifty years old, was seriously ill. He was cast as the tough editor Walter Burns in *The Front Page* and put himself on a punishing diet to lose twenty-five pounds. As it turned out, the diet wasn't necessary. Wolheim had advanced stomach cancer and collapsed on the set in the early stages of production. Doctors performed an operation, but Wolheim never recovered. He died two weeks later on February 18, 1931.

Wolheim's movie career did not stretch into what many regard as Hollywood's Golden Age. However, that definition depends on one's perspective. Wolheim began work at the moment narrative film was invented, played many roles in the classic silent era, and made talkies before "the Code" restricted what films could say. During his lifetime more Americans proportionately went to the movies than at any later time. For about a decade Wolheim was easily Cornell's most recognizable graduate.

Arthur Augustus Allen

✒ CLASS OF 1907

Celebrated as "the greatest bird behaviorist in North America," Arthur Allen, the first professor of ornithology in the United States, created the Laboratory of Ornithology at Cornell, where he taught ten thousand students and supervised more than one hundred M.A.s and Ph.D.s. With his bird biographies, color photographs, motion pictures, and sound recordings, Allen helped make birding a popular pastime for millions of Americans.

Arthur Augustus Allen was born in Buffalo, New York, on December 28, 1885, the son of Anna Moore Allen and Daniel Williams Allen, a businessman who specialized in railroad and land development. After "a youth spent robbing birds' nests about Buffalo," according to the *Cornell Class Book,* "A3" entered Cornell's College of Arts and Sciences in 1903 to pursue a career as an ornithologist. He joined Gamma Alpha fraternity and rowed crew, was a member of the Agassiz Club, the Biology Club, the Arts Feed Committee, and Sigma Xi honor society. More than anything else, however, he enjoyed walking the campus and the gorges in search of birds. After receiving his B.A. in 1907, Allen remained at Cornell, "chasing bats (Vespertilionidae, he calls them) for an M.A. degree, and teaching the adolescent mind the joys of five A.M. bird excursions." In 1911 he received a doctorate. His dissertation, "The Red-Winged Blackbird: A Study in the Ecology of a Cattail Marsh," was praised by Frank Chapman, chairman of the Department of Ornithology at the American Museum of Natural History, as "the best, most significant biography which has thus far been prepared for any American bird." Allen's work, with its detailed examination of a species interacting with its environment, became a model for monographic studies in the field.

Tapped by Chapman to lead an American Museum of Natural History expedition to Colombia, Allen had to cut his trip short after

a few months when he contracted malaria. He returned to the United States in 1912 with an appointment as instructor in zoology at Cornell, where he would remain for forty-one years. In 1913 he married Elsa Guerdrum. In the early years of their marriage, she raised their five children, but as her own interest in ornithology deepened she earned a Ph.D., accompanied her husband on field trips, and provided significant assistance in his research and publications.

A superb teacher, Allen built a comprehensive and much-copied program in ornithology. His *Laboratory Notebook* (1927) went through five editions, and his textbook, *The Book of Bird Life* (1930), was reprinted a dozen times, with a final revision in 1961. The doctoral program in ornithology developed by Allen was the first (and until the 1940s the only) one of its kind in the nation. A founder and the second president of the Wildlife Society, he was the first to offer a college course in wildlife conservation. At Cornell, Allen set up the "Grad Lab," located first in McGraw Hall, then on the top floor of Fernow, where "practically around the clock" students, faculty, and visiting scholars exchanged ideas about ornithology. Out of this initiative came the "Laboratory of Ornithology," which became a formal entity at Cornell in 1955. Its own building, flanking a ten-acre pond and facing Sapsucker Woods, was completed two years later. Still used for research and observation, the "Lab of O" reaches out to the general public as well.

During the 1920s Allen's research focused on the relatively new field of game management. He devised methods for raising the ruffed grouse in captivity and studied diseases of this bird for the American Game Association. For this work he won the *Outdoor Life* Gold Medal in 1924. Allen then did pioneering research on the sex rhythms of the ruffed grouse and other species, including cowbirds, house wrens, Canadian geese, yellow warblers, and song sparrows.

By the 1930s "Doc" Allen, a fixture on the lecture circuit, had a national reputation. He continued to do field work with trips to Labrador, Hudson Bay, and Panama. He did research in Mexico on jungle acoustics for the Office of Scientific Research and Development in the War Department. In 1935 he led an expedition in search of vanishing birds that located the rare ivory-billed woodpecker in Louisiana. Thirteen years later, in Alaska, he found the nest of the bristle-thighed curlew, for which he received the Franklin L. Burr Award from the National Geographic Society. But he devoted most of his time and energy to bringing an informed appreciation of birds to lay audiences. Allen's stories about birds, written initially for the magazine *Bird-Lore* (which became *Audubon* magazine), became the basis for two books, *American Bird Biographies* (1934) and *The Golden Plover and Other Birds* (1939), that contained charming life histories of forty-seven American species. Between 1934 and 1962 Allen also contributed eighteen articles to the *National Geographic,* often adorned with photographs he had taken. Among his most famous bird photos was one of a peregrine falcon against the background of Taughannock Falls. He turned one of his essays, "Stalking Birds with a Color Camera," into a very popular book with the same title.

In 1929 Allen helped a motion-picture crew film and record three species of wild birds singing in Stewart Park. The equipment they used was bulky and expensive, but Allen was excited by the prospect of a permanent record of bird sounds. With the encouragement and financial assistance of retired stockbroker Albert Brand, Allen produced a phonograph record of bird songs, a film of drumming ruffed grouse with the sounds synchronized, and in 1935 made a sound recording of the songs of endangered species in the south and southwestern United States. *American Bird Songs* and *Voices of the Night* followed, in 1942 and 1948. In his greatest coup, Allen carried recording equipment on a jeep and in a dense fog snuck up to within three hundred yards of the shy whooping crane. He became the first to record the loud bugle note of America's tallest bird, made with its long and curled windpipe, nature's trombone.

Some ornithologists believed that Allen misrepresented birds in his efforts to humanize them for a lay audience. He insisted, for example, that birds were shocked and sometimes angered when they saw their own images in mirrors. In claiming that the mental states of birds were as important as those of humans, Allen wrote that, like people, they suffered from inferiority complexes.

Allen retired from Cornell in 1953. According to a colleague he relished puns, occasionally played Ping-Pong with his graduate students, and hunted waterfowl once or twice each fall. But politics, literature, music, religion, and sports "seldom distracted him for any length of time." He continued to lecture, travel, and, with Paul Kellogg, to produce phonograph records. *Songbirds of America, Bird Songs in Your Garden,* and *Dawn in a Duckblind* appeared in bound books with color illustrations. Allen spent considerable time as well at his beloved "Lab of O," looking out the window at the ducks settling in on the pond to feed. He died in Ithaca on January 17, 1964.

Adolph Coors Jr.

✒ CLASS OF 1907

When his father fell or jumped from a ledge on the sixth floor of the Cavalier Hotel in Virginia Beach, Virginia in 1929, Adolph Coors Jr. became the president of Coors Brewing and Manufacturing Company. He kept the business solvent during Prohibition and the Depression, then made "the little giant" of Golden, Colorado, one of the most successful breweries in the United States. Skilled, single-minded, and secretive, Coors produced a beer that inspired devout consumer loyalty and a company that some Americans love to hate.

Junior was born in Golden on January 12, 1885, one of six children of Adolph Sr. and Louisa Weber Coors, both immigrants from Germany. Tall, taciturn, and painfully thin, Adolph Jr. was destined almost from infancy to join the family business. His father sent him to Cornell in 1903 to study chemistry, so that, his classmates joked, he could learn how to "manufacture 'beverage' for rejuvenation parties in the West." They remembered a student who thought "he had to work on the Hill every day, all day, and study every night, almost all night." Adolph, however, was anything but a hermit. The *Cornell Class Book* documents his extracurricular activities: Delta Theta Pi, Sphinx Head, Aleph Samach, Alembic, Nalanda, Junior Smoker Committee, Sophomore Cotillion Committee, Sunday Night Club, and leadership in the Anti-coeducation Society.

After graduating in 1907, Adolph spent nearly three years in Vienna and Munich learning the latest brewery methods. When he returned to Colorado, his father made him a partner. In 1913, Adolph Jr. married Alice May Kistler and settled into a domestic life that would include four children. A strict disciplinarian, who kept notes on his children's misdeeds and meted out punishment on Sundays, Coors was not really happy unless he was working.

When the nation "went dry" in 1920, Adolph Sr. was despondent, but his son was ready. Although the sales of near beer—Coors Golden and Mannah—were a fraction of pre-Prohibition sales of real beer, the Chemical Porcelain Company that Coors had founded was an industry leader, making everything from cooking utensils to scientific items. Much later, Coors Porcelain would manufacture the heat-resistant nose cones used in guided missiles and the ceramic materials used in bulletproof vests. In the 1920s it provided much-needed revenue. Adolph also helped his brother Grover set up a malted milk plant and persuaded Mars Candy Company, the manufacturer of Milky Way, to make Coors their main supplier.

By 1923 Junior was running the Coors Corporation, and he became president after his father died in 1929. When Prohibition ended in 1933 Coors beer got a new lease on life. Though Adolph Jr. kept the company regional, he ordered a major expansion of the plant, the modernization of equipment, and began selling beer in Arizona and California as well as in its pre-Prohibition markets in Colorado, Wyoming, and New Mexico. To keep the dries at bay, he had the company maintain a low profile. "We don't show people in our ads," he said as late as 1953. "We don't want to remind the prohibitionists that people actually drink beer."

Coors boasted that his beer was not produced by "old-world craft" but was "scientifically controlled" and "protected from human contact." At the same time, he approved advertisements reminding consumers that it was "brewed with pure Rocky Mountain spring water." When an artificial waterfall was built for tourists near the plant, he had it redone so that it would actually use the spring water.

Convinced that young men preferred lighter beer, he donned an apron and, along with his son Bill, experimented with different quantities of rice, malt, yeast, and hops. The first Coors Light appeared in 1941. Coors decided to emphasize that Coors Light, which became known as "Colorado Kool-Aid," had 13.8 fewer calories per serving. Coors Light was discontinued during World War II when grain was rationed and hops were impossible to get. Coors often ambled into bars during the war to get bottle caps the company might reuse (during Prohibition, to save on envelopes, he had asked employees to return their pay envelopes to the bursar's office). After the war, he decided to reduce the alcohol content of Coors regular beer from 4.5 percent to 3.6 percent so people would have to drink more of it to get the same buzz.

Coors led the way in finding an alternative to beer bottles. In 1936 a tin can line at the plant filled 150 containers a minute. Tin cans weighed less than bottles, required no deposit, and kept sunlight away from the contents. Unfortunately, tin cans caused the beer to cloud and gave it a metallic taste. Thanks to Bill Coors, "inventor of the aluminum can" and Modern Metal Man of the Year, Coors in 1959 became the first U.S. beverage company to use aluminum cans. By 1990, the company had the largest aluminum can plant in the world.

By instinct a paternalist, Coors enjoyed spending time with his employees, giving out Christmas bonuses, and ladling out eggnog at company parties. But he loathed unions. During a strike by the United Mine Workers in 1954, he switched from coal to natural gas and then established his own energy company. To avoid interruptions in supplies of bottles and cans, he set up the nonunion Coors Container Company. In 1957, following a three-and-a-half-month strike, Coors gave his employees a fifteen cent an hour increase (their wages, according to some reports, were seventy-five cents below the company's competitors in the region) but insisted that the union be prohibited from punishing workers who crossed picket lines.

The animus Coors had toward unions increased in 1960, following the kidnapping and murder of his son, Adolph III, who had been running the company for some years. He suspected that unions were somehow involved in the murder. Adolph Jr. resumed the title of chairman and ordered that no one sit in Adolph III's seat at board meetings, each one of which he began by reading a eulogy and the announcement that "this company will never be the same."

During the 1960s, Coors instituted preemployment polygraph tests for workers. According to one journalist, the company provided counseling for employees and then reviewed the notes of psychologists to discern what they were up to. At this time, as well, several members of the family began to involve themselves in ultraconservative political causes.

As the '60s ended, Coors was the fourth largest brewery in the United States, with annual sales of $160 million, even though it operated only one plant and sold its products in only eleven states. Tightly controlled by the family, the company remained much like the man who built it, a curious mix of the traditional and the innovative. Making use of state-of-the-art engineering and chemistry, Coors produced the only canned beverage in the United States without a ring pull top. Adolph Coors Jr. was actively involved with the management of the company as well as various philanthropic activities in the community until his death on May 18, 1970.

Kenneth Lewis Roberts

CLASS OF 1908

"You write those books," Theodore Roosevelt told him. "There aren't enough of that sort being written by Americans." Kenneth Roberts responded with some of the most popular historical novels of the first half of the twentieth century.

Kenneth Lewis Roberts was born in Kennebunk, Maine, on December 8, 1885. Roberts never referred in print to his father, Frank Roberts, a traveling salesman. The family of his mother, Grace Tibbets, arrived in New England in 1639 and boasted two captains in the Continental Army during the American Revolution, one member of Benedict Arnold's expedition to Quebec, and a privateer in the War of 1812.

Roberts attended school in Malden, Massachusetts, where his family had moved. Expelled from public school for saying geometry gave him "a pain in the neck," Roberts finished high school at the Charles Wellington Stone preparatory school in Boston and entered Cornell in 1904. An undistinguished student, he participated in a breathtaking number of social and literary activities. He presented light musicals for the Masque Club and the Savage Club; he was a cheerleader and wrote two football songs, "Fight for Cornell" and "Carnelian and White"; he joined Chi Psi fraternity and served as president of Kappa Beta Phi, a campus drinking club with an engraving of a beer stein on its key. He also belonged to Undine, Dunstan, the Mummy Club, Aleph Samach, and Quill and Dagger. Roberts wrote for the humor magazine, the *Cornell Widow,* and served as its editor in chief, splitting $10,000 in profits with the business manager when he graduated in 1908. And he founded and published at least eight issues of the *Cornell Deadly Sin,* a parody of the campus newspaper.

After graduation Roberts worked briefly in a wholesale leather company in Boston before joining the *Boston Post* as a reporter in 1909.

In addition to his news work, he created the character Professor Morton Kilgallen, whom many readers thought a real person. In one of many inside jokes, Roberts timed his account of Professor Kilgallen's marriage to coincide with his own wedding, in 1911, to Anna Seiberling Mosser of Boston. The couple had no children.

By the second decade of the new century, Roberts's humor pieces were appearing in *Puck, Life,* and *Judge* magazines, and he placed short stories with *Collier's Weekly* and the *Saturday Evening Post.* In 1917, he left the *Post* to devote himself to fiction, but when the United States entered World War I, he enlisted, receiving a commission as captain in army intelligence. Roberts traveled to Siberia with the Siberian Expeditionary Force, which was formed to support the anti-Bolshevik forces after the Russian Revolution, and reported on the mission for the *Saturday Evening Post,* which he joined in 1919 as a staff writer.

Roberts made several extended trips to Europe for the *Post* between 1919 and 1922. Disgusted with the disorder he saw around him and attracted by fascism, Roberts, in eleven articles for the *Post,* two books, *Why Europe Leaves Home* (1922) and *Black Magic* (1924), and several appearances before Congress, urged the United States to adopt a restrictive immigration policy. "The American nation," he argued, "was founded and developed by the Nordic race, but if a few more millions of members of the Alpine, Mediterranean and Semitic races are poured among us, the result must inevitably be a hybrid race of people as worthless and futile as the good-for-nothing mongrels of Central America and Southeastern Europe." Roberts believed his efforts were partly responsible for the congressional legislation of 1924 that drastically reduced immigration quotas from eastern and southern Europe.

After completing a book on the land boom in Florida in 1926, Roberts turned to historical fiction. In several novels set during the American Revolution and the War of 1812 Roberts celebrated the people who were "in his blood." The assistance of Booth Tarkington, author of *Penrod* and winner of two Pulitzer Prizes, was crucial. Until his death in 1946, Tarkington remained his literary mentor, editor, friend, and surrogate father. Roberts felt so indebted to Tarkington that he offered him coauthorship of *Northwest Passage* and half the royalties.

Roberts's novels are highly readable, reliable about details applicable to the period, and chock-full of action. A "choleric man when he was in good spirits, which was not often," as one acquaintance put it, Roberts believed "our historians have bitched, botched and buggered the facts of American history to an astounding degree." He would use historical fiction to set the record straight. In fiction, he wrote, where "the gauge of truth is applied to everything," including conversations, characters, and action, "falsities" are abundantly apparent to readers. In two books, *Arundel* (1930) and *Rabble in Arms* (1933), Roberts, ever the contrarian, chronicled the military exploits of Benedict Arnold, who he passionately defended as a "rare and

solitary genius," fighting against England because the alternative was subservience to France. He set *Lively Lady* (1931) and *Captain Caution* (1934) during the War of 1812, drawing on the experiences of his ancestors in creating what the critic Orville Prescott called "vivid close-ups of history."

These four novels had solid but unspectacular sales. A disappointed and dyspeptic Roberts wrote *For Authors Only, and Other Gloomy Essays,* taking to task Pulitzer Prize committees for ignoring Joseph Pulitzer's instruction that awards be given to novels that "present the wholesome atmosphere of American life." Under this criterion, he argued, neither Thornton Wilder's *The Bridge of San Luis Rey* nor Pearl Buck's *The Good Earth* qualified.

After conferring with Tarkington, Roberts returned to fiction, settling on a novel about Major Robert Rogers, a hero of the French and Indian War who also searched unsuccessfully for an overland route from the Atlantic Ocean to Oregon and the Pacific. Published in 1937, *Northwest Passage* was a Book-of-the-Month Club selection and, in 1940, a film starring Spencer Tracy, Walter Brennan, and Robert Young. Kenneth Roberts had become a literary phenomenon.

Several more novels followed. In *Oliver Wiswell* (1940), an ambitious work that covered the entire Revolutionary War, Roberts viewed the conflict through the eyes of a Loyalist. To mark its publication, *Time* magazine presented a cover story on the author. Selected by the Book-of-the-Month Club and the Literary Guild, and subsequently made into a motion picture, *Lydia Bailey* (1947) examined Toussaint L'Ouverture's uprising against the French in Haiti and the war with Tripoli fought by the United States in the early nineteenth century. Roberts's last novel, *Boon Island* (1956), told the story of the wreck of a ship off the coast of Maine in 1710.

Roberts continued to write nonfiction as well. *Trending into Maine* (1938), a book of reminiscences, included a diatribe against the billboards that despoiled the landscape. During the last decade of his life, Roberts grew fascinated—some thought obsessed—with water dowsing, the ability to locate underground water by using a forked stick. He recognized that his commitment to "water witching" subjected him to ridicule and, no doubt, relished it, contemplating as a subtitle for one of the three books he wrote on the subject, "How to Lose Friends and Alienate People."

In 1957 Roberts received a special citation from the Pulitzer Prize committee for writing novels that helped create "greater interest in our early American history." In July, Roberts had a heart attack. He died in Kennebunkport on July 21, 1957. Roberts was buried, as he had requested, in Arlington National Cemetery, alongside the soldiers he admired, who had fought for a nation that so often disappointed him.

Alice Catherine Evans

❧ CLASS OF 1909

Alice Evans lived a quiet life but pursued her work as a bacteriologist with steely determination. She waged two important battles: the first, to convince skeptical scientists that she had found a harmful bacillus in the nation's milk supply; the second, to force the profit-conscious dairy industry to safeguard the products it sent to market. Largely because of her efforts, Americans began to pasteurize their milk.

Evans was born in the agricultural community of Neath, Pennsylvania, on January 29, 1881. Her father, William Howell Evans, farmed, and her mother, Anne B. Evans, taught school. Not many opportunities loomed on her horizon, and when she graduated from Susquehanna Collegiate Institute, Evans followed her mother into teaching. Four years later she enrolled in a two-year course in nature study for rural teachers offered by Cornell's College of Agriculture. The move to Ithaca changed her life.

At Cornell, Evans became interested in science and completed a B.S. degree in 1909. She served as president of the Girls' Agricultural Club (women were a rarity in the ag school) but otherwise concentrated on her studies. From Ithaca she went to Madison where in 1910 she received an M.S. degree in bacteriology from the University of Wiscon-

sin. She declined an offer to continue her studies for a doctorate. Perhaps that was a mistake. The lack of a Ph.D., as well as her gender, hampered her early efforts to influence other scientists. On the other hand, had she stayed in her graduate program, she might not have done the work that made her famous.

She was drawn away from school by a job offer from the dairy division of the U.S. Department of Agriculture. Her charge was to study the bacteriology of milk and cheese.

For three years she worked in Washington, D.C., and in Wisconsin, where she looked for microbes in the milk of healthy cows. Three years later she became the first woman to receive a permanent position at the USDA.

In 1917 Evans discovered a Bang bacillus in the milk of cows. Named for the Danish veterinarian Bernhard Bang, the bacillus was known to cause abortion in cows. However, scientists did not think it harmful to humans. Evans disagreed. She concluded that the Bang bacillus was identical with the Bruce bacillus, discovered by Sir David Bruce during the Crimean War when it disabled thousands of British soldiers. If Evans was right, then what she had found in the milk consumed by ordinary Americans most definitely was harmful to them. It was the major cause of undulant fever, a disease that although usually not fatal caused severe flu-like symptoms in humans. It had no cure and often became chronic. Its victims, over their lifetimes, suffered a recurrence of fever, arthritis, and debilitating fatigue. Meningitis and infections of the heart lining were among the possible nasty consequences.

Evans reported her findings in 1917 to the Society of American Bacteriologists and published them in the *Journal of Infectious Diseases.* Her findings were ignored, in part because American doctors detected no widespread incidence of undulant fever in the country. The dairy industry strongly encouraged that point of view, since any alarm raised about the country's milk threatened to cost dairy producers large sums of money. Undulant fever did, in fact, exist in the United States, but since it was easy to confuse with other diseases, it was often misdiagnosed. Besides, the United States had a far more serious health problem at the time with the lethal strain of flu that swept the world after World War I.

In 1918 Evans moved to a division of the U.S. Public Health Service that later became the National Institutes of Health. She used her post to advocate for pasteurization of the nation's milk supply, but nothing happened until Karl Meyer, working at the University of California in 1920, concluded that Evans was right in equating the Bang and Bruce bacilli. He proposed a new bacillus, brucella, that affected both humans and most animals and that could be passed from tainted dairy products to humans. Undulant fever and the disease that caused abortions in cows and other animals were renamed brucellosis. With that knowledge Charles Carpenter of Cornell and other important scientists and public health officials backed Evans's drive to pasteurize milk, the only way to kill brucella bacteria. By the 1930s federal laws required the dairy industry to pasteurize milk and all products made with milk.

Brucellosis is now a rare disease in the United States in both humans and animals. Unfortunately, its decline came too late to spare Evans, who became one of its victims. Contracting the illness in the course of her research, she suffered from its effects for over twenty years. "It seems," she said, "as if those bugs had a special animosity toward me, since I made that discovery."

Evans remained at the National Institutes of Health for twenty-seven years. She worked on other projects and published many papers in the *Journal of Bacteriology,* the *Journal of Immunology,* and *Science.* Even without a Ph.D. she had become a respected scientist. In 1928 she was elected president of the Society of American Bacteriologists, the first woman to attain that post. In 1930 she was a delegate to the first International Microbiological Congress in Paris. The Woman's Medical College of Philadelphia conferred on her an honorary degree in 1934, a year after she had been inducted into the National Women's Hall of Fame. Fittingly, the University of Wisconsin awarded her a doctorate in 1936, twenty-six years after she left the graduate program there. It was an honorary degree, but her work in science had surely made her worthy of it.

Evans lived for thirty years after her retirement from NIH in 1945. She never married, and had no children or grandchildren to fill her days. Work continued to occupy her, and she was elected to a number of honorary posts. From 1945 to 1957 she was president of the Inter-American Committee on Brucel-

losis. In frequent lectures she urged women to pursue scientific careers. She was living in Alexandria, Virginia, when she died on September 5, 1975.

Martha Van Rensselaer

CLASS OF 1909

"Hang up the dishpan and the broom," Martha Van Rensselaer advised housewives in 1904. "Let the family forego the benefits of more laborious cooking and live on plain bread and butter occasionally." An uninspired cook herself, the First Lady of Home Economics education in the United States recommended labor-saving utensils to women who crowded forty-eight hours of work into twenty-four, and whose lives were "made up of men, men, and mud." She believed that modern technology gave women the gift of time for "other duties in and out of the home," including self-improvement, leisure, and intellectual stimulation.

She was born in Randolph, New York, on June 21, 1864. Her father, Henry Killian Van Rensselaer, was a storekeeper, Republican officeholder, and trustee of the Chamberlain Institute, a Methodist coeducational school. Arvilla Owen Van Rensselaer, a former schoolteacher who was active in the Methodist Church and the temperance and suffrage movements, had a profound influence on her daughter. An average student, "Mattie" graduated from the Chamberlain Institute in 1884 and for the next decade taught in various schools in western New York and Pennsylvania, while taking summer school classes in Latin, Greek, and English literature at the Chautauqua Institute. Appointed teacher-preceptress at Chamberlain, where she taught physical culture, rhetoric, English literature, and teacher training, Van Rensselaer was elected—thanks to the support of the Woman's

Christian Temperance Union—one of two school commissioners of Cattaraugus County in 1894. (Women were never barred from running for office in New York, and in some areas they could vote for school officials.)

As she inspected schools throughout the district, driving a horse and buggy over rough roads in all kinds of weather, Van Rensselaer was appalled by the primitive conditions—no running water, electricity, or even mail delivery—under which rural families lived. Determined to do something about it, she accepted an invitation from Cornell professor Liberty Hyde Bailey in 1900 to organize an extension program for farmers' wives. Working out of a small basement office in Morrill Hall, she produced her first publication, "Saving Steps," which was distributed to five thousand women in 1901.

Issued about five times a year, "Miss Van's" subsequent bulletins dealt with sanitation, interior decorating, nutrition, dressmaking, and child care. Within a few years, twenty thousand women subscribed, many of them enrolling as well in local study groups. In 1903, the year Liberty Hyde Bailey became dean of the College of Agriculture, Van Rensselaer began offering home economics instruction for credit on the Cornell campus. In 1907, with the addition of Flora Rose, an expert in foods and nutrition, Bailey and Van Rensselaer overcame the opposition of President Jacob Gould Schurman—"Cooks on the Cornell faculty," he exploded. "Never."—and established the Department of Home Economics.

Van Rensselaer and Rose were a terrific team, working so well together that they also ran a tea shop in downtown Ithaca. According to Schurman, Van Rensselaer and Rose were "the only successful double-headed administration in the academic world," with the former concentrating on administration and extension work, the latter on research and teaching. In 1911, the Cornell faculty grudgingly appointed Van Rensselaer and Rose to professorial rank.

To supplement her own knowledge, Van Rensselaer began taking courses in bacteriology, dairy farming, and agricultural chemistry while she was a lecturer in home economics. She wanted to learn about the bacteriology of the dishcloth, she told one of her professors, "so I can explain to the farm women why it must be kept clean." "Oh, they don't need to learn about bacteriology," he replied, "just teach them to keep their dishcloth clean because they are nicer that way." Undeterred, she completed her Cornell undergraduate degree in 1909, at the age of forty-five.

By 1917, the home economics department offered a full four-year curriculum leading to a degree, published monthly bulletins, sponsored hundreds of study clubs and extension courses throughout New York State, and helped organize Cornell's annual Farm and Home Week. Two years later the department became a school, and in 1925, with a big assist from Van Rensselaer's friend Eleanor Roosevelt, the legislature passed and Governor Alfred E. Smith signed a bill creating the New York State College of Home Economics.

Van Rensselaer was recognized throughout the nation and the world as the pioneering figure in the field of home economics. She was president of the American Home Economics Association from 1915 until 1916. With Flora Rose and Helen Canon, she wrote *A Manual of Homemaking* in 1919. And she served as homemaking editor of the *Delineator* magazine from 1920 to 1926.

During World War I, she worked for Herbert Hoover, who was then head of the U.S. Food Administration. As codirector of the Home Conservation Division she organized campaigns to teach women to can, dry, and preserve foods, and to conserve wheat, meat, and sugar. After the war, she advised the Belgian government on education for women, impressing the queen so much that she made her Chevalier of the Order of the Crown. In 1923 a committee of the National League of Women Voters selected Van Rensselaer as one of the twelve most distinguished women in the United States.

She remained active almost to the day of her death on May 26, 1932, from a lymphoidal sarcoma. She helped President Hoover plan two White House conferences, one on child health and protection, the other on home building and ownership. During the early Depression years, she worked tirelessly to make farm families aware of low-cost, nutritious foods and ways to reuse old clothing, furniture, and discarded household items.

Two weeks after she died, Cornell's president, Livingston Farrand, presided over a simple ceremony to lay the cornerstone for new quarters for the College of Home Economics. Provided with classrooms, an auditorium seating six hundred, an amphitheater for two hundred, and a cafeteria open to students and the general public (which was closed in 2002), the building was to be named Martha Van Rensselaer Hall. It would stand, Flora Rose predicted, as a permanent memorial to the woman who "conceived of home economics education as a means by which women's minds could be trained, their capabilities released, and their deepest desires satisfied through growth in understanding and direction of their own normal social functioning."

Thomas Midgley Jr.

CLASS OF 1911

In his search for an antiknocking agent for internal combustion engines, Thomas Midgley Jr. tested thousands of chemical compounds, "from melted butter and camphor to ethyl acetate and aluminum chloride, and most of them had no more effect than spitting in the Great Lakes." Finally he found a metallo-organic compound, tetraethyl lead (TEL), that suppressed the knock completely. His discovery fed the nation's four-billion-gallon-a-year gasoline habit and made possible high-compression automobile and airplane engines. Despite his insistence that TEL was not toxic and his public demonstrations to prove the point—the *New York World* reported that he "frequently bathed in it"—leaded gasoline carried health risks. When they became apparent, environmentalists placed Midgley in their hall of shame.

Thomas Midgley Jr. was born on May 18, 1889, in Beaver Falls, Pennsylvania. His mother, Hattie Louise Emerson, was the daughter of the man who invented the inserted-tooth circular and band saws. Thomas Midgley, his father, managed a bicycle factory, owned an automobile tire company, and held patents on a woven-wire wheel with detachable tires and a puncture-proof collapsible tire. After completing his secondary education at Betts Academy in Stamford, Connecticut, Thomas Jr. entered Cornell's College of Engineering in 1907. He did not leave much of a mark on the institution. He did not join a fraternity, society, or club, and received no honors. Professor W. H. Barnard, the director of the Sibley School of Mechanical Engineering, noted that Midgley almost "busted out," given his "inexactitude as regards attendance" and his proclivity for "chasing up some loss of energy in a problem to the exclusion of the rest of his work." Because a few professors "appreciated his ability" he was allowed to graduate in mechanical engineering in 1911.

Without waiting for commencement exercises, Midgley took a job in the inventions department of the National Cash Register Company in Dayton, Ohio. He was in love with Carrie Reynolds of Delaware, Ohio, and needed a steady paycheck to marry her. On August 3, 1911, they exchanged vows and, Midgley said, "like all good fairy tales, we lived happily ever afterwards," with two children. After brief stints at NCR and at his father's tire company, Midgley joined the Dayton Engineering Laboratories Company (Delco) in 1916. Charles Kettering, director of research and development at Delco, became his mentor, collaborator, and lifelong friend. Kettering assigned him the task of eliminating knock in gasoline engines, a malfunction that reduced efficiency and power. By designing a more precise engine indicator, Midgley quickly discovered that the fuel, not the engine, caused the knock. During World War I, he put aside this investigation, however, to help devise systems to control the direction of aerial torpedoes. Working with scientists at the Bureau of Mines, he developed a high-octane synthetic fuel for Liberty airplane engines. The war ended before it was put into production.

When Midgley returned to civilian research, General Motors had acquired Delco. As head of the fuel section of the research lab, he prepared tetraethyl lead, which, on December 9, 1921, ended the search for an anti-knock agent. Although lead poisoning had forced him for several months "to drop all work and get a large supply of fresh air," Midgley took an active role in bringing "ethyl" gasoline to market. As vice president and general manager of the Ethyl Corporation (Kettering was president), formed in 1924 by GM and Standard Oil of New Jersey, he went back to the lab when road tests showed that TEL fouled spark plugs and exhaust valves. Finding a chemical corrective, ethyl bromide, he helped develop a procedure to extract bromine from the sea and concluded an agreement with Dow Chemical to produce it. When four workers were killed and dozens hospitalized in a 1924 accident at a TEL plant in New Jersey, Midgley helped ward off restrictions on the sale of leaded gasoline by arguing, from his own studies of mechanics and garage workers, that the compound was no more hazardous than many other chemicals.

Midgley also worked on synthetic rubber in the 1920s. His findings, presented in nineteen research papers, defined the structures of natural and synthetic rubber and the chemistry of vulcanization. Although a drop in the price of rubber prevented commercial applications of his work until later, Midgley regarded it as his most important contribution to science.

At the request of the Frigidaire Division of General Motors, Midgley turned next to artificial refrigeration, a burgeoning but fragile industry in the 1920s because the gases used in refrigerating systems—ammonia, sulfur dioxide, and methyl chloride—were highly toxic or flammable. In the search for a safer compound, Midgley relied on a periodic table arranged according to Irving Langmuir's theory of atomic structure. He found that flam-

mability declined as one moved from right to left on the table and that lighter elements were less toxic than heavier ones. The safest refrigerant, he concluded, was a fluorine compound, dichlorodifluoromethane, or "Freon 12." The research, including tests on the compound's physical properties and toxicity, was completed in three days—not nearly enough time, as later events demonstrated, to test its effects.

Ever the showman, Midgley demonstrated the nontoxicity and nonflammability of Freon at the annual meeting of the American Chemical Society in April 1930. He inhaled a mouthful and slowly breathed it out to extinguish a lighted candle. He helped manufacture and market Freon as vice president of the Kinetic Chemical Company, formed by GM and DuPont in 1930. The most widely used refrigerant for domestic use by the end of the decade, Freon also became an aerosol propellant. In the 1970s, scientists began to discover its unfortunate consequences for the ozone layer. Ironically, Midgley's search for a safe refrigerant led to a product as dangerous as TEL.

A self-taught chemist, credited with more than one hundred patents, Midgley won many of the major awards bestowed by the discipline: the Nichols (1923), Longstreth (1925), Perkin (1937), Priestly (1941), and Gibbs (1942) medals; election to the National Academy of Sciences (1942); the chairmanship of the board of directors for a decade and in 1944 the presidency of the American Chemical Society; and honorary doctorates from the College of Wooster (1936) and Ohio State University (1944). An outgoing man, "fond of all sorts of people," Midgley relished his role as an apostle of progress. In a speech in 1935 celebrating the tercentenary of chemistry in the United States, he predicted that the next century would see a two-hour workday, an end to indigestion, colds, flu, tuberculosis, and possibly cancer, sleep tablets that banished bad dreams, the sluicing of three quadrillions worth of gold out of seawater, eggs the size of footballs and cows the size of mastodons, throwaway cellulose pajamas, and interplanetary travel.

Midgley was stricken with polio in 1940. Some hinted darkly that the tragedy was somehow related to the chemicals with which he had worked. Confined to a wheelchair,

Midgley tried to remain active. But he became depressed, began to drink heavily, and on November 2, 1944, at his home in Worthington, Ohio, he strangled himself in a harness he had designed to help him arise from bed.

Edward L. Bernays
CLASS OF 1912

Few Cornellians have had as dramatic and enduring an impact on American life as Edward L. Bernays. More than anyone else, he developed the principles and practices of public relations. A pioneer of advertising, Bernays, according to one historian, "orchestrated the commercialization of American culture."

His parents, Anna Freud Bernays (a sister of Sigmund Freud) and Ely Bernays, emigrated to the United States in 1892, eight months after Edward (the middle initial doesn't stand for anything) was born in Vienna. A grain merchant in New York City with a seat on the produce exchange, Ely Bernays was convinced that the future of the United States lay in scientific farming. So he sent his son, who had done exceedingly well at Dewitt Clinton High School, to the new agricultural college in Ithaca that had been established by the New York State legislature in 1904. Edward Bernays came to Cornell in 1908 and was miserable from the minute he moved into his $4.50-a-week rooming house on the steep incline of Williams Street until graduation, when he took the train back to Manhattan. His Cornell years, where he pursued a degree in agriculture, involved, in his words, "little stimulation and less learning," "listless boredom," "agonizing courses," and "professors who droned on." In Ithaca he was a "city cat, an outsider" in a world of farmers, ROTC drills, and fraternity privilege.

After a quick stint writing for the *Cornell Countryman,* he returned to New York where his first job was with the *Dietetic and Hygienic*

Gazette. He wrote editorials on such "advanced" topics as the case against corset stays, the need for taking showers, and the value of sex education for children. These editorials provided the springboard for his career in public relations. He was approached by an actor, Richard Bennet, who was producing a play, *Damaged Goods,* which dealt with venereal disease. Bernays's magazine supported the venture, and in a move that augured the strategy that would make him famous, he organized a "sociological fund," inviting progressive-minded leaders of government, industry, and society to give four dollars apiece to support the cause of sex education. In return, Bernays publicized their support and provided first-night tickets to the play. The play was a success, and Bernays seemed set on a career as a theater publicist.

He organized the publicity for several visiting Russian ballet companies before World War I and did the publicity for New York's Metropolitan Opera, turning the Met's relatively obscure Italian tenor, Enrico Caruso, into a household name in America. But it was the war that laid the foundation for Bernays's phenomenal career. He worked for the Committee on Public Information, the first federal propaganda agency, where he designed slogans to persuade the public to support the war against "the Huns."

Convinced the same approach could be used in peacetime, in 1919 Bernays opened an office in New York as a "public relations counselor," a term he would popularize. For the next forty-two years Bernays shaped the new profession of public relations and the purchasing practices of Americans. In 1922 he married Doris E. Fleischman, who remained at his side all those years as his wife and business partner. She retained her maiden name and became the first married woman to get a United States passport in her own name.

A short, rumpled, scholarly looking man, Bernays made his case for "public relations" in several books in the 1920s, *Crystallizing Public Opinion* (1923) and *Propaganda* (1928). The public relations counselor was hired not only to convey information to the public, he insisted, but to "engineer consent." Doing this involved understanding social tastes and habits, which he assessed through the scientific surveys and polls that he pioneered. It also made use of Freudian insights about authority and the role of the unconscious in human behavior, which led to innovations that included the use of experts and celebrity endorsements.

Many of Bernays's public relations campaigns are legendary. He convinced Americans that it was respectable for women to smoke in public by organizing demonstrations in which debutantes gathered on street corners to smoke Lucky Strike cigarettes, which he called "torches of freedom." When his surveys showed that women were reluctant to buy Luckys because its green package with a red bull's-eye clashed with the colors of their clothes, Bernays made green fashionable by underwriting green fashion luncheons, green balls with green gowns, and female mannequins in New York store windows clothed in green suits and dresses. Sales of Lucky Strikes to women soared.

Women were often Bernays's targets. For a client who made luggage, he spread the idea that three changes of clothing were necessary for a weekend trip. For the Venida hairnet company, whose sales plummeted when women started to bob their hair in the 1920s, Bernays got experts to urge that women working near machinery wear hairnets for their own safety. Several states even passed laws requiring them. He persistently used "science" to "engineer" the purchasing patterns of mothers. He used panels of doctors claiming that in the home only disposable cups were truly sanitary to launch a campaign for Dixie cups in the 1930s. To get mothers to bathe their children, and buy Ivory soap, Bernays mobilized pediatricians to endorse the values of a nightly bath. His real coup for the soap company, however, was to organize a national soap carving contest, which for years had millions of school children submitting carvings to a national sculpture committee for an array of awards.

One of Bernays's most legendary successes was aimed at men. In the 1920s, the Ingersoll Company manufactured an inexpensive wristwatch that only women bought; men resisted, convinced apparently that pocket watches were more masculine. Bernays discovered through contacts in the Department of War that in World War I soldiers had carried pocket watches to battle and read them at night by striking matches, thus endangering their lives. Using this research, Bernays convinced Army officials to issue Ingersoll wristwatches with luminous dials as standard equipment. Masculine enough for rugged fighting men, Ingersoll watches became fashionable for all men.

Not surprisingly, Bernays did political public relations as well. He was hired by supporters of President Coolidge to transform their cold, frugal, and taciturn hero into a sympathetic, if not jovial, personality. Undaunted, Bernays staged a news story, bringing forty Broadway stars from New York on the night train to Washington for breakfast at the White House. It worked. Accounts were on the front pages across the country: "Actors Eat Cakes with the Coolidges" read one headline; "President Nearly Laughs," read another. His political efforts were not always so benign. In the 1950s he helped the United Fruit Company convince Americans that the Guatemalan government of Jacobo Arbenz, which wanted to distribute unused company land to landless peasants, was full of communists. The campaign helped generate public support for the CIA's overthrow of Arbenz in 1954.

In 1962 Bernays moved to Cambridge, Massachusetts, apparently to retire to an old house on Lowell Street. There he wrote *Biography of an Idea: Memoirs of Public Relations Counsel Edward L. Bernays* (1965). It was there that his wife died in 1980. In 1983 Bernays returned to Cornell for his first visit since commencement in 1912; he returned several times more to speak with students and faculty of the School of Communications. Until he was one hundred, Bernays represented clients, who paid him a thousand dollars an hour. Soured on the profession he founded, he also lobbied unsuccessfully for legislation that would require the licensing of public relations practitioners. "It seems," he wrote, "anyone can use the term to try to make money, any nitwit or crook or anti-social person can use the name." His last years were marred by a bitter dispute between his two children (one of whom is the novelist Anne Bernays) and his live-in housekeeper, Joan Vondra, over his power of attorney and the control of his estate. The widely publicized affair included charges of kidnapping, fraud, and sexual misadventures, and was finally resolved when his daughters were named conservators of his estate. It was a sad ending to a life of historic achievement. The "father of public relations" was himself a salacious item in the news when he died on March 9, 1995, in Cambridge, Massachusetts.

Millar Burrows

❧ CLASS OF 1912

That Millar Burrows in 1947 was among the first to see the newly discovered ancient texts, written by a Jewish sect at the time of Christ, was pure coincidence. His role in naming them and two popular books in which he explained their significance to the general reader attached him forever to the "Dead Sea Scrolls."

Millar Burrows was born in Wyoming, Ohio, on October 26, 1889. Edwin Jones Burrows, his father, was a carriage manufacturer. Millar's love for the piano, composing, and singing songs came from his mother, Katharine Douglas Millar Burrows, an amateur musician and painter. In 1897 the Burrowses moved to Buffalo, where Edwin Burrows got a job with the McKinnon Dash

Company and his son began his formal education. Millar completed the high school requirements in three years but stayed on to prepare for the state scholarship examinations. The extra work paid off, and he entered Cornell in 1908 with a tuition scholarship.

While compiling an academic record that earned him a Phi Beta Kappa key, Burrows remained popular with his peers. "I have no fear of your getting into bad company," Edwin Burrows wrote his son. "You need companionship, though, and as you want to help others, you must have a kindly feeling for everyone, making allowances for the things you don't like in others." Millar did just that. He joined the Deutscher Verein, acted in a production of *Wilhelm Tell,* and used his musical skills to teach "short horns" to students in Barnes Hall. His magic act (with the patter he had practiced for years) was a big hit at the Sophomore Vaudeville Entertainment, on a program that also featured film star Adolphe Menjou (who later played editor Walter Burns in *Front Page,* the role that Cornellian Louis Wolheim had begun just before his death). Celebrating his "naturally sweet disposition" ("I think the world was made for love," he wrote in his diary), the editors of the Class of 1912 Cornell Yearbook noted that "Cherub" had studied "ancient languages, philosophy, music, black and dramatic art, and fussing, with pronounced success in each."

With ministers on both sides of his family, Burrows got the "call" while at Cornell and entered Union Theological Seminary in 1912. He received his bachelor of divinity degree and was ordained as a Presbyterian minister in June 1915. A month later he married Irene Belle Gladding, a Cornell classmate who he had met while playing catch in front of his boarding house at 208 Dryden Road in Ithaca. The couple had one son. Assigned to a rural church in Wallace, Texas, the "Buffalo Cowboy" found the fundamentalist ideology of his congregation at odds with his more ecumenical, liberal beliefs. Burrows retained his desire to "know Jesus," but Christ seemed to him "so much like an ardently admired stranger." Burrows left Wallace in 1919 to supervise a rural church survey in Texas for the Interchurch World Movement. In 1920 he became college pastor and professor of Bible at Tusculum College in Greenville, Tennessee. Three years later, he completed his odyssey from minister to scholar, enrolling in the doctoral program at Yale. In 1925 his thesis, "The Literary Relations of Ezekiel," was accepted and Dr. Burrows was appointed assistant professor of Biblical Literature and History of

Religions at Brown University. In 1932 he became department chairman.

Trained at Yale in Aramaic and Syrian, the languages of Palestine in the first century A.D., Burrows became fascinated with the archeology of the Middle East during a stint as visiting professor at the American University of Beirut from 1930 to 1931. "Because I was close by and available," he modestly claimed, he was appointed director of the American School of Oriental Research in 1931, a position he held in 1931–32 and 1947–48, serving as president from 1934 to 1948. Well connected and well published (*Founders of Great Religions* appeared in 1931), Burrows was named Winkley Professor of Biblical Theology at Yale Divinity School in 1934. Eventually, from 1950 to 1958, he served as chairman of the Department of Near Eastern Languages and Literature at Yale.

During the 1930s, as a member of the Standard Bible Committee, a group of experts commissioned by the National Council of Churches, Burrows began work on the monumental and controversial task of preparing the Revised Standard Version of the Bible, one intended to replace the King James Bible widely used by Protestants. Even among biblical scholars, Burrows was distinguished by his expertise in the Old and New Testaments. He was the only member of the original team to help with the new translations of both parts of the Bible as well as the Apocrypha, the ancient Jewish books not included in the Protestant canon of Scripture. The complete *Revised Standard Version* was published in 1954, the year Burrows was president of the Society of Biblical Literature and Exegesis.

Burrows was working in Jerusalem when a treasure trove of material was unearthed at Qumran, on the northwest coast of the Dead Sea. Although he had little experience with excavation, he understood the importance of the find immediately. Rejecting the suggestions that the material be called "Essene Texts" or "Qumran Scrolls," Burrows gave the "Dead Sea Scrolls" their dramatic, though slightly inappropriate name, contributing mightily to the popular reception they received and, perhaps unwittingly, securing his own reputation. "He has never sought the headlines," a colleague wrote, "though he has been getting them." In 1955 Burrows's book, *The Dead Sea Scrolls,* became a best-seller. A second account of the discovery, *More Light on the Dead Sea Scrolls* (1958), also reached a large audience. A careful scholar, Burrows identified for interested lay readers similarities and differences between the Jews who wrote the scrolls and early Christians. He dismissed as speculation claims that Jesus and/or John the Baptist were members of the Qumran community and that the scrolls might well be Christian texts. Burrows embraced his role as a popularizer. When his two books were combined in one volume, *Burrows on the Dead Sea Scrolls,* the author quipped, "sounds like ham on rye."

With the creation of the state of Israel in 1948, Burrows became a vocal advocate of the rights of Palestinians. In 1949 he published *Palestine Is Our Business.* From 1954 to 1957 he served as president of American Middle East Relief, an organization that assisted Palestinian Arab refugees.

A fellow of the American Academy of Arts and Sciences, Burrows received honorary doctor of divinity degrees from Oberlin, Brown, and Yale following his retirement in 1958. Union Theological Seminary altered his 1915 degree to read "Master of Divinity." "Now, I'm really retired," he wrote in the 1960s. "Present interests: keeping going and puttering in the garden. State of the Church? I'm sorry, but I wouldn't know. State of the world? Same, only much more so." In 1967, Irene Gladding Burrows died. Devastated, Burrows soldiered on, driving a car until he was past ninety and making himself a favorite of the staff at the Holiday House restaurant in Winter Park, Florida. In 1977 he completed *Jesus in the First Three Gospels* "because I promised Irene." But he described himself in a poem, "Lugubrious Lament," as "A stranded hulk upon the shore,/ abandoned now, to sail no more,/ creaking I roll from side to side,/ obeying the relentless tide,/ while pieces of me day by day,/ come loose, drop off, and wash away." After a stroke in 1980, Burrows agreed to move in with his son and daughter-in-law. He died on April 29, 1980, in Ann Arbor, Michigan.

Georgia Elma Harkness
CLASS OF 1912

In 1972 a delegate to the General Conference of the United Methodist Church rose to speak. She got no further than her opening line, "I am Georgia Harkness," before being interrupted by sustained applause. It was a spontaneous tribute to an eighty-one-year-old woman who had played an important role in opening American Methodism to the ordination of women ministers. In the early 1940s, when she had said, "The church is the last stronghold of male dominance," her reception had been less enthusiastic.

Georgia Elma Harkness was born on April 21, 1891, in Harkness, New York, a small town

in the Adirondacks named for her grandfather. Both of her parents, Joseph Warren Harkness and Lillie Merrill Harkness, worked the family farm. It was, she recalled, "a definitely Christian home." Among the books she voraciously consumed as a child were Methodist conference minutes amassed by her father, a Methodist lay leader. Even so, nothing pointed to a religious vocation. Harkness received the necessary classical training at nearby Keeseville High School to enter Cornell University on a scholarship in 1908. Cornell was not known as a school one attended to study religion, since it had neither a divinity school nor a curriculum of classes in religious subjects.

Harkness majored in history and political science. Outside of the classroom, she participated in Cornell's YMCA, housed in Barnes Hall, and its Student Volunteer Movement. The latter organization, associated with another Cornellian, John R. Mott, encouraged careers in missionary work. Harkness gave that option serious consideration, but when she graduated in 1912 with Phi Beta Kappa honors, she chose instead to teach school for a few years in small New York towns. Ambitious to teach on the college level, she enrolled in Boston University in 1918. In 1920 she received at the same commencement two master's degrees, one in arts and one in religious education. One of her master's theses, "The Church and the Immigrant," later became the first of her thirty-seven books. It reflected Harkness's commitment to the Social Gospel credo of liberal churchmen, a credo that pushed the church toward programs of social reform that included, in the tradition of noblesse oblige, helping "Americanize" the people who passed through Ellis Island. In 1923 Harkness received a Ph.D. from Boston University in the philosophy of religion.

Harkness began her distinguished career in higher education at Elmira College where she served as an assistant professor of the philosophy of religion and religious education from 1922 to 1926 and then until 1937 as professor of philosophy. During that period she held

teaching fellowships at Harvard, Yale, and Union Theological Seminary. In 1937, the same year she became the first female member of the American Theological Society, she accepted an offer to teach in the Department of the History and Literature of Religion at Mount Holyoke. Two years later she moved to Garrett Biblical Institute, a Methodist school in Evanston, Illinois, where she became the first woman in the United States to hold a professorship in theology. The official designation of her post was "applied theology." Although Harkness later said that "applied" meant nothing in particular, the title recognized her interests in practical church matters. Churches, she thought, existed for laypeople and not for academics who wrestled with fine points of doctrine.

Despite her many publications, which included books that more or less fell within the field of systematic theology, Harkness was not a profound theologian. She did, however, write in a clear, organized fashion that enabled her to reach a general audience. She also had an unmistakable point of view in her strong endorsement of liberal ecumenicalism. Churches, in her opinion, should be forces for bringing people together in constructive action, not for driving them apart. Harkness's strengths and weaknesses were also apparent in her several books of religious verse, the most notable being the 1935 volume *Holy Flame,* which received tepid notices from people who cared about poetry. Nonetheless, through her publications Harkness gained an influence second to none among women in American religion. One of her books, *Understanding the Christian Faith,* stayed in print for forty years. She gained many opportunities to lecture around the country and in 1946 returned to Ithaca during Holy Week to speak in Barnes Hall and several local churches. Her final teaching post was at the Pacific School of Religion in Berkeley, California, where she was a professor of applied theology from 1950 until her retirement in 1961.

Over her long career, Harkness joined in many crusades. She became a pacifist in 1924.

She modified her stance during World War II, but in 1950, at a conference of the Federal Council of Churches that issued a position paper, "The Christian Conscience and the Weapons of Mass Destruction," she signed a minority statement that took exception to the majority's approval of the use by the United States of "atomic weapons or other weapons of parallel destructiveness in retaliation for the use of such weapons against this nation or its friends." That action, in the context of the Cold War, constituted sufficient provocation for the FBI to open a file on Harkness. Her ecumenical interests made Harkness a delegate to many worldwide church gatherings in the 1930s and 1940s, including one in Amsterdam in 1948 that launched the World Council of Churches. In these endeavors she met John Foster Dulles, the staunchly Christian man who would become secretary of state under President Eisenhower. Dulles praised her "felicitous gift of phrasing" that made draft "documents say exactly what was meant."

In 1926 Harkness was ordained as a "local elder" of the Methodist Church, which under certain restrictions allowed her to administer the sacraments and to preach but not to be a full member of the Methodist conference. Her longest struggle, then, became one to win full equality for women within her church's ministry. She was not afraid to speak boldly, as she demonstrated in a famous debate about the status of women in the church with the Swiss theologian Karl Barth in 1948. She chose, however, on most occasions to pursue a tactic of moderation, in part because in her personal experiences in ecclesiastical affairs, "I can honestly say that I have had more encouragement than opposition." This, despite the laughter from male delegates that routinely greeted motions to secure women's equality. At the 1956 meeting of the Methodist General Conference that finally endorsed full equality for female ministers, Harkness allowed "able and discerning men" to do the speaking. Despite the crucial role she had played in bringing her church to this point, she kept silent because "I had long since learned that this is often the surest way to get something passed." She approached the podium to express her pleasure only after the resolution had carried.

Harkness's public face was always one of sunny optimism, but she was subject to depression and physical illness, including painful arthritis that made it difficult for her to sit and write. She never married, but her personal loneliness eased when she began to share her home with Verna Miller in 1944. In Berkeley, they maintained a seven-room house with a magnificent view of San Francisco Bay. Harkness enjoyed gardening and entertaining her students with home-baked cookies and pies. Each summer she returned to New York where she stayed in a cabin near Lake Champlain. There she visited with members of her brothers' families and revisited the area that had been her childhood home. She died, apparently of a heart attack, on August 21, 1974. In her honor, Elmira College and Garrett Biblical Institute endowed professorships in her name.

John Merrill Olin
☙ CLASS OF 1913

John M. Olin, the distinguished industrialist and sportsman, left his greatest mark on American society when he established the Olin Foundation. One of the first avowedly conservative "think tanks" in the United States, the Olin Foundation played an important role in changing political ideology and behavior in the United States during the 1970s and 1980s.

John Merrill Olin was born on November 10, 1892, in Alton, Illinois, the second of three sons of Mary Mott Moulton Olin and Franklin Walter Olin. A graduate of Cornell in civil engineering in 1886, Franklin Olin had recently founded one of the companies that became the Olin Corporation, a large diversified manufacturing conglomerate. He expected his sons to enter the family business, sending all of them to Cornell to study chemistry or engineering. John went to the Cascadilla School before entering Cornell in 1909. A member of Kappa Sigma fraternity and a chemistry major, he worked for his father every summer before graduating in 1913. His first full-time job was with Olin's Western Cartridge Company. In 1917 Olin married Adele Levis, with whom he had three children. The couple divorced in 1935, and five years later he married Evelyn Niedringhaus.

Between 1919 and 1944 Olin served as vice president of Western Cartridge, while remaining active in the design and manufacture of arms and ammunition. He was one of the few executives at that time with extensive training as a scientist. Among the two dozen patents he held or shared was one for the use of progressive burning powder in shot shells, which resulted in a "Super X" cartridge with a greater velocity and range than its competitors. The Super X was a commercial success as well as a technological breakthrough.

In 1931, when the Winchester Repeating Arms Company went bankrupt, Olin acquired one of the largest sporting arms plants

in the world for the bargain basement price of eight million dollars. When Olin Industries was founded in 1944, he became president. His company's work on hydrazine, a rocket propellant, provided significant assistance to the U.S. effort to launch a satellite into space. In 1954, following a merger with Mathieson Chemical Corporation, Olin became chairman of the board of a multibillion-dollar complex of chemical, metal, sporting arms, paper, and real estate enterprises. Among the companies he acquired were Squibb Pharmaceuticals and Ecusta Paper Corporation of North Carolina.

An avid skeet and trap shooter, hunter and fisherman (he bought his first fly rod when he was seven), Olin was named to the Hunting Hall of Fame in 1974. He was a leading breeder of horses and dogs as well. His Labrador retriever, King Buck, at the time the only dog ever to appear on a U.S. stamp, was the breed's national champion in 1952 and 1953. His thoroughbred, Cannonade, won the Kentucky Derby in 1974.

Olin's commitment to nature and wildlife preservation, and his efforts to preserve the Atlantic salmon, resulted in appointments to the board of trustees of the American Museum of Natural History and Keep America

Beautiful. On 550 acres near Alton, Ohio, Olin built Nilo (Olin spelled backward) Kennels, a superb Labrador retriever training and breeding center, and subsequently a wildlife preserve.

Before he stepped down as chairman of Olin-Mathieson in 1957 Olin turned to philanthropy. A member of the Cornell Board of Trustees, he made a series of gifts to the university, endowing a professorship in veterinary medicine and funding a microbiology building for the Veterinary Virus Research Institute and the Research Laboratory for Diseases of Dogs. When the cornerstone was set in place in 1960 for the graduate-faculty research library at Cornell that he primarily funded and that bears his name, it was one of the world's largest university libraries, with study facilities for eight hundred scholars and the capacity to house two million volumes.

A staunch believer in free enterprise capitalism, he was convinced that the public had to be awakened "to the creeping stranglehold that socialism had gained here since World War II" and to the centralization of political power in Washington, D.C. In 1953, he founded the John M. Olin Foundation. During the 1960s, under his personal direction, the foundation began to support the economic, political, and philosophical principles known as "neoconservatism." By the mid-'70s, Olin was distributing $1 million a year to conservative scholars and writers.

In 1977, Olin appointed William E. Simon, who would later serve as secretary of the treasury under Ronald Reagan, as president of the Olin Foundation "because his fundamental thinking and philosophy are about identical with mine." Under Simon, the foun-

dation aggressively supported conservative causes, including grants to the journal *The Public Interest*, to William F. Buckley Jr.'s television program *Firing Line*, to student newspapers (most famously the *Dartmouth Review*) and campus magazines across the country, to young faculty and graduate students, and to conferences and seminars dedicated to freedom and free enterprise.

Olin supported public policy institutions in and near Washington, including the American Enterprise Institute, the Cato Institute, the Center for Strategic Studies, and the George Mason School of Law. Seed money was provided to establish think tanks in thirty state capitals dedicated to influencing state legislators and local officials. Ideologically coherent and consistent, the Olin Foundation served as a veritable godfather of the conservative resurgence in American politics and society. Its beneficiaries made up an all-star team of the right: Irving Kristol in public policy, Robert Bork in law, Allan Bloom in education, Jeanne Kirkpatrick in international relations, and Milton Friedman in economics.

When John Olin died at his home in East Hampton, Long Island, on September 8, 1982, Ronald Reagan was president and, thanks in no small measure to Olin's money and his mission-driven foundation, the Reagan Revolution was well under way. William Buckley provided an epitaph Olin would have liked: "John Olin was blessed by inherited wealth which he creatively expanded, devoting himself to industry and to attempting to understand the freedoms within which industry, and employment, and economic progress flourish."

Y. R. Chao (Chao Yuen Ren)

❧ CLASS OF 1914

When Y. R. Chao translated Lewis Carroll's *Alice's Adventures in Wonderland* into Chinese in 1922, he laid claim to being the first person to write the Chinese language exactly as it was spoken. In so doing, he became part of the Chinese literary revolution launched by his Cornell classmate Hu Shih, a revolution that replaced classical Chinese with the written vernacular. These two Cornell graduates, both in the same class, helped change the cultural and political face of China.

Chao was born November 3, 1892, in Tientsin, the only child of an old family from the Changchou district of Kiangsu Province. On a form he filled out for Cornell's Alumni Office many years later, he claimed descent from the first emperor of the Sung dynasty. Perhaps that is why his wife said that he was thoroughly spoiled. Spoiled or not, he was well educated. Following the death of both his parents when he was eleven, he lived with relatives in Soochow. From 1907 until 1910 he attended the progressive Kiangnan Higher School at Nanking.

In 1910 Chao competed for one of the Boxer Indemnity Scholarships. Placing second in the national ranking, he entered Cornell in the fall of 1910 with several of his countrymen, most notably Hu Shih but also Chao's roommate Hu Ming Fu, who became a distinguished mathematician. When Chao graduated four years later with Phi Beta Kappa honors in mathematics and physics, he decided to spend a fifth year in Ithaca studying philosophy. He participated actively in the Cornell Chinese Students Club and the Cosmopolitan Club, but Chao's greatest accomplishment during his Cornell years was his work with two other Cornell students, H. C. Zen and Yang Ch'uan, to bring Western scientific knowledge to China. In 1914 they organized the Science Society of China and a year later the first issue of its journal, *K'o-hsueh* (Science), appeared. Edited for a few years in the United States,

first in Ithaca, and printed in Shanghai, it became extraordinarily important in China's efforts to learn from the West. It is still printed today and halted publication only in 1950, following the victory of the Communists.

From Cornell, Chao moved to Harvard for his doctorate; while there, in addition to his main work in physics, he took courses in philosophy and musical composition. After receiving his Ph.D. in 1918, he accepted a year's traveling fellowship and then returned to Cornell as a physics instructor during the 1919–20 academic year. After ten years in the United States, he returned to China in 1920 to teach mathematics at Tsing Hua University in Peking. He was back in the company of Hu Shih and caught up, like Hu, in the political and cultural ferment of the May Fourth Movement. When John Dewey came to China, Hu Shih acted as his interpreter. When Bertrand Russell arrived in Peking, it was Chao's turn. Through the winter of 1920, he traveled with Russell around China and translated his lectures into various Chinese dialects. The success of that endeavor turned him, more or less by accident and without formal study, toward the field of linguistics, where he achieved his greatest academic distinction.

Another momentous change in his life occurred in 1921 when he met and married Buwei Yang. Both Yang, who had studied medicine in Japan and ran a hospital, and Chao were long betrothed by their families to other people. They abruptly broke their engagements and married without a ceremony by inviting two friends to dinner (Hu Shih being one) and having them sign the marriage certificate as the price of the hospitality. The couple saw it as a "new-style wedding of new-style people" and a very successful union. Yang's considerable talents much enriched Chao's life. She raised four daughters without much domestic help from Chao (he preferred to buy new dishes rather than wash the old ones), practiced medicine when she could, worked to introduce birth control methods to China, and wrote her autobiography and a classic Chinese cookbook for westerners, *How to Cook and Eat in Chinese.*

Buwei Yang best described the split scholarly personality of her husband that was apparent in his study of the Chinese language. Acting from one side of his brain, he was a reformer who joined Esperanto clubs, sat on committees on the unification of the Chinese language, devised a romanized Chinese alphabet, and prepared a textbook for a standardized national spoken language along with an accompanying set of phonograph records. On the other hand, Chao also believed that whatever existed needed to be studied. In this mood, he saw classical Chinese not as something to be fought against but as something to be understood. Similarly, he regarded dialects not as dissonance that needed to be abolished but as national heritages that had to be recorded and compared. Chao was known for his perfect pronunciation of all the languages he learned to speak.

Shortly after his marriage, Chao returned to the United States to teach Chinese at Harvard, the first time that language had been offered at Harvard in forty years. He stayed in Cambridge until 1924, teaching and auditing courses in linguistics and music. He then re-

turned to Peking after a year of travel in Europe. He remained in China, where he directed the phonology division of the Institute of History and Philology of the Academia Sinica until war broke out with Japan in 1937. He then accepted a series of posts in the United States, first at the University of Hawaii, then at Yale from 1939 to 1941, again at Harvard from 1941 to 1946, and finally at UC Berkeley where he was the Agassiz Professor of Oriental Languages from 1948 to 1963.

During his active career, Chao was not only the leading scholarly authority on the Chinese language but also a major influence on how Chinese was taught in the United States. At Harvard he directed the Chinese-English dictionary project of the Harvard-Yenching Institute, ran the Chinese language program of the School for Overseas Administration established during World War II, and published three books of applied linguistics, *Concise Dictionary of Spoken Chinese, Cantonese Primer,* and *Mandarin Primer: an Intensive Course in Spoken Chinese.* He served as president of the Linguistic Society of America and of the American Oriental Society. He was a fellow of the American Academy of Arts and Sciences and received honorary doctorates from Princeton and the University of California.

Even while living in the United States, Chao retained strong ties with China. From 1945 until 1947 he served as the Chinese representative to UNESCO, and he continued to direct the study of linguistics at the Academia Sinica. When he went to Taiwan in 1959 as a Fulbright lecturer, he was treated not as a "returned American" but as a towering figure in Chinese studies.

Chao expressed his emotions always through his intellect. When Hu Shih, his close friend of fifty years, died in 1962, Chao honored Hu with an essay about the dialect of his native district in Anhwei Province. Chao's life, so filled with satisfactions, knew one great disappointment. His translation of Carroll's *Through the Looking Glass,* which he regarded as his finest literary achievement, was lost in a fire in Shanghai during China's war with Japan. Chao's fascination with Carroll may seem an odd avocation for a man regarded by many as formal and reserved. His wife quipped that he was "a linguist who can keep silent in seven languages." Yet Chao loved humor. He collected popular music and composed songs for children as well as songs based on contemporary Chinese poetry. One of his compositions became the title song of a Chinese movie. His studies in linguistics won him respect in China, but his music carried his fame beyond the university and into the lives of ordinary people.

Not long before his death Chao seized a chance to visit mainland China with two of his daughters. He died on February 24, 1982, at the age of eighty-nine, a year after the death of his wife. All four of his children became college professors, and one of them, Bella Chao Chiu, earned her graduate degree in physics at Cornell. Chao himself had returned to Ithaca many times to lecture and to attend reunions, including his sixtieth reunion in 1974.

William Frederic Friedman

ᴥ CLASS OF 1914

On occasion, William Friedman regretted that he had been "seduced from an honorable profession" — genetics — "to one with a slight odor." But virtually all Americans who lived through World War II were delighted that the man who broke the infamous Japanese "Purple" code had decided to become a cryptologist.

Wolfe (later William) Frederic Friedman was born in Kishinev, Russia, on September 24, 1891. His father, Frederic Friedman, worked for the Russian postal service. Rosa Trust, his mother, was the daughter of a prosperous wine merchant. To escape a country beset by anti-Semitic laws and pogroms, in 1893 the Friedmans emigrated to Pittsburgh, where Frederic Friedman found work as a door-to-door salesman of Singer sewing machines and Rosa took a job as a clothing peddler. Interested in engineering and agriculture, William took up telegraphy in his teens so that he and his buddies could send messages to one another from their homes. He graduated from Pittsburgh Central High School in 1909 at the top of his class, briefly attended Michigan Agricultural College in Lansing, and in 1911 transferred to the College of Agriculture at Cornell to pursue a career in genetics. An excellent student, Friedman

found time to join Phi Epsilon Pi fraternity, serve as secretary of the Eugenics Society, and play in the Agricultural Music Club and the Banjo Club. He received a B.S. in 1914 and remained in Ithaca for graduate work.

In 1915 Friedman ended his studies at Cornell to take a job as head of the Department of Genetics at Riverbank Laboratories, which was on an estate thirty miles from Chicago owned by George Fabyan, a grain merchant and eccentric millionaire. Hired to develop tougher strains of wheat, Friedman found himself drawn into Fabyan's obsessive effort to prove that Francis Bacon was the illegitimate son of Queen Elizabeth and the author of the plays attributed to William Shakespeare by deciphering messages thought to be incorporated in each text. Friedman was attracted to cryptography, which at this time was dominated by dilettantes, because he believed it required "unusual powers of observation, inductive and deductive reasoning, much concentration, perseverance, and a vivid imagination." Fabyan also assigned to the project

Elizebeth Smith (Elizebeth with an "e" because her mother did not want her to be called Eliza), in whom Friedman found a soul mate in cryptography who shared his doubts about the claims made for Francis Bacon. The couple married in 1917 and had two children.

After the United States entered World War I, Fabyan offered the services of the Riverbank cryptologists to the federal government. The Friedmans taught U.S. Army officers the scientific and statistical techniques of code making and breaking. They tested a British enciphering machine, and in five hours came up with five messages, one of which began "This cipher is absolutely indecipherable." While assisting Scotland Yard in an investigation of ties between the German government and Hindu nationalists, the Friedmans uncovered an essential principle of cracking codes and ciphers—the frequency of the use of key letters in messages. Sent to France in 1918 with the Code and Cipher Solving Section of the General Staff, William Friedman helped break the ADFGVX cipher. The Germans, he noticed, often showed an "unintelligent pedantry," failing to alter the form or punctuation of messages and making the sometimes fatal mistake of sending proverbs as practice messages.

During and after the war, Friedman, sometimes in collaboration with his wife, published essays and books, including the four-volume *Elements of Cryptanalysis* (1926) and *The History and the Use of Codes and Code Languages* (1928) that became the primers for students of cryptology. According to David Kahn, author of *The Codebreakers,* Friedman's theoretical work, especially his pamphlet, "The Index of Coincidence and Its Applications to Cryptography," revolutionized the science of cryptanalysis in ways that "can only be described as Promethean."

The Friedmans came to Washington, D.C. in 1921, when William was appointed chief cryptanalyst in the War Department, a post he would occupy for twenty-five years, and Elizebeth was hired by the Treasury Department, where she helped break the codes of liquor smugglers during Prohibition. Dubbed

a Midas because "everything he touched turned to plaintext," William translated the messages used by the conspirators in the Teapot Dome scandal and throughout the 1920s and 1930s studied mechanical ciphering devices to learn how to construct and decode them. In 1930 he became chief of the Signal Intelligence Service of the Army Signal Corps, which built a network of radio listening stations around the world to gather data.

Friedman also patented devices for ciphering and deciphering messages that would become essential to the systems used by the United States. He was the first person to use an IBM card for cryptographic keying purposes. In 1939, as war became more and more likely, Friedman was relieved of administrative duties to devote all of his time to breaking the Japanese "Purple" code. He was not allowed to discuss the project with anyone, including his wife. In September 1940, Friedman's team came up with its first ungarbled message and soon built a replica of the Angooki Taipu A machine out of $684.85 worth of spare parts.

Because of a catastrophic series of coincidences and misjudgments (none of the eight Purple machines the SIS constructed was sent to Hawaii), the messages that might have alerted the military to the attack on Pearl Harbor did not reach them in time. But Friedman's code breaking played a pivotal role in the Battle of Midway; in the shooting down of a plane carrying Admiral Yamamoto, the commander-in-chief of the Japanese fleet; and in providing advance knowledge of Germany's military plans when they were communicated to the Japanese. In 1945 Friedman picked up "peace feelers" from Japan. Had he been able to send them directly to President Truman, he lamented years later, he would have recommended "that he not drop the [atomic] bomb—since the war would be over within a week."

Friedman appeared at work each day, punctually, with a starched shirt and tie, trim suit, and two-tone shoes. But his dapper figure and formal but cordial manner concealed turmoil within. The pressure to produce and the need for secrecy—the government even classified as "restricted" his essay "Jules Verne as Cryptographer," published in the *Signal Corps Bulletin,* and forbade the Jules Verne Society to review it—were unrelenting. In 1941 the overwork and mental strain of breaking the Purple code resulted in a nervous breakdown, the first of several he would endure.

When World War II ended, Friedman tried to get the patents for his nine inventions of cryptographic machines declassified. When the U.S. government refused, he sought legislative relief. Since national security prevented him from selling his cipher machines to other governments, Congress in 1956 passed a bill to pay him $100,000 in lieu of profits he had been unable to realize. Friedman also received the highest honors awarded by the United States government: the War Department's Commendation for Exceptional Civilian Service in 1944; the Medal for Merit, the civilian equivalent of the Distinguished Service Award for military personnel, in 1946; and the National Security Medal in 1955.

Friedman remained active in cryptanalysis during the 1950s, helping create the National Security Agency, where he served briefly as assistant to the director, and undertaking three secret missions to Europe to coordinate allied code breaking during the Cold War. But as their workload diminished, the Friedmans took time to return to the Shakespeare cipher project. Their devastating critique of the evidence used to discredit the authorship of the Bard's work won the Friedmans the Folger Shakespeare Award in 1955. Two years later they published *The Shakespearean Ciphers Examined,* a work that combined sophisticated literary criticism with cryptographic rigor.

In 1955 Friedman had a massive heart attack. For the rest of his life he was beset by depression and poor health and disenchanted by what he thought the overzealous behavior—its intrusiveness and its impact on individual liberties— of the National Security Agency. William Friedman died on November 2, 1969. Only in the obituaries did he emerge fully from the shadows of secrecy, as the man who helped create the profession of cryptanalyst, and as the greatest code breaker in the United States.

Hu Shih
❧ CLASS OF 1914

If a future Chinese government moves in the direction of liberal political principles, Cornell may claim a small role in the transformation. Hu Shih (listed in the *Cornellian* as Suh Hu) graduated in 1914 and after several more years in the United States returned to China to play a leading part in the May Fourth Movement. Named after a 1919 protest, this movement of urban intellectuals opposed foreign domination and backward Chinese traditions and wanted to learn from the West to create an independent, modern, industrial nation. For the next two decades he was among the most influential intellectuals who sought

to guide the cultural and political turmoil that changed China. Hu Shih is without question one of the great scholars of twentieth-century China.

Hu Shih was born on December 17, 1891, in Shanghai, where his father, Hu Ch'uan, served as a minor functionary in the imperial Chinese bureaucracy. Hu and his mother, the third wife of Hu Ch'uan, followed the father on a new assignment to Taiwan but returned without him to the family home in Chihsi in 1895. Later that year, Hu's father died. Hu, a precocious child who knew over eight hundred Chinese characters before he went to the local school in Chihsi, returned to Shanghai and attended the China National Institute, where he received his first instruction in English and in Western math, science, and philosophy. Most of Hu's fellow students considered themselves radicals and embraced the changes that swept China during its revolution of 1911.

However, Hu Shih would not be in China to witness the fall of the Ch'ing dynasty. In 1910 he traveled to compete for one of the Boxer Indemnity Scholarships, which had been created from money China was forced to pay to the United States and other Western powers after they had defeated the anti-foreigner Boxer Uprising of 1898–1900. With seventy other successful candidates, including Y. R. Chao (Chao Yuen Ren), who would become his close friend at Cornell, Hu Shih sailed for the United States in August. When he enrolled at Cornell, he was nineteen and equally conversant in traditional Confucian philosophy and Darwinian science (Shih, the adult name he chose for himself, means "fit").

Hu Shih enrolled in Cornell's College of Agriculture because he believed that China most needed technical expertise. However, Hu's idealized vision of plowing and sowing did not match the dull reality of his study, and in 1912 he transferred to the College of Arts and Sciences to study philosophy. Many years later he showed Professor Knight Biggerstaff, Cornell's distinguished sinologist, the exact chair in Goldwin Smith Hall where he was

seated when he decided to change majors. Hu, who graduated with Phi Beta Kappa honors, the Hiram Corson prize in English for an essay about Robert Browning, and the nickname "Doc," spent a postgraduate year in Ithaca studying philosophy. He then began a doctorate at Columbia under the guidance of the American pragmatist John Dewey.

Hu's lifelong complaint about himself was that he got involved in many activities that detracted from scholarship. He was gregarious and unable to ignore life outside the university. At Cornell, he was president of the Cornell Chinese Students Club. During the 1912 U.S. presidential election, he became an ardent supporter of Theodore Roosevelt's Bull Moose Party. He became even more enthusiastic about the progressivism of the winning candidate, Woodrow Wilson. Perhaps Hu's most significant extracurricular interest at Cornell was the Cosmopolitan Club, an international organization that was founded at Cornell in 1904. As president of the Cornell chapter, Hu participated in discussions that reinforced his pacifism and forged in him an enduring opposition to all narrowly conceived nationalisms. He often studied while sitting on a stone bench that still stands in front of Goldwin Smith Hall. On it are carved the words "Above All Nations Is Humanity."

Critics would later say that Hu returned to China thoroughly Westernized—a man with a Chinese body but an American brain. Certainly his graduate study with Dewey had made him a firm believer in experimentalism and the methods of Western science. He criticized the Chinese for their lack of individualism and their unexamined adherence to traditions that shackled individual choice. In part because of the influence of the daughter of a Cornell faculty member who was his close friend, Hu advocated the liberation of Chinese women. He admired the optimism of Americans and their insistence that every problem had a rational solution. For all that, Hu Shih felt his Chinese roots deeply and tried both in his doctoral dissertation and in later work to demonstrate that what he admired in Western philosophy was also present in Chinese philosophy, especially in neo-Confucianism.

Hu Shih's greatest scholarly achievement was in leading a literary movement that replaced China's classical written language with vernacular literature (*pai-hua*), a movement as important as western Europe's break with using Latin. As "father of the literary revolution," Hu recovered a wealth of vernacular writing from China's past, helped destroy the monopoly on literacy held by "the aristocratic few," and made printed material accessible to ordinary Chinese citizens. Arguably the revolution started on Beebe Lake when three Chinese Cornell undergraduates overturned in a canoe and waded ashore. Agreeing to commemorate the event by writing poetry, two of them created verse in classical Chinese. The other, Hu Shih, wrote his poem in the vernacular and justified the experiment in an essay, "Tentative Proposals for the Reform of Chinese Literature." Published in China in 1917, the essay became instantly famous.

In 1917 Hu returned to China as a professor of philosophy at Peking University, and later became the chancellor. He became a leading voice in the New Culture movement that flowed into the May Fourth Movement, which began in Peking's Tiananmen Square in 1919. He hosted John Dewey and Bertrand Russell during their celebrated stays in China in the early 1920s. Following a trip to Europe and the United States in 1926–27 and a three-year teaching assignment in Shanghai, he served from 1931 until 1937 as dean of the College of Arts at Peking.

In politics, Hu led the "no party, no faction" intellectuals. From the beginning, Hu opposed the Chinese Communists, who did not understand—in Hu's famous and controversial phrase—that the reconstruction of a society is "created bit by bit and drop by drop." During the 1920s, he was almost as critical of the Nationalist Party (Kuomintang) that Chiang Kai-shek led after the death of Sun Yat-sen. The problems with the Kuo-

mintang lay in its nationalism and its authoritarianism. During those years of his greatest influence, especially as editor of *The Independent Critic* during the 1930s, Hu championed liberal political values.

At the outbreak of the Sino-Japanese War in 1937, Hu Shih left China. When he addressed the Cosmopolitan Club that year in Ithaca, he said that the doctrine of pacifism he had long advocated was no longer tenable in the face of Japanese aggression. Though he never joined the Kuomintang, he moved closer to Chiang Kai-shek, who named him the Chinese ambassador to the United States in 1938 ("I have degenerated into an ambassador," he said). He was the second Cornellian to hold that post, the first being Dr. Alfred Sao-ke Sze, class of '01, who represented China in Washington from 1932 to 1935. Hu's diplomatic career ended in 1942, although he later served as a member of the Chinese delegation to the United Nations Conference on International Organization in London.

Hu Shih returned to China to participate in the writing of the new constitution of 1947, which was designed to end the period of Kuomintang tutelage and one-party rule. He was elected to the National Assembly. In 1948, Chiang Kai-shek, now badly needing unconditional support from the United States, tried to enhance his democratic credentials by asking Hu to run for the presidency. Hu declined, saying that a scholar who could not even keep his desk in order had no business trying to manage a government.

It was too late in any case. Chinese Communist forces pushed the Nationalists from the mainland in 1949, and Hu returned to the United States to live in semiretirement. During these years, he supported America's Cold War stance toward the Chinese Communists and gave encouragement to the China Lobby, which accused the U.S. State Department of having deserted Chiang Kai-shek.

Returning often to Cornell, whose campus he loved, he was honored by his graduating class in 1939 at his twenty-fifth reunion with the Class of 1914 Award for Eminent Achievement. To packed audiences, he delivered the Messenger Lectures in 1946.

In 1958, Hu Shih went to Taiwan where Chiang Kai-shek had appointed him president of the Academia Sinica. On February 24, 1962, he died unexpectedly of a heart attack. His wife Chiang Tung-Shiu, whose marriage to Hu had been arranged by Hu's mother when Hu was eleven, survived him. Hu's older son, Tsu-wang, graduated from Cornell in 1942 and settled in the United States. The younger son, Sze-tu, stayed in the People's Republic of China and became an outspoken critic of his father. Ironically, the Communists were major beneficiaries of the language revolution that Hu had spearheaded.

The Chinese students who gathered in Tiananmen Square in 1989 to renew the spirit of the May Fourth Movement after seventy years were heirs to the independent spirit of Hu Shih, a scholar who spent his life trying to "think well." As Martin Sampson, Cornell's legendary English professor, remarked of the gifted alum, "It is entirely possible that a thousand years from now Cornell may be known as the place where Hu Shih went to college."

Leroy Randle Grumman

❧ CLASS OF 1916

"The name Grumman on a plane or a part," said Vice Admiral John S. McCain, deputy chief for Naval Operations-Air, "is like sterling on silver." During World War II, Grumman Aircraft Engineering Corporation produced 18,768 airplanes, more than any other company, meeting or surpassing its quota every month. In 1948, Leroy Grumman, the founder of the company, became the first aircraft manufacturer to receive the Presidential Medal of Merit.

Leroy Randle Grumman was born in Huntington, New York, on January 4, 1895, the son of George T. Grumman, a carriage shop owner, and Grace Conklin Grumman. A talented student, who graduated second in his class from Huntington High School, Leroy decided to take his father's interest in transportation in a new direction, discussing in his salutatorian address the infant aircraft industry. At Cornell, which he entered in 1912, "Herk" played some baseball, but concentrated on his mechanical engineering courses and Eta Kappa Nu, the electrical engineering society. After graduation he took a job with the New York Telephone Company, then

joined the Navy in June 1917, two months after the United States entered World War I. Accepted for aviation duty, he did not see action overseas, serving instead as a flight instructor, test pilot, and project engineer for the Naval Aircraft Factory in Philadelphia.

In October 1920 Grumman resigned his commission and took a job with Albert and Grover Loening, pioneering aviators he had met in the navy. The next year he married Rose Marion Werther (a 1919 graduate of

Cornell), with whom he had four children. Grumman rose quickly through the ranks at Loening Aeronautical Engineering Corporation of New York, from test pilot to plant manager to general manager, playing an important role in the construction of the Loening air yacht, an amphibious biplane. When the Loenings decided to relocate to Bristol, Pennsylvania, as part of the Keystone Aircraft Company in 1929, Grumman took $17,000 of his own money and, with five other Loening employees, formed the Grumman Aircraft Engineering Corporation. With 46.7 percent of the voting stock, he became president and chairman of the board of a company with sixteen employees that was located in a converted garage in Baldwin, New York.

Grumman decided not to construct airplanes for personal or commercial use, but to focus exclusively on aircraft for the military. His strategy paid off in 1930, when the company produced an amphibious plane with landing gear that recessed fully when retracted. Lighter than the "float-without-wheels" then in use, the seacraft inaugurated for Grumman a long and lucrative association with the Navy. From its more spacious headquarters in Valley Stream, Long Island, Grumman designed and built two-seat fighter planes with potbellied fuselages that resembled bumblebees. They were dubbed "Fi-Fis" (for FF-1s) by fliers who found them rugged, fast, and maneuverable, lavishing praise as well on their state-of-the-art landing gear and gun mounts. In 1934 the Navy purchased fifty-five single-seat planes, the F2F; three years later, eighty-one F3F biplane fighters rolled off the assembly lines. Navy orders for Grumman's biplane fighters led to gross sales of $2.2 million in 1937. The company, with its five hundred workers, had weathered the Great Depression.

When the United States entered World War II, Grumman Aircraft was ready. One of the first recipients, in 1940, of an emergency plant facilities contract, which provided government funds for expansion of facilities, Grumman had by 1945 added 2,650,000 square feet of floor space to its plants, most of it paid for by U.S. taxpayers. In 1941, employee rolls jumped from two thousand to seven thousand; by 1943 they had reached twenty-five thousand. While other companies debated designs, Grumman rolled "Wildcats" off the assembly lines. With a folding wing—which Grumman himself conceived of to increase the number of aircraft that could be accommodated on a carrier—the Wildcat was the Navy's only operational fighter for the first thirty months of the war. According to Undersecretary of the Navy James Forrestal, Grumman Wildcats "saved Guadalcanal." Exempt from the wartime freeze on new design and large-scale experimental work, Grumman added the "Hellcat" to the fleet in August 1943. Hellcats shot down 5,156 enemy aircraft during the war—55 percent of all the planes destroyed by the Navy and Marine Corps—while only 270 of them were lost. Pilots loved the durable plane they called the "Grumman Iron Works." Said one flier: "If my Hellcat could cook, I'd marry it."

Grumman built more airplanes in a single month—664 in March 1945—than any other U.S. competitor. It made 65 percent of the fighter planes and, with the TBF "Avenger," 98 percent of the Navy's torpedo-bombers. Grumman workers produced more airframe pounds per employee than any other airplane manufacturer. Leroy Grumman's paternalistic management style accounted in no small measure for the company's ability to meet its production schedule. A quiet man, with a spartan office, where hundreds of model airplanes hung from the ceiling, Grumman worked in shirtsleeves and was rarely seen without his pipe. He encouraged his employees to visit him if they had a suggestion or a complaint. Grumman instituted one of the most generous noncontributory pension funds in the United States for his employees, while also providing bonuses, nurseries for the children of women workers, a "green car" service for anyone with an errand to run or an emergency, and inexpensive hot meals, dancing, volleyball, baseball, and handball during lunch hour. This approach kept unions out and Grumman free of strikes or slowdowns during the war. At less than 3 percent, worker turnover was about half the rate for the rest of the industry.

Shortly before the war ended, Grumman caught a cold that developed into pneumonia. Without asking about allergies to medication, a doctor injected him with penicillin. It so severely and permanently impaired his eyesight that he stepped down as president of the company in 1946. Remaining an active chairman of the board, he anticipated the lean postwar years and promoted diversification. Before he retired in 1966, the company was producing aluminum canoes, crop dusters, and the lunar module. The Cold War allowed Grumman to continue its lucrative relationship with the Navy. During the Korean War, his company produced the F9F Panther (a jet fighter) and, later, the swept-wing Cougar, the supersonic Tiger, and the A-6A Intruder attack bomber.

For his contributions to aeronautics, Grumman received many honors. In 1948 he was awarded the Daniel Guggenheim Medal. He received the first Hunsacker Medal from the National Academy of Sciences in 1968. He was named to the National Aviation Hall of Fame in 1972 and the International Aerospace Hall of Fame in the following year.

Grumman was an active Cornell alumnus, serving as a member of the board of trustees for more than a decade and contributing funds for the construction of the Grumman Squash Courts and Grumman Hall, the home of aerospace engineering. In 1961 he donated his red and white DC-3 to the university. Called *Far Above,* the plane flew staff and faculty, athletic teams, special student groups, government officials, and foreign ambassadors in and out of Ithaca until it was sold in 1970.

Grumman's health deteriorated in the 1970s and he stopped visiting his alma mater and the assembly lines and boardrooms of his company. On October 4, 1982, the man who had wanted to create "a small, intimately manageable, and innovative" aircraft company and built a billion dollar aerospace empire instead died at North Shore University Hospital in Manhasset, Long Island.

Laurens Hammond

CLASS OF 1916

In March 1937, in the chapel of the University of Chicago, officials of the Federal Trade Commission, fifteen undergraduates, and a jury of nine professional musicians listened to parts of thirty compositions played in an unannounced sequence sometimes on a pipe organ and sometimes on an instrument invented by Laurens Hammond. The students could not determine which selections came from the Skinner pipe organ and which were from the Hammond electric. The experts fared only slightly better. As a result the FTC decided that Hammond could use the word "organ" in advertisements. Hammond had brought the machine age to music.

Three years after Laurens's birth on January 11, 1895, in Evanston, Illinois, his banker father, William Andrew Hammond, died, and Idea Strong Hammond took the family to Paris, Geneva, and Dresden, where she could paint beautiful landscapes and let her four children be taught by followers of Friedrich Froebel, father of the kindergarten. The family returned to Evanston when Laurens was ten. By the time he was sixteen he had already filed two patents, one for an automobile transmission and the other for a barometer that could be sold for one dollar. In 1912 Hammond entered the College of Engineering at Cornell. Although he joined Delta Upsilon fraternity, he appears to have spent most of his time in Ithaca studying mechanical engineering. He received a B.S. in 1916.

After graduation, Hammond served in France during World War I with the Sixteenth Engineering Regiment. Discharged as a captain in 1919, he took a job with the Gray Motor Company of Detroit and experimented with diesel engines. In 1920 he set up shop in Chicago as an independent inventor. In 1924 he married Mildred Anton-Smith. The couple had two children. In the 1920s, Hammond invented several machines that produced three-dimensional (3D) movies. The "Teleview" placed a device in front of each spectator that blocked the vision of the left and then the right eye at such a speed that no obstruction could be detected. The result was a stereoscopic effect that appeared to be three dimensional, making close-ups of love scenes, according to one critic, "almost embarrassing." Hammond's demonstration film, *Hello Mars,* received favorable notice, but Hollywood showed no interest in purchasing the special cameras and projectors needed to produce the effect. Hammond's "Shadowgraph" was only slightly more successful. It produced a three-dimensional illusion by projecting red and green shadows on the screen, which audience members viewed through lorgnettes with red- and green-colored lenses. Florenz Ziegfeld used the Shadowgraph for

his Follies, but no filmmaker was willing to invest.

Hammond's inventions kept coming, including a tickless alarm clock and an electric bridge table that shuffled and dealt the cards. His first big success came in 1929 with an electric clock with a reliable, simple, synchronous motor conducive to mass marketing. Unfortunately, although Hammond had patents on his motor, rival companies developed similar devices. By 1932 over one hundred manufacturers were selling electric clocks. The inventor added month and day indicators to his clock, but the competition and the Depression produced large deficits for the Hammond Clock Company and the prospect of bankruptcy.

Hammond found another use for his synchronous motor. Although not a musician, he remembered the pipe organ at St. Luke's Episcopal Church in Evanston, where he had been an altar boy, and decided to develop an electric organ for commercial and residential use. In contrast to the bulky, expensive, and temperamental pipe organ, the Model A that Hammond offered for sale in 1935 weighed about 275 pounds, cost $1,250 (the price for the cheapest pipe organ was $6,000), was not affected by temperature or humidity, and as long as the voltage remained constant delivered a pitch that did not vary and required no tuning. With its drawbar system of tone control, the Hammond produced millions of different sounds, making it as suitable to jazz and rock as it was to classical music. The company also published instructions for producing the sounds of chimes, bongo drums, and marimbas on the organ. George Gershwin bought the first instrument manufactured by Hammond. Leopold Stokowski, conductor of the Philadelphia Orchestra, did not buy one, but acknowledged that with four Hammond organs he could re-create the sound of an entire symphony orchestra.

Although some critics complained that the sound produced by the electric organ was colorless and monotonous, Hammond sold 1,763

Model A organs in 1936—a year when only 583 pipe organs were sold. At first churches bought most of the organs, but within a decade theaters, roller skating rinks, baseball parks, and restaurants were major buyers. Radio stations used Hammond organs to provide background music for soap operas and for such popular adventure serials as *The Shadow* and *The Cisco Kid*. By 1950, dealers, who stressed how easy "music's most glorious voice" was to play and offered free lessons, sold a majority of Hammond organs for use in private homes.

With the success of the electric organ, Hammond developed variations on the theme. In 1939, in the auditorium of the Commerce Department in Washington, D.C., he gave a demonstration of the "Novachord." Designed to simulate the sound of any known or hypothetical instrument, the Novachord, enclosed in a case that resembled a spinet, had seventy-two keys and two sets of controls, one to vary the "envelope" (the instrument), the other to adjust the tone. Unlike the electric organ, in which the alternations in current (the electrical equivalent of notes) were regulated by a motor driving a shaft that ran the width of the console, the Novachord used grids in vacuum tubes that pushed impulses through at a desired frequency. The next year Hammond introduced the "Solovox," an attachment to the piano keyboard that enabled amateurs to project the melody in organ-like tones. And in 1950 Hammond gave more assistance to nonmusical musicians with a "chord organ" that supplied harmonies whenever a button was pressed.

Until his retirement in 1960, Hammond presided over a company that dominated the electric organ market, despite competition from Wurlitzer and others. He remained as much an inventor as a businessman. Concerned that Americans were spending too much time at the movies or listening to the radio, he experimented with "the self-reading" book. Placing a sixty-thousand word novel on a cellophane sound track four and a half inches in diameter and an inch and a half wide, Hammond hoped to entice people to sit comfortably in the living room as a spool placed in a little cabinet read aloud in a clear, pleasant voice. He even envisioned a self-reading Book-of-the-Month Club, open to illiterates as well as the reading public. Like 3–D movies, the "self-reading" book was an idea ahead of its time.

During World War II Hammond was a consultant to the guided-missile section of the Army Air Force. During peace and war, while working or in retirement, he knew how to live the good life, at the poker table or on a yacht with his family. Hammond died in Cornwall, Connecticut, on July 1, 1973, just before Hammond Organ discontinued its traditional line of electromechanical instruments and Suzuki purchased the company. Although the machine age has given way to the era of digitization, some old models survive, sought out by amateurs and professionals who like the sound of a Hammond.

H. C. Zen (Jen Hung-chün)
❧ CLASS OF 1916

H. C. Zen (Jen Hung-chün) was one of the remarkable group of Chinese who, in the second decade of the twentieth century, studied at Cornell under the Boxer Indemnity Scholarship program. In funding the program, the United States hoped to shape the future leaders of a country it viewed as a potentially lucrative trading partner. To a point the gambit succeeded. It produced an impressive cadre of intellectuals who returned home seeking to modernize China with ideas learned at universities in the United States. From his student days at Cornell until the end of his life, H. C. Zen played a crucial role in promoting the methods and spirit of Western science in his homeland.

Born into a gentry family in Szechwan Province on December 20, 1886, Zen attended a modern public school where he was trained both in classical Chinese studies and some aspects of Western thought. After graduating from middle school in Chungking in 1906, he taught briefly before continuing his studies at the China National Institute in Shanghai and the Higher Technical College in Tokyo. In 1911, when the revolution that toppled the Ch'ing Dynasty took place, Zen returned to China from Japan to serve in Sun Yat-sen's presidential office in Nanking. Zen, in fact, drafted Sun's manifesto to the nation. When the revolution went off course and the provisional government dissolved in 1912, Zen looked to opportunities outside China. In January 1913, he arrived in Ithaca to begin studies in chemistry.

On June 10, 1914, nine Chinese Cornell students, including Y. R. Chao (Chao Yuen Ren), met in H. C. Zen's room to hold the first meeting of the Science Society of China and to found the journal *K'o-hsueh* (Science). "In today's world," Zen said, "a nation cannot become powerful without science. It is our responsibility to introduce modern science into China." The inaugural issue of the journal, edited in a boarding house in Ithaca and written in classical Chinese, was published in Shanghai in January 1915. The first Chinese scientific journal written and published by Chinese scientists rather than Western missionaries, *K'o-hsueh* is still printed today and ceased publication only in 1950. In October 1915 Zen became president of the society, a post he held until 1923 and then again from 1934 until 1936 and from 1947 until 1950. Nicknamed "Sage" by his classmates, Zen graduated from Cornell in 1916. After receiving an M.A. from Harvard in chemistry, he returned to China to begin a career as a teacher and academic administrator.

However, before leaving Ithaca, Cornell had one more decisive effect on his life. In the summer of 1916 Sophie H. Chen (Ch'en Heng-che), a student at Vassar, vacationed in Ithaca and was drawn into the circle of H. C. Zen and Hu Shih, Zen's Cornell classmate, who were editing the *Chinese Students Quarterly* and debating the merits of using vernacular Chinese as a medium of literary expression. Chen was in the United States under the auspices of the Boxer Indemnity program with the first group of Chinese women allowed to compete for one of the fellowships. Elected to Phi Beta Kappa at

Vassar, she studied history at the University of Chicago before returning to China to become the first woman professor in the country. In 1920, she married Zen; theirs was a long union that produced three children.

In 1920, Zen, teaching science at Peking University, complained to Hu Shih, now chancellor of Peking University, that the cultural and political ferment that swept China after 1919 had neglected the natural sciences. His mission was to change that. Along with Y. R. Chao, he acted as one of Bertrand Russell's translators during Russell's visit to China in 1921 and used the Science Society to publicize Einstein's theory of relativity. In 1925, when the U.S. government returned the balance of the Boxer Indemnity fund to China, Zen worked hard to see that the money was used to promote scientific research and education. His efforts resulted in the China Foundation for the Promotion of Education and Culture, of which he was executive director from 1929 to 1934 and from 1942 to 1948. He also played a leading role in launching the prestigious research institution Academia Sinica in 1927 and served as its secretary general from 1939 to 1942.

Interspersed with his Foundation appointments, Zen held several university positions. From 1923 until 1925 he taught chemistry and served as vice-chancellor of National Southeast University, a new institution in Nanking intended to be especially strong in the natural sciences. Several other members of the faculty had studied at Cornell and almost all of them were members of the Science Society. In 1935 Zen returned to the province where he was born and became chancellor of the National Szechwan University in Chengtu. The experience was not altogether happy. His wife, shocked by the poverty and misrule in Szechwan Province, wrote a series of critical articles about its politics. The local press in turn unleashed a torrent of abuse on her, attacks so severe that she decided to go to Peking and leave her husband with the task of trying to reform the university. Zen did enjoy some success before his resignation in 1937, bringing a number of highly qualified scholars to Chengtu, especially in science and agriculture. The agricultural faculty contributed to important improvements in southwest China's grain production.

Zen's proselytizing for science always eschewed politics. He never joined the Kuomintang (Nationalist Party) and opposed any attempt to inject party indoctrination into education. When Japan and China went to war in 1937, Chiang Kai-shek reached out to Zen and appointed him as an academic representative to the People's Political Council. Zen continued to spend most of this time, however, trying to fund scientific research during the lean war years when he was separated from his family.

Zen spent the year 1946–47 in the United States and then returned to Shanghai where his wife joined him. Dismayed and angered by the corruption and hoarding among the officials of the Nationalist government, they elected to remain in Shanghai after the Chinese Communist victory in 1949. For a few years Zen served the government of the People's Republic in several capacities. The Science Society ceased to exist, but Zen became a member of the All China Federation of Natural Science Societies.

From the mid-1950s until his death on November 9, 1961, he lived quietly. Like many Chinese who studied in the United States, Zen had learned from the West without losing a love for his own culture. He wrote poems in classical Chinese (despite his long friendship with Hu Shih, who championed the vernacular), became a talented calligrapher, and was a connoisseur of Chinese art. Zen argued that the notions of Western empiricism he had first championed at Cornell were compatible with Chinese values, even if at times science entailed the overturning of tradition. His life followed a creed that he enunciated in 1919: "If the established teachings and words of ancients clash with what I perceive as truth, then even if it means great difficulties and going through water and fire, I will fight them until death and without regret."

George Joseph Hecht

☙ CLASS OF 1917

Cornell can hope that George Joseph Hecht is one of its few alums who lived to attend his fiftieth reunion and found it a "great disappointment." Nonetheless, it was at Cornell that Hecht first honed the skills that made him one of America's leading publishers. His empire centered on *Parents* magazine, a journal that in the mid-1960s enjoyed a paid circulation of over two million. Hecht was an economics major but, with the exception of Benjamin Spock, for much of the twentieth century he may have had as much influence on the attitude of parents in the United States as any trained child expert.

Hecht's childhood home in New York City, where he was born on November 1, 1895, stood on the site of the future Radio City. His father, Meyer Hecht, of German Jewish descent, ran a prosperous hides and skins business, and his mother, Gella Stern Hecht, was prominently associated with a number of New York charities. Hecht and his sister Beatrice attended the Ethical Culture School in New York. Felix Adler, the famous founder of that institution, had taught philosophy at Cornell, but his contract was not renewed, probably because of his Jewish origins. Students at the Ethical Culture School were strongly urged to consider careers in public service. Hecht did, in fact, devote his life to helping others and made a great deal of money in the process.

Hecht entered Cornell's College of Arts and Sciences in the fall of 1913. He became active in a number of extracurricular activities. He joined the Cosmopolitan Club and played for two years on the basketball team. However, his major interest was the monthly literary magazine, the *Cornell Era*. He become the journal's business manager in his junior year. By gaining more advertising for the *Era* than any other collegiate magazine, Hecht made it possible for the *Era* to expand its size and use half-tone pictures of consistently high quality.

Hecht received his B.A. from Cornell in June 1917, two months after the United States declared war on Germany. He left Ithaca to become the volunteer head of the financial department of New York's office of the American Ambulance Field Service, a group organized by Americans in Paris to aid French and English soldiers. For the next year he worked as a civilian for a number of war-related activities. He became one of the so-called four-minute speakers for the National Committee of Patriotic Societies, which promoted the sale of Liberty Bonds. He also worked as a researcher for the War Trade Board and led an initiative to convince American cartoonists to publish work that supported the war effort. The last activity evolved into a bureau under the Committee of Public Information headed by his Cornell classmate Alfred M. Saperston. In 1918 Hecht joined the army as a private, but the armistice prevented his being called to active service. His last act of war patriotism was to publish *The War in Cartoons,* a collection of one hundred works by twenty-seven of the country's most prominent cartoonists.

Hecht returned to New York to work for his father, but he grew far more interested in editing a monthly social welfare publication, *Better Times,* for New York City's settlement houses. In this nighttime, unpaid job, he turned a miniscule monthly journal of eight pages into a successful, influential weekly that represented some two thousand private and public charitable agencies. He kept that journal ("A Little Paper with a Big Purpose") going until 1931, and in 1925 he founded the Welfare Council of New York City, one of the many charitable organizations he associated himself with throughout his life. His special interest was the welfare of children, an interest he developed before his 1930 marriage to Frieda Epstein, a Johns Hopkins graduate with a degree in child psychology, and had two children of his own.

In 1924 the unmarried Hecht had a chance conversation aboard an ocean liner with the mother of a grown family. She lamented her failures as a parent, saying that she had had no books to guide her. Intrigued, Hecht went to the ship's library and found books about raising cattle, dogs, and flowers, but nothing about the rearing of children. Actually, if Hecht had gone to a better library he would have found plenty of references, but then he might never have gotten the idea for *Parents Magazine.* He took his idea for a journal devoted to helping parents rear their children to the Laura Spelman Rockefeller Memorial Foundation, which made grants to four universities—Yale, Iowa, Minnesota, and Columbia Teachers College—to purchase stock in Hecht's proposed company. The masthead of the new journal listed many prominent educators as advisory editors, including Cornell's president, Livingston Farrand. The first issue appeared on September 23, 1926, and carried a newsstand price of 25 cents. Designed for fathers as well as mothers ("we hope both parents will read it together"), in the first year of publication the journal ran articles and features whose subjects ranged from clothing, educational behavior, health, spiritual problems, toys, housing plans, and family relation-

ships. Hecht attached to his creation the slogan "On Rearing Children from Crib to College."

Almost an instant success, by the early 1930s *Parents Magazine* was used as a study guide in more than nine thousand PTAs and Mothers' Clubs. Hecht walked a delicate line in trying to keep the journal entertaining but based on science. He said that "its medical advice is sound, but it isn't written in the language of the American Medical Journal. . . . It reads like a professor on a holiday." He wanted to restore to parenthood "the fun, the humor and the sense of well-being which undigested advice from experts has sometimes tended to diminish." Though some academic critics dismissed it as "innocuous," it gained the largest circulation of any magazine in the world devoted to child rearing and allowed Hecht to launch a number of other journals, with varied formats, aimed at parents and children. These included *The Boy's and Girl's Newspaper, Your New Baby,* and the children's magazine with the largest circulation in the United States, *Humpty Dumpty. True Comics,* an effort "to present the most exciting and interesting stories of current and past history" in comic book form, was one of Hecht's few commercial disappointments.

In other successful business ventures, Hecht bought control of Baker and Taylor Company, the largest book wholesaler in the country, and of F. A. O. Schwarz, New York's famous toy store. What Hecht never achieved was a close relationship between his enterprises and Cornell. Although President Farrand served as an advisory editor of *Parents Magazine,* he refused other opportunities to endorse Hecht's projects. President Edmund Day was only slightly more attentive in responding to overtures from Hecht. Efforts made in the 1970s to interest Hecht in extension programs run by Cornell's College of Human Ecology came to naught. Hecht criticized Cornell for not having schools of social work or of education and acidly said that the publications of one of its best-known child psychologists would not have been accepted if submitted for publication in *Parents Maga-zine.*

In truth, Hecht felt slighted by Cornell, but solace for his considerable ego came from many other sources that recognized his tire-less work for progressive causes on behalf of children. He served as chairman of the Child Welfare League of America, and in 1947 he es-tablished the American Parents Committee, the only lobby group in Washington that worked exclusively for children's legislation. Hecht was particularly proud of the role he played in promoting the National Defense Education Act of 1958, which provided federal funds for schools. Active well into his 70s, he died on April 23, 1980. His philanthropy had produced many concrete results, though per-haps not for two of the causes that he had most generously funded—Esperanto and world population control.

Howard Winchester Hawks

❧ CLASS OF 1918

Because of his deceptively straightforward style ("If I can make five good scenes and not annoy the audience, I've got a good picture"), Howard Hawks had to wait until the 1960s to be recognized as a great Hollywood director. Since then he has been acclaimed as a self-consciously "modernist" artist and a "giant of the American cinema."

Howard Winchester Hawks was born on May 30, 1896, in Goshen, Indiana, the son of Frank Hawks, a wealthy businessman, and Helen Howard Hawks. Hawks studied at Pasadena High School and the elite Phillips Exeter Academy before matriculating at Cor-nell in 1914. According to a classmate, he spent more time playing craps at his frater-nity, Delta Kappa Epsilon, than studying. During summer vacations he went to Califor-nia where he worked in the prop room at Paramount Studios. When the United States entered World War I in April 1917, Hawks left Cornell to enter the Army Air Corps. He was not sent overseas. Hawks was awarded a de-gree in mechanical engineering in absentia in 1918.

After the war and after a brief stint as a race car driver, Hawks returned to Holly-wood. His wealth and therefore ability to fund movies helped him get work as a pro-duction editor, producer, and then director.

Hawks quickly established himself as a suc-cessful filmmaker, with an engineer's ability to "visualize" a scene and a knack for making brilliant and occasionally counterintuitive casting decisions. In the eight silent and forty talking films he directed, Hawks specialized in variety, and migrated from studio to studio. No matter what the genre, however, he re-turned repeatedly to stories involving either male camaraderie or characters unencum-bered by a spouse and children who relish the innuendo-laden exchanges between men and women made equal, at least rhetorically, by the sexually electric feelings they have for one another.

A Girl in Every Port (1928), the story of two soldiers who are friends and romantic rivals, was his signature silent film. In the role of a conniver who takes a male friend's money and then two-times him, Hawks cast Louise Brooks, who was beautiful, direct, and a touch rebellious, with her hair in a sharp bob, bangs hanging just above her eyebrows. After he saw *A Girl in Every Port,* the German director G. W. Pabst selected Brooks for the lead in *Pandora's Box,* the film that made her a cult legend.

The transition to sound was relatively easy for Hawks, who scored with *Dawn Patrol* (1930) and *The Criminal Code* (1931), before making his favorite film, *Scarface* (1932), based on the career of Al Capone. Casting Paul Muni as the lead, and the novice George Raft as his henchman, he added a playfulness to the brutality of the gangsters by having Muni whistle an operatic tune before committing a murder and inventing Raft's celebrated bit of constantly flipping a coin. Although Hays Office censors forced Hawks to change the ending (Muni, once a defiant mobster, ready to shoot it out to the end, became "yellow" without his gun), *Scarface* was a hit at the box office and has been a model for directors of gangster films ever since.

In the 1930s, Hawks, at his directorial peak, helped introduce the "screwball comedy," a romance with rapid fire dialogue, improbable situations, characters from different social classes, and a sophisticated understanding of the relationship between love, sex, and social power. For *Twentieth Century* (1934) he enlisted John Barrymore ("It's the story of the biggest ham on earth and you're the biggest ham I know") and plucked Carole Lombard, a former Mack Sennett bathing beauty, from relative obscurity. When Lombard stiffened in scenes with the legendary Barrymore, Hawks claimed he took her aside and suggested she "do any damn thing that comes into your mind that's natural, includ-

ing a kick in the balls." For *Bringing Up Baby* (1938), a comic masterpiece, Hawks brought together Cary Grant and Katharine Hepburn in a story about a paleontologist, a rich society woman, and a pet leopard. *His Girl Friday* (1940) was a remake of the play *The Front Page,* this time with a woman, Hildy Johnson (played by Rosalind Russell), engaged in professional and romantic combat with Walter Burns (played by Cary Grant). Perhaps because it had "normal" characters with whom audiences could identify, *His Girl Friday* was much more popular than Hawks's other screwball comedies.

Ironically, Hawks, who loathed Franklin Roosevelt and was lukewarm about the United States entering World War II, scored his greatest success at the box office with *Sergeant York* (1941). The true story of a man from the Tennessee hills who overcomes his pacifist beliefs to become a hero in World War I, the film was condemned by isolationists as interventionist propaganda but emerged as the third most popular film in the history of cinema until then. Hawks received what would be his only Academy Award nomination for *Sergeant York,* but lost.

Throughout the '40s Hawks produced hit after hit. Made with the cooperation of the War Department, *Air Force* was Warner Brothers' fourth biggest earner in 1943. For *To Have and Have Not* (1944), Hawks took a novel by his friend Ernest Hemingway and hired his friend William Faulkner to work on the screenplay. He discovered Lauren Bacall, added the second "l" to her stage name and advised her to speak with a "mannish" voice. Hawks claimed that he wrote Bacall's "whistle" scene—"You know how to whistle, don't you, Steve? You just put your lips together and blow."—to test whether the eighteen year old would stand up to costar Humphrey Bogart. "In every scene you play with her," he told Bogart after the test, "she's going to walk out and leave you with egg on your face." After this film, Bacall became "The girl with 'the Look.'" Although he had a crush on her, Hawks brought Bogie and Bacall together again in *The Big Sleep* (1946), and thus was probably as responsible as anyone for making them a couple.

After World War II, Hawks was unable to sustain his string of successes. His biggest hit was *Gentlemen Prefer Blondes* (1953), though he could barely tolerate Marilyn Monroe's chronic lateness, neurotic habits, and dependence on drama coaches. His best films were Westerns. In *Red River* (1948), he persuaded John Wayne to play an older man put in his place by his surrogate son. In the contemplative, hypersensitive Montgomery Clift, Hawks found the perfect contrast to Wayne's over-the-top physicality. Hawks taught Clift to hop a little in the saddle, suggested he chew on a stalk of wheat, and got a sore arm "from trying to show him how to throw a punch." In *Rio Bravo* (1959), Hawks coaxed fine performances from Wayne, Ricky Nelson, and Angie Dickinson in a subtle exploration

of self-respect, self-control, and male bonding. Other films—*Land of the Pharaohs* (1955), *Hatari!* (1962), *Red Line 7000* (1965)—failed to attract audiences, and after 1970 Hawks stopped making films.

Hawks was married and divorced three times—to Athole Shearer Ward (Norma Shearer's sister), Nancy Raye Gross, and Dee Hartford. He had four children. A "man's man," he had numerous affairs, with Ann Dvorak, Jean Harlow, Ann Sheridan, and Ella Raines, among others. He drank, gambled, hunted, rode motorcycles with his buddies in the Moraga Spit and Polish Club, and was, depending on his mood and the audience, either a reserved, understated man or an "inspired liar."

The subject of a retrospective at the Museum of Modern Art in 1962, Hawks received an honorary Academy Award in 1974. He died on December 26, 1977.

Arthur Hobson Dean

❧ CLASS OF 1919

When he invited Arthur Dean to the signing ceremony in Moscow of the Limited Nuclear Test Ban Treaty in 1963, John F. Kennedy acknowledged the diplomat's role as architect of United States policy on testing and weapons limitation. "After all," the president said, "it's your treaty."

Arthur Hobson Dean was born in Ithaca, New York, on October 16, 1898, the son of Maud Campbell Egan and William Cameron Dean, an assistant in an engineering laboratory. Educated in the public schools of Ithaca, "Hob" entered Cornell's College of Arts and Sciences in the fall of 1915. To pay for his education, he worked as a night clerk at a hotel and as a bookkeeper in a bank. These jobs left little time for extracurricular activities outside of his fraternity, Phi Delta Phi. When the United States entered World War I, Dean

joined the Navy, returning to Cornell in 1919 and completing his B.A. in 1921. After graduation, he enrolled in the Cornell Law School, where he was managing editor of the *Cornell Law Quarterly.*

In 1923 Dean joined the prestigious firm of Sullivan and Cromwell and soon became the protégé of John Foster Dulles, one of the senior partners. During the 1920s he accompanied Dulles to the financial capitals of Europe to negotiate business deals for American clients. In 1927 and 1928 Dean worked out a $9 billion bond issue for the Nippon Power Company in Japan, which was then opened to investors in the United States.

Sullivan and Cromwell rewarded him with a full partnership.

Dean married Mary Talbott Clark Marden in 1932. The couple had two children. In 1933 Dean took the first of many leaves from Sullivan and Cromwell when President Roosevelt appointed him to a commission to help draft what became the Securities and Exchange Act of 1934. He also had a hand in writing the Bankruptcy Act of 1938, the Trust Indenture Act of 1939, and the Investment Company Act of 1940. An officer in the Coast Guard Reserve during World War II, Dean taught classes in piloting and navigation.

In 1945 he returned to Sullivan and Cromwell. That same year he was appointed a trustee of Cornell University, the beginning of a lengthy tenure that would include service as chair of the board. The *Cornell Daily Sun* reported that Dean turned down several requests by the board that he succeed Edmund Ezra Day as president of the university. In 1949 Dean's book *Business Income under Present Price Levels* appeared. A year later, when the federal government brought an antitrust action against seventeen investment banking firms in *U.S. v. Morgan,* Dean led the successful defense team.

In September 1953, Dulles, by then President Eisenhower's secretary of state, appointed Dean special deputy secretary of state with the rank of ambassador, charged with representing the seventeen nations whose troops had formed the United Nations Command during the Korean War in the post-armistice talks. The *New York Herald Tribune* called it "one of the most important diplomatic roles ever assigned to an American." Negotiating with the North Koreans and Chinese in a tent in the freezing latitudes of Panmunjom turned out to be exhausting, dreary, and frustrating. Dean was instructed to secure an exchange of prisoners and a framework for a conference to establish a permanent peace between North and South Korea. Despite several ingenious formulations, he could not get the parties to agree about whether to seat nonbelligerents, in-

cluding the Soviet Union, alongside the combatants at the conference. Although he tried to listen without showing "any sign of being impatient, angry, or annoyed," he lost his temper when the Chinese and North Koreans accused the United States of "deliberate treachery" in conspiring with South Korea to release thousands of North Korean prisoners of war who refused repatriation. He called them "Soviet agents," determined to sabotage a permanent peace. At one point he cried out, "Don't you listen to me? Don't you hear what I say?" At another, a colleague recalled, "he was like pom-poms, firing off verbal rockets."

After seven weeks of stalemate, Dean broke off the talks. The Communists, he wrote in a report to the American people, had used the negotiations as a forum for their propaganda. "It's all part of their psychological war. They insult you all day long. . . . They are determined to keep North Korea politically and economically integrated into their own economy. They believe that at a long drawn out conference the American negotiators will be forced by American public opinion to give in." Cold War animosities were so deep, however, that Senator Herman Welker of Idaho accused Dean of "appeasement," apparently because he was willing to talk with the Chinese Communists at all. Dean defended himself in a press conference, branding communism "repugnant to every idea for which I stand."

President Eisenhower called on Dean again in 1958, this time to serve as head of the U.S. delegation at the Geneva Conference on the Law of the Sea. Dean blocked a proposal by the Soviet Union to expand the size of "international waters" but reached agreements on fisheries and rights of access to the sea by landlocked nations.

Impressed with Dean's skill and experience, President Kennedy, a Democrat, asked the Republican lawyer to lead the U.S. delegation to the Conference on Discontinuance of Nuclear Weapons Tests, which met from February 1961 to January 1962, and the

Geneva Disarmament Conference, which convened in January 1962 and adjourned in February 1963. In these capacities, and as U.S. representative to the United Nations General Assembly, Dean shaped government policy on nuclear weapons. He helped draft the legislation creating the Arms Control and Disarmament Agency. At Kennedy's request, Dean drafted the nation's first comprehensive test ban treaty proposal. Although he remained committed to "reliable verification" as the "sine qua non" of disarmament, his plan included several concessions to the Soviets: it reduced the number of inspections mandated each year; provided that equal numbers of inspectors on each team be drawn from the West and the Communist bloc; and dropped a demand that each inspection in the United States require one in the Soviet Union. When the Soviets rejected this plan in 1961, a frustrated Dean saw in the delegates' behavior "the ultimately hostile and revolutionary nature of Soviet goals."

Nonetheless, he continued to work, not only for nuclear disarmament but for reductions in conventional forces as well. The Soviets rejected as "utterly unacceptable" his proposal to gradually reduce armies and navies to levels needed to keep internal order. In August 1962 Dean drafted two more plans, one for a comprehensive test ban treaty that mandated on-site inspections, and another for an agreement banning tests at sea and in the atmosphere at high altitudes. Again Premier Khrushchev, who believed that the Soviet Union had to continue to test weapons if it was to achieve nuclear parity with the United States, said no. But talks between the two nations continued. In the summer of 1963 Undersecretary of State for Political Affairs W. Averill Harriman completed the work Dean

had begun. On August 5, 1963, President Kennedy signed the Limited Nuclear Test Ban Treaty, the first significant agreement on the control of nuclear weapons between the two superpowers.

In *Test Ban and Disarmament: The Path of Negotiation* (1966) Dean looked back on his experiences as a negotiator. President Johnson would not let him contemplate retirement from public service. In 1964 and 1965 he chaired the National Citizens Committee for Community Relations and the Lawyers Committee for Equal Rights under the Law, watchdog groups to monitor compliance with civil rights legislation. Dean also served on a panel on nuclear proliferation, which he called "the overriding arms problem of our time." In 1968, as a member of the Senior Advisory Group on Vietnam—the so-called Wise Men—he evaluated proposals to send 206,000 more American troops to Vietnam. The group is credited with helping to persuade President Johnson to halt the bombing of North Vietnam and propose peace talks.

Dean retired from government service and the practice of law in 1976. He continued to sit on the board of dozens of corporations and philanthropic organizations. A knowledgeable collector of Americana and rare books, Dean provided financial assistance to Cornell to acquire an archive of material related to the career of the Marquis de Lafayette. Talented horticulturists and gardeners, Mr. and Mrs. Dean turned their estate in Oyster Bay into a showplace for flower lovers. On Nantucket Island, where they maintained a summer home, the Deans created a wildlife sanctuary around Sesachacha Pond. Arthur Dean died in Glen Cove, Long Island, on November 30, 1987.

Isidor Isaac Rabi

❧ CLASS OF 1919

At I. I. Rabi's retirement party from Columbia University in 1967, the physicist Jerrold Zacharias displayed the "Rabi Tree" to illustrate his transformational impact on modern physics. Rabi's experimental work formed the main trunk, with the branches representing the research inspired by him. Nested within the branches were the names of twenty men who, like their mentor, were Nobel laureates.

Israel (later Isidor) Isaac Rabi was born on July 29, 1898, in Rymanov, Galicia (then in the Austro-Hungarian Empire, but historically part of Poland). When he was an infant, the family emigrated to New York City, where they lived in a small apartment behind the grocery store where David and Sheindel Rabi eked out a living. Raised as an Orthodox Jew, Israel discovered astronomy as he browsed the *A* section at the local library. He became fascinated with electricity as well, building his own telegraph station and, while in elementary school, had a paper published in *Modern Electrics*. By now convinced that "the whole Jewish thing" was superstition, Rabi insisted, much to his parents' dismay, on the topic "How the Electric Light Works" for his bar mitzvah speech. For high school, he chose Manual Training High School, with its shop-oriented curriculum, over Boys High, where most of the smart Jewish boys matriculated. And in 1916 he won a tuition scholarship to go "way out West" to Cornell to study engineering.

Living on one dollar a day, Rabi lost several teeth to malnutrition because he "didn't see wasting the money on vegetables." Unable to afford membership in a fraternity, he amused himself with long walks and participation in an amateur theater group. Uninspired by engineering, Rabi switched to chemistry, but even then he "didn't have a single teacher who really interested [him], or who was very good." Ever the contrarian, he almost never studied, preferring to read a book by Freud to completing his assign-

ments. He received only one A, and that only to win a bet. When the United States entered World War I in 1917, the patriotic Rabi (had the family remained he Europe, he said frequently, "I probably would have become a tailor") tried to enlist in the Army Air Corps, but his mother prevailed on him to remain in school. Rabi graduated in 1919, one year early, having completed a senior thesis on the chemistry of the element manganese.

With good jobs in chemical companies closed to Jews, Rabi worked briefly for Lederle Laboratories, analyzing furniture polish and milk, and in a law office dealing with accounts receivable. He returned to Cornell for a year as a graduate student, but when he did not get a fellowship in 1923, he decided to follow "the most beautiful girl in the world," Helen Newmark, a friend of his sister Gertrude, to Columbia. Caught up in the revolution in physics, and the prospect of new ways of thinking about time, space, and matter, Rabi changed fields for the last time: Physics "filled me with awe, put me in touch with a sense of original causes. Physics brought me closer to God." To pay his expenses, Rabi taught physics at the City College of New York. In 1926 he received his doctorate for experiments measuring the magnetic susceptibility of crystalline substances called Tutton salts. The day after he submitted his dissertation, Rabi married Helen Newmark. The couple had two daughters.

Aware that the best work in quantum mechanics and atomic structure was being done in Europe, Rabi applied for and won a Barnard fellowship to study with leading physicists there. For two years he worked with the great scientists of the era, including Niels Bohr, Wolfgang Pauli, Otto Stern, and Werner Heisenberg. Stern introduced Rabi to molecular beam technology, which isolated molecular or atomic systems from interactions with adjacent atoms or the walls of a container. On Heisenberg's recommendation, Columbia offered Rabi a position as lecturer in quantum mechanics in 1929. He was the first Jewish faculty member in the physics department.

Rabi, often a dreadful lecturer but a fabulous teacher of graduate students, was especially proud of his award from the American Association of Physics Teachers. Bored by data collection, he could be lazy in the lab, but his creativity and intuition—what colleagues called his "street smarts"—led to extraordinarily important discoveries in the 1930s. He "appears to ride around on the electrons within an atom," a colleague remarked, and "through sheer force of character" gets them to bend to his wishes. Rabi's magnetic resonance method measured the properties of atoms, including the magnetism of their component parts, one hundred times more accurately than any existing method. It became the standard technique in all molecular and atomic beam experiments and, along with his work on radio frequency spectroscopy, made possible the construction of atomic clocks, guidance systems for missiles and satellites, and the medical diagnostic technique of magnetic resonance imaging. In 1944 Rabi won the Nobel Prize in physics.

With war raging in Europe, the U.S. military recruited Rabi to work on radar at MIT in the fall of 1940. After the attack on Pearl Harbor, Rabi was appointed associate director of the "Rad Lab," which became, according to MIT President (and physicist) Karl Compton, "the greatest cooperative research establishment in the history of the world." The Rad Lab devised systems to guide bombers to their targets and back in overcast weather; to detect enemy aircraft at long range; and to allow shipboard radar to see beyond the horizon. Radar was essential in eliminating the threat of German submarines and in operations ranging from the Battle of Midway to the D-Day landing. "The bomb ended the war," concluded Lee DuBridge, director of the Rad Lab, "but radar won the war."

A senior advisor to the Manhattan Project, Rabi drew on his experience at the Rad Lab to convince the director, J. Robert Oppenheimer, and General Leslie Groves not to run Los Alamos as a military installation. With civilian control, he insisted, there would be less friction, higher morale, and more creativity. Rabi declined Oppenheimer's request that he become associate director at Los Alamos, citing his family's reluctance to move. Equally important was his sense that the chances of building a fission bomb were "iffy" and his ambivalence about developing weapons of mass destruction. To be sure, he supported any idea that would help defeat Hitler—"How many Germans will it kill?" Rabi often asked at the Rad Lab—but he remained unsettled about dropping atomic bombs on civilians. Nonetheless, when the first atomic bomb was detonated at Alamagordo, New Mexico, in 1945, Rabi was there. At first "jubilant," he soon said he had "gooseflesh all over me when I realized what this meant for the future of humanity."

When the war ended, Rabi returned to Columbia as chairman of the Department of Physics and helped build a distinguished program in nuclear physics. When he stepped down in 1949, he had four colleagues who would later win Nobel Prizes. Rabi also played a major role in founding the Brookhaven National Laboratory at Yaphank, Long Island, the first advanced high-energy physics facility on the East Coast. Although he continued to do important work on the impact of electromagnetic fluctuations of the vacuum on atomic systems, Rabi found that the intensity was gone. "Unless you are very competitive," he noticed, "you aren't likely to function with the same vigor" after winning the Nobel Prize.

Rabi used his connections in physics, the

military, and in politics, and his status as elder statesman to promote research and the responsible use of nuclear power. In 1946, he helped devise the Baruch plan for international cooperation and control of the peaceful development of atomic energy, believing that "it was our finest moment in America. . . . We should have gone back to the Russians when they said no." He was a member of the General Advisory Committee of the Atomic Energy Commission from 1947 to 1952. Rabi persuaded President Eisenhower to create the office of Special Assistant to the President for Science and Technology. He was the originator of the idea for CERN (Conseil Européen pour la Recherche Nucleaire), a high-energy physics research center in Geneva, Switzerland, which was instrumental in the rebirth of science in postwar Europe. In 1957, with Detlev Bronk, president of the National Academy of Sciences, and James Killian, president of MIT, Rabi proposed a new division of NATO to promote science and technology in the member nations and was appointed the first U.S. delegate to the NATO Science Committee.

Rabi became an outspoken critic of the nuclear arms race. "The more you talk about arms control," he said, "the more you become morally obtuse. You have to recoil from the horror of it." In 1949 he joined with Enrico Fermi in opposing research for a fusion thermonuclear "Super" bomb: "The fact that no limits exist to the destructiveness of this weapon makes its very existence and the knowledge of its construction a danger to humanity as a whole." Rabi never forgave President Truman for "buckling under pressure" and approving the hydrogen bomb. Five years later, the feisty five-feet four-inch physicist provided a spirited defense of Oppenheimer at hearings of the Atomic Energy Commission, which ultimately revoked the security clearance of the former director of the Manhattan Project over doubts about his loyalty to the United States. Enraged at "pygmies trying a great man," he cited Oppenheimer's role in building atomic bombs: "What more do you want—mermaids?"

Active well into his eighties, Rabi gave little thought to making money, never thinking to patent any of his ideas, including the atomic clock. In the 1930s, when friends asked him what he would do with a million dollars, he thought and thought and finally said, "I think I'd buy a new hat." Rabi died at his home on Riverside Drive in New York City on January 11, 1988.

Colston Estey Warne

CLASS OF 1920

Long before there was Ralph Nader, Colston Estey Warne led the consumer movement in the United States. In 1936 he founded the Consumers Union, the publisher of *Consumer Reports,* and was its first and only president for the next forty-three years. His weapons against the "artificial product differentiation and romantic fantasies" of American advertising were testing and "unadulterated truth."

Warne was born in Romulus, New York, on August 14, 1900. His father, Clinton Arlington Warne, pursued a variety of jobs, and

his mother, Harriet Ellsworth Estey, worked for women's rights in Seneca County. Warne entered Cornell in 1916, having prepared at Ithaca High School. He chose economics as his major with the intention of becoming a banker. Two unorthodox teachers in Cornell's otherwise orthodox economics department changed his mind about his career. One of them, Edward Zeuch, was an instructor demoted to paper grader because of his criticisms of capitalism. Warne recalled that Zeuch lined the margins of his essays with references to R. H. Tawney, Karl Marx, and John Hobson and in long conversations made him aware of a long tradition of American radicalism. His other mentor was Herbert J. Davenport who wore a "ten year old Sears Roebuck suit and plow shoes to class." Davenport, a close friend of Thorstein Veblen, taught Warne about "conspicuous consumption" and the perverted ways of manufacturers who substituted planned obsolescence for good design.

In 1920, the year of his graduation from Cornell, Warne married Frances Lee Corbett, a student of Martha Van Rensselaer in the College of Home Economics. She would be Warne's partner in early product testing. Her zeal for standards won her the reputation of being the only woman who, at a cocktail party, discussed the nature of the lining needed in one's water heater.

Warne stayed at Cornell another year and earned an M.A. in economics. He then took a teaching position at the University of Pittsburgh. While there, he observed steelworkers who put in twelve-hour shifts and lived in "bleak rows of wooden shacks." The experience awakened him to the labor movement and moved him even farther away from the attitudes he held when he began study on that "cloistered hilltop above Lake Cayuga." He returned to graduate school at the University of Chicago. There he studied with Paul Douglas, the future United States senator whose economic views placed him on the liberal left, and earned his Ph.D. in 1925. At the same time Warne took part in a variety of progressive causes—the League for Independent Political Action, where he worked with John Dewey; the League for Industrial Democracy; and Roger Baldwin's fledgling American Civil Liberties Union.

At Douglas's urging Warne wrote his thesis on the consumer cooperative movement in Illinois. *Your Money's Worth,* a book by Stuart Chase and F. J. Schlink, profoundly affected his thinking about the need to use consumer product testing as an antidote to advertising. The example of a Methodist church club in White Plains, New York, caught his attention. Members of the club listed the products they liked and did not like. For one dollar, they offered to send to anyone a mimeographed copy of the club's lists.

For most of his academic career, from 1930 until 1969, Warne taught at Amherst College, although he often abandoned the classroom for his work as consumer advocate. It was at Amherst where he and his wife and a group of academic women did their first testing of can openers. In 1928 Warne had been one of the founders of Consumers Research, but when labor troubles split that organization in 1935, Warne joined with a group of strike supporters on the staff and founded the Consumers Union for the United States (CU). In 1936, the first issue of the product-testing journal, *Consumer Reports,* evaluated soaps (large size Ivory was a "best buy" at nine cents a cake), cereals, stockings, toothbrushes, high-octane gasoline, and the alleged virtues of Alka-Seltzer ("they vanish like gas bubbles in the air"). From three thousand charter subscribers and a staff of ten, Warner created a journal that at its peak in 1980 employed four hundred and had a paid circulation of over two million. It did not accept advertising, the lifeblood of most American periodicals.

After World War II, CU somewhat surprisingly found itself under attack as a subversive organization. The House Un-American Activities Committee seemed to think that questioning the claims of American manufacturers was part of a communist conspiracy to overthrow the government. Warne was not a communist or even a socialist. He was, however, a nonconformist who had no patience with the anticommunist hysteria of the late 1940s and early 1950s. He condemned criminal prosecution of communists ("mere advocacy of an idea is not indictable"), and when serving as a consultant to President Truman's Council of

Economic Advisors, he became one of the first government employees to refuse to sign a loyalty oath. He said: "This Executive Order is so repugnant to the political institutions of our country that I cannot comply with its terms." Despite his refusal to sign the oath, he did not lose his job. Warne attacked advertising, the American pharmaceutical industry, and tax benefits for the rich. But his radicalism had nothing to do with the Soviet Union. He described himself as an upstate New York Yankee who lived in a small New England town trying to carry on the American democratic tradition.

Ralph Nader, who resigned from CU in the mid-1970s, complained that the organization was not sufficiently political. He suggested that Warne's brush with the forces of anticommunism had made him overly cautious in directing the policies of CU in his later career. In fact, Warne and Nader were men of very different styles. Warne wore three-piece suits, spoke softly, and at a lean six-feet three-inches behaved more like a well-bred British gentleman than a confrontational activist. Even so, at his Cornell class reunion in 1975, Warne told his classmates that he em-

pathized with the student rebels of the 1960s. Praising their antiwar protests, their struggle for civil rights for minorities and women, and their criticism of the unchecked power of multinational corporations, he said that he was happy to let today's youth try to solve the problems of the world for which his own Class of 1920 had found no adequate answers.

Warne's consumer advocacy made him part of dozens of government panels and private organizations. In 1960 he brought together sixteen consumer groups from fourteen countries to form the International Organization of Consumers Unions. Headquartered in The Hague, the IOCU appropriately chose Warne as its first president. Already retired from teaching, Warne stepped down from his leadership role at CU at the age of seventy-nine. His three children had now provided him and his wife with grandchildren. She died in 1982, five years before Warne's own death on May 20, 1987. By then the trouble-making journal he had started during the Depression had become a standard reference work for the American middle-class, professional family.

Laura Z. Hobson

ᕗ CLASS OF 1921

Laura Z. Hobson helped put anti-Semitism on America's post–World War II social agenda with her immensely popular novel *Gentleman's Agreement*. Her experience at Cornell, she claimed, provided the idea for her best-seller.

Born on June 19, 1900, in New York City, she was the child of Russian immigrant intellectuals who were active in New York's then flourishing Jewish socialist circles. Her father, Michael Zametkin, an editor of the Jewish *Daily Forward,* America's premier Yiddish newspaper in the early decades of the twenti-

eth century, was also active in trade union politics, while her mother, Adella Kean Zametkin, was a regular columnist for another Yiddish language paper, *The Day*.

Like many talented young women, Hobson's route to Cornell was paved by a New York State Regents Scholarship, which had to be used in the Empire State. She enrolled first at Hunter College, but after two unhappy years there she transferred to Cornell where she flourished in the College of Arts and Sciences. Winning letters in both crew and field hockey, she also played the romantic male lead in the annual play of the Women's Dramatic Club. She excelled in academic work, as well, winning the Barnes Shakespeare Prize in 1921, her senior year.

Much to her regret, she was not inducted into Phi Beta Kappa. In her autobiography, *Laura Z.: A Life*, published in 1983, Hobson blamed anti-Semitism at Cornell for her failure to make the prestigious honor society. She wrote that Harry Caplan, then a young assistant professor, destined to be loved by future decades of Cornellians, confided to her that some trustees and faculty felt that too many honors were going to students "from New York City": "It's a Jew clean-up . . . they don't call it that, but that's just what it is." Not making Phi Beta Kappa was "the great wound of my youth" she wrote in 1983, put to rest only, she added "when I began to write my second novel, *Gentleman's Agreement*."

After Cornell, Laura Z. returned to New York City where she worked as an advertising copywriter. Then, like her parents, she turned to journalism, not for the Yiddish press, but through most of the 1920s for the *New York Evening Post*. Her life and career took a dramatic turn in 1930 when she married Thayer Hobson, a young publisher, whose classmate and friend from Yale, Henry Luce, hired her to write for *Time, Life,* and *Fortune* magazines. She worked for Luce publications throughout the 1930s and also wrote her first full-length fiction, two pulp Westerns coauthored in 1933 and 1934 with her husband.

Hobson and her husband divorced in 1935, and she remained unmarried for the rest of her long life. She had several well-publicized and long-lasting relationships with fellow writers, most significantly with Ralph Ingersoll, an editor of *Time* and then publisher of the left-liberal magazine *P.M.,* and with Eric Hodgins, the brilliant but clinically depressed and alcoholic author of *Mr. Blandings Builds His Dream House*. Hobson adopted a son, Michael, in 1936. In 1941 she found herself unexpectedly pregnant and, never revealing the father, gave birth in secret to a son, Christopher, who she then formally adopted, telling friends that, like her first son, he had come from an adoption agency.

It was as a mother of two small sons that Hobson wrote her first solo work of fiction in 1941, a children's book, *A Dog of His Own*. Her first adult novel, *The Trespassers*, published in 1943, dealt with the impact of immigration quotas on the love affair of two refugees from Hitler's Europe trying to enter America. Its plot set the pattern for all of her eight later novels: social and political themes initially felt by her characters as private and personal injustice turn out to be matters of pressing community-wide concern. Nowhere is this developed more powerfully than in her second novel, *Gentleman's Agreement*, published in 1947. It spent six months on top of the *New York Times* best-seller list, sold over a million copies in its first year of publication, and was eventually translated into thirteen foreign languages. *Gentleman's Agreement* was the story of an ambitious journalist, Phil Green, a widower, who undertakes the writing of an exposé of anti-Semitism in the United States for a crusading liberal magazine. Seeking an "angle" for his story, the gentile Green pretends to be Jewish to discover how Jews "feel" about being discriminated against. He has ample opportunity to learn as he is turned away from "restricted" resort hotels and denied housing in suburbs where "gentlemen's agreements" keep out Jews. Meanwhile, Green's young son is beaten up at school and called a "dirty Jew." His girlfriend, who knows he is not Jewish, almost breaks up with him when he insists she not blow his cover with her Darien, Connecticut, family. Green's articles that reveal the humiliation he suffered when, as he writes, "I was a Jew for eight weeks," caused a public sensation.

So did Hobson's novel. Originally serialized in *Cosmopolitan* magazine, it struck a responsive chord in a country fresh from its long and bitter war against Hitler and just learning about the extermination of European Jewry, despite the fact that nowhere in the book are Hitler or concentration camps mentioned. Reinforcing the popularity of the novel was its almost immediate transformation into an equally popular movie, produced by Darryl F. Zanuck. With its star-studded cast led by Gregory Peck, the film *Gentleman's Agreement* won the Academy Award as the best film of 1947. Elia Kazan won the Oscar for best director as did Celeste Holm for best supporting actress.

None of Hobson's later novels ever matched the phenomenal success of *Gentleman's Agreement*. She wove the plots of these books from the fabric of her own life. Her *First Papers* (1964) is the tale of an immigrant family, much like her own; the father is a socialist journalist and the daughter is off to college, a thinly veiled Cornell, by the end of the book. *The Tenth Month* (1971), which centers on a single mother's decision to bear her child and then adopt him, was made into a TV movie. In *Consenting Adult* (1975) Hobson used her son Christopher's homosexuality as the focus of a moving story about a mother's acceptance and love of a gay son. This, too, became a TV movie.

Hobson was politically outspoken

throughout her career. She refused to accept an award in 1947 from the Jewish Book Council for *Gentleman's Agreement* as "The Best Jewish Novel of the Year," insisting that the book was not a "Jewish novel" but a "book about an American problem of special interest to Jewish people." In the McCarthy era, her double-barreled criticisms of both red-baiting and Soviet Communism put her in the company of her fellow founders of the Cold War liberal organization, Americans for Democratic Action (ADA).

A colorful figure, with many friends in New York's literary and publishing elite, Hobson lived into a vigorous old age, the last thirty years of which found her at 923 Fifth Avenue, from where well into her eighties she bicycled daily in Central Park. She remained an active writer, working on the second volume of her autobiography until shortly before her death from cancer on February 28, 1986. Four years earlier, *Perspectives,* a magazine published by the United States Commission on Civil Rights, asked her to write an article about what she might change if she were writing *Gentleman's Agreement* in 1982. She would leave most of the book intact, she wrote, merely "changing the word Jew to black or Puerto Rican or gay or Mexican American." She ended the essay with an optimistic flourish, saying, "Equality . . . will eventually come for all people."

Hobson may not have been a literary writer of the highest order, but she was certainly a successful one, with a book whose popular impact most authors would die for, a book that, to hear her tell it, had its roots in her senior year at Cornell.

E. B. White

✣ CLASS OF 1921

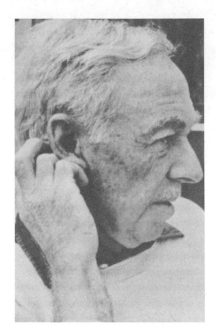

E. B. White wrote better sentences than any American of his time and used them to craft essays that reminded one critic of Montaigne. He became a famous author, but his essays seldom concerned literary subjects. White once said that he owned only one book, Thoreau's *Walden.* He hated pretension and made very little of his achievements. Probably what he would have most wanted said about himself he said about a remarkable spider he named Charlotte: "It is not often that someone comes along who is a true friend and a good writer."

White claimed that his parents had run out of names when they got to the youngest of their six children, born on July 11, 1899. Once he was away from home he let no one call him Elwyn Brooks. White was grateful to Cornell for many things, but none more important than the nickname "Andy," a moniker bestowed on students named White to honor Cornell's first president, and one that E. B. kept. White's father, Samuel Tilly White, headed a successful company that made pianos, and his mother, Jessie Hart White, was the daughter of the painter William Hart. White grew up in prosperous circumstances in Mount Vernon, New York, and attended the local schools. He spent summers with his family in Maine, wonderful summers that awakened his love for the natural world and for the rhythms of rural life.

White discovered his vocation early. He remembered "really quite distinctly, looking at a sheet of paper square in the eyes" and thinking "this is where I belong." Before he was ten, he won a literary prize from *Woman's Home Companion* for a poem about a mouse. He won more prizes from *St. Nicholas* magazine, one at age eleven for his first published piece, "A Winter's Walk," and another at age fourteen.

In the fall of 1917, just months after the United States entered World War I, White left home to attend Cornell, where his two older brothers had been students. Though he

thought about enlisting, he was a scrawny kid who did not weigh enough to pass the physical. He joined Phi Gamma Delta fraternity and became its president. However, the most important focus of his undergraduate activities was the *Cornell Daily Sun,* whose staff he joined as a freshman, rising to become editor in chief in the spring of his junior year. His commitment to the campus newspaper brought him into close, almost familial, contact with Bristow Adams, a professor of journalism who invited students to his home on Monday nights. White was strongly influenced by three other Cornell teachers: William Strunk Jr., whose English course gave White his religious respect for the rules of grammar; Martin Sampson, who presided over the Manuscript Club, which encouraged the writing of both faculty and students; and George Lincoln Burr, whose courses in history indelibly impressed upon White the value of freedom.

White also met his first girlfriend at Cornell. His awkward courtship of Alice Burchfield revealed a shyness that affected all of White's personal relationships—his difficulty in expressing his feelings, often casting his letters in the voice of a third person or even a pet dog; his frequent need to retreat into himself; his sometimes desperate insecurities. Andy White was gregarious and deeply kind, but he was not an easy person to know well.

With a Cornell degree earned in 1921 and membership in three honor societies, Aleph Samach, Quill and Dagger, and Sigma Delta Chi, White headed for New York City to become a journalist. He landed jobs—the first was with United Press—but did not last long in any of them. He discovered that he did not like writing about the things that interested his editors. At a time when some other young American writers were discovering "art" in Paris, White took off for the West Coast with a friend who had just flunked out of Cornell. He stayed for over a year, working without satisfaction for a Seattle newspaper and traveling to Alaska. He collected experience but not much else. Without a job and fearing that he was not cut out to be a journalist, White returned to New York in 1923 and sold his talents for a while to an ad agency.

On February 21, 1925, the first issue of the *New Yorker* appeared. In its ninth issue, it carried E. B. White's first contribution to the magazine, a parody that drew on his work as an ad man. The *New Yorker*'s editor, Harold Ross, offered White a staff position in 1926; it was an affiliation that White cautiously accepted and that lasted until very near the end of his life. The job at the *New Yorker* brought White into close contact with Katharine Angell, Ross's key associate. Unhappily married, Angell was a graduate of Bryn Mawr, had two children, was older than White, and far better read. The attraction between the two was immediate. In 1929, after Angell got a Nevada divorce, she and White married, without telling anyone and without either of them missing a day of work. Their close marriage continued until she died in 1977. They had one son together.

White, Angell, Ross, and a few others made the *New Yorker* quite simply the best magazine published in the United States. James Thurber was the most important of the few others. He and White shared a tiny office and laughed at each other's paragraphs. In 1929 they coauthored *Is Sex Necessary?*, a send-up of self-help manuals that contained Thurber's first published drawings. White did many things for the *New Yorker*. His most trivial task, though it continued for fifty-five years, was to edit the magazine's celebrated "newsbreaks," little excerpts from newspapers containing a gaffe to which White added a wry comment or a caption. Many unsigned contributions by White appeared in "Talk of the Town," the signature (and most read) opening section of the magazine. Sometimes he supplied captions for the magazine's celebrated cartoons, including the famous exchange between mother and child: Mother, "It's broccoli, dear;" Child, "I say it's spinach and I say the hell with it."

White's work at the *New Yorker* did not always bring him satisfaction even if Ross believed that "there is no purpose to which words can be put that White was unable to master." White took more than one leave of absence to get over the feeling that he was "a failure at the writing racket." In 1938, sensitive to the charge that while many Americans suffered economic hardship he made a nice income writing humorous whimsy, White gave up most of his work at the *New Yorker* to write a signed monthly column, "One Man's Meat," for *Harper's* magazine. When war swept over Europe, he spoke out strongly about the need to defend freedom—"the right to speak our minds, haul our own [lobster] traps, mind our own business, and wallow in the wide, wide sea." When he returned to editorial duties at the *New Yorker* toward the end of the war, he crusaded for world government and wrote bravely against the anticommunist frenzy that gripped the country after the war.

White loved New York City, but he loved Maine more. In 1933 he and Katharine moved to a forty-acre farm on the Maine coast, even though she had to give up her career as fiction editor of the *New Yorker* to do so. They moved back to the City in 1943 but returned to Maine in 1957, this time for good. On his farm, living amid his "private zoo," White perfected some stories that he had originally made up for his nieces and nephews, stories about animals or animal-like people. White's moral values were transparent in these books. *Stuart Little,* which was published in 1945, recounted the adventures of a courageous mouse-like child who dealt with broken dreams and a damaged canoe to learn, along with young readers, that the essential thing was to "be headed in the right direction." In 1952 White published *Charlotte's Web,* an unforgettable tale that will endure as a classic for as long as children read books. It is about sacrifice and loyalty and a pig named Wilbur who is saved from the farmer's ax by a resourceful spider who spins words of praise for Wilbur into her webs. When White's *The Trumpet of the Swan* appeared in 1970 and rose to the top of the *New York Times* list of best-selling children's books, *Charlotte's Web* still held the No. 2 position.

White enjoyed a good income from his royalties. Collections of his essays sold well as did *A Subtreasury of American Humor,* a collection that he put together with his wife.

One of his most lucrative projects was also his most influential. In 1959 he published a revision of *The Elements of Style,* a writing manual published in 1918 by his now-deceased Cornell English teacher, William Strunk Jr. By 1982 that slim volume, now as much White's as Strunk's, had sold over five million copies. Nearly every American college student in the last part of the twentieth century who learned to write a satisfactory essay read it and took to heart its mantra, "A sentence should contain no unnecessary words."

White was the recipient of many honorary degrees and awards, not all of which he bothered to pick up. Among them were the Presidential Medal of Freedom, the Gold Medal of the National Institute of Arts and Letters, and a special Pulitzer Prize in 1978 for his entire body of work. He died on October 1, 1985, at his home in Maine, not far from where his son's family lived. He was bedridden at the end, but into his eighties he continued to rise early, work around the farm, and feel lucky, like Louis his trumpeter swan, "to inhabit such a beautiful earth."

Barbara McClintock

↪ CLASS OF 1923

Before she died, Barbara McClintock's career had gained almost mythical status. The myth speaks of a lonely scientist who pursued her vision undeterred by the jeers of uncomprehending colleagues, who was denied prestigious academic appointments because of her gender, and who waited over thirty years for recognition of her discoveries. The truth is more interesting. McClintock was controversial, but fellow scientists recognized the brilliance of her work from her first published articles. Many of the eccentricities of her career were self-chosen and arose from her fierce desire for independence from rules, from institutions, and from personal attachments.

Eleanor McClintock was born in Hartford, Connecticut, on June 16, 1902 (the third of four children), but grew up in Brooklyn. Her parents, Sara Handy, who traced her ancestry back to the *Mayflower,* and Thomas Henry McClintock, a physician, started to call her Barbara because they thought the name somehow suited her tomboy nature. (The name stuck, although it was not legally changed until 1933.)

Graduating from Erasmus Hall High School in 1919, McClintock bucked her mother's opposition to a university education for her daughter and entered Cornell, in her opinion the only good school in the East that admitted women. Interested in plant and animal breeding, she enrolled in the College of Agriculture. She took up smoking, bobbed her hair, and played banjo in a jazz combo. Though elected president of the women's freshman class, she refused a bid to join a sorority. "I have never been able to function well in an organized group," she said later. Her academic transcript was filled with Zs— marks indicating that she had withdrawn from many courses, ones that she did not like. She failed one course in music but overall earned just under a B average.

If not a stellar student in all subjects, McClintock was already, as an undergraduate, enrolled in graduate courses in cytology and genetics. She received her bachelor of science degree in 1923 and segued effortlessly into Cornell's graduate division. Genetics, a field then based on Gregor Mendel's discovery of dominant and recessive genes, was producing a cadre of gifted young scientists. Among McClintock's peers at Cornell were George Beadle, who went on to head the biology division at Caltech and to win a Nobel Prize, and Marcus Rhoades, who also rose to preeminence in genetics and was McClintock's lifetime supporter. Her Cornell mentor, Rollins A. Emerson, directed her toward research on maize. For the next sixty-nine years her carefully cultivated fields of Indian corn, with their complex patterns of variation, supplied McClintock with her research material.

After receiving her Ph.D. in 1927, McClintock remained at Cornell as an instructor. In 1929 she published her Ph.D. dissertation as a long article in *Genetics,* the foremost journal in the field. Within two years of her doctorate, McClintock had published six other articles in major journals, all making important contributions to knowledge about the location of genes on chromosomes. Academic jobs were scarce during the Depression, and no prime post was offered to McClintock. However, in 1931, she won a two-year fellowship from the National Research Council, which allowed her to work at a series of important science centers across the country. A Guggenheim Fellowship, which she won in 1933, took her to Germany where she established an important association with Richard Goldschmidt, a Jewish scientist who headed Berlin's Kaiser Wilhelm Institute for Biology and who left Germany in 1936.

After two more years at Cornell on a Rockefeller Foundation grant, in 1936 McClintock accepted a position as assistant professor at the University of Missouri. She quit the post in 1941, claiming later that the university was about to deny her tenure. Evidence suggests, however, that her tenure was never in doubt. McClintock simply did not like teaching students "dumb as they may be" or being pressed into academic duties that interfered with her research. In any case, in the same year that she left Missouri she was offered a position as a permanent staff member of the Department of Genetics at Cold Spring Harbor Laboratory. Cold Spring Harbor, which spread over fifty acres of coastal Long Island, was founded in 1890 to rival the Marine Biological Laboratory at Woods Hole. Funded by the Carnegie Foundation of New York, Cold Spring Harbor had no students and offered its researchers complete independence. It suited McClintock's temperament, and she was based at Cold Spring for the rest of her career.

McClintock's high standing in her discipline was affirmed in 1944 by her election to the National Academy of Sciences. She was only the third woman so honored, and at age forty-two, she was a young inductee for either sex. In the same year, she became the first woman elected president of the Genetics Society of America. Two years later, she won the Achievement Award from the American Association of University Women. All this recognition came before McClintock entered her most significant period of scientific discovery.

In the late 1940s McClintock's observation of the variations that appeared on the ears of her maize crops convinced her of several things. What geneticists called mutation was not the result, or at least always the result, of chemical changes in the gene. Rather, genes or genetic material were moving about, transposing their position on the chromosome. Moreover, she decided that these changes could not be fully understood if they were regarded only for their role in producing mutant abnormalities. They were part of normal development. In 1948 McClintock made her first explicit description of what were later called, somewhat inaccurately, "jumping genes." It directly challenged those who believed that chromosomes had a stable structure, that they were strings of carefully fixed genetic pearls.

McClintock's first public presentation of her theory came in an unrefereed paper published in 1950 in the *Proceedings of the National Academy of Sciences*. She also read a paper about the transposition of genes in 1951 at a celebrated symposium at Cold Spring Harbor. The myth holds that other geneticists laughed at McClintock's "jumping genes" and paid no attention to her work. The truth is that other scientists almost immediately confirmed the hypothesis. What was controversial, and not generally accepted, were McClintock's speculations about the relationship of genetic transposition to development and to purposeful adaptations of the cell to changes in its environment. Despite stiff opposition to McClintock's broader conclusions, she often was invited to speak at leading universities.

A fuller appreciation of the implications of McClintock's work was not possible until

molecular biologists entered the field of genetics and discovered DNA and RNA. This was ironic because McClintock, with no training either in chemistry or molecular theory, played no role in this important breakthrough in genetics. By the 1960s she was something of an old-fashioned scientist, a small, wiry woman, just under 5'2", with short hair, loose-fitting clothes, and large glasses. Her scientific equipment included a microscope, fields of Indian corn that she personally tended, and a brain that seemed to be able to rearrange its enormous store of information in sudden flashes of inspiration. With that equipment she moved ahead of others in the 1950s in sensing that genetic transposition, normal development and adaptation to changes in the environment, and evolution were linked. No biologist today would disagree with McClintock's insights that the genome is dynamic, that genes interact with other chromosomal elements, and that the development of the cell is influenced by the world outside the cell.

Long after her best research was complete, the new context for genetics brought a fresh round of prizes to McClintock. In 1967, the year she formally retired, she won the Kimber Genetics Award from the National Academy of Sciences. Cornell named her an Andrew Dickson White Professor, a visiting post. The Genetics Society of America in 1981 gave her its Thomas Hunt Morgan Medal. In the same year, the Wolf Foundation awarded her its $50,000 prize in medicine; the MacArthur Foundation named her its first MacArthur Fellow, the so-called genius award that brought with it $60,000 annually, tax free, for life; and she shared the Albert Lasker Basic Medical Research Award. Finally in 1983, when she was eighty-one, McClintock won the Nobel Prize for medicine or physiology. She was the third woman to receive an unshared Nobel Prize in the sciences (the other two being Marie Curie and Dorothy Hodgkin).

Some colleagues found McClintock's logical leaps from her empirical data to her theories hard to follow and judged her something of a mystic. This view gained currency because McClintock was interested in ESP and gave the writing of Immanuel Velikovsky (about the collision of the planet Venus with the earth in biblical times) a warmer reception than other scientists thought was warranted. McClintock was not a mystic, although, like the American philosopher William James, she thought that too many scientists were afraid to look at phenomena they could not readily understand.

McClintock had many associates but few close friends and no confidantes that she made part of her personal life. She never married and once said that she never went "through the experience of requiring" marriage. She also claimed that at times, when totally invested in her work, she forgot her own name. McClintock was still working when she died on September 2, 1992. McClintock suffered from bouts of depression during her career, but what she told a journalist in 1983 rings true: "I've had a very, very satisfactory and interesting life."

Gregory Goodwin Pincus
～ CLASS OF 1924

"Test Tube Babies Come Step Nearer," the *New York Times* announced in 1941 in a story about Dr. Gregory Pincus's technique for implanting female rabbits with eggs fertilized "without benefit of the male of the species." This experiment, Pincus predicted, would shed light on human sterility as well as conception. Within twenty years he would be hailed—and scorned—as "the father of the birth control pill."

Almost from birth in Woodbine, New Jersey, on April 9, 1903, Gregory Goodwin Pincus aspired to become a scientist. His father, Joseph W. Pincus, was a teacher and editor of a farm journal. The brother of his mother, Elizabeth Lipman, was director of the New Jersey State Agricultural Experiment Station and the founding editor of *Soil Science* magazine. An honor student at Morris High School, Pincus entered the College of Agriculture at Cornell in 1921. In addition to superb work in class, he was a founder and editor of the *Cornell Literary Review* and a member of the Cosmopolitan Club. A few months after receiving his B.S. in 1924, "Goody" married Elizabeth Notkin, with whom he had two children.

Pincus earned a master's degree and a doctorate in physiology and genetics from Harvard in 1927. That year, he won a three-year fellowship from the National Research Council that allowed him to study at Cambridge University with scientists specializing in reproductive biology and at the Kaiser Wilhelm Institute with the renowned geneticist Richard Goldschmidt. Pincus returned to Harvard in 1930 as an instructor, then became an assistant professor in 1931. At Harvard and then at Clark University, whose Department of Experimental Zoology he joined in 1938, Pincus studied the effect of hormones on reproduction in mammals. In 1939 Pincus set forth his method for achieving the first fatherless birth of a mammal: he had taken an ovum from a female rabbit, stimulated it parthenogenetically (without fertilizing the egg with sperm), and placed it back in the uterus of the female, who then carried the fetus to term.

When other researchers could not duplicate and therefore verify Pincus's experiment, they began to refer to the procedure, with a sneer, as "Pincogenesis." Attacks on Pincus grew when the press accidentally omitted the "not" from his claim that his work was not the beginning of efforts to produce human test-tube babies. Shrugging off his critics, he continued his research at Clark; the Worcester Foundation for Experimental Biology, which he cofounded in 1944; Tufts Medical College, which he joined in 1945; and Boston University, where he became a research professor in 1950.

As director of laboratories and then research director at the Worcester Foundation, Pincus supervised research on the relationship between hormones in general and individual steroids and reproduction. Aware from his own work that overdoses of progesterone caused infertility in rabbits, he came to believe that fertility could be inhibited physiologically. In 1951, Pincus had several important conversations with Margaret Sanger, the founder of the American Birth Control League, who described the problems resulting from overpopulation and the impact, especially on the poor, of inadequate and dangerous methods of birth control. Pincus collaborated with Min Chueh Chang, a researcher at the Worcester Foundation, who had discovered that the female hormone progesterone inhibited ovulation by thickening the walls of the Fallopian tubes and womb and rendering the mucus of the lower reproductive tract resistant to the intrusion of sperm. Pincus and Chang experimented with more than two hundred substances as sources for synthetic progesterone before discovering that three steroid compounds derived from the roots of a wild Mexican yam prevented ovulation in laboratory animals.

Pincus had the insight to recognize the implications of these findings for the social control of human fertility, and the skill and contacts to design experiments, evaluate results, and produce a product for the marketplace. With philanthropic foundations reluctant to allocate funds to controversial experiments and field tests, he secured substantial financing from Katharine McCormack, a friend of Margaret Sanger, who believed that an effective contraceptive could liberate women in family relationships and in society at large. After combining forces with John Rock, a Roman Catholic gynecologist and obstetrician who was using progesterone in work with childless patients, Pincus contacted the G. D. Searle pharmaceutical company, where he had been a consultant, and organized clinical tests of a contraceptive pill on hundreds of women in Brookline, Massachusetts; Puerto Rico; and Haiti. In 1957 the Food and Drug Administration authorized the marketing of these steroids in cases of miscarriage or menstrual disorder. Three years later, the FDA licensed Enovid, a contraceptive pill that became celebrated for its effectiveness and relative safety.

An ambitious and by no means modest man, Pincus remained an outsider in the scientific community. His work was recognized with the Albert D. Lasker Award in Planned Parenthood (1960), the Modern Medicine Award for Distinguished Achievement (1964), election to the American Academy of Arts and Sciences (1939) and the National Academy of Sciences (1965), and the American Medical Association's Scientific Achievement Award (1967). He was permanent chair of the Laurentian Hormone Conference, which he founded in 1944 and which has become a major forum in the field of endocrinology. But he never won the Nobel Prize, which he coveted, and election to the National Academy of Science came in 1965, inexcusably late in his view. Not a single institution, moreover, ever gave him an honorary degree.

Friends and colleagues attributed the belated recognition of Pincus in part to anti-Semitism, in part to the fact that his colleagues did not much like him, and in part to religious opposition to birth control. In Massachusetts, where Pincus worked, it was against the law until 1972 to assist a woman with contraceptive devices. The Roman Catholic Church and other religious groups strenuously opposed honoring a researcher who tried to give human beings control over their own reproduction.

It is almost impossible to overestimate the impact of Pincus's pill. Without it, attempts to stop overpopulation would be even more difficult. By virtually eliminating the risk of pregnancy, it transformed the lives of hundreds of millions of people, ushering in the "sexual revolution" of the 1960s and '70s. "I can still remember the feeling of elation," recalled one woman, who felt, at long last, that she could enjoy sex without fear of getting pregnant. Contraception contributed as well to weakening the "double standard," which had applied more severe sexual restrictions to women than to men. In doing so, the birth control pill contributed to the movement that demanded equal rights for women in the workplace as well as in the bedroom.

Pincus was the author of two books, *The Eggs of Mammals* (1936) and *The Control of Fertility* (1965). During the last decade of his life he traveled extensively to promote the responsible use of birth control pills. He accepted membership in biological and endocrinological societies in Portugal, France, Great Britain, Chile, Haiti, and Mexico. He died in Boston on August 22, 1967, of myeloid metaplasia, a bone-marrow disease, which according to some scientists may have been caused by exposure to the organic solvents so essential to his experiments with contraception.

Julian Haynes Steward

CLASS OF 1925

Julian Steward first encountered cultures radically different from his own when he was sixteen. He never thereafter considered a career other than in anthropology. To him anthropology was both an effort to describe the unique features of individual cultures and a search for cultural regularities that crossed space and time. His ambitions were large—perhaps too large for one lifetime.

Steward said little about his boyhood in Washington, D.C., except that it had no importance in forming his ambitions. Born on January 31, 1902, he was the younger of two sons in the family of Grace Garriot and her husband Thomas G. Steward. Steward's father, without college training, rose to become chief of the Board of Examiners of the U.S. Patent Office. Steward's parents were Christian Scientists, a circumstance that surely gave the boy some sense of cultural distinctiveness. However, the watershed in his young life came in 1918 when he entered the newly established Deep Springs Preparatory School (now Deep Springs College) near Death Valley in California. The school, founded by Lucien L. Nunn, a mining and hydroelectric power magnate, had, and still has, the goal of forming a group of twenty-six young men at a time into moral and intellectual leaders. Steward and his classmates read books, did manual labor, and explored the surrounding rugged environment, which happened to be the home of the Paiute and Shoshone. Their ways of life deeply interested Steward.

Deep Springs, through the Telluride Association, had a connection to Cornell. When Steward graduated from Deep Springs in 1921, many of his classmates headed for Ithaca. Although Steward joined them a year later, he first carried his interest in American Indians to UC Berkeley where as a freshman he took a course in anthropology taught jointly by Alfred Kroeber, Robert Lowie, and Edward Gifford. They were young luminaries in the field who had studied with Columbia's great ethnologist Franz Boas. Steward transferred to Cornell to live in the intense intellectual environment of Telluride House. He belonged to the Varsity Debate Club and the Glee Club. Because Cornell had no anthropology department, he majored in zoology and biology. By luck, Cornell's president, Livingston Farrand, was an anthropologist. When Steward graduated in 1925 Farrand helped Steward to get in to UC Berkeley where he began doctoral work in a small but innovative anthropology program. The faculty members who had taught him as a freshman were still at the cutting edge of the field.

As a graduate student, Steward continued to focus on American Indians. His dissertation, a study of clowning (the "ceremonial buffoon") in the rituals of several tribes, was his first venture into cross-cultural studies. With a Ph.D. earned in 1929, Steward traveled back across the country to the University of Michigan where he taught the first courses in anthropology offered at Ann Arbor. In 1930 he moved again, this time to the University of Utah, where he met his future wife, Jane Cannon. They married in 1933, started a family of two sons, and together conducted field research near Deep Springs as well as in Nevada, Idaho, and Oregon. Much of Steward's early published work was as much archaeology as cultural anthropology. Steward, in fact, believed that the two subjects, when properly pursued, were closely related.

In 1935 Steward received an appointment as associate anthropologist in the Bureau of American Ethnology (BAE) of the Smithsonian Institution. For a few years in the mid-1930s he also worked under John Collier in the Bureau of Indian Affairs. In the latter agency, Steward discovered some practical applications of anthropology. He and Collier began a "New Deal" for American Indians intended to restore their lands to tribal ownership and to help perpetuate Indian cultures. At the former agency, the BAE, Steward found time to spell out some of the theoretical implications of his work. He wanted to explain social systems in terms of their accommodations to environmental circumstances. The differing applications of similar technologies in different habitats dictated the organization of work in a given group. Work forms in turn affected most other aspects of culture. "Cultural ecology," the name Steward gave to the study of how the environment, technology, and patterns of work interacted to shape human societies, did not amount to cultural determinism. Although environment and available technology acted to constrain what was possible to express culturally, the constraints weakened as societies became more complex.

Related to his understanding of cultural ecology was Steward's belief in "significant regularities" observable in processes of cultural change, regularities that could not, according to Steward, be explained by diffusion of traits from one group to another. He rejected the model of unilinear evolution promoted by Lewis Henry Morgan in the nineteenth century. Morgan had tried to show how groups exposed to progressive levels of technology moved inexorably from primitive to civilized societies. Instead, Steward spoke of multilinear evolution, a theory positing that given similar conditions certain basic types of culture develop in similar ways. Culture, he claimed, was "an orderly domain," guided by discoverable causalities rather than by random and endless divergence. He nonetheless recognized that few concrete aspects of culture appear among all groups of mankind, that "no cultural phenomena are universal."

While at the BAE Steward prepared and edited his most enduring work of scholarship—the six-volume *Handbook of South American Indians.* The project, involving the cooperation of many social scientists, began while Steward served as the first director of the Institute of Social Anthropology at the Smithsonian and ended after he left Washington in 1946 to accept a position at Columbia. In his new university post Steward continued to urge anthropologists to work in teams. His focus was now on cultural change within large areas and over time. He and his graduate students studied different aspects of Puerto Rican history and culture and in 1956 published *The People of Puerto Rico.* Stewart saw it as an example of area studies, an important trend in postwar scholarship that Steward had promoted in his 1950 book *Area Research: Theory and Practice.*

In 1952 Steward became University Professor at the University of Illinois, a research post that relieved him of undergraduate teaching duties. He organized an ambitious study of peasant agricultural systems that had been exposed to wage labor and other modern social and economic forms. In this search for "cross-cultural regularities" in cultural

evolution, he stationed researchers in Latin America, Africa, and East Asia. The book that resulted from this collective labor, *Contemporary Change in Traditional Societies,* appeared in 1967 and was Steward's last major effort to find "the larger context" for cultural phenomena. He remained at the University of Illinois until his death on February 6, 1972.

Steward was a major figure in expanding the popularity of anthropological study in the United States after World War II. He worked with others to reorganize the American Anthropological Association and made its research endeavors part of the enterprises sponsored by the National Science Foundation. In 1954 he became one of the first social scientists elected to the National Academy of Sciences. The following year the Wenner-Gren Foundation named him the recipient of the Viking Fund Medal, then considered the most prestigious award in American anthropology.

Steward believed that facts only mean something in the context of theories. Scientific investigation ended necessarily in the need for more investigation—never in immutable truth. That consideration called for modesty in the scientist, a quality that Steward, ever since his days at Deep Springs, had found indispensable in trying to understand other cultures too easily misread as "primitive."

Andrew John Biemiller

❧ CLASS OF 1926

George Meany, president of the AFL-CIO, often said that "if he picked a child to train as a lobbyist, and brought him all the way through, he couldn't have found anyone with a better background than Andrew Biemiller had." He may well have been right.

Andrew John Biemiller was born on July 23, 1906, in Sandusky, Ohio. His father, Andrew Frederick Biemiller, a traveling salesman

who supplied dry goods to general stores, was a political activist and chairman of the Republican Party central committee in Sandusky. When her husband died in the influenza epidemic of

1918, Pearl Weber Biemiller ran a boarding-house to support the family and make it possible for Andrew to attend the College of Arts and Sciences at Cornell.

Active in his fraternity, Delta Kappa Epsilon, Andy Biemiller was also president of the Freshman Debate Club and one of a group of upperclassmen that advised first-year students. When he received his B.A. in history in 1926, he seemed intent on a career as a university professor. He was an instructor at Syracuse University for two years and then did graduate work at the University of Pennsylvania between 1928 and 1931, with the British trade union movement as the focus of his research. In 1929, Biemiller left the Episcopal Church to become a Quaker and married Hannah Perot Morris, with whom he had two children.

Like many Americans, Biemiller moved politically to the left in response to the Great Depression. In 1932, he left graduate school, without a degree, to take a job as a reporter with the *Milwaukee Leader,* a socialist newspaper. Biemiller immersed himself in the labor movement in Wisconsin, serving during the next decade as labor relations counselor, organizer, and member of the executive board of the Milwaukee Federation of Trade Councils and the State Federation of Labor. He was active, as well, with the Newspaper Guild and the American Federation of Teachers. Biemiller later broke with his socialist colleagues because they were isolationists. He was elected to the Wisconsin legislature in 1936 as a Progressive Party member. He remained in the Assembly until 1942, including serving a two-year stint as floor leader, before accepting a position in Washington, D.C., as assistant to Joseph Keenan, vice chairman of the War Production Board.

In 1944 Biemiller was elected to Congress as a Democrat representing a district closely divided between Democrats and Republicans. He lost his seat in 1946, regained it two years later, and was defeated again in 1950. After another loss in 1952, he never again sought elective office. In the House of Representa-

tives, Biemiller faithfully supported New Deal legislation and also learned from Sam Rayburn, the legendary Speaker of the House, how to use parliamentary rules "to get things done or keep things from being done." As a lobbyist, he made good use of those lessons.

As a member of the Resolutions Committee at the Democratic National Convention in 1948 Biemiller worked for an explicit commitment by the party to equal rights for African Americans. He drafted the strong civil rights plank that Hubert H. Humphrey, mayor of Minneapolis, brought to the floor. When the draft was adopted and President Truman endorsed it, Governor Strom Thurmond of South Carolina led the so-called Dixiecrats out of the convention hall. It was a defining moment for the Democratic Party. Biemiller fought for civil rights for the rest of his professional life. Testifying in favor of a civil rights bill before Congress in 1959, he argued that "prejudice and bigotry are personal, subjective things. But discrimination, lawlessness, and inequality are social acts—and this society has a right and a duty to eliminate them as rapidly and as thoroughly as possible." Biemiller later pushed President Kennedy to add an equal employment provision to the civil rights legislation drafted by his administration and then mobilized AFL-CIO support behind the path-breaking Civil Rights Act of 1964.

After leaving Congress in 1952, Biemiller remained in Washington, first as a special assistant to the secretary of the interior and then as a public relations consultant. In 1953 he joined the legislative staff of the AFL and became director of the legislative department of the newly merged AFL-CIO three years later. "Don't beg, don't threaten, and don't assume you are 100 percent right," George Meany advised when he appointed him. In more than two decades on Capitol Hill Biemiller learned that a lobbyist could not succeed if he always abided by these precepts. A large man with a fresh rose in his lapel and a deep, professorial voice, he knew when to plead or flatter, how to apply pressure, and the importance of spreading conviviality as well as information. "Once a year Andy would come around with a fifth of scotch," Frank Thompson Jr. of New Jersey, chairman of the House Labor-Management Subcommittee, remembered. "Presumably that was trying to make up for all he drank in my office during the year. He should have brought a gallon."

Convinced that a strong labor movement and effective collective bargaining were essential forces for progressive reform, Biemiller rejected arguments that labor stick to a narrow agenda. "We are American citizens as well as members of trade unions," he insisted. Labor must be "the people's lobby" because in a modern, industrial economy virtually all legislation affected workers: "Trade is related to jobs, labor law reform to the Senate's filibuster rule, occupational safety and health to budgets and appropriations." As labor's top lobbyist, he pushed for increases in the minimum wage, comprehensive health insurance, federal aid to education, clean water and air, federal regulation of hazardous materials,

preservation of forest lands, and extension of national parks. Biemiller did not always get what he wanted, but his imprint appears on much of the social and economic legislation enacted during the quarter century following World War II.

With the election of Richard Nixon as president in 1968 Biemiller found himself, more often than not, in the opposition. He took considerable satisfaction in his successful effort to defeat the nominations of Clement F. Haynsworth and G. Harrold Carswell to the U.S. Supreme Court. Convinced that "neither of those guys were fit to serve on the Court," given their records on civil rights as well as the welfare of workers, Biemiller claimed that "labor carried the load" using "the simplest kind of lobbying"—the truth. "It was a good battle."

Expressing satisfaction with what he had accomplished, Biemiller retired at the end of 1978. He and his wife lived quietly in Bethesda, Maryland, until his death from congestive heart failure on April 3, 1982.

Leon (Lee) Pressman

⌘ CLASS OF 1926

Lee Pressman dressed in expensive, pin-striped suits and looked more like a well-paid corporate lawyer than a man of the people who devoted the most important part of his career to the labor movement. Everyone who worked with him or against him recognized his brilliance. To those who knew about and deplored his communist sympathies, his talents made him a dangerous man.

Pressman was born on July 1, 1906, on Manhattan's lower East Side. He grew up in New York City and graduated from Stuyvesant High School. His father, Harry Pressman, and his mother, Clara Rich Pressman (age fifteen when Pressman was born), were part of the late nineteenth-century Jew-

ish immigration from Russia. When Pressman entered Cornell on a scholarship in 1923, he started a very different life.

At Cornell, Pressman joined Omicron Alpha Tau, a largely Jewish fraternity, and was on the varsity wrestling and swimming teams. Courses with Sumner Schlichter, an eminent economist, kindled Pressman's interest in American workers. In 1926, after three years of study, Pressman received his B.A. degree with Phi Beta Kappa honors. He was not yet twenty years old. From Cornell he went to Harvard Law School where he was one of a handful of young men who dazzled Felix Frankfurter. Among his friends on the *Harvard Law Review* was Alger Hiss.

After receiving his law degree from Harvard in the same year as the stock market crash, he joined the prestigious New York legal firm of Chadbourne, Stanchfield and Levy. Jerome Frank, Pressman's sponsor at the firm, called him "probably the best lawyer I have ever met." Pressman stayed in corporate practice for three years and seemed headed for a conventionally successful life. In 1931 he married Sophia Platnick and started a family of three children. (One of his daughters later attended Cornell.) However, with the onset of the Depression Pressman sensed a new tide in history, a tide that he believed would one day make human beings truly free. He left New York for Washington, D.C., in 1933 to join the New Deal. Jerome Frank, who had recruited Pressman to corporate law, now recruited him to become assistant general counsel to the Agricultural Adjustment Administration (AAA).

Pressman and several of his Harvard-trained peers at the AAA were later accused of being part of a Communist Party cell. Many of the facts surrounding this charge remain in dispute, but Pressman, by his own testimony, was a party member from the end of 1934 through 1935 and remained allied in ideology with the Communist Party for the next fifteen years. Henry Wallace, the secretary of agriculture, fired Pressman and several others in 1935, not for alleged Communist links but for trying to get the AAA to support sharecroppers—which was deemed a radical initiative. Pressman, in fact, never knew much about farming and, according to one of his detractors, had demanded at a meeting of macaroni producers to know what a proposed code would do for the macaroni growers.

The "purge" at AAA did not harm Pressman's career. He served briefly as general counsel to the Works Progress Administration and the Resettlement Administration,

before a career opportunity opened outside of government. John L. Lewis, president of the United Mine Workers and the principal force behind the new Congress of Industrial Organizations (CIO), discovered that he needed a good lawyer on his team. Pressman was retained as general counsel first of the Steel Workers Organizing Committee and subsequently of the CIO.

Pressman's close ties to Lewis and to his successor, Philip Murray, became the basis of many allegations about the influence of communism on the American labor movement. Lewis, warned by Labor Secretary Frances Perkins about Pressman's communist leanings, did not care. Pressman's legal skills were irreplaceable. Pressman secured the lifting of court injunctions against autoworkers engaged in a sit-down strike against General Motors in 1937. He drew up the first contract between steelworkers and U.S. Steel, which was then headed by Myron Taylor, another Cornell graduate. He won a Supreme Court case against Republic Steel that forced the company to reinstate and pay back-wages to strikers. He secured the first wage agreement that pegged wages and prices to inflation. To some conservatives at the time, all of these victories were Communist inspired. They were, instead, important benchmarks in making collective bargaining an essential part of American capitalism.

Without doubt communist policies influenced Pressman's views on foreign policy, and he resolutely opposed FDR's war-preparedness measures when nonintervention best served the interests of the Soviet Union. Hitler's invasion of the Soviet Union in 1940 changed the equation, and Pressman's switch to the interventionist side caused a rift with Lewis, who had, for his own reasons, broken with FDR on foreign policy issues and supported Wendell Wilkie in 1940. That mistake and a heart attack suffered by Lewis brought new leadership to the CIO. Philip Murray was Catholic and ardently anticommunist, but he, like Lewis, judged Pressman much too valuable to sacrifice to anticommunists in the union who wanted his ouster. Pressman later claimed that his Communist sympathies had no impact on the legal work he did for labor. As proof, he noted that in his role as mediator among various factions within the CIO, he drafted many resolutions denounced by the Communist Party.

Pressman's balancing act ended in 1948. Murray, determined to repeal the worst features of the antilabor Taft-Hartley Act, put the CIO squarely behind the election of President Truman as the candidate most likely to achieve that goal. Pressman decided to support Henry Wallace, his old boss at AAA who had fired him but who now was running for president as the Progressive Party candidate, with the backing of the Communists. To Murray, the association was unacceptable. Pressman resigned his position at the CIO just moments before Murray pushed him out. Arthur Goldberg succeeded him. Pressman still thought he was riding the tide of history and ran for Congress from Brooklyn on the Progressive Party ticket. Both Wallace and Pressman suffered crushing defeats and, according to Murray Kempton, Pressman awoke on the morning after the November 1948 election to find that he had fallen out of history.

Pressman had no money problems. He had always charged the CIO high fees for his services, and when Murray allowed Pressman after his removal to continue a small part of the legal work challenging Taft-Hartley, Pressman billed the CIO for over $80,000. He supported himself in private legal practice until his death on November 19, 1969. But his fame and influence disappeared during the anticommunist hysteria of the early Cold War. Named as a leading Communist by Whittaker Chambers in 1948, Pressman was summoned by the House Un-American Activities Committee to testify in its investigation of Alger Hiss. Pressman pleaded his right under the Fifth Amendment to not incriminate himself. HUAC summoned him again in 1950. Before this appearance, Pressman acknowledged to the press that he had belonged to the Communist Party for one year while he worked for the New Deal and had been a fellow traveler until recently. His press release further announced that he had definitively broken with communism, that he had resigned from the American Labor Party, and that he supported the United Nations police action against North Korea.

His emergence as a champion of American democracy did not make him a hero to the members of HUAC. He gave them the names of three people, including his once close friend and law partner Nathan Witt, but HUAC already had those names. The name they wanted was that of Alger Hiss, and Pressman disappointed them. "I have no knowledge," he said, "regarding the political beliefs or affiliations of Alger Hiss. I do know that for the period of my participation [in a Communist Party cell] he was not a member of that group."

In a 1957 interview Pressman lamented the lack of idealism in the labor movement. If that were so, he, perhaps, bore some of the blame. His victories for the CIO, won when he held anticapitalist convictions, helped wed "big labor" to the American system. It was a major achievement, however filled with irony.

Margaret Bourke-White
~ CLASS OF 1927

Margaret Bourke-White entered Cornell partly to get away from a bad marriage and partly because she had heard that the university had waterfalls. Her experiences "in the midst of one of the most spectacular campus sites in America" turned her passion for taking pictures into a career. Three years after her graduation in 1927 she was a celebrity in the new field of photojournalism. By the end of her life she had provided Americans with enduring images of the best and the worst moments of the mid-twentieth century.

Bourke-White was born in New York City on June 14, 1904, the daughter of Minnie Bourke and Joseph Edward White. (She adopted her hyphenated surname in 1927; at Cornell she was Margaret White.) Her father, who worked as an inventor for a company that manufactured printing presses, introduced her to nature, especially snakes, which were part of childhood lessons in overcoming fear; to the dramatic beauty of factory machines; and to the possibility of recording everything through the eye of a camera. Only one thing about her father seems to have embarrassed her. For her entire life she went out of her way not to mention that he was the son of Orthodox Jewish immigrants.

After graduating from Plainfield High School in New Jersey, she entered Columbia University. During her second semester, in addition to her Columbia courses, she took a photography course at a school established by Clarence H. White, one of the country's most respected "artistic" photographers. Her mother gave her a $20 used camera with a cracked lens. With it, working as a camp counselor, Margaret organized her first photography business. Little campers and their parents eagerly bought her pictures as a way to remember their summer. Her father's sudden death from a stroke left the family in bad financial straits, but Margaret White continued her education at the University of Michigan, studying herpetology. There, at age nineteen, she met a graduate student, Everett Chapman, who shared her interest in photography. They married, took pictures together, and moved to Purdue University where "Chappie" landed a teaching job. The couple fought, reconciled, and finally separated. When she transferred to Cornell in the fall of 1926, she told no one about her not-yet-divorced husband. She worked briefly as a waitress, but then decided she could repeat the success of her camp counseling days by selling pictures of Cornell to undergraduates. She sat before campus buildings for hours, waiting for the best light, and then spent all night developing her images, striving for the still fashionable soft-focus effect that lent photographs a painterly quality. She later dismissed her Cornell photographs as pseudo-Corots, but they sold. The Cornell *Alumni News* put her on a small commission, and at commencement her stock "went like a blaze." Because of credits earned at other universities, Bourke-White received her degree in biology after only one year at Cornell.

Encouraged by Cornell-trained architects

who had seen her work in the *Alumni News*, Bourke-White moved to Cleveland, where her mother now lived, and opened a photography business. She received a variety of commissions from wealthy clients, mostly to capture images of their homes and gardens, but her passion lay in photographing Cleveland's industrial landscape. In the 1920s many photographers and painters explored the "machine aesthetic," but no one exploited the drama of industrial America with a flair comparable to Bourke-White's. After much badgering and a certain amount of flirting, Bourke-White was allowed into the Otis Steel Company to photograph the process of steel production. For a time, the darkness of the mill interior stumped all of Bourke-White's efforts to create readable photographs, but finally she recorded in riveting images the startling contrast between the blackness of the interior and the fiery light of the molten steel. Henry Luce, creator of *Time* magazine, saw the photographs and called Bourke-White with a job offer. Luce was about to launch a new, expensive journal to celebrate American industry.

It was arguably bad timing, since the first issue of *Fortune* appeared in February 1930, only a few months after the stock market crash. But the journal was a success, and in Luce's mind it succeeded in good measure because of Bourke-White's photographs. For several years, Bourke-White worked for *Fortune* while continuing her commercial photography, including assignments to photograph the construction of the Chrysler Building and to provide advertising photographs for Goodyear. However, when Luce on November 11, 1936, added another magazine, *Life*, to his empire, Bourke-White's career came to be centered on Time, Inc. Her photograph of the Fort Peck dam in Montana, one of the projects of the Public Works Administration, graced the first cover of *Life*, and her photo essay on the men who built the dam was the lead article.

The list of her projects is extraordinary. In the early 1930s she became the first non-Soviet citizen allowed to photograph the achievements of the first Five Year Plan, a project that led to a book, *Eyes on Russia*, and two documentary films. When World War II engulfed Europe, she was the only journalist from the United States in Moscow when the Nazis bombed the city. She also documented the bombing of London. As the first woman photographer accredited by the U.S. Air Force, she photographed her own rescue from a torpedoed boat, the campaign in North Africa, the fighting in the Cassino Valley in Italy, and the Allied advance into Germany. Her photographs of the surviving victims of Buchenwald shocked the world. After the war, she spent almost two years in India, capturing the agony of the partition that created the new independent nations of India and Pakistan. She had many opportunities to photograph Gandhi and interviewed him for the last time only hours before his assassination. In the 1950s she made celebrated photographic missions to Korea during the "police action" and to South Africa where her photograph of two sweating and bare-chested workers in a gold mine deep below the earth's surface became an important document in the struggle against apartheid.

To the people who did not like Bourke-White, and there were many, her photographs were slick and superficial, aimed more at publicizing herself than at calling thoughtful attention to her subjects. Her detractors charged that she got opportunities to photograph dramatic events because she slept with generals and other powerful men and that the quality of her work depended on the talents of people back in New York who developed her underexposed negatives. Bourke-White was undeniably flamboyant, and she did relish publicity and the company of men. However, she was also passionate about her work, which more and more reflected a strong social conscience.

Perhaps the most celebrated project of her career was one she undertook in 1936 with Erskine Caldwell to record the blighted lives of southern tenant farmers. The resulting book, *You Have Seen Their Faces* (1937), combined

Bourke-White's photographs and the biting social commentary of Caldwell. It was a critical and commercial success, prompting Walker Evans and James Agee, photographer and author of the contemporaneous and now more celebrated but then neglected *Let Us Now Praise Famous Men,* to criticize Bourke-White for exploiting her subjects. Bourke-White made no apology for using the camera as an intrusive instrument and for putting aside feeling when recording images of tragedy and grief. It was the only way she knew to shock her viewers into a response. Her leftist sympathies were sufficient for the FBI to begin a file on Bourke-White, and during the McCarthy period she was the target of attacks by the red-baiting journalist Westbrook Pegler.

Bourke-White and Caldwell wrote two other books together, and after a lengthy affair married in 1939. It was a brief union, for Bourke-White recoiled at Caldwell's efforts to dominate her. She loved children but decided that "mine is a life into which marriage doesn't fit well." Her several miscarriages were probably self-induced. She was not a feminist and had few women friends other than her own sister. She was, however, a strong, independent person. She had to be. In 1951 she experienced the first symptoms of Parkinson's disease, a cruel illness she battled for the rest of her life, a battle memorably recorded by her friend Alfred Eisenstaedt for a feature article in *Life.* With rigorous exercise and two operations, she was able to continue working for another decade. However, the crippling effects of Parkinson's gradually wore her down. Following a terrible fall at her home in Darien, Connecticut, she died on August 27, 1971. A promise she had wrested from Luce, to allow her to be the first *Life* photographer to go to the moon, went sadly unfulfilled.

Nathaniel Alexander Owings

❧ CLASS OF 1927

"I was totally unprepared for the miracle of the cathedrals," Nathaniel Alexander Owings said, recalling the "most important vision" of his life when in August 1920 he stood before Notre Dame de Paris. He was a seventeen-year-old Boy Scout who had won a Rotary fellowship to attend an international Scout jamboree in London and to tour the Continent. The Gothic structures he saw in France determined his career as an architect, although he sought to build in idioms appropriate to twentieth-century America. By the time the American Institute of Architects awarded him its Gold Medal in 1983, Owings had played a major role in turning American architecture away from the past toward the cool, elegant modernism of Bauhaus design.

Owings was born in Indianapolis on February 5, 1903, and named for his father, a suc-

cessful importer of fine wood. However, his father's death in 1914 placed the burden of family support on Owings's mother, Cora Alexander, who worked for a bookstore. In

1921, with $900 of his mother's savings, he enrolled in the College of Architecture at the University of Illinois. A life-threatening illness—Bright's disease—interrupted his education, and his mother sent him off to Oklahoma where he was supposed to benefit from a hot, dry climate. There, he worked for thirty-five cents an hour unrolling steel wire used to reinforce concrete pipes that carried water to Tulsa. His effort to imagine his job as equivalent to building Roman aqueducts failed, and his thoughts turned back to school. A Mrs. Churchyard filled him with passion for her alma mater, Cornell University, and a chance encounter with a Cornell trustee, Nicholas Noyes, while he worked as a counselor at a Boy Scout camp, helped secure his Cornell admission.

Owings entered Cornell in 1922 and graduated in 1927 with a B.S. in architecture. He earned money waiting tables and as student manager of Willard Straight Hall. He joined the Sigma Chi fraternity and found time to uphold the reputation of Cornell architects as "screwballs" who were expected to "cause excitement, provide entertainment, and, hopefully, land in trouble." His social skills did in fact aid his career, but so did his success as a student. He was elected to Gargoyle, the architectural honor society. With the other twelve members of his architecture class, he relished the attention of Dean Franke Bosworth who "did more for the students than all the other professors and critics and architects I have known."

After graduating, Owings headed to New York where he worked without pleasure at the "old-fashioned" architectural firm of York and Sawyer. He left that job and teamed with a Cornell classmate, Arthur Winkler, who had landed a contract to design a jail in New Jersey. That budding partnership failed when Winkler was tragically killed in a swimming accident, and Owings began an association with Louis Skidmore, a gifted architectural graduate of MIT who had just married his sister Eloise. Through a connection with Raymond Hood, the architect of Rockefeller Center, Skidmore became the chief of design for the 1933 Chicago World's Fair, and Owings served as the fair's development supervisor. The Depression sharply curtailed plans for the "Century of Progress" exhibition, but Skidmore and Owings took satisfaction, even with cheap building materials, in giving the fair a modern look. Owings felt that he had repaid a debt to Louis Sullivan, Chicago's great architect, who had championed functional design in the late nineteenth century only to see his urban vision betrayed by the Beaux Arts composition of the 1893 Chicago Columbian Exposition.

When the fair closed, Owings traveled around the world with his wife Emily Hunting Otis, whom he had married in 1931. At the end of a long trip, mostly through Asia, Owings and his wife joined Skidmore and his wife in London. While waiting for a train in Paddington Station, Skidmore and Owings decided to form a partnership, one that they hoped would become a modern Gothic builder's guild that emphasized teamwork, anonymity, and painstaking attention to detail. Skidmore and Owings opened their first office in Chicago in 1936. Adding the architect-engineer John Merrill to the list of partners several years later, Skidmore, Owings and Merrill (SOM) quickly expanded with large offices in Chicago, New York City, San Francisco, and Portland. During Owings's career, no other architectural firm in the United States received as many contracts for major work and none won more awards for design.

Although most of the projects during the 1930s were small, SOM did a number of buildings for the 1939 New York World's Fair. In 1942 the government hired SOM to design an entirely new town, Oak Ridge, Tennessee, a project so cloaked in secrecy that the architects did not know that the purpose of the town was to house people working to refine uranium. An even more influential project was Lever House, completed on New York City's Park Avenue in 1952. A slender glass-enclosed shaft, wide enough for two sets of offices and a corridor between, rose twenty-one stories over only a small portion of the available building site. What might have been rental office space was consigned instead to urban plaza and open air. The elegant design of Lever House was left to Gordon Bunshaft, perhaps the greatest architect to be nurtured by SOM and one of the first prominent Jewish architects in America. However, Owings took credit for the plaza concept. His dictum that "the only true economic value is beauty" was evident in later and much larger skyscrapers designed by SOM—the Chase Manhattan Bank in lower Manhattan and the John Hancock Building and Sears Tower, both in Chicago. The much-imitated Lever House revolutionized the skylines of American cities.

Owings once proudly claimed that "I as an individual cannot point to any major building for which I am solely responsible." He preferred to think of himself as a cajoler and educator, someone who could sell the vision of the designer to a client. In that respect no project taxed his skills more severely than the new campus of the U.S. Air Force Academy in Colorado Springs. Owings fought for SOM's modern design against skeptical senators and congressmen from small towns with "narrow but fixed ideas . . . often aesthetically influenced by their local pseudo-Colonial library." One critic called the proposed chapel "an assembly of wigwams" and "an insult to God." However, Owings viewed the church as an homage to Mont St. Michel, the great French religious site he had seen as a young Scout. The completed Academy became one of SOM's most celebrated projects.

Owings's constant travel and socializing took a toll on his personal life. His wife and the mother of their four children divorced him in 1953. That same year he happily married Margaret Wentworth Millard, although he was by now a heavy drinker. In the early 1960s Owings checked himself in to an alcohol rehabilitation center. Interestingly, this man who was so closely associated with building cities preferred not to live in them. He had moved with his first wife from Chicago to Santa Fe, and with his second he built a dramatic home in Big Sur. There they led passionate and successful fights against California developers. Owings's conservation efforts continued when he bought a ranch in New Mexico and gave money to restore colonial adobe churches.

Owings remained at SOM until 1976, longer than either Skidmore or Merrill. But in his later years he became less interested in large building projects. He poured his energy into urban planning with the aim of creating environments "where man can live in harmony with nature." He successfully led a fight against the building of a superhighway in Baltimore that would have cut the city off from its harbor and prevented the later rejuvenation of the waterfront. In 1962 President John Kennedy appointed him chair of the Presidential Advisory Committee on Pennsylvania Avenue. Serving in that capacity for over a decade, Owings oversaw the avenue's rebirth as well as the restoration of the Great Mall.

Owings died in Santa Fe on June 13, 1984, but not before he had renewed his connection with Cornell. He served as an advisor to the College of Architecture and in 1979 endowed the Nathaniel and Margaret Owings Chair. SOM designed two buildings on the Cornell campus, the Newman Laboratory of Nuclear Studies and Uris Hall. Rational, functional design was the hallmark of an SOM project. Owings, however, following the lead of Louis Sullivan and Henry Adams, two men he admired enormously, insisted that instinct rather than intellect mattered most in the creative process. He would not have understood the critique by postmodernist architects of SOM's work as cold. To him it represented an "economics of wonder and of harmonious living."

Franchot Tone

CLASS OF 1927

His best claim to immortality may be as "Mr. Joan Crawford," an appellation he despised. But until his political activism caught up with him, Franchot Tone was known as the Millionaire Star, an actor from a privileged background who was attractive to critics as well as audiences.

Stanislas Pascal Franchot Tone was born in Niagara Falls, New York, on February 27, 1905. His father, Frank Jerome Tone, rose from a position as an engineer to become president of the Carborundum Company of America. His mother, Gertrude Franchot, a suffragette, was a political mentor to Franchot, who would become an outspoken liberal.

Tone attended Miss Otis' School and a boys academy, the Hill School, in Pottstown, Pennsylvania, from which he was dismissed for being "a subtle influence for disorder throughout the fall term." With a half semester of high school remaining, he entered Cornell University, where his brother had been a student. Fluent in French and blessed with a photographic memory, Tone graduated in 1927 with a major in Romance languages and a Phi Beta Kappa key. Active in his fraternity, Alpha Delta Phi, "Pamp" was passionate about drama. He was trained by Alexander M. Drummond, who shared his love of French Canadian poetry and who was then beginning what would be a legendary career at Cornell. Tone appeared in dozens of plays, including Shaw's *Arms and the Man* and Shakespeare's *A Midsummer Night's Dream*. When he displayed his thespian talents in French class, Professor Mason admonished him, saying, "Now, now, Barrymore."

After graduation Tone considered a career in teaching but instead joined a theatrical company in Buffalo. In 1928 he got his big break when the New Playwrights Company in Greenwich Village cast him to appear alongside Katharine Cornell, one of the great

ladies of the theater, in *The Age of Innocence.* Soon after his first starring role, in *Green Grow the Lilacs,* Tone joined the revolutionary Group Theater, where, he would always claim, Lee Strasberg taught him more about acting than he thought he could ever learn.

In 1932, after receiving critical acclaim for his role as a businessman in *Success Story,* Hollywood in the form of MGM decided to make this tall, sophisticated, gracefully handsome man into a movie star. In the pages of *The New Republic,* the critic Stark Young lamented Tone's departure from the stage. He wondered whether Hollywood, with its "perpetual blast of wonders, stars, mysteries, and pinnacles . . . sideshow barkers, dazzling or monstrous marvels" was the right place for an actor of Tone's "particular possibilities in range." Tone, however, was attracted to a medium where "you can do something with the flick of an eyelash" because the camera directs the audience right to it. He made his debut in *Gabriel over the White House* (1933), a Depression-era fantasy about a hack politician who becomes president of the United States, and then, deranged by an auto accident, institutes sweeping reforms of the banking system and international relations. That same year Tone played Ronnie Boyce-Smith in *Today We Live,* with Gary Cooper and Joan Crawford. In 1935, he married Ms. Crawford, with whom he would make several more films. After a tempestuous four years the couple, who had no children, divorced.

Although Tone was no match for Crawford, professionally or personally, his career flourished through most of the 1930s. He was nominated for an Academy Award for his portrayal of Lieutenant Forsythe, opposite

Gary Cooper, in *The Lives of a Bengal Lancer* (1935), and in the same year appeared with Charles Laughton and Clark Gable in *Mutiny on the Bounty.* He liked *Bengal Lancer* so much that every year he asked the Museum of Modern Art to screen it for him. Toward the end of the decade, however, Tone's agent stopped calling. Besides being active in the Group Theater he supported the anti-Franco coalition (which included Communists) in the Spanish Civil War and took an activist role as director and vice president of the Screen Actors Guild. In 1940 he landed on the front page of the *New York Times* when he was accused in testimony before the Los Angeles County Grand Jury, along with James Cagney, Humphrey Bogart, and other Hollywood heavyweights, of contributing regularly to the Communist Party. According to an informant, the actor was a member of a Communist study group and gave between $75 and $150 per month to the party. Hauled before the House Un-American Activities Committee in Washington, D.C., later in the year, Tone denied the charges. However, he found himself consigned to B pictures and returned to New York City and the stage, appearing first for the Group Theater in *Gentle People,* as a menacing man who "protects" his neighbors, and in 1940 as an ex-journalist and counterespionage agent in Hemingway's *The Fifth Column.* The *New Yorker* singled him out in the latter for "maturity and a disregard for romantic attitudes that would never have got him anywhere in Hollywood."

In 1941, Tone married the actress Jean Wallace. When the couple divorced seven years later, he was awarded custody of their two sons. In 1951 Tone's image suffered when he was mauled in a highly publicized brawl with ex-boxer and would-be actor Tom Neal over actress Barbara Payton. Shortly after that fight, he was booked on suspicion of battery after an encounter with columnist Florabel Muir in a Sunset Strip nightclub. Muir mumbled something uncomplimentary, and he responded, "I'm so mad I could spit in your face. As a matter of fact, I will." The colum-

nist then slapped him. Tone had lost two fights, although he briefly won Miss Payton. After extensive plastic surgery to repair the damage done by Neal, he married Payton and fifty-three days later divorced her. His last try at matrimonial bliss was with actress Dolores Dorn-Heft in 1958. Dorn obtained a divorce in Mexico two years later.

No longer suited to roles as a leading man, Tone rediscovered his skills as a character actor as the McCarthyite Red Scare faded. He appeared on Broadway in *A Moon for the Misbegotten* and *Strange Interlude.* In 1958 he played Astroff, the wearily disillusioned doctor in *Uncle Vanya,* in the first film adaptation in English of a Chekhov play. He returned to Ithaca for a pre-premier showing of the film. He also financed the film, which was aimed at art houses, because he wanted to "immortalize" a production that had begun as a play in the tiny Fourth Street Theater in New York City. Still working, Tone won praise in Hollywood for his performance as the dying president of the United States in *Advise and Consent* (1962) and appeared in *In Harm's Way* (1965) and *Mickey One* (1965). In 1965 and 1966 Tone's character replaced Sam Jaffe's in the popular television program *Ben Casey,* and he appeared in a classic episode of *The Twilight Zone,* "The Silence." Television, Tone said, was "a lovely way to coast," providing more time for him to spend with his sons.

On September 18, 1968, not long after he had purchased the movie rights to *My Father, Renoir* by Jean Renoir, the renowned film director and son of the painter, Franchot Tone died of lung cancer. The *New York Times* obituary gave his friend, actor Burgess Meredith, the last, perhaps too modest word, on an actor who had made scores of films and appeared in dozens of plays: "His problem, aside from his obsession with lovely women, was, I suppose, that he really had too many graces. If he had had a little less money, a little less looks, he might have made a larger mark. But I can't think of a man who enjoyed his life more."

Sidney Sonny Kingsley

⮞ CLASS OF 1928

Every drama set in a police station or a hospital owes a debt to Sidney Kingsley, whose plays *Men in White* and *Detective Story* established him as a trenchant and realistic critic of contemporary American society.

Sidney Kingsley was born Sidney Sonny Kirschner in New York City on October 18, 1906. Educated in the public schools of Manhattan, he began writing one-act plays even before he won a scholarship to Cornell University, which he entered in 1924. At Cornell, he was a member of the Debate Team, but his first love remained drama. Kingsley appeared in several plays with Franchot Tone and continued to write. His play *Wonder-Dark Epilogue* won the prize for the best one-act drama by a student in 1928, the year he graduated.

Kingsley returned to New York City to try his hand at acting with the Tremont Stock Company. He also worked as a scenario writer for Columbia Pictures, while doing research for his play *Men in White*. To make sure that he had mastered clinical details, Kingsley prowled around Lebanon, Montefiore, Bellevue, and Beth Israel hospitals, masquerading more than once as an intern. Cosponsored by the experimental Group Theater (the troupe that Franchot Tone joined around the same time), *Men in White* opened at the Broadhurst Theater on September 26, 1933. The contrast between the matter-of-fact routine of the hospital staff and the life-and-death situations they faced fascinated audiences. The play pivoted on the story of a young woman who dies from a botched abortion. *Men in White* ran on Broadway for 351 performances, was a hit in Europe, and in 1934 appeared as a film, with Clark Gable and Myrna Loy. It also won the Pulitzer Prize. The award was tarnished, but only a bit, by the revelation that the advisory board of the Columbia School of Journalism, which makes final recommendations for awarding the prize, had overturned the Pulitzer jury's

unanimous recommendation that it go to Maxwell Anderson's *Mary Queen of Scots.*

Kingsley followed his successful debut as a playwright, and this time as director too, with *Dead End,* the story of a gang of kids living in the slums of the lower East Side. Kingsley's philosophy—that man "can create his own environment and thereby create himself"—left him open to the charge of sentimentalism in this play and others, but many were moved by Kingsley's juxtaposition of luxurious apartment houses and run-down tenements and convinced that the speech of street waifs, policemen, and prostitutes was realistic. In an inspired bit of staging, Kingsley turned the orchestra pit into the East River. When the young toughs jumped in to cool off, the stage manager released a geyser of water, and the audience could not see the net into which they landed. The assistant stage manager rubbed them down with oil, so when they reappeared on stage they glistened as if they were wet. The boys of *Dead End*—Huntz Hall, Billy Halop, Leo Gorcey, and Gabriel Dell—were not, as many thought, imports from the East Side, but graduates of New York City drama schools. They appeared with Humphrey Bogart in the film version of the play in 1937, and, for many years afterward in movies that billed them as the "Dead End Kids." *Dead End* was the first play to receive a command performance at the White House and was credited by Senator Robert F. Wagner Sr. with building support for slum clearance legislation.

With *Ten Million Ghosts* (1936), a preachy denunciation of munitions merchants starring George Coulouris and Orson Welles, Kingsley had his first flop. *The World We Make*

(1939), the story of a young woman who escapes from a mental institution and heals herself by living among normal people, was a modest success. Reviewers singled out a remarkable scene of work in a steam laundry and a brilliant performance by the actress Margo (she had no last name) as Virginia McKay. Kingsley's biggest success in 1939 was his marriage to actress Madge Evans, a union that lasted until her death in 1981. The couple had no children.

Kingsley served as an Army lieutenant during World War II, where, amid doubts about democracy's capacity to survive, he got the idea for a play about the work of Washington, Hamilton, and Jefferson in creating the government of the United States. *The Patriots* (1943) endorsed Jefferson's belief that each generation must rediscover and reshape democracy. The play won the New York Drama Critics Circle Award.

Drawing on eighteen months of observation of policemen, *Detective Story* (1949) was vintage Kingsley, with shoplifters, street people, and hardened criminals in a single setting, the shabbily utilitarian detective squad room. As he had in *Men in White,* Kingsley explored the fatal consequences of laws prohibiting abortion. The 1951 film, which was directed by William Wyler, starred Kirk Douglas and Eleanor Parker, with Lee Grant and Joseph Wiseman reprising the roles they created in the play.

Kingsley was to have one more success, earning a second New York Drama Critics Circle Award for his adaptation of Arthur Koestler's novel about Soviet communism, *Darkness at Noon* (1951). That same year, the American Academy of Arts and Letters presented him with an Award of Merit Medal for Outstanding Work in Drama.

Kingsley's last plays, *Lunatics and Lovers* (1954), a farce featuring Buddy Hackett, and *Night Life* (1962), a melodrama about the habitués of a key club, including a movie star with a death wish and a labor leader willing to kill to achieve power, closed rather quickly. He continued to write, working intermittently on a play about Robert Oppenheimer and the atomic bomb that he never finished. In the last decades of his life, Kingsley was showered with honors. He was inducted into the Theater Hall of Fame in 1983 and received the William Inge Award for Lifetime Achievement in the American Theater in 1988. In 1985, he returned to Ithaca for a performance of *Darkness at Noon* by Theater Cornell. Kingsley remained active in promoting the arts. A former president of the Dramatists Guild, he served on its awards panels. He was also on the boards of the Martha Graham Dance Company and Café La Mama. Through the latter affiliation he manifested his interest in experimental drama and promoted Off Off Broadway productions.

A soft-spoken, thoughtful man, Kingsley enjoyed painting, sculpture, woodworking, and collecting Americana. On March 20, 1995, at his eighteenth-century clapboard farmhouse that overlooked the Ramapo River in Oakland, New Jersey, Sidney Kingsley died. He was fortunate, during his long life, in finding both his calling and his livelihood in playwriting. With more exhilaration than resignation, Kingsley claimed that he finished revising a script only "when the curtain goes down on opening night." And when George Bernard Shaw asked him why he had chosen "this godless profession," Kingsley replied, with a fatalism absent in his plays, "The gods chose me," exerting a "mighty gravitational force."

Allen Funt

◈ CLASS OF 1934

In his classic book, *The Lonely Crowd* (1950), Harvard professor David Riesman ranked Allen Funt, after Paul Lazarsfeld, as the "most ingenious sociologist in America." Before most Americans could afford a TV set, acclaim, fame, and fortune had come to the man behind—and in front of—the "candid camera."

Allen Funt was born in Brooklyn, New York, on September 16, 1914, a year after his parents, Isadore and Paula Saferstein Funt, had left Russia for the United States. An excellent student, Funt skipped several grades and graduated from New Utrecht High School when he was fifteen. Interested in a career as an artist, he attended Pratt Institute in Brooklyn before transferring to Cornell in 1932. With his father's once-lucrative diamond business in decline during the Depression, Funt waited on tables to help pay for his tuition. He hustled to complete a B.A. in fine arts in two years, spending the little leisure time he had as a member of the boxing team.

After graduation, Funt took some courses in business administration at Columbia and worked in an advertising agency art department before discovering an interest in radio. For a brief time, he wrote continuity for a program that featured First Lady Eleanor Roosevelt. Soon he found his niche as a "gimmick man" who created ideas for audience participation shows. His biggest success (and "the stupidest show on radio," he later recalled) was *The Funny Money Man,* in which the master of ceremonies gave a small sum— rarely more than ninety-nine cents—to a person who sent in an unusual item, such as a strand from a mop, half a mothball, or the shirt off somebody's back.

In 1943, Funt joined the Army. He trained Nisei infantrymen and produced entertainment programs for the Special Service before the Signal Corps tapped him to record messages from the soldiers to their families. Finding that many servicemen were tongue-tied,

he started the tape recorder without telling them. Their natural, informal, and colorful monologues gave Funt the idea for a radio show that would demonstrate "the beauty of candid speech and gesture." After his discharge from the Army, he refined the idea when he was bugging a dentist's drill for his radio show and a woman, who mistook him for a dentist, asked him to examine her wisdom teeth. Funt inspected his "patient" and told her that she had no wisdom teeth. The woman's reaction—she exploded and stomped out of the dentist's office—convinced Funt that a contrived situation, and an instigator, provoked entertaining reactions. *Candid Microphone* was launched on ABC radio in 1947, moving to television as *Candid Mike* a year later, and then, shuttling among the three networks from 1949 to 1954, as *Candid Camera.* After a hiatus, the show returned to CBS from 1960 to 1967, with Funt joined by Arthur Godfrey, then Durwood Kirby, and finally, by Bess Meyerson as co-hosts. Among the highest-rated shows on television, it introduced into the language the phrase, "Smile. You're on *Candid Camera.*"

Candid Camera provided viewers and voyeurs with the pleasure of watching subjects cope with puzzling or embarrassing situations. Funt's genius, as a writer and sometimes on-air prankster/provocateur, was in creating a small crisis for an average person: a passerby is addressed by a talking mailbox; a locksmith is asked to remove chains from a secretary tied to her desk; a gas station attendant is asked to check the water and oil of a car with no engine under the hood. Because most people, even when placed in these surprising situations, fail to react with sufficient irritation or apoplexy, the crew, on average, shot 9,000 feet of film to get the 450 they needed for a five-minute episode. The show, Funt claimed, provided evidence of "man's ability to laugh at himself" and of his fundamental decency and integrity. *Candid Camera,* he insisted, never depicted something a person wanted to conceal. If a subject did not sign a release, the producers did not even develop the film that had been shot.

Nonetheless, some critics thought the subjects were "victims." In an essay in the *New Yorker,* Philip Hamburger denounced the show as "sadistic, poisonous, anti-human, and sneaky," a pseudo-documentary that robbed people of their dignity by placing them in situations where they had no choice but to look foolish. Nine years later, in the same magazine, John Lardner acknowledged that "Mr. Funt understands the world better than nine-tenths of the entertainers who make television one long round of bird song and good fellowship." Nonetheless, he lamented that Funt targeted the man in the street rather than applying "his great gift for aggressiveness to men in public life, beginning at the top."

Funt's many fans recognized that *Candid Camera* contained valuable insights into human behavior. Scores of corporations, including Simmons, Seagrams, Bristol-Myers, and Nash-Kelvinator, hired Funt to make training films for their sales staff. *Candid Camera*'s "sidewalk sociology" made its way into hospitals as "laughter therapy" and into college courses throughout the country. One course at Monterey Peninsula College in California, taught by Funt himself, used clips from the show to illustrate group pressure, vanity, dishonesty, and cognitive dissonance.

When *Candid Camera* was at the height of its popularity, Funt changed families. After seventeen years of a marriage that produced three children, he divorced Evelyn Kessler in August 1964. A month later Marilyn Ina Laron, who had been Funt's secretary, became his wife. The couple had two children.

In the three decades following its cancellation, *Candid Camera* refused to die. Funt added *Candidly, Allen Funt* to the two books he had published earlier, *Eavesdropper at Large* and *Candid Kids.* In the early 1970s, he produced two feature-length films, *What Do You Say to a Naked Lady?,* a hidden-camera study of sexuality, and *Money Talks.* In addition to forty movie shorts and seven record albums, he produced for television two short-lived variations on the candid-camera theme, *Tell It to the Camera,* where viewers knew they were on the air, and *Candid Candid Camera,* a cable program with risqué material. *Candid Camera* itself returned to television, in several specials, in syndicated versions that ran in the '70s, '80s, and early '90s, and again on prime time in 1998, hosted by Funt's son Peter. That *Candid Camera* was an enduring icon of popular culture was demonstrated when a man hijacked a plane (which later landed safely) on which Funt was a passenger, and the other passengers stood up, looked for the hidden camera, and cheered.

Funt continued to run the *Candid Camera* empire until he suffered a stroke in 1993. Given six months to live, he battled for six years, supplementing medication with laughter therapy. Before he died, on September 5, 1999, "reality TV," which he had helped invent, dominated the airwaves, but in a form he deplored. *Real People* and *That's Incredible,* Funt believed, used "unreal people," "freaks and aberrations" with whom audiences could not really connect. He predicted, quite wrongly, that the new programs would not last. "When people are smiling," he said, "they are most receptive to almost anything you want to teach them. I think that can be applied industrially, academically, technically and almost every other way." Funt's proudest achievement was being able to go almost anywhere in the world and have people say, "Thanks, Allen. You made us smile."

Margaret Morgan Lawrence
~ CLASS OF 1936

From its founding Cornell had no color bar. Ezra Cornell and Andrew Dickson White wanted to offer a college education for any person, man or woman, white or black. But, that did not mean you had an easy time if you were one of the handful of black students in Cornell before World War II. For Margaret Morgan Lawrence, who became one of America's most distinguished and influential pediatric psychiatrists, her time at Cornell was bittersweet; they were years of humiliation and of achievement.

The path to Cornell was circuitous. Her mother, Mary Smith Morgan, a schoolteacher, and her father, Sandy Morgan, an Episcopal priest, lived in Virginia. Mistrusting segregated southern hospitals, in 1914 Mary temporarily moved in with her mother and sisters, who lived in Harlem, where her daughter was born on August 19. Margaret's childhood, however, was spent primarily in Vicksburg, Mississippi, where her father's next congregation was located. She grew up a precocious child, reading at three and living in a middle-class black neighborhood with her educated parents.

Every summer she visited her aunts in Harlem, and at the age of fourteen she decided she wanted to live with them so she could go to a better high school. She had already decided to be a doctor, which she told people was because her older brother had died in infancy before she was born, and she wanted to save babies from dying. With her parents' blessing she moved to Harlem and attended the Wadleigh School, one of the two classical high schools for girls in New York City that then had entrance exams. Margaret excelled at the predominantly white high school, and on graduation day the top prize in Greek and Latin was awarded, as the principal put it, to "the Negro girl from Mississippi." She received scholarships from Cornell, Hunter College, and Smith and chose Cornell because of her Regents Scholarship, its strong reputation in the biological sciences, and also, as she told friends, because it had men.

When she came to Cornell in the fall of 1932 Margaret Morgan was the only black student in Arts and Sciences. She was not allowed to live in the women's dormitory, but the dean of students found her a room with a business family at 209 Hudson Street. There, in order to pay for her room and board, she worked as a servant, wearing a uniform and waiting on the dinner table while she herself ate separately in the kitchen. She was also responsible for the housecleaning, washing, and ironing. She lived in this South Hill house for two years, sleeping in an uninsulated attic.

In Morgan's junior year she moved in with a faculty family on East Hill where she had a large, comfortable room, but where once again she earned her keep as the household maid. Her luck changed in her senior year when she was taken in by Hattie Jones, a legendary figure in Ithaca's tiny black community. Married to a big-time gambler and driven around town in her flashy car by a good-looking young chauffeur, Hattie rented rooms in her big comfortable house and cooked huge dinners for students she called "young Negroes coming up." Years later, Margaret Morgan would recall the wonderful dinners and finally finding an Ithaca home in Hattie Jones's rooming house.

Determined to be a doctor, Morgan preferred courses in organic chemistry and astronomy to those in ancient history or sociology, and in her senior year she worked as a technologist for a researcher in the College of Agriculture. The job paid the rent at Hattie's and taught her how to prepare tissue specimens for microscopic study. She received excellent grades in her courses and was told by the dean of the medical school, located at that time in Ithaca, that she had done "very well" on the Medical Aptitude Test. Medical school seemed certain and she chose Cornell's.

Cornell Medical School rejected her application. The very same dean who had praised her told a stunned Morgan that several meetings of the Admissions Committee had been devoted to her application. Although she was a very good student and a promising physician, they were still turning her down. The dean told her, in words she would always remember, that twenty-five years earlier the medical school had conducted "an experiment," by admitting a Negro, "and it didn't work out. He got tuberculosis."

She was accepted at Columbia, however, and when she entered in 1936 Margaret Morgan became the third black student in the medical school's history. During her four years there she was the only African American in the school. She did well in her courses and won the respect of her teachers and classmates. Meanwhile, to pay for her meals at the residence hall for medical students, she worked in the kitchen drying silverware.

Her life's goal was still to save babies, so Morgan—now Lawrence; she had married Charles Lawrence, a college professor, in 1938—sought a residency in pediatrics. Her top choice was New York's Babies Hospital, affiliated with Columbia Medical School. Her application was rejected, because, as she was told and never believed, married interns could not live in the hospital's quarters, even though her husband, Charles Lawrence, was studying and living in the South at Atlanta University. Instead, she did her pediatric internship at Harlem Hospital and then took a master's degree in public health from Columbia in 1943.

In 1943 she left New York and returned to the South for four years, teaching pediatrics and public health at Meharry Medical College in Nashville, Tennessee, then the premier medical school for black Americans. She was back together with her husband, who taught sociology at nearby Fisk. Margaret and her husband moved to New York City in 1948, never to leave, and after psychoanalytic training at the Columbia Psychoanalytic Institute (she was the first black person to go through the institute) she settled into a career of research, teaching, and clinical work at Harlem Hospital and Columbia Medical School, where she distinguished herself, while her husband became an eminent sociologist at Brooklyn College.

A lucky break that helped put her on the path to professional distinction was her association with a young pediatrician, Dr. Benjamin Spock, during the year she worked for her master's degree in public health at Columbia. Spock opened Lawrence's eyes to the link between physical health and psychological well being. From Spock, who was also trained in psychoanalysis, she learned to look at the social and family context of childhood disease. She put these insights to work at Harlem Hospital where she worked tirelessly to reconstruct the shattered lives of young black children through treatment and therapy provided in the Developmental Psychiatry Clinic, which she founded and ran for many years.

Lawrence's most important contribution to child psychiatry was her pioneering advocacy of placing therapeutic teams composed of psychiatrists, neuropsychologists, social workers, and nurses in schools. Her first book, *The Mental Health Team in the School* (1971), describing how visiting teams of mental health specialists could serve children in school, is recognized as a milestone in pediatric psychiatry, as are the programs in child psychiatry she developed in day-care centers and hospital clinics.

Throughout her career Margaret Lawrence was passionately involved in the antipoverty and civil rights movements, always seeking to improve, as she never tired of putting it, "the impoverished lives of black babies." She was particularly interested in how poor urban black families coped with adversity and how some black children were able to develop ego strength under stress, themes she explored in her second book, *Young Inner City Families* (1975).

Margaret and Charles Lawrence had three children, one of whom, the Harvard education professor Sara Lawrence Lightfoot, has written a moving biography of her mother, *Balm in Gilead: Journal of a Healer* (1988). In 1984, after her retirement at age seventy from Harlem Hospital and Columbia University Medical School, Lawrence continued her private child psychiatry practice in Rockland County while remaining an active crusader for improved mental health care for economically disadvantaged children. She has been awarded many honorary degrees and in 1992 received the Cornell Black Alumni Award. Cornell, which would not let her live in its dorms, nonetheless, with its labs and lectures, laid the foundation for her distinguished career.

In the spring of 2002, at the age of eighty-seven, Lawrence returned to Ithaca to give a talk; the lecture room was packed with students and members of the Cornell community. She told the rapt audience that she had made it despite her difficulties as a student because "I knew who I was, and I knew my own gifts."

Arthur Laurents

⌘ CLASS OF 1937

In giving serious attention to street gangs and racial prejudice, *West Side Story* violated the "sacred code of show business: musicals are for nonthinking joy." Author of the books for *West Side Story* and *Gypsy,* two outstanding Broadway musicals, Arthur Laurents won acclaim as a leading dramatist, librettist, and screenwriter in the second half of the twentieth century.

Arthur Laurents was born in Brooklyn, New York, on July 14, 1918, the son of Irving Laurents, a lawyer, and Ada Robbins Laurents, a teacher. As a teenager at summer camp, Arthur became "wildly stagestruck" after he was picked for a part in *The Crow's Nest* because he was "agile enough to climb up the mast of a ship and bright enough to re-

member some lines." While a student at Erasmus Hall High School in Brooklyn, he regularly attended the theater in his neighborhood as well as in Manhattan.

In 1933, Laurents entered Cornell. With encouragement from Raymond Short, his freshman English teacher, he decided to become a writer rather than to follow his father into the legal profession. A theater major, Laurents (who would be dubbed "the meanest mouth in show business") was not impressed by the faculty or the curriculum in the department. The reading course he designed for himself, "The Socially Conscious Drama since 1848," was, he thought, "one of the pathetically few [classes] I took at Cornell that I enjoyed or from which I learned anything." When Professor Alexander M. Drummond advised students never to begin a play with a telephone ringing, Laurents defied him by writing a first act that did just that. He knew he was declaring war, but dismissed Drummond as a "casually overt anti-Semite." Not surprisingly, Drummond suggested that Laurents give up playwriting.

Although Laurents remembers his undergraduate years with little affection, they were formative. As assistant editor and drama critic of the *Cornell Daily Sun,* he wrote regularly about topics that interested him. As a member of the liberal-socialist American Student Union, he gained firsthand experience with progressive politics and red-baiting. He also met Fanny Price, the frizzy-haired Young Communist Leaguer whom he would later make the model for Katie Morosky, the heroine of his film *The Way We Were.* In 1937 Laurents attended the peace strike organized by the Young Communist League, which featured placards calling for "Peace at Any Price, Except Fanny Price."

Following graduation in 1937, Laurents performed in a nightclub revue and wrote a few radio scripts. When the United States entered World War II, he enlisted in the Army. Assigned at first to a paratroop unit at Fort Benning, Georgia, he spent most of the war writing scripts for military training films and radio scenarios about the rehabilitation of veterans and the problems of returning servicemen. Drawing on his research in veterans hospitals, Laurents wrote his first Broadway play, *Home of the Brave,* in 1945; it's the story of an Army psychiatrist and a Jewish soldier whose amnesia is the result of guilt over the death of his possibly anti-Semitic buddy. Praised by some as bold and important, the play closed after sixty-nine performances. In 1949 United Artists released a film version of *Home of the Brave,* rewritten as an exploration of prejudice against blacks rather than Jews.

After his next play, *Heartsong,* flopped during pre-Broadway trials in 1947, Laurents moved to Hollywood. He produced the screenplay for Alfred Hitchcock's *Rope* (1948), a script for Anatole Litvak's *The Snake Pit* (1948), and worked on *Caught* (1949) and *Anna Lucasta* (1949). Laurents returned to Broadway in 1950 with another flop, *The Bird Cage,* but scored an impressive hit two years later with *The Time of the Cuckoo,* a comedy-romance set in Venice that is about the relationship between an American spinster — brilliantly played by Shirley Booth — and a married Italian shopkeeper. The play was subsequently turned into a film, *Summertime,* with Katharine Hepburn, and a musical comedy, *Do I Hear a Waltz?,* with music by Richard Rodgers and lyrics by Stephen Sondheim.

Blacklisted in Hollywood as a "fellow traveler" for much of the 1950s, Laurents fled to Paris. In mid-decade, he returned to the Broadway theater. Despite a fine performance by Kim Stanley, *A Clearing in the Wood* closed after less than a month in early 1957. In the fall, however, he was part of a great Broadway triumph. *West Side Story,* with music by Leonard Bernstein, the book by Laurents, lyrics by Sondheim, and conception, choreography, and staging by Jerome Robbins, electrified audiences. Laurents won praise for updating the story of the star-crossed lovers, Romeo and Juliet, seamlessly integrating the dialogue and plot with the music, creating for the Anglo Jets and Puerto Rican Sharks the "talk of the juveniles, or a reasonable facsimile," and weaving it into "a magic fabric."

Following the success of *West Side Story, Gypsy,* with lyrics by Stephen Sondheim and a score by Jule Styne, enjoyed a two-year Broadway run, spawned a film that was a smash hit, and became one of the most frequently staged musicals in the United States. Based on the memoirs of stripper Gypsy Rose Lee, Laurents's libretto concentrated on Gypsy's ambitious, overbearing stage mother, played by Ethel Merman. In 1973 Laurents directed a revival of *Gypsy,* this time starring Angela Lansbury, for which he earned a Tony nomination and a Drama Desk Award.

The 1960s were somewhat less kind to Laurents. He directed a musical comedy version of Jerome Weidman's play *I Can Get It for You Wholesale* in 1962, a musical remembered only because it marked the Broadway debut of Barbra Streisand. Two years later he was librettist and director for *Anyone Can Whistle,* a show with music and lyrics by Sondheim that lasted for only nine performances. In 1967, Laurents wrote the musical libretto for *Hallelujah, Baby!,* which examined race relations through the lives of a young black couple played by Leslie Uggams and Robert Hooks. Despite lackluster reviews, the show ran for nine months, and Laurents picked up another Tony.

In the 1970s Laurents scored his biggest commercial successes with his screenplays for *The Way We Were* (1973) and *The Turning Point* (1977). *The Way We Were* allowed Laurents to explore the anticommunist witch-hunt in Hollywood during the 1950s, through a romance between Streisand, playing a left-wing intellectual, and Robert Redford, playing a WASP novelist. Columbia Pictures considered, then rejected, Cornell as the setting for Katie Morosky's college days.

Acclaimed as "literate, mature, and compelling," *The Turning Point* featured stellar performances by Anne Bancroft, as a prima ballerina on the verge of retirement, and Shirley MacLaine, as a talented dancer who gave up her career to raise a family. The film earned Laurents an Oscar nomination for best screenplay.

A gay man, Laurents took special pleasure in directing *La Cage aux Folles* (1983), the musical about the homosexual owners and transvestite stars of a nightclub in Saint-Tropez. He worked hard to ensure that "people and emotions" remained at the heart of this often bawdy play. A box-office smash, *La Cage aux Folles* won six Tony Awards, including best musical.

Laurents remained active in the 1990s, writing several plays: *Nick and Nora* (1991), a musical; *Jolson Sings Again* (1995), a treatment of the Hollywood blacklist; *The Radical Mystique* (1995); and *My Good Name* (1997). Although none of them found an audience, Laurents became the center of attention again, in 2000, with the publication of *Original Story By,* a candid, acerbic, even fierce memoir of his life in the world of art, love, and politics, that concludes, "I'm still sexual, still skiing, still crusading . . . [and] I have begun a new play, of course."

Charles Cummings Collingwood

CLASS OF 1939

Edward R. Murrow would have hired Charles Collingwood as a reporter for CBS radio during their first meeting but for the orange argyle socks he wore during the interview. As Murrow guessed, Collingwood was a dandy. He was also a superb war correspondent and would be among the first on television to combine the roles of broadcast journalist and "entertainer."

Charles Cummings Collingwood was born June 4, 1917, in Three Rivers, Michigan, the son of Jean Grinnell Cummings (the daughter of a Michigan state senator) and George Harris Collingwood, an official of the U.S. Forest Service, who moved the family to Washington, D.C., soon after Charles's birth. The eldest of six children, Collingwood grew up with a frugal, cultured gentility. "I am so conscious of my shabbiness that I want to cover it with a fine cloak," he wrote in his diary, and from the money earned on summer jobs as a deckhand on a freighter and a cowpuncher in California, he purchased the well-tailored clothing that would earn him the nicknames "Bonnie Prince Charlie" and the "Duke of Collingwood."

In 1935 Collingwood won a scholarship to Deep Springs School, the two-year experimental school near Death Valley, California, that combined Oxford-style seminars with work on a cattle ranch. In 1937 he transferred to Cornell, with free room and board provided by the Telluride Association at the house donated by Lucien Nunn, the founder of Deep Springs. A law and philosophy major, fluent in French, Collingwood was a member of Book and Bowl, a literary and drinking society. He graduated cum laude in 1939 and was awarded a Rhodes Scholarship, which took him to Oxford. Although intrigued by medieval law, Collingwood was swept up by the war in Europe. Convinced that this was "not to be a world conducted by pale scholars," he left the university in the

summer of 1940 to work for the United Press wire service. He covered the London Blitz, watching the skyline with field glasses and then inspecting neighborhoods for bomb damage. Impressed by his courage and intellect, Edward R. Murrow hired him for CBS radio. As one of Murrow's Boys, a group of foreign correspondents that included William Shirer, Eric Sevareid, and Howard K. Smith, Collingwood covered Operation Torch, the Anglo-American invasion of North Africa in 1942, breaking the story of the assassination of Admiral Jean Darlan, head of the French government there, for which he won the George Foster Peabody Award, and arousing the ire of General Eisenhower by revealing American support for the Vichyites.

Collingwood cut quite a figure in North Africa. The only man who knew where to get a suit pressed, he chased secretaries and female military drivers (and with his curly hair and matinee-idol looks he caught more than a few) and gambled on just about anything, including the Eisenhower Cup, which went to the correspondent first to get his story out to the wire services. The "first" with an eyewitness account of the liberation of Tunis, Collingwood left North Africa the envy of colleagues and competitors, none of whom knew he had gonorrhea.

On D-Day, Collingwood was at Utah Beach with the Navy. After the landing, he told listeners that he could now pick up a handful of sand and say, "This is France." An intensely competitive man, who liked living on the edge, he sent to London via military pouch his story about the liberation of Paris, featuring the valiant struggle of Resistance fighters, before it happened. Collingwood's explanation of this serious breach of the rules of journalism convinced no one. The other Murrow Boys marveled not only that he was not fired but that he was allowed to remain in Paris, where he dined with royalty, politicians, and CBS president William Paley, decked out, as Howard K. Smith remembered, like "a twentieth-century replica of an eighteenth-century Beau Brummel." Collingwood spent much of his time in Paris visiting galleries and acquiring Picassos that he had to sell to pay gambling debts.

In 1946, Collingwood married Louise Allbritton, a statuesque actress he had met on a blind date three years earlier. The couple had no children. In the United States, he served as the CBS correspondent for the founding meetings of the United Nations and hosted *The Big Question,* a television program about domestic and foreign affairs. In 1952 he took a leave to serve as special assistant to Averill Harriman at the Mutual Security Administration. There, he joined the poker game hosted by President Truman. In the decade following his return to CBS in 1953, Collingwood was actively involved in television journalism. He filled in for Douglas Edwards on *CBS News;* he hosted the TV science series *Adventure,* winner of several Peabody Awards; acted as host-narrator of the *Chronicle* series and as a reporter on *Eyewitness.* From 1957 until 1959 he was CBS's London correspondent; and in 1959 he succeeded Murrow as host of the popular *Person to Person.* Not sur-

prisingly, CBS chose the charming Collingwood to accompany Jacqueline Kennedy on her televised tour of the White House in 1962.

During the 1950s Collingwood spoke out against McCarthyism. Elected president of the New York chapter of the American Federation of Television and Radio Artists in 1955 on a slate pledged to end blacklisting, he vigorously defended John Henry Faulk, a variety and talk show host. Faulk was the unfortunate victim of an attack by AWARE, Inc., an organization that identified "subversives" and, for a fee, helped them clear themselves. A key witness in the libel case brought by Faulk, Collingwood lambasted networks and sponsors who lacked "the guts" to hire performers and journalists whose patriotism was under attack.

In 1962 Collingwood hoped to be named anchor of the *CBS News* and was devastated when Walter Cronkite got the assignment. In 1964 he returned to Europe and for eleven years served as CBS's chief foreign correspondent. In that capacity he traveled widely to cover the major stories of the era: the six-day Arab-Israeli war of 1967; the Soviet invasion of Czechoslovakia in 1968; Nixon's visit to China in 1972. Collingwood made eighteen trips to Vietnam and hosted several specials, titled *Vietnam Perspective.* In 1968, he became the first American network journalist to visit North Vietnam, winning an Overseas Press Club Award for his reports. Collingwood gave Americans their first glimpse of life in Hanoi: "This is the country the United States is fighting: poor, shabby, doctrinaire, but resourceful and still undefeated." He drew on his impressions of the North Vietnamese in a novel, *The Defector.*

Collingwood stepped down as a foreign correspondent in 1975. Before he returned to the United States, he was awarded the Order of the British Empire and made a chevalier of the French Legion of Honor. Mentor to many CBS correspondents, including Dan Rather and Morley Safer, Collingwood spoke out in the late 1970s against the rise of "happy talk" in television journalism, and he was not given many special assignments by CBS executives.

Louise Allbritton died in 1979. Collingwood retired two years later, and in 1984 he married an old girlfriend, Tatiana Jolin, a Swedish singer. On October 3, 1985, the man who had been the golden boy of CBS died in New York City.

Jerome Heartwell Holland

◈ CLASS OF 1939

Jerome Heartwell Holland, class of 1939, played football for Cornell and was named to all-American teams in both his junior and senior year. He was the first Negro—a term he preferred to "black"—to play for the Big Red. Had a color line not existed in professional football, he might have made his living in that still not well-paid sport. Instead, he became a distinguished educator and diplomat, in the process breaking through many other color bars for himself and for later generations of African Americans.

Holland was born on January 9, 1916, in Auburn, New York, a town not far from Ithaca that was known mainly for its state penitentiary. His parents, Robert and Viola Bagby Holland, had thirteen children, but illness took the lives of most of them while they were young. In 1970, only Brud (so nicknamed by his many sisters), one brother, and three sisters survived. Holland's father was a gardener and caretaker for several families in Auburn, skills he had learned in Ithaca where his own father has worked on the property of Andrew Dickson White, Cornell's first president. Holland recalled that his parents were very religious and very poor. They lived in a ward among first-generation Italians and Poles and second- and third-generation Irish. If there had been racial discrimination of a painful sort, Holland chose not to remember it, saying that he was conscious of race as a child, because of the Negro church and Negro fraternal or-

ders, but not because of racial prejudice in Auburn's integrated schools.

In 1935 Holland entered Cornell's College of Agriculture. Although he had been an outstanding football player at Auburn, he was not offered a scholarship. Recognizing that as a racial snub, Holland refused a later offer of financial assistance. Even so, he played football in all four years and established himself as Cornell's finest athlete to that time. Cornell's coach, Carl Snaveley, put Holland on the line because of his large size. But he also placed him at an end position and devised plays to take advantage of Holland's speed. Alumni had reason to remember Holland's "end around" runs in which he dropped back from his end position, received the ball from a member of the backfield, and raced around the other end and up field. In Holland's senior year, Cornell won the Ivy League crown, losing only to Syracuse. In 1965, although he never played professional football, Holland was elected to the National Football Hall of Fame.

Holland had to work as a student. He lived in the basement of an all-white fraternity and fed coal into the furnace. However, he excelled in his studies and found time to volunteer at the South Side Community

Center, which was devoted to the interests of Ithaca's sizable black population. In New York City, he successfully sought contributions for construction of a new building for the center. When ground was broken, Eleanor Roosevelt attended the ceremony, escorted from her car by Holland. He was elected to the junior and senior honorary societies, Aleph Samach and Sphinx Head, and received his B.S. degree with honors. In 1969 he recalled that, although he had been an outstanding campus citizen, he was the only one of his peers not offered a job by a corporate recruiter. He had, in fact, not been granted a single interview.

In 1939 Europe went to war, and all young men faced difficult decisions. Until 1942, Holland served as an instructor in sociology at the mostly black Lincoln University in Oxford, Pennsylvania, while he worked on his master's degree in that field, which Cornell conferred on him in 1941. A first marriage produced two children but ended in divorce. After the United States entered the war, Holland was summoned to work in a critical industry that employed 16,000 black workers. He was the director of personnel for the #4 Yard of the Sun Shipbuilding and Drydock Company in Chester, Pennsylvania, from 1942 to 1946—work that Holland used as the basic research for a doctoral dissertation at the University of Pennsylvania in 1950.

While he was director of the Division of Political and Social Sciences at Tennessee A & I University in Nashville from 1946 to 1951, his personal life took a happy turn. In 1948 he married Laura Mitchell, a fellow educator with an M.A. degree from Radcliffe who taught at nearby Fisk University. They had two children, a daughter, Lucy, and a son, Joseph. Joseph later attended Cornell, played football, graduated with distinction in history, and earned a law degree at Harvard. (Holland's daughter from his first marriage, Pamela, also went to Cornell and worked for a number of years in the Office of Alumni Affairs.) From 1951 to 1953, Holland served as a consultant to the Pew Charitable Trusts, whose family members had close ties to Cornell. However, in 1953, Delaware's governor asked Holland to leave that job to save a predominantly Negro college that had just lost its accreditation. Holland became president of Delaware State College, got its accreditation back in 1957, and stayed until 1960 when he was asked to lead another predominantly black institution, Hampton Institute in Virginia.

Holland served Hampton with distinction, doubling the size of its physical plant, improving its student body and faculty, and making its endowment the largest of any of the nation's historic black colleges. However, no college president got through the 1960s unscathed. Holland was committed to the idea of integration and brought white students to Hampton. In his 1969 book *Black Opportunity* Holland urged young black college graduates to seek jobs in the private sector, heralding a newly formed partnership "between educated Negroes and corporate industry as a 'mirror of hope' . . . one of the most remarkable advances in human relations in this century." Holland's book endorsed many private and public programs designed to help blacks, so long held back. But he focused on the opportunities now open to educated blacks, opportunities that had not been available to him in 1939. His critics said he neglected the problem of continuing discrimination. Angry young black militants read his book as an uncritical endorsement of the American Creed. Attracted by the Black Panthers, who wanted to empower the black community, they rejected Holland's program of black power through social integration. They organized a takeover of Hampton's administration building in 1969 and demanded Holland's resignation. Although Holland survived the challenge without calling in the police and with the support of the majority of the student body and faculty, he was, in 1970, ready to step down. "In all candor," he mused in a rare mood of pessimism, "the contemporary college scene encourages one to reconsider . . . continuing in an administration capacity."

In 1970, Holland had no publicly declared political affiliations. However, he was friends with William P. Rodgers, Nixon's secretary of state and a graduate of the Cornell Law School. Rodgers's wife Adele had been Holland's classmate. Rodgers told his boss that Holland was looking for a new assignment and was someone who exemplified what Republicans sought in black leadership. Holland became Nixon's choice for ambassador to Sweden, a difficult post that had remained vacant for over a year because of strained relations between the two countries. Sweden offered asylum to American men fleeing service in Vietnam and had just recognized the government of North Vietnam. Holland's son, Joe, who was thirteen when the family arrived in Stockholm, remembered a sea of jeering protestors that had come to the airport to boo and make racial taunts at the new ambassador. For six months Joe and his sister were driven to school under tight security. Holland's charismatic personality and visible participation in Swedish life finally eased the tension and greatly improved relations between the United States and Sweden.

When Holland returned to the United States in 1972, he turned to business. He had already become the first black to serve on Cornell's board of trustees and also served on the MIT board. He became the first African American to serve on the board of the New York Stock Exchange. He also was on the boards of a dozen large corporations, including AT&T, Chrysler, Union Carbide, and General Foods. He maintained his leadership roles in many charitable and other nonprofit organizations, including the Urban League, the Experiment in International Living, Planned Parenthood, and the United Negro College Fund. President Carter named him chairman of the Board of Governors of the American Red Cross, a position he continued to hold into the Reagan years.

Brud Holland died of cancer on January 13, 1985. He was sixty-nine. Cornell, which had named its International Living Center for him in 1985, was not free of racial troubles at that time, but at least it was home to many more African American students than in 1939. Holland had lived through and helped bring about a social upheaval that he courageously and correctly designated as progress in America's race relations.

Constance Knowles Eberhardt Cook

♘ CLASS OF 1941

"I don't admire mavericks at all," Constance Cook maintained. "It's very easy to get headlines, to take a dramatic, beautiful position, and accomplish nothing. That's not the name of the game. The name of the game is compromise, as a result of very hard negotiation. To do that you have to be in; you can't work on the outside." A pragmatist with strong values, Cook in 1970 engineered the passage through the New York State legislature of the most liberal abortion law in the United States.

Constance Knowles Eberhardt was born in Cleveland, Ohio, on August 17, 1919. Her father, Walter Eberhardt, a civil engineer, moved the family to New York City when Connie was ten.

Catherine Sellmann, Connie's mother, worked as a secretary until she married, regretted not going to college, and encouraged her daughter to get an education and become a professional. By the time Connie entered the prestigious, female-only Hunter College High School, she had decided on a career in law. In 1937, she followed her brother to Cornell. An excellent student, Connie Eberhardt majored in government. She was a first-rate athlete as well, playing hockey and serving as captain of the fencing team. Sensitive to the discrimination that women faced, she served as president of the Women's Student Government Association. When officers of the Civilian Pilot Training Program barred her from flying because she was a woman, Eberhardt kicked up a fuss until they relented. Before graduation in 1941, she applied to Harvard Law School, only to be told by the dean that the institution was not open to women. Fortunately, Cornell Law School accepted females. Placed in an accelerated program, she received her law degree in 1943.

With so many young male professionals in the armed forces during World War II, managing partners in many law offices, who had previously refused even to interview women attorneys, decided to hire them and Eberhardt took a job with a prominent Wall Street firm, Shearman and Sterling. She worked there for five years, until 1949, when Mary Donlon, a friend, fellow lawyer, and trustee of Cornell, helped her secure a position on the legal staff of New York's governor, Thomas E. Dewey. The first woman on the staff, she found the work "fascinating." In 1951, she received a Fulbright grant to study international law at the Nobel Institute in Oslo and the Hague Academy of International Law. When she returned to the United States, she did not rejoin Shearman and Sterling, preferring to open her own practice in Ithaca and to manage property her parents had left her in the town. In 1953, she became an assistant to Republican Assemblyman Ray Ashberry, a position she held for nine years. She married Alfred Patterson Cook, the vice president and part owner of Honeybutter

Products, Inc., in 1955. The couple had two children.

When Ashberry announced that he would not run for reelection in 1962, local Republican leaders did not even think of her as his successor: "When I proposed that I run, the chairman responded that it was impossible, that they would never elect a woman out of Tompkins County." With her "dander up," Cook ran anyway, even though she was pregnant. She bested four men in the GOP primary, then won the election handily. If voters expressed skepticism that she could be a wife, mother, and a representative in the Assembly, she invited them to her home to see for themselves. Had the legislative session in 1962 been longer than three months, she later acknowledged, she might not have run.

In the Assembly, Cook concentrated on employment, education, and health issues. It was important for women to assume responsibility in these traditional areas, she argued, "not for equality alone, not for feminist reasons, but because there is tremendous need." A shrewd politician, who won respect for her accuracy in "counting noses," she supported Perry Duryea in his race for Speaker of the Assembly. When he prevailed, he named her to the powerful post of chair of the Education Committee in 1968.

By then, Cook had become involved in a movement to decriminalize abortion. Aware of the issue "at a very, very low level" throughout the 1960s, she had her consciousness raised at a meeting of the New York chapter of the National Organization for Women at the apartment of Betty Friedan in 1967. She joined NOW and agreed to sponsor pro-choice legislation. Careful always to emphasize that she was not personally in favor of abortion, Cook argued that the issue was not whether there would be abortions, but where, and under what conditions, abortions would be performed: "This is a matter of conscience and medicine." As she listened to debate on a reform bill that required pregnant women to consult with psychiatrists, social workers, and priests, and then get the permission of a committee of doctors and/or hospital administrators, Cook grew angry: "The speeches were so outrageous, and so male oriented that I decided, 'Oh, I'd love to show them what a real bill is.'" Women would rouse themselves, she decided, only in support of a bill to eliminate all restrictions on abortion. Her principal contribution to abortion reform, she later recalled, was in "drawing the distinction politically between repeal and reform."

In what the *New York Times* called a "tailored, matronly manner," she was enormously effective as well in enlisting support for her bill in a legislature dominated by men (only four of 207 representatives were women), more than a third of whom were Roman Catholics. Although she claimed she "never, never" voted against her conscience, Cook was willing to compromise to secure the votes of a majority of her colleagues. She refused to add amendments making abortion contingent on the consent of a husband or parents. But she did agree to provisions mandating that a doctor perform the procedure and setting a limit of twenty-four weeks, after which an abortion would be illegal. As she lobbied assemblymen and senators in Albany, Cook also worked with NOW, Planned Parenthood, the National Abortion Rights Action League, Hadassah, the Unitarian Universalist Association, the Empire State Federation, New York State Women's Clubs, and other organizations to keep the pressure on. She gave pro-choice activists political cues, telling them where to go, who to talk to, and how to spend their time.

In 1970, three years of "plain hard work"

paid off. Cook suffered the indignity of having the bill introduced first in the Senate, in part to prevent her name from appearing on it, in part because Majority Leader Earl Brydges hoped a bill legalizing abortion would die there. He miscalculated. After an emotional, five-hour debate, the Senate passed the bill 31–26. Brydges sat slumped in his chair, dissolved in tears. It was even closer in the Assembly, but Assemblyman George Michaels, a Democrat from the heavily Catholic city of Auburn, assured passage in a vote that, he recognized, "is the termination of my career." When Speaker Duryea added his "yea," the margin was 76–73. As soon as it reached his desk, Governor Rockefeller signed the bill, which went into effect July 1, 1970. In an interview with a reporter for the *New York Times,* Cook called the legislation "the final stage of an inevitable victory for women." Cook remained in the Assembly until 1974. But she never became "one of the boys." Although she worked well with fellow assemblymen, she was never once invited to join them at a dinner. This isolation, and the vilification that accompanied her pro-choice activities, "made life hard in Albany." After considering a run for Congress or the New York State Court of Appeals, she decided to retire. Irked at her independence and her liberalism, and embarrassed by her association with "abortion on demand," her fellow Republicans, she thought, were "happy" with her decision. For almost three decades she has lived in relative quiet in Ithaca, with a brief flurry of public activity as Cornell's vice president for land grant affairs, the first woman ever to be a Cornell vice president.

Henry Jay Heimlich

✍ CLASS OF 1941

His handiwork is posted on a wall in nearly every eating establishment in the United States. "As long as people choke and drown and have asthma," claims the designer of "the hug of life," "they'll all know Henry Heimlich."

Born on February 3, 1920, in Wilmington, Delaware, Henry Jay Heimlich soon moved with his family to New Rochelle, New York. Henry often accompanied his father, Philip Heimlich, a prison social worker, to the maximum security prisons of the state. Encouraged by his mother, Mary Epstein Heimlich, to help humanity by becoming a doctor, Henry entered Cornell in 1937. His interest in music began in childhood when he studied clarinet and piano and continued at Cornell where he was Cornell's drum major, leading the Big Red Band, decked out at football games with high hat and chin strap, whistle, baton, and boots. After graduation in 1941, Heimlich entered Cornell Medical School and received his M.D. in two years. He began an internship at Boston City Hospital, but within a year joined the Navy, volunteered for hazardous duty, and served as a surgeon behind Japanese lines with Chinese guerrillas in the Gobi Desert and Inner Mongolia. In 1984, China's ministry of health recognized him for his contributions to the Chinese people.

After the war, Heimlich held surgical positions at the Veterans' Administration Hospital in the Bronx, Mount Sinai and Bellevue in Manhattan, and Triboro Hospital in Jamaica, Queens. From 1950 to 1969 he was attending surgeon at Montefiore Hospital in New York City. He got the idea for his first medical innovation, a procedure for constructing a new esophagus from a section of a patient's stomach, while attending a meeting at Montefiore in 1950. With only a sketch on a paper napkin, he persuaded his colleagues at New York Medical College, where he served as assistant

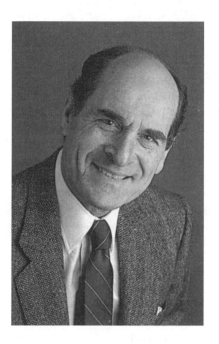

clinical professor of surgery, to provide him with $300 to experiment on dogs. It took five years, and collaboration with researchers in Bucharest, Romania, to try it out for the first time on humans, but the operation became the standard procedure in the United States.

For his second major innovation, Heimlich drew on his experiences during World War II, where he had seen the need for an emergency device to replace the standard drainage bottle used with an electrical suction pump to extract air and fluid from soldiers with chest wounds. In a toy store he found a Japanese-made noisemaker with a flutter valve and adapted it to prevent regurgitation of fluids. The Heimlich valve for chest drainage was used extensively on the battlefields of Vietnam.

By 1969, Heimlich and his wife, Jane Murray, the daughter of the dancing duo Arthur and Katherine Murray, decided to take their four children out of New York City. As director of the Jewish Hospital in Cincinnati, he began to work on the technique that would bring him international recognition. Choking, primarily on food, Heimlich discovered, was the sixth leading cause of accidental death in the United States, responsible each year for about four thousand fatalities, many of them children. The measures recommended by the Red Cross and the American Heart Association—hitting victims on the back with an open hand, putting fingers in their mouths to dislodge the food, or administering mouth-to-mouth resuscitation—often forced the objects deeper down the throat.

Heimlich guessed that by compressing the air in the chest, one might produce enough force to blow the object out through the mouth. Using dogs in a laboratory, he perfected a procedure for "sub-diaphragmatic pressure" and published his findings in the *Journal of Emergency Medicine*. Heimlich advised good Samaritans to stand behind the victim and wrap their arms around his/her waist; place a fist against the abdomen, slightly above the navel and below the rib cage; grasp the fist with the other hand and press it into the abdomen with a quick upward thrust. In 1975, the American Medical Association endorsed the procedure and gave it its name, the "Heimlich Maneuver." Publicized by science writers in newspapers around the country, the procedure saved perhaps ten thousand people within a dozen years.

Testimonials from ordinary citizens and the rich and famous made Heimlich a household name. After political consultant Michael Deaver forced a peanut out of Ronald Reagan's mouth in 1976, the future president endorsed the maneuver. New York Mayor Ed Koch was saved from gagging on Chinese food, and director Robert Altman applied the maneuver on Cher. In 1986, a five-year old-boy from Lynn, Massachusetts, saved a playmate by applying the maneuver, after seeing it demonstrated on a TV sitcom. Listed in *Webster's, Random House,* and the *Oxford American* dictionaries, the Heimlich Maneuver enabled its inventor to become a star on the lecture circuit and a guest on *The Tonight Show, The Today Show, The David Letterman Show,* and *Good Morning America*. Author in 1980 of *Dr. Heimlich's Home Guide to Emergency Medical Situations,* he produced in that same year the Emmy Award-winning one-minute cartoon series for children on ABC television, *H.E.L.P.* (Dr. Henry's Emergency Lessons for People).

In 1977 Heimlich was appointed professor of advanced clinical sciences at Xavier University in Cincinnati, which also established the Heimlich Institute. Over the next decade, he devised a procedure for stroke victims who could not "remember" how to swallow, and with several colleagues, including former astronaut Neil Armstrong, designed the Heimlich Micro-Trach, a portable oxygen system for patients suffering from emphysema and other chronic lung ailments. His search for a cancer cure was less successful. Heimlich believed that at very high temperatures, perhaps 102–104 degrees Fahrenheit, the body produces immune substances, carried through the circulatory system, that wipe out cancer. One way to produce such a fever, he suggested, was to give the patient malaria. Once the cancer cells were destroyed, the malaria could be treated with quinine and other drugs. But Heimlich was unable to counteract the devastating impact of the immune substances on healthy cells in the body.

Heimlich's grandest scheme, however, had nothing to do with medicine. Impressed with the power and pervasiveness of communications technology, he promoted a "Computers for Peace" program to end the Cold War. If the people of the Soviet Union and the United States could learn, via the computer, that trade between the superpowers was beneficial to them, they would reduce armaments. "Wars," he insisted, "all seem to be based on economic factors. This is good old free enterprise in a planned fashion." Undaunted by the skepticism of government officials, who questioned the assumption that people react rationally and in their own self-interest, Heimlich besieged politicians in the United States with letters about "Computers for Peace," and briefly considered seeking the Republican presidential nomination in 1984 on a peace platform.

Now in his eighties and long retired from surgery, Heimlich has remained active in research as well as on the tennis court. He has continued work on a malaria-based cure for cancer, Lyme disease, and AIDS, and has studied the usefulness of the Heimlich maneuver for patients suffering asthma attacks.

He has jousted with the Red Cross, contending that his maneuver, which can purge water from the lungs, should be the first step in aiding drowning victims, rather than a follow-up to mouth-to-mouth resuscitation. Among the honors he has received are the presidency of the National Cancer Foundation, the Albert Lasker Public Service Award, the Golden Plate Award of the American Academy of Achievement, and selection to the Engineering and Science Hall of Fame.

Samuel Riley Pierce Jr.

◁ CLASS OF 1944

At a reception in 1981 Ronald Reagan greeted his Secretary of Housing and Urban Development by saying, "Hello, Mr. Mayor." The incident was as embarrassing (and instructive) for Samuel Pierce, the African American lawyer and political figure who made a practice of being "first," as it was for the president.

Samuel Riley Pierce Jr. was born on September 8, 1922, in the thoroughly Republican town of Glen Cove, Long Island, where his parents, Sam Sr. and Hettie Armstrong Pierce, made a comfortable living in the dry cleaning and real estate businesses. Salutatorian of his high school class, Sam Pierce entered Cornell in the fall of 1940. A superb student who was awarded a Phi Beta Kappa key after his junior year, he was also a star halfback on the football team, leading the Big Red in scoring despite a pulled tendon suffered in a game against Colgate. When the United States entered World War II, Pierce exchanged his football jersey for an officer's uniform. He spent three years in North Africa and Italy, serving as the only African-American member of the Army's Criminal Division for the Mediterranean Theater.

After the war, Pierce returned to Cornell and received a bachelor's degree with honors in 1947. Inspired by Professor Robert Cushman's course on constitutional law, he decided to become an attorney and received a degree from Cornell Law School two years later. Pierce loved to compete. Every morning, a classmate remembered, he bet his housemates a nickel or a dime that he would be the first to get to class. In 1948, he won the race for the affections of fellow Glen Cove native Barbara Penn Wright, a graduate of Mount Holyoke and the Columbia College of Physicians and Surgeons. An internist, Wright worked for years on the staff of the Metropolitan Life Insurance Company. Married for fifty-two years, the couple had one daughter.

Equipped with a unique set of characteristics—an African American with an Ivy League education, a lawyer, and a staunch Republican—Sam Pierce had no shortage of offers for work in public-service law. From 1949 to 1953 he was an assistant to District Attorney Frank S. Hogan of New York City, and from 1953 until 1955 he served as assistant United States Attorney for the Southern District of New York. In 1955, Arthur Larson, a Cornell professor who had just been appointed undersecretary of labor, brought his former student to

Washington, D.C., as his assistant. Shortly after he began work, Pierce ran into Arthur Sutherland, another former professor, who promptly recommended him to Representative Kenneth Keating, ranking Republican on the House Judiciary Committee, as counsel to the antitrust subcommittee. When Keating ran for the U. S. Senate in 1958, Pierce became his campaign treasurer.

With a Democrat in the White House in 1961, Pierce found himself in private practice, at Battle, Fowler, Stokes, and Kheel (which eventually became Battle, Fowler, Jaffin, Pierce, and Kheel), as the first black partner in a major New York City law firm. In 1964 he was the first black to join the board of a major American corporation, U.S. Industries. Six months later, Prudential Insurance Company tapped him for its board. Then, and later, when Pierce discussed his contributions as a board member, he mentioned his expertise in labor law, taxes, and antitrust, but never his race. Meanwhile, Pierce's Republican friends sought a place for him in the judiciary of New York State. Governor Nelson Rockefeller twice appointed him to fill vacancies on the Court of General Sessions, but Pierce was unable to win election to a full term in overwhelmingly Democratic Manhattan.

In 1970 President Richard Nixon appointed Pierce general counsel to the U. S. Treasury, another "first" for that position. He served three years, supervising a staff of nine hundred lawyers and helping negotiate a government bailout of Lockheed Aircraft Corporation, before returning to his law firm and to the faculty of the New York University School of Law.

In 1980 a twist of fate brought Pierce back to Washington. After Philip V. Sanchez declined appointment as President Reagan's secretary of housing and urban development, a hurried search for a member of a racial minority to fill the post resulted in an offer to Sam Pierce. E. Pendleton James, the President's personnel director, cited Pierce's "very distinguished background," but acknowledged that a desire for "a black in the Cabinet played a role."

Pierce was the only member of the cabinet to stay through Reagan's two terms as president. He presided over a transformation of federal housing programs. Conservatives hailed the administration's policy of ending government support for housing construction for low-income families, replacing them with rent vouchers to be used in the open market. While Pierce was HUD secretary, the number of employees in the department dropped from 15,300 to 12,300, and the budget for housing for the poor was slashed from $33 billion to $15 billion. The conservative magazine, *National Review*, declared him the "Unsung Hero of the Reagan Revolution." To liberals, Pierce was "the dud at HUD." Lawrence Simons, federal housing commissioner under President Carter, gave him an F for promoting housing opportunities for low-income Americans. According to Representative Barney Frank, Pierce operated on the principle that "he runs the Department of Housing, and homeless people don't have any housing, so they are not his responsibility." The secretary insisted that "we have done more with less," pointing to a 34 percent increase in the number of families receiving housing aid and a forceful stand in favor of legislation to outlaw discrimination against minorities in housing.

Pierce was a loyal member of the cabinet. He defended the administration's attack on racial quotas, saying that those who advocated them "demean those they purport to help. For what they are saying is that minority citizens can't make it on their own." In his own department, in cabinet meetings, and in appearances before Congress, he was not a forceful advocate of housing and urban development. Pierce earned the nickname "Silent Sam" because he delegated and deferred to subordinates and failed to use the bully pulpit to rally public support for his policies, as his successor Jack Kemp did. He did not protest when the Reagan administration refused to allow him to select his own people for key positions in the department, or when Budget Director David Stockman eliminated federal matching funds for investment in low-income neighborhoods. Pierce stayed on, year after year, his friends believed, because he hoped President Reagan would appoint him to the Supreme Court.

After he left office, criticism turned deadly serious, with allegations that the Department of Housing and Urban Development was a swamp of mismanagement, influence peddling, and corruption. After a five-year investigation by special counsel Arlin Adams produced sixteen convictions and $2 million in fines, Samuel Pierce acknowledged that his meetings with friends lobbying for federal housing funds and hoping to receive large consulting fees "sent signals to my staff that such persons should receive assistance." Theodore Kheel, Pierce's law partner and fellow Cornellian, acknowledged that his friend might not have had administrative skills "equal to running a department the size of HUD," but told reporters "Sam is very honorable."

Although he denied that he had received "a single improper benefit for my actions," Pierce took responsibility for contributing to "an environment in which these events could occur." In return for his cooperation, and because of Pierce's age and health and a lack of criminal intent, Adams agreed not to prosecute. Sam Pierce died on October 31, 2000, in Silver Springs, Maryland.

Cornell in the Postwar Era, 1945–1975

ORNELL EMERGED from World War II in precarious economic shape but with a profound conviction that universities must play a critical role in securing the future of democracy both in the United States and around the world. President Edmund Day pressed forward with initiatives that the war had placed on hold. The Industrial & Labor Relations School (I&LR) was the fulfillment of an idea of Irving Ives, the majority leader of the state Assembly, who won enabling legislation for the new venture in 1944. New York's Governor Thomas Dewey opened the school in 1945, declaring, "It is a school which denies the alien theory that there are classes in our society and that they must wage war against each other." I&LR moved into makeshift wooden barracks, and conducted its business there for the next seven years. Not until 1960 did it find a permanent home, in Ives Hall. Another deferred project important to Day was the opening of the School of Business. Authorized by the trustees in 1942, it welcomed its first students in 1946 and settled its small staff in Goldwin Smith Hall.

Through a long and sometimes unplanned process, but in a pattern now confirmed by legislation, Cornell had become two distinct halves, one comprising statutory or state units and one comprising endowed units, both halves joined under Cornell's own board of trustees and central administration. A Cornell education was considerably more expensive for some students than for others. Whether statutory or endowed, however, all students and all programs in the years immediately after the war lacked adequate space for living and for working. Cornell, like other universities, felt a strong obligation to returning veterans who took advantage of the generous provisions of the G.I. Bill. In the fall of 1946 enrollment, which had never been much more than seven thousand, rose to 10,560. Seventy-seven percent of all male students were veterans. They were older and definitely more experienced than any group of Cornell undergraduates before or since. Many of them had wives and children, and Cornell erected more wooden barracks to give them a home. Even a number of the students enrolled in the College of Home Economics were women who had served in the armed forces.

Statler Hall had a practice inn, faculty club, and library. (Courtesy Kroch Rare and Manuscript Collections, Cornell University.)

President Day was determined to put Cornell in the forefront of nuclear physics. With a distinguished physics faculty that included Hans Bethe, Robert Bacher, Richard Feynman, and Robert Wilson, he launched a $2 million project to build the Newman Laboratory of Nuclear Studies. Graduate studies grew by leaps and bounds following the war. Cornell built new programs in all of the sciences as well as in the humanities and social sciences. Cornell's area studies programs in East Asian and Southeast Asian Studies, complete with language training, gained reputations for excellence equaled only by similar initiatives at Harvard.

The College of Engineering underwent a strong resurgence, with enrollment rising from eight hundred, where it had stagnated since the mid-1930s, to 2,667 in the 1946–47 academic year. Its dean, S. C. Hollister, who wanted to make Cornell engineers literate, introduced a five-year degree program—the first in the country—so that engineering students could take courses in the College of Arts and Sciences. Plans for a new engineering quad, ordered by the trustees in 1940, acquired greater urgency with the multiplication of specialized engineering fields. The difficulty of financing the expensive new facilities delayed those plans until 1953 when Kimball Hall and Thurston Hall were completed. The other engineering buildings erected in the 1950s—Phillips, Carpenter, Upson, Grumman, and Hollister—shifted Cornell's architecture toward modern design. Anabel Taylor Hall, built in 1953 with a gift from Myron Taylor to house Cornell United Religious Work, was Cornell's last Gothic-inspired structure. It was located next to the law school.

The College of Engineering quadrangle. (Courtesy Kroch Rare and Manuscript Collections, Cornell University.)

President Day's declining health prompted him to retire in 1949. For two years Cornelius de Kiewiet, Cornell's provost and former dean of the College of Arts and Sciences, served as acting president. He officiated in 1950 at the opening of the Statler Hall and Auditorium, and the Department of Hotel Administration became the School of Hotel Administration. Two years later it was separated from the College of Agriculture to become an independent academic unit. While de Kiewiet was in charge, the flood tide of returning veterans abated. Many of the temporary structures erected for housing and classrooms began to come down, and the university started the construction of six dormitories that became known, unfortunately, as U Halls.

In July 1951 Dean Waldo Malott became Cornell's sixth president. He had a bachelor's degree from the University of Kansas, an MBA from Harvard, business experience as vice president of Hawaiian Pineapple Company, and university administrative experience as president of the University of Kansas. He remained at Cornell until 1963.

Malott took office during the heated part of the Cold War, which gave rise to the witch-hunts led by Senator Joseph McCarthy. Universities, which are supposed to make a virtue out of encouraging outspokenness in students and faculty, were under pressure to root out communists. In the early 1950s Cornell had its fair share of radical student organizations and of professors critical of American domestic and foreign policy. Paul Gates, a populist-minded member of the history department who in his courses on the American West championed small farmers, became a controversial figure because he had supported the presidential campaign of Henry Wallace in 1948. Knight Biggerstaff, another historian and a leading sinologist, fell under suspicion outside the university because while living in China before the Communist takeover he had known Mao Tse-tung and Chou En-lai. In 1952 and 1953, the House Un-American Activities Committee (HUAC) accused two Cornell professors, a physicist and a biologist, of being Communist Party members. President Malott was not eager to have communists on his faculty, but he strongly defended his faculty against unsubstantiated charges. Academic freedom at Cornell weathered the chill of the anticommunist crusade better than it did at many other leading American universities.

Cornell's faculty benefited from the postwar decline in anti-Semitism and welcomed important scholars who happened to be Jewish to its ranks. Before World War II, Harry Caplan and Simon Bauer had been the two best-known faculty members out of a handful of Jews who got through the unwritten agreements that had, despite Cornell's claim to neutrality in religious matters, imposed a religious test on faculty appointments. Now M. H. Abrams, Max Black, Milton Konvitz, and many others joined them. A few fraternities at Cornell cautiously began to admit Jewish members. Other aspects of the faculty did not change, however: outside of the College of Home Economics, there were no women on the professorial staff. But unlike its major competitors, which also remained societies of "old boys," Cornell had female students. By the mid-1950s almost one-quarter of the students were women.

Student life at Cornell during the 1950s had a nonserious side. Athletics, despite the de-emphasis placed on big-time sports by the Ivy League, were popular. Teagle Hall opened in 1954. Sometimes parties got out of hand. Panty raids on women's dormitories were a distressing feature of the social life of fraternity boys. In 1957, after a particularly wild weekend during which a drunken student died in a fall from a rooftop, President Malott decided to crack down on student drinking and what he viewed as permissive dating. He tried to strengthen Cornell's system of parietal rules, which required women to be in the dormitories by a fixed hour and sharply limited the visiting rights of males to those dorms. Suddenly, student rights became a major issue. The editors of the *Cornell Daily Sun* and other student leaders protested. In 1958 a large group of students marched to the president's house and egged it. Malott and his faculty allies had to retreat, recognizing that the days of the university acting in loco parentis were numbered. Cornell nonetheless required women undergraduates to live in dormitories or approved campus housing until 1965.

The 1960s began with the opening in 1961 of the John M. Olin Library to house Cornell's large research collections. The College of Agriculture had dedicated Mann Library almost a decade earlier, in 1953. Olin Library symbolized Cornell's determination to stay in the front ranks of American research institutions. The shock of the Soviet launch of Sputnik had opened the eyes of Congress to the vital need for science instruction and an expansion of higher education. Although the goal was to give the United States technological superiority over the Soviet foe, the government money that poured into research institutions benefited and prompted growth in every sector of the university. Even departments in the humanities doubled or tripled in size during the 1960s. The Baby Boomers had arrived, giving Cornell's student population greater diversity than it had ever had before. More students from public schools, from parochial schools, and from areas outside the Northeast came to Ithaca. They took advan-

The end of the occupation of Willard Straight Hall. (AP/Wide World Photos.)

tage of the new federally funded student loan program, established in 1965, and got an Ivy League education despite steadily rising tuition fees.

There was of course another side to the 1960s, a tumultuous side marked by protests against racial discrimination and American military involvement in Vietnam. The man who succeeded Dean Malott as university president in 1963 profoundly influenced how Cornell navigated those contentious years. James Perkins looked like someone born to lead a major American institution. Tall, poised, and elegantly patrician, he was a man of committed, progressive social views. After receiving a Ph.D. in political science from Princeton, Perkins had worked in the Office of Price Administration during World War II, in various administrative posts at Swarthmore, his alma mater, and at the Carnegie Corporation of New York. He had been a leader in the civil rights movement, promoting the cause of racial integration when segregation in one way or another dominated American social practice, and not just in the South. When he took office, Cornell had four black students in an entering class of 2,300.

In a bold initiative, Perkins committed Cornell to a policy of actively recruiting minority students. He created the Committee on Special Education Projects (COSEP) for that purpose. Under Perkins's plan, in the fall of 1969 Cornell was to welcome 170 African Americans into the new class. Perkins prepared the way for the creation of Cornell's largely autonomous Africana Studies and Research Center and for Ujamaa, a residential program based on African American identity established in 1970. These steps divided the campus in ways Perkins failed to control, in part because the civil rights struggle turned in a direction he had not expected. His ideal of liberal integration collapsed during the 1960s under the pressure of militant racial separatism.

To add to his woes, Cornell's very active chapter of the white-led Students for a Democratic Society (SDS) had a broad revolutionary agenda to restructure the university, the nation, and individual consciousness. In 1965 it led efforts to disrupt a speech by Averill Harriman, the U.S. ambassador to South Vietnam. Matters escalated from there with students trying to extirpate military recruiting and the Reserve Officers Training Corps (ROTC) from campus. When Cornell's 100th anniversary arrived in 1968, the school was in no mood to hold a celebration, and the anniversary passed unmarked.

When members of the Afro-American Society marched out of Willard Straight Hall with guns in April 1969, they ignited a chain of events that bitterly split the faculty and prompted some of them to quit. Many accused President Perkins of abandoning the university's commitment to free speech and to an uninhibited atmosphere of open inquiry. Vilified on his right and on his left,

The John M. Olin Library and Uris Library for undergraduates. (Courtesy Kroch Rare and Manuscript Collections, Cornell University.)

Perkins was forced by the trustees to step down. Only much later was he honored for what he had tried to do.

Despite the troubles of the 1960s a lot of more or less normal projects had moved ahead. The university vastly expanded its science facilities, including Clark Hall, the Space Science Building, and the Wilson Synchroton Lab. New high-and low-rise dormitories, now for men and women, opened on North Campus. In 1969 the College of Home Economics, recognizing that the new movement for women's liberation had undermined what had been the progressive meaning attached to that school's name, re-christened itself as the College of Human Ecology and expanded its operations into a large new wing of Martha Van Rensselaer Hall. It continued to provide unique opportunities for women students and faculty at Cornell, but the other colleges were beginning to search for women teachers. Affirmative action programs in the early 1970s slowly but definitively moved women into faculty appointments. In 1972 they launched the Women's Studies Program.

The youngest of our Cornell notables matriculated a year after Dale Corson was recruited to take over the university presidency in 1970, at a time when few wanted the job. Corson was a distinguished physicist and longtime member of the Cornell faculty. When he stepped down in 1977, replaced by Frank H. Trevor

Rhodes, this unassuming man with an enormous capacity to inspire trust had re-stored comity to the university community. Our youngest notables were on campus when Cornell's football team won the Ivy League crown in 1971, when the last campus elm trees were felled, when Uris Hall opened in 1971 (the design of the prominent architectural firm of Skidmore, Owings and Merrill, one of whose founding partners was a Cornell graduate), and when the soaring re-search tower of the College of Veterinary Medicine marked the east end of the campus. Beyond that lay the Cornell Plantations, one of the glories of the Cor-nell landscape and a favorite target of alumni giving. Under construction was the Johnson Museum of Art, opened in 1975, the design of I. M. Pei.

In the early 1970s Cornell's enrollment reached 18,000, about two-thirds of it in the undergraduate divisions. The Cornell population included representa-tives from many of the world's cultures. The youngest of our Cornell notables, like all Cornell students before them, had enormous freedom to choose their courses. In the College of Arts and Sciences, they could invent their own pro-gram of concentration, an Independent Major, or apply to the College Scholars Program, which exempted them from all requirements except physical educa-tion. Although cows no longer roamed the central campus, dogs without own-ers romped among pedestrians and wandered into classrooms to sleep at the feet of tolerant professors. Our youngest Cornell notables could eat at Johnny's Big Red Grill, swim in Fall Creek Gorge under the suspension bridge, and live with men and women in a run-down Collegetown apartment. Thanks to concerts mounted by Cornell's music department, the ambitious programs of Cornell Cinema, and the productions of the theatre department, our youngest Cornell notables had no reason to spend one day without culture. Ithaca no longer had passenger rail service and the county airport was a tiny structure with two gates—one glass door for departing passengers and an adjacent glass door for ar-riving passengers. Ithaca was isolated. But, on a beautiful October day when the colors of autumn almost blinded the eyes, or during the long winter after a blan-ket of fresh snow covered the campus (without canceling classes), or on a rare day of spring when students shed most of their clothes to play Frisbee or lie in perfect sunshine, one really did not care.

Joyce Bauer Brothers

CLASS OF 1947

She has been called "America's Therapist," the "Mother of Media Psychologists," and "Mary Poppins for the Psyche," all with good reason. In her more than three decades in the media, Joyce Brothers personified psychology for millions of Americans, becoming one of the most visible celebrity professionals in the last half of the twentieth century.

Joyce, the eldest daughter of Morris and Estelle Bauer, of Far Rockaway, Queens, was born on October 20, 1927. Her parents, who were both lawyers who emphasized academic success, encouraged Joyce to become a studious child; she was constantly reading or doing her homework. There could have been an explosion in the house and she wouldn't have heard it, her father recalled years later. When Joyce was twelve, she worked as a counselor at a summer camp for disturbed adolescents, an experience that helped forge her later vocation: "I got lots of very pleasant feedback from helping others." A top student at Far Rockaway High School who skipped several grades, she entered Cornell's College of Home Economics in 1943 at the age of sixteen.

At Cornell Joyce Bauer joined the Yacht Club, worked at WVBR, and was a member of Sigma Xi Tau. She majored in psychology and graduated with honors. She also fell in love with fellow Cornellian Milton Brothers and the two married in 1949, honeymooning in Ithaca. He went to medical school in New York (and eventually became a distinguished specialist in endocrinology and diabetes), and Joyce Brothers entered the graduate program in psychology at Columbia University. She taught at Hunter College and Columbia while she worked for her Ph.D., which she received in 1953. When their only child, Lisa, was born the next year Brothers decided to remain at home and raise her daughter, which, as she tells the story, reduced the couple's earnings to her husband's modest

monthly check as a medical resident. So she devised a plan to augment their income by winning money on a TV quiz show.

The CBS television program *The $64,000 Question* premiered in June 1955 and quickly became America's top-rated TV program. Every Tuesday night, millions of Americans watched the amiable quizmaster Hal March ask a set of increasingly difficult questions in an area of expertise chosen by the contestant, who stood alone in a dramatically lit isolation booth. Each answer doubled the prize money and, if the contestant declined to stop and keep the winnings, the tenth question brought the then unprecedented jackpot of $64,000. Contestants, ordinary people with extraordinary knowledge in unlikely areas, became famous overnight, like the New York City policeman who was an expert on Shakespeare, the shoemaker opera buff, and the soldier who knew gourmet food cold.

Brothers, already an astute student of human nature and popular culture, knew that the producers would jump at the chance to have as a contestant an attractive female psychologist who was an expert on boxing. She wasn't, but she made herself one. She read all the back issues of *Ring* magazine and, as she took care of her infant daughter, memorized a twenty-volume boxing encyclopedia. As she later recounted it, "I had good motivation because we were hungry."

Brothers sailed through her audition and in late 1955 was accepted as a contestant. An immediate success who knew every answer, she built up her winnings week after week, until she won the $64,000 in December, the second person and the only woman ever to win the top prize. On *The $64,000 Challenge* in 1957, which had replaced *The $64,000 Question,* she won yet another jackpot. Two years later the quiz shows were rocked by scandal after revelations that contestants had been coached or made to lose, but Brothers was not implicated. The grand jury hearings revealed, on the contrary, that Brothers had defied the producers by winning when they wanted her to lose and be off the show because she answered the questions too crisply, without letting suspense build up. The sponsor, Revlon, was also angry that Brothers did not wear lipstick. Unlike celebrity winner Charles Van Doren, Brothers emerged from the scandal an even more respected national figure.

Brothers never left television after her quiz show triumphs. For a short while she was co-host of *Sports Showcase,* a program on which she interviewed athletes and commented on sports events. Her breakthrough occurred in 1958 when NBC decided to repackage her intelligence, charm, and attractiveness with her professional training in psychology and launch her career as "America's Therapist." She was given an afternoon TV show on which she offered advice and counseling about love, marriage, sex, and raising children. *The Dr. Joyce Brothers Show* was a phenomenal success, lasting five years, followed by other TV programs: *Consult Dr. Joyce Brothers, Ask Dr. Joyce Brothers,* and *Living Easy with Dr. Joyce Brothers.*

Brothers filled a niche in TV programming, popularizing psychology and exploring human relationships. A late-night program was added, allowing her opportunities to discuss and advise people on such hitherto taboo topics on television as impotence, frigidity, sexual satisfaction, and menopause. Then in 1966 came her live radio call-in show, the first of its kind. Its popularity soared in 1971 when she dissuaded a would-be suicide by talking with her for almost three hours, ninety minutes of it on the air. Her psychological advice was everywhere. For years she wrote a weekly column, syndicated in 350 newspapers, as well as a monthly piece for *Good Housekeeping* magazine. She wrote ten books that have been translated into twenty-six languages.

As a professional celebrity, Brothers was constantly available for interviews and talk shows, which were eager to have such an intelligent and lively woman guest. When Johnny Carson retired in 1992, a list of his most frequent guests revealed that Brothers was seventh with ninety-two appearances. She became an iconic fixture of American popular culture, showing up on *The Simpsons, Captain Kangaroo,* and in Mel Brooks movies. An accessible and acceptable intellectual, she took the relatively new and threatening subject of psychology and made it less scary. She was named as one of the ten most admired American women in a 1969 poll of students at one hundred college campuses. In the late 1970s, contestants on the TV game show *A Family Feud* were asked to name a smart person. Dr. Joyce Brothers was second, after Einstein.

Mental health clinicians are divided on Brothers's professional achievement. They acknowledge her enormous influence; her role in popularizing psychology; her ability to give advice in simple, understandable, jargon-free language; and the appeal of her programs and writings with her sympathetic responses to the lonely, troubled, and despairing. They credit her for the revolutionary frankness of her public discussions of sexuality and intimacy. However, some contend that her advice is too sugarcoated and inspirational, offering simplistic solutions to complex problems, and too glibly offered without knowing the details of the caller's or correspondent's life.

Brothers has not forgotten Cornell. She spoke on campus at her fiftieth reunion and has given her papers, which fill nearly two hundred boxes, to the Rare Books and Manuscripts Collection in Cornell's Kroch Library.

Future scholars who write about the woman the *New York Times* credited with bringing "the lessons of psychology, for better or for worse, to millions of Americans" will fittingly enough have to journey to Ithaca to study this notable Cornellian.

James Whitman McLamore
CLASS OF 1947

James McLamore was never as well known as Ray Kroc, Dave Thomas, or Colonel Sanders. But when Kroc said he had named "the Big Mac" for the cofounder of Burger King, he was acknowledging a fast-food titan who, for good and ill, enticed American families, whether or not they could stand the heat, to get out of the kitchen.

James Whitman McLamore was born in New York City on May 30, 1926, to a troubled family. His mother, Marian Floyd Whitman McLamore, was committed to a sanatorium two years later, and died in 1933. Thomas Milton McLamore, James's father, saw a fortune amassed as an executive in the Whitman family textile business wiped out in the stock market crash of 1929, and moved his children to Central Valley, New York, fifty miles from Manhattan. Educated at Mount Hermon School for Boys in Massachusetts, James McLamore made the honor roll and played on the football, basketball, and baseball teams. Interested in playing for the then-powerhouse "Big Red" eleven, he entered Cornell in 1943, choosing the School of Hotel Administration because it had a program in business. He defrayed expenses by gardening for Professor Herbert Whetzel, chairman of the Department of Plant Pathology in the College of Agriculture, who also helped the young man secure loans to pay his tuition. In 1944 McLamore interrupted his studies to enlist in the Navy—only to be assigned to

NROTC back at Cornell. He resumed his seat on the bench as the third-string quarterback, married Nancy Nichol, whom he had met on campus, and graduated in August 1947, a few months after his classmates.

In his first job, as director of food service at a YMCA in Wilmington, Delaware, McLamore developed a successful banquet business. At $267 a month, his salary barely met the needs of a family that would soon include four children, and in 1950 he decided to open a restaurant in Wilmington. Featuring hamburgers, french fries, pancakes, waffles, and eggs, the Colonial Inn netted McLamore what then seemed like the princely sum of $15,000. The McLamores relocated to Miami, Florida, Nancy Nichols's hometown, and opened the Brickell Bridge restaurant. The eatery struggled until McLamore stationed the brother of the dishwasher on the street in an immaculate white chef's uniform and tall chef's hat, as "Dinner Bell Charlie." Plenty of patrons paid for the bargain steak dinner Charlie advertised.

With his eyes still on the main chance, McLamore in 1954 joined David Edgerton, another Cornell "Hotelie," as owner of an Insta Burger restaurant acquired from two entrepreneurs in Jacksonville, Florida. Part of the burgeoning fast-food phenomenon that depended on the post-World War II explosion of mobile, suburban families, Insta Burger used a Rube Goldberg contraption to cook the burgers, dip them in sauce, and toast the bun. Edgerton decided to change the name to Insta Burger King and designed the king-on-the-bun symbol that would become the company's trademark.

Within three years the partners had acquired seven restaurants in southern Florida. But sales were slow and the enterprise teetered on the brink of bankruptcy. Edgerton's new flame broiler, designed to get the burgers quickly to customers, helped. The breakthrough came when McLamore decided to offer a big, juicy, well-garnished hamburger called "The Whopper" and announced, with a sign atop each restaurant, that customers were approaching "The Home of the Whopper." Offered for thirty-seven cents apiece, double the price of a "regular-sized" burger, the Whopper was an instant success. McLamore and Edgerton dropped the "Insta," severed their connections with the Jacksonville businessmen, and became the parent company of Burger King.

McLamore soon recognized that a lot more money could be made by selling franchises than if the partners ran all the restaurants themselves. He and Edgerton wrote specifications for food products and equipment. Franchisees were trained at "Whopper College" in southern Florida. McLamore set up three companies essential to the operation. Distron produced and delivered food and other supplies to each franchise. Davmor Industries became one of the largest manufacturers of restaurant equipment in the United States, even though it had only one customer, Burger King. And First Florida Building Corporation built each restaurant. McLamore

was a pioneer in taxing each franchisee 4 percent of sales to support local and national advertising. By 1965 Burger King restaurants were opening at the rate of one per week and millions agreed that a Whopper, fries, and a Coke was the great American meal. McLamore, by now the president and CEO, and Dave Edgerton, his partner, owned a fast-food phenomenon.

But Burger King remained a distant second to McDonald's. For the company to catch up, it needed capital to purchase real estate and to build restaurants. When he was told that a public stock offering was not feasible, McLamore persuaded Edgerton to merge with the Pillsbury Company in 1967. To his dismay, Pillsbury cut back on franchising and real estate development—and Burger King lost any chance it had had to catch up to McDonald's. If only he had not failed the course in corporate finance at Cornell, McLamore would subsequently say, the history of Burger King might have been different. He hung on as president and CEO for five years, before stepping down in 1972. By the time he retired, Burger King had opened eight hundred restaurants, not one of which had to be shut down.

McLamore maintained his connections to the company, as chairman of the board of directors and occasionally as a consultant. He remained active in the industry, most visibly as president of the National Restaurant Association in 1974. But most of his time was spent on charitable activity and public service. As chairman of the board of trustees at the University of Miami, he led a fund-raising campaign that brought in more than $500 million. He resumed his fascination with horticulture, begun at the home of Professor Whetzel, by becoming president of Fairchild Tropical Gardens. And as a director of WPBT-Channel 12, the public television station in Miami, he got the idea of offering a business news program. Since its debut in 1979, *The Nightly Business Report* has become one of the most popular programs on public television. McLamore died on August 9, 1996.

Robert William Fogel

⮰ CLASS OF 1948

When he was an undergraduate at Cornell and president of the Marxist Discussion Group, Robert Fogel was already something of an intellectual agitator. In a distinguished career culminating in the Nobel Prize in economics, he has remained one, as a founder of "cliometrics" and coauthor of one of the most controversial books about slavery published in the twentieth century.

Robert William Fogel was born in New York City on July 1, 1926, four years after his parents, Harry and Elizabeth Mitnick Fogel, migrated to the United States from Odessa in the Soviet Union. While the Fogels scraped together their savings to establish the first of several small businesses, they inculcated a love of learning in their sons, Robert and Ephim (who became a professor of English at Cornell University). Incensed by the social dislocation of the Great Depression, Robert became a passionate opponent of capitalism. Although he concentrated on physics and chemistry at the prestigious Stuyvesant High School, he switched to economics and history when he matriculated at Cornell in the fall of 1944.

An inveterate joiner as an undergraduate, Fogel took part in many mainstream activities. He was a member of the History Club, the Independent Council, the Model United Nations, the Willard Straight Committee, and Hillel. But he also made his mark as a campus radical, with the Cornell chapter of the NAACP, the American Youth for Democracy, the Young Progressive Citizens of America, and the Marxist Discussion Group. In speeches, public debates, and letters to the *Cornell Daily Sun,* Fogel proclaimed that communists "fight for anybody that will help the majority of the people" and lambasted the administration for failing to hire professors who believed in Marxism and for requiring all student organizations to file membership lists at a time when "having a subscription to *The*

New Republic is considered a basis for suspicion of loyalty."

Fogel graduated from Cornell in 1948, a committed radical, convinced that by combining a study of history and economics he might discover the fundamental forces responsible for social instability and inequality. In 1949, he married Enid Cassandra Morgan, a Sunday school teacher and leader of youth organizations at St. Phillip's Episcopal Church who had headed a Harlem youth group supporting the election of presidential candidate Henry Wallace in 1948. An interracial couple, the Fogels struggled to find landlords who would rent apartments to them and suffered the indignity of department store personnel who refused to allow Enid to try on clothes. They persevered, with Enid raising their two sons and helping support the family while Robert worked for the Labor Youth League. Asked by the House Un-American Activities Committee to describe his duties, Fogel invoked the First and Fifth Amendments in 1955. Eventually, Enid became a dean of students and director of student life at the University of Rochester, Harvard, and the University of Chicago.

Fogel enrolled in graduate school in the late '50s. He received a master's degree in statistics at Columbia in 1960, with a thesis about the financing of the Union Pacific Railroad and its economic impact. Intrigued by the new mathematical and statistical methods of economics, he moved on to Johns Hopkins for his Ph.D., where he came under the influence of the great economist Simon Kuznets. While working on his dissertation, which he completed in 1963, Fogel was appointed to the faculty at the University of Rochester.

Fogel's first book, *Railroads and American Economic Growth* (1964), was a tour de force, a foundational text in what would come to be called "cliometrics" (the use of economic theory and statistical methods by historians; in Greek mythology, Clio is the muse of history). Challenging the prevailing wisdom that railroads were essential to economic development in the United States, Fogel posed a counterfactual proposition: What if railroads had not been used in the nineteenth century? Using sophisticated models and a vast amount of data, he concluded that railroads accounted for only 3 percent of economic growth.

A leader in the movement to apply economic theory and quantitative methods to history, Fogel was appointed to the faculty of the University of Chicago in 1964. Except for a stint at Harvard from 1975 until 1981, he has remained there throughout his career. In 1974, with the publication of *Time on the Cross,* coauthored with Stanley Engerman, Fogel touched off an intellectual conflagration. With the scholarly details relegated to a second volume, subtitled *Evidence and Methods, Time on the Cross* mobilized mountains of data (from accounts of slave auctions to plantation medical records to crop yields) in an audacious, and some said shocking, reinterpretation of slavery in the United States. The "peculiar institution," Fogel and Engerman argued, was generally quite profitable, yielding rates of return that compared favorably with manufacturing businesses in the North. Their data promoted a long list of controversial propositions: slave agriculture was 35 percent more efficient than the northern system of farming; slaves worked harder and were more efficient than northern workers; slave owners encouraged the stability of slave families because it was in their interest to do so; the material conditions of slaves, including diet and housing, compared favorably with those of free industrial workers; although slaves were certainly exploited, slave owners spent 90 percent of the income that slaves' work generated on their upkeep; slavery was

not stagnating between 1840 and 1860 and would not have ended without a war or some form of political intervention.

Greeted as the most important book in American history published in the previous decade, "destined to become a classic," *Time on the Cross* was awarded the Bancroft Prize in 1975. It also became the target of unrelenting, withering criticism. Although Fogel's aim, as articulated in the last sentence of the book, had been to reveal "not only to blacks, but to whites as well . . . the record of black achievement under adversity," critics read the book as an apology for slavery. Professional historians devoted whole conference sessions to it. They wrote reviews, essays, and books denouncing it as "simply shot through with egregious errors," "vulnerable not only to attack—but to dismissal," and suitable for consignment "to the outermost ring of the scholar's hell, obscurity." One scholar questioned the import of Fogel and Engerman's quantification of the whipping of slaves. Although a particular slave might have been whipped, on average, 0.7 times a year, he pointed out that on large plantations someone was whipped every 4.56 days, so slaves would have *seen* another slave whipped every five days, and suffered the resulting terror that induced. The debate spilled into the popular press, and Fogel found himself grilled by journalists and on television talk shows. Stung by charges that *Time on the Cross* was racist, Fogel clarified his findings in a subsequent book, *Without Consent or Contract: The Rise and Fall of American Slavery* (1989), which emphasized his belief that slavery was morally repugnant.

Time on the Cross clearly had an impact. Some of its findings—that slavery was profitable and viable, and that slave agriculture compared favorably with the productivity of free labor—are now accepted by most economists and historians. Equally important, the book led to a substantial body of research, using sophisticated economic tools, on such issues as the standard of living of slaves. *Time on the Cross* may or may not have been, as one critic called it, "a flash in the pan, a bold but now discredited work." But it certainly established cliometrics as an important and enduring subdiscipline.

In 1993 Fogel shared the Nobel Prize in economics with Douglass North, another seminal figure in economic history. "Bob wants to be known as the supreme empiricist, the great numbers person, the person who establishes what a fact is," said Claudia Golden, professor of economics at Harvard. "It just so happens that the facts he establishes are rather controversial." Fogel remained defiant in defense of his work. "If you want me to say [slavery] was unprofitable and inefficient, I won't," he said at a press conference announcing his Nobel Prize. "But I don't think anyone would say it was moral."

Throughout the 1990s and into the new millennium, as the Charles R. Walgreen Distinguished Service Professor of American Institutions in the Graduate School of Business and a member of the Department of Economics and the Committee on Social Thought at the University of Chicago, the brilliant intellectual incendiary has continued to investigate the fundamental forces responsible for instability and inequality. His current research is on nutrition, longevity, and the changing patterns of aging in the United States.

Wilson Greatbatch

CLASS OF 1950

Wilson Greatbatch is an independent inventor with a passionate faith in technology. Many of his projects had only limited success, including an atomic battery, an electric bladder stimulator, and a process to encourage bone growth. He once modified his pickup truck to run on alcohol. On his seventy-second birthday he coursed 120 miles on New York's Finger Lakes in a solar-powered canoe that he developed but never tried to market. However, one of the more than one hundred and fifty patents he holds is among the great achievements of biomedical engineering. Greatbatch invented the implantable cardiac pacemaker.

Greatbatch was born in Buffalo, New York, on September 6, 1919. As a child everything having to do with electricity caught his interest. Hooked on the new phenomenon of radio, in his early teens he built a shortwave receiver that allowed him to tune in to England. He got a radio amateur's license when he was sixteen and joined the Sea Scout radio division of the Boy Scouts. Some of the young men in that Scout unit, including

Greatbatch, enlisted in the Naval Reserves in 1939 and volunteered for active duty in 1940. The entry of the United States into World War II at the end of 1941 determined Greatbatch's career for the next four years. He repaired electronic equipment on a destroyer, operated a radio on merchant ships, taught in a Navy radar school, and finally served as a rear gunner in carrier-based bomber planes.

Released from the service in 1945 and newly married to Eleanor Wright, Greatbatch went to work for the New York Telephone Company. A year later the G.I. Bill made it possible for him to enter the School of Electrical Engineering at Cornell, where he earned his degree in 1950. With three children during his Cornell years, he might have been excused had he kept his academic commitments to a minimum. But "after all that time in the dive-bombers, it was such a joy to wander around the campus, to go to class, and to learn something." Cornell provided him with knowledge, from nuclear physics to electronic circuit design and welding, that he later used in his inventions. To "feed my family," Greatbatch ran the university AM/FM transmitter (WHCU) on weekends and took a job at the psychology department's Animal Behavior Farm in Varna.

During the summer of 1951, after his graduation, Greatbatch shared brown-bag lunches with two cardiologists who were working at the Animal Behavior Farm. They talked about procedures that doctors were developing to treat cardiac arrests. The best technology at the time relied on impractical, television-set-sized devices that sent a painful shock to the chest. While he worked for the Cornell Aeronautical Laboratory in Buffalo (until 1952) and then as an assistant professor of electrical engineering at the University of Buffalo, Greatbatch set his mind to imagining a better mechanical treatment that would permit cardiac patients to lead normal lives.

He became interested in the new technology of transistors and spent part of his time in the early 1950s working with two doctors at Buffalo's Chronic Disease Research Institute. One of them needed a machine to record fast heart sounds, and Greatbatch built an oscillator using a single transistor. But he made a mistake putting the oscillator together, changing the function of his creation. He inserted the wrong resistor into it, unexpectedly causing the circuit to pulse, then stop, and then

pulse again. "I stared at the thing in disbelief," Greatbatch recalled, "and then realized that this was exactly what was needed to drive a heart." And it was smaller than a TV set.

With $2,000, Greatbatch put it "to the Lord in prayer" and decided to take time off from his job and devote all his energy to developing a surgically implantable device to control a patient's heartbeat. Working in an old cedar-sided barn behind his house that was heated by a woodstove, Greatbatch created by hand his first fifty cardiac pacemakers. In the spring of 1958, after Greatbatch had been rebuffed by several physicians who saw no value in the proposed technology, Dr. William Chardack, chief of surgery at Buffalo's Veterans' Administration Hospital, concluded that the device could save ten thousand lives a year. Within three weeks, on May 7, 1958, Chardack, using one of Greatbatch's handmade products, implanted the first self-powered cardiac pacemaker in an experimental animal.

The dog lived for only a few hours, but later that year a Swedish team successfully implanted a device in a man who lived more than forty years, dying in January 2002 at age 86 after outliving twenty-six pacemakers. Greatbatch and Chardack, using what proved to be a more successful design, did their first human implants in 1960. Greatbatch formed a partnership with Medtronic, a small company in Minneapolis that had tested wearable, battery-operated heart stimulators. Medtronic switched to Greatbatch's steadily improving devices and became the world's top producer of therapeutic implantable devices.

Many technical problems with cardiac pacemakers persisted, mostly having to do with the zinc-mercury batteries that lasted for only 18 to 24 months. In the 1970s Greatbatch developed a corrosion-free lithium battery to power the pacemaker, a technological breakthrough as important as the pacemaker itself. In most patients the pacemaker with the new lithium battery was permanent, requiring no further surgery. Greatbatch severed his connections with Medtronic and formed an independent company in Clarence, New York, that was soon selling more than 90 percent of the world's pacemaker batteries.

Greatbatch likes to recall "the way it was," simple times when his wife Eleanor tested transistors by tapping them in their bedroom with a calibrated pencil. He worried that his five children might miss out in a world in which accomplishment so often depended on being tied to a bureaucracy. Greatbatch regards professional service almost as a religious mission, a calling that is not driven by the desire for fame, financial reward, or peer approval. "Just immerse yourself in the problem and work hard," he said. "The true reward is not in the results but in the doing."

However, although Greatbatch never got "a swelled head over success," his enterprises became very big business. By 1968, he no longer worked behind his house but in a manufacturing plant on a thirty-acre site in Clarence, New York. His peers and many pacemaker recipients who lived to enjoy their grandchildren have recognized his achievements. Greatbatch has received the Holley Medal of the American Society of Mechanical Engineers, the Chancellor Morton Medal of the University of Buffalo, and from President George Bush in 1990 the National Medal of Technology. He has been named to the National Inventors Hall of Fame, the U.S. Space Technology Hall of Fame, and the Science and Engineering Hall of Fame. Perhaps the most prestigious honor came in 1996 when the Massachusetts Institute of Technology gave him the Lifetime Achievement Award granted by the Lemelson-MIT Prize Program, an award established to recognize the nation's most talented inventors. Greatbatch was then 76 and working with John Sanford of Cornell on a way to block replication of HIV, the virus that causes AIDS. The number of pacemakers implanted yearly had risen from 10,000, a figure that Greatbatch had thought was wildly optimistic back in 1958, to over 600,000.

Harold Irving Bloom

&. CLASS OF 1951

Harold Bloom, a towering figure in American letters, is prodigiously productive, creative, and controversial. Anointed by *Newsweek* "the best known literary critic in America," he is also one of the most influential interpreters of Western literature in the latter half of the twentieth century. One scholar has labeled Bloom's *Anxiety of Influence: A Theory of Poetry* (1973) "one of the most discussed books of literary criticism for the last 300 years." He has his detractors, though, Hilton Kramer among them, who dismissed Bloom as an "author of numerous works of supererogatory obfuscation."

Bloom was born on July 11, 1930, the youngest of the five children of William, a garment worker, and Paula Bloom, who emi-

grated to the Bronx from Eastern Europe. He had an Orthodox Jewish upbringing and spoke only Yiddish until he was five. Bloom quickly became a voracious reader of English, falling in love especially with poetry. Between the ages of eight and twelve he read all of Hart Crane and Walt Whitman. His passion for literature persisted through his years at the prestigious Bronx High School of Science, which he later referred to as "that ghastly place." Finishing first in the statewide Regents exam, Bloom was awarded a full scholarship to the Cornell College of Arts and Sciences in 1947. He majored in English and studied with the distinguished literary critic M. H. Abrams, a recent arrival on the faculty, to whom Bloom would dedicate his second book, *The Visionary Company: A Reading of English Romantic Poetry* (1961). At Cornell, Bloom's brilliance was legendary, with classmates marveling at his fluency in eight languages and his capacity, drunk or sober, to recite Milton's "Paradise Lost" or Hart Crane's "The Bridge" "frontwards, then backwards, quite like a tape recorder running wild." A Phi Beta Kappa graduate in 1951, Bloom went to graduate school at Yale.

Bloom received his doctorate from Yale in 1955 and was hired to teach on its English faculty. In 1977 he split from the English department to form his own department, becoming Yale's only Professor of Humanities, and has been the Sterling Professor of Humanities since 1983. In recent years he has had a professorial appointment at New York University as well. Bloom has written nearly twenty-five books of literary and cultural criticism, each displaying dazzling religious, philosophical, historical, and psychological erudition. In addition to his one novel, *The Flight to Lucifer: A Gnostic Fantasy* (1979), he has also edited *Stories and Poems for Extremely Intelligent Children of All Ages* (2000). A regular contributor to the *New York Times Book Review* and the *New York Review of Books,* he is the mastermind behind one of the late twentieth century's most ambitious literary projects. As the general editor of the Chelsea House Publishers series of critical essays on British, American, and European writers and texts, Bloom has personally edited and written introductions for nearly two hundred and fifty volumes.

Bloom is an insomniac who still writes in longhand on yellow pads. His books go from his typist directly to print, since he refuses to be copyedited. "No one edited Emerson or Carlyle," he insists. He quotes authors from memory and eschews footnotes. A cultivated eccentric, Bloom has been known to write in the middle of parties. He is a Zero Mostel look-alike with a sad, shaggy, epicene face and a soft, oversized body and a mesmerizing lecturer who can switch from Nietzsche or the kabbalah to baseball statistics and vampire movies. In 1985, Bloom was named as a MacArthur Fellow, one of twenty-four people with a track record of creativity in their fields chosen each year by the MacArthur Foundation to receive a so-called genius grant, now at $500,000 over five years, to support their work. He married his wife, Jeanne Gould, in 1958. They have two sons, Daniel Jacob and David Moses.

Bloom emerged as an important literary critic in the 1960s with several books on English Romantic poetry. He rescued Shelley, Blake, Wordsworth, Byron, Coleridge, and Keats from the neglect of the New Critics—some of them his colleagues at Yale—who preferred the metaphysical and religious poets of the seventeenth century. Bloom insisted that the Romantics were not mere poets of nature but of consciousness and imaginative vision. They constituted the central tradition of poetry in English, looking back to Milton and forward to Yeats and Wallace Stevens. *The Anxiety of Influence* marked Bloom's arrival as an intellectual superstar. In it, he challenged the conventional understanding of the term *literary tradition.* Bloom argued that literature was founded on rivalry, with each generation of writers wrestling with writers of the past, locked in an oedipal struggle, striving to surpass and replace the dead champions that preceded them. Far from a continuity of unfolding inspirations and influences, the "literary tradition" doomed poets to the "anxiety of indebtedness," forever seeking to create themselves as original and first, not derivative and belated. While not abandoning his iconoclastic rereading of literary influence, Bloom transformed himself in the 1980s and 1990s from literary enfant terrible to unabashed traditionalist. He has, for example, written a series of books sympathetic to religion. Strongly influenced by Jewish kabbalistic mysticism and the early Christian gnostics,

Bloom wrote a spirited autobiography in 1996, *Omens of Millennium: The Gnosis of Angels, Dreams, and Resurrections,* in which he classified himself as an "agnostic Jew." He has written one book tracing belief from the Bible to the present and another on American religion. In 1990 he suggested, in *The Book of J,* that a woman wrote significant portions of the Bible. The book landed on *The New York Times* best-seller list.

Bloom enlisted as Shakespeare's champion as well. In his *Shakespeare: The Invention of the Human* (1998) he found in each of the bard's thirty-seven plays something pertinent to the human, and the modern, condition: "He reads us more deeply than we can read him." Shakespeare is central to Bloom's defense of high culture. He indicts the university, which he sees evicting Shakespeare from the curriculum, for its "contamination and deterioration of taste" and for allowing humanistic subjects in general to be "taken over by people who resent the aesthetic." The university, he writes, "has a captive audience, and it therefore will present any type of gibberish and then hide behind academic freedom." It's bad enough when "the destruction of intellectual and aesthetic standards in the humanities and the social sciences occurs in the name of social justice." But, surely the barbarians are at the gates when "the appreciation of Victorian women's underwear replaces the appreciation of Charles Dickens and Robert Browning" in English departments.

Bloom defends the barricades. In *The Western Canon: The Books and Schools of the Ages* (1994) and *How to Read and Why* (1999), he proclaims himself "one of a dwindling elite" who lament the loss of "a certain form of culture and ways of reading." His 2002 book *Genius* provides one hundred of history's most brilliant and creative people offering an exemplary honor role of the heroes of literature. He was appalled by the phenomenon of Harry Potter, a book series he described as "long on clichés and short of imaginative vision." His review in the *Wall Street Journal* concluded with sad resignation: "At a time when public judgment is no better and no worse than what is proclaimed by the ideological cheerleaders who have so destroyed humanistic study, anything goes. The cultural critics will, soon enough, introduce Harry Potter into their college curriculum and the *New York Times* will go on celebrating another confirmation of the dumbing-down it leads and exemplifies." This curmudgeonly blast at popular culture was almost certainly written by hand on his yellow pad, pressed against a clipboard which, Bloom told a magazine writer in 1998, he had bought when he was nineteen and a freshman at Cornell.

Clifford Michael Irving

❧ CLASS OF 1951

"World-class con man," trumpeted the CBS Web site in May 1999, announcing a *60 Minutes II* interview with the man who had pulled off "the literary hoax of the century." Clifford Irving protested, telling the *New York Times* that he had seventeen books to his credit; to label him "a con man" was analogous to calling an alcoholic who had been sober for twenty-two years a drunkard. Nearing sev-

enty, the lanky, still boyish-looking Irving was, indeed, a well-known writer whose novels in the 1990s sold a solid ten or fifteen thousand copies each. After four marriages (which produced three sons, Joshua, Ned, and Barnaby), he had apparently settled down, with his fifth wife, Maureen. But for most people watching *60 Minutes II* in 1999, Clifford Irving meant one thing—colossal fake.

Clifford was born on November 5, 1930, in Manhattan, the son of Dorothy and Jay Irving, the latter a cartoonist who created Pete the Cop in the comic strip "Pottsy." A graduate of New York's Music and Art High School, Irving entered Cornell in 1947, where he was a member of the freshman crew and Pi Lambda Phi fraternity. He majored in English in the College of Arts and Sciences and received his bachelor's degree in 1951. After Cornell, Irving worked intermittently as a TV correspondent in the Middle East and as a creative writing teacher at UCLA while establishing himself as a novelist. His first novel, *On a Darkling Plain,* was set at Cornell with tales of drunken parties in an apartment on Linden Avenue. The publisher heralded it as introducing "a brilliant new writer who shows outstanding ability to speak for contemporary young America." Irving, alas, never became his generation's spokesman.

His second novel, *The Losers,* and his third, *The Valley,* a Western, went unnoticed. His fourth novel, *The Thirty-Eighth Floor,* received more attention. A tale of Cold War politics, it centers on John Burden, a black American who is suddenly elevated to acting secretary general of the United Nations, with an office on the thirty-eighth floor of the UN building.

Irving turned next to nonfiction and did well enough in the 1960s to live a comfortable expatriate life in a large house on the little island of Ibiza, off the coast of Spain. He wrote the *Battle of Jerusalem* based on the Six Day War of June 1967, and then in 1969, the quite successful *Fake!,* the story of Hungarian art forger Elmyr de Hory. Serialized in *Look* magazine, *Fake!* was featured along with its author in an Orson Welles movie of the same name. Describing his fascination with the forger, Irving wrote presciently in 1969, "All the world loves to see the experts and the establishment made a fool of, and everyone

likes to feel that those who set themselves up as experts are really just as gullible as anyone else." He set out to prove his point.

In December 1971, McGraw Hill announced with great fanfare that it was about to publish the autobiography of Howard Hughes, compiled from over a hundred hours of secret interviews that Clifford Irving had conducted with the eccentric millionaire and famous recluse. Rights to print excerpts from the book were quickly sold to *Life* magazine and it was selected by the Book of the Month Club. McGraw Hill also lined up a lucrative paperback contract with Dell.

There was one problem. Several weeks into 1972 Howard Hughes held a telephone press conference from his secret hideaway in the Bahamas. He had never heard of nor met any Clifford Irving, he told reporters, and insisted that the manuscript was a fake. Meanwhile, three checks totaling $650,000, money McGraw Hill had given to Irving to pass on to Hughes as an advance on the book, turned up in a savings account in the Swiss Credit Bank in Zurich. Swiss authorities ascertained that the checks were endorsed "H. R. Hughes" and deposited in an account opened by a slim brunette who resembled Irving's wife Edith. She had used a Swiss passport with the name Helga R. Hughes.

As the elaborate hoax unraveled, McGraw Hill and *Life* offered embarrassed apologies. Irving was sentenced to two-and-a-half years in prison, his wife Edith to two years, both on charges of grand larceny, conspiracy, perjury, mail fraud, and possession of forged documents. Irving spent sixteen months in federal prison in Danbury, Connecticut, before being paroled. His wife's sentence in New York was reduced to two months but she was then imprisoned for fourteen more in Switzerland.

It emerged at their separate trials that Irving had forged letters from Hughes to himself and fabricated replies to his interview questions using a manuscript life of Hughes written by a California writer, James Phelan. Edith Irving had used an out-of-date Swiss passport altered by her husband, which included a photograph of herself in a wig and glasses. Irving showed no remorse, telling the press: "I never thought I was getting into a criminal thing. I thought it was a big gag. I never for one moment thought I would be sent to prison. The worst I thought could happen was that I might be severely embarrassed."

The couple divorced after their nearly two years of forced separation. Edith returned to Ibiza to run an art gallery. With unabashed chutzpah, Irving tried to pay back his huge debts to McGraw Hill by setting up a business called Literary Developments, Inc., which offered legitimate Clifford Irving ghostwritten autobiographies to anybody who would pay him $25,000. When there were no takers, Irving made a living writing travel columns and public relations pieces.

He returned to novels in 1978 with a spy story, *The Death Freak,* about a CIA agent who wants to retire, written with a friend, Herbert Burkholz, under the pseudonym "John Luckless." Using his own name in the 1980s and 1990s, Irving wrote another eight books. *Tom Mix and Pancho Villa* (1982) was an historical romance set in Texas and Mexico. *The Angel of*

Zin (1984) was based on a 1943 revolt in a Polish concentration camp. In the 1990s he produced three crime novels, *Trial* (1990), set in Texas; *Final Argument* (1993), about a country lawyer and an execution in Florida; and *Spring* (1996), involving a criminal trial set in Colorado mining country. He did well enough to resume an expatriate's life, dividing his time between Mexico and France with occasional stays in Santa Fe, New Mexico.

Irving's *Autobiography of Howard Hughes* was published in 1999 as an "imaginative biography." Having tried unsuccessfully for nearly twenty-five years to persuade mainstream commercial presses (including McGraw Hill) to publish the book as fiction, Irving published the book himself on-line with Terrificbooks.com, a Santa Fe–based company he co-owns that sells books directly to customers over the Internet. He labeled it "the most famous unpublished book of the 20th century." In an interview in the *New York Times* "Media Talk" column, Irving reflected on the crime that made him notable: "I probably did it because I was bored and it was a challenge and it was an adventure and I was stupid."

Ruth Bader Ginsburg

CLASS OF 1954

The 107th Justice of the United States Supreme Court, sworn in on August 10, 1993, was particularly pleased "to be the *second* woman on the Court." It meant that women were no longer singular symbols and tokens, "a wonderful sign of change in society," Ruth Bader Ginsburg told the press.

Ruth Joan Bader was born on March 15, 1933, in the Flatbush neighborhood of Brooklyn. Her father Nathan, a furrier and haberdasher, and her mother Celia (Amster), a homemaker, were first-generation Jewish Americans. Her six-year-old sister Marilyn

died of meningitis when Ruth was one and her mother, who profoundly influenced her, died of cancer in her senior year. Ruth acquired a love of learning from her mother. First in her class at P.S. 238, she went on to edit the school newspaper and graduate sixth in her class at Brooklyn's James Madison High School. She played cello in the orchestra and was a baton-twirling cheerleader.

Winning a New York State Regents scholarship, Ruth Bader entered Cornell in 1950 and majored in government in the College of Arts and Sciences. She was a member of Phi Kappa Phi sorority, the "Student-Faculty Committee," and a dorm captain. Graduating first in her class in 1954, she was elected to Phi Beta Kappa as well. Shortly after her Cornell graduation in 1954, she married Martin Ginsburg, whom she had met in her freshman year when he was a sophomore.

The couple spent the next two years at Fort Sill in Lawton, Oklahoma, where Martin, who had been drafted, was assigned to military service. It was here that Ginsburg first experienced employment discrimination against women. In her application for a civil service job she revealed that she was pregnant and was assigned a position lower than the one for which she was qualified.

In 1956 the Ginsburgs, with their young daughter Jane, moved to Cambridge, Massachusetts, where she entered Harvard Law School, one of nine women among the five hundred students admitted that year. Her husband, returning to his second year at the law school, was diagnosed with cancer, and Ruth took notes in his courses and typed his papers during his successful medical treatment even as she juggled motherhood and her own studies. Undaunted, Ginsburg worked so hard as a student that she won election to the editorship of the *Harvard Law Review.* When her husband, fully recovered, was offered a job in a New York law firm in 1958, Ginsburg transferred to Columbia Law School for her final year, where she made the *Columbia Law Review* as well, graduating in 1959 tied for first in her class.

Not a single law firm in New York City offered Ginsburg a job because, in her words,

she was "a woman, a Jew, and a mother to boot." Nor could she obtain a prestigious clerkship. Supreme Court Justice Felix Frankfurter, who was not willing to hire a woman, refused to interview her. Finally she secured a two-year clerkship with a federal district judge in New York. From 1961 to 1963 Ginsburg was associated with Columbia Law School's Comparative Legal Studies project, writing about and becoming an expert on Swedish legal procedure. In 1963 she became the second woman on the Rutgers University School of Law faculty; she was among the first twenty women to teach in an American law school.

During the nearly ten years she taught at Rutgers her legal interests changed from comparative law to gender discrimination. She attributes the move to her residual anger at having had to disguise her figure in oversized clothes during her pregnancy with her son James in 1965, to listening to the complaints of her female students, and to reading Simone de Beauvior's pathbreaking book *The Second Sex* in the late 1960s. In 1971 Ginsburg received national attention for successfully arguing *Reed v. Reed,* the first case in which the Supreme Court decided a sex bias claim in favor of women, overturning an Idaho law that gave preference to men over women as estate executors on the assumption that they were more capable in that position.

During the 1970s, after her move to Columbia Law School, as its first tenured female professor (1972), and after becoming director that same year of the American Civil Liberties Union's Women's Rights Project, Ginsburg's litigation had a profound impact on the law of sex discrimination, changing dramatically the legal status of men and women in America. She did this by winning five of the six cases she argued before the Supreme Court. An Air Force policy requiring the discharge of pregnant officers was overturned as were federal laws giving male servicemen certain spousal and family benefits that were not given to the spouses of female soldiers. Her arguments led the Court to reject state laws that distinguished between men and women regarding jury service as well as to declare unconstitutional unequal Social Security benefits for widows and widowers. Her successful strategy was, in her words, "to attack the most pervasive stereotype in the law—that men are independent and women are men's dependents."

Ginsburg's legal quest in the '70s, the "egalitarian feminist" ideal of ending all legal distinctions between the genders, bothered some women's rights activists. Equally convinced that the law should accept legitimate distinctions between men and women, they feared the loss of benefits related to motherhood and child care. She has also crossed swords with fellow feminists in her restrictive views on *Roe v. Wade* (1973). Rather than seeing the right to abortion as a privacy issue, as the Court did, she sees it as necessary to women's equality and thus a sex discrimination issue.

In 1980 Ginsburg was appointed by President Carter to the U.S. Court of Appeals for the District of Columbia where she became the judicial colleague of, among others, the conservatives Robert Bork and Antonin Scalia. Over the next thirteen years she wrote more than three hundred moderate and nuanced opinions on such issues as abortion and gay rights, affirmative action, freedom of religion, and free speech.

Ginsburg's centrist, non-strident liberalism and her deep commitment to judicial restraint recommended her to President Clinton in 1993 when for the first time in twenty-six years a Democratic president had a Supreme Court appointment. Her confirmation hearings were unusually non-controversial and her nomination was approved by the Senate on August 3, 1993 by a vote of 96 to 3, with Republicans Jesse Helms, Don Nickles, and Bob Smith citing her support of abortion rights as the basis for their opposition.

After a trying first year on the Court in which she attracted unfavorable notice for defying the tradition of freshman reticence with persistent questioning—often, in fact, interrupting lawyers and other justices—Ginsburg has become one of the Court's hardest-working and most-respected justices. She usually sides with her "middle" colleagues, David Souter and Anthony Kennedy. Ginsburg was operated on for colon cancer in 1999 and returned to the Court seventeen days after her surgery.

Justice Ginsburg lives in Washington, D.C., with her husband Martin, who is now a professor of tax law at Georgetown University Law Center. Her daughter Jane is a professor at Columbia Law School and her son James is a producer of classical recordings. Her hobbies include listening to opera (she once appeared on the Texaco-Metropolitan Opera Saturday radio quiz), reading mysteries, golf, horseback riding, and water skiing. She remains connected to Cornell, where she first studied government, speaking to Cornell alumni gatherings and annually hosting a Supreme Court visit for Cornell-in-Washington students. In 2002 she was inducted into the Women's Hall of Fame in Seneca Falls, New York.

For most Cornellians, as for most Americans, the most indelible sense of Ruth Bader Ginsburg was crafted by her words on June 14, 1993 in the White House Rose Garden when President Clinton informed the nation that he had chosen her for America's highest court. She dedicated her nomination to her mother: "the bravest and strongest person I have known, who was taken from me much too soon. I pray that I may be all that she would have been had she lived in an age when women could aspire and achieve and daughters are cherished as much as sons."

Sheldon Lee Glashow
❧ CLASS OF 1954

Most immigrants who came to the United States never realized the dream of rapid upward social mobility. Rags to riches in a single generation is a myth. Nonetheless, many spectacular true stories keep the myth alive, including that of Sheldon L. Glashow. The son of Jewish immigrants who left Czarist Russia in search of opportunity and freedom from religious persecution, Glashow rose to become one of the most famous physicists of the late twentieth century.

By the time he was born on December 5, 1932, in New York City, Glashow's father Lewis had established a successful plumbing and heating business. He and Glashow's mother, born Bella Rubin, encouraged their three sons to pursue careers related to science. Samuel and Jules, who were eighteen and fourteen when Sheldon was born, chose medicine and dentistry. Their baby brother went in a more theoretical direction. Glashow's father, who patented several inventions important to his business, built his youngest son a chemistry lab in the basement of their house, just as Sheldon entered the elite Bronx High School of Science. On the subway to and from school, Glashow and his classmates Gerald Feinberg and Steven Weinberg talked about physics, the field in which all of them would make a mark. Glashow loved billiards, which he viewed as an art of controlling motion. Thinking about billiard balls was one way into theoretical physics. In his senior year Glashow was a finalist in the national Westinghouse Science Talent Search.

In 1950 he entered Cornell to study physics and received his degree on schedule four years later. He later told an interviewer that Cornell was a "letdown," calling its faculty unimpressive and saying their courses were not challenging. He never forgot a bureaucratic requirement that forced him to take an undergraduate course in electricity

and magnetism when he had already finished a graduate course in the same subject. Nonetheless, Cornell had prepared him well enough so that he succeeded brilliantly in his graduate work at Harvard. He earned his Ph.D. in physics in 1958.

At Harvard Glashow worked with Julian Schwinger, a physicist who would win the Nobel Prize in 1965. "Getting Schwinger's ear," Glashow recalled, "was as difficult as it was rewarding." His thesis, "The Vector Meson in Elementary Particle Decay," was his first step toward a theory unifying two of the four fundamental forces in nature, the subatomic weak force responsible for the slow decay of a nucleus and the much more observable force of electromagnetism. He and Schwinger drafted a paper on the subject in 1958 and then lost the manuscript. The world would wait several more years before Glashow published something relevant to what became known as electroweak theory (the unification of electromagnetism and the weak force).

During his last year at Harvard Glashow won a National Science Foundation postdoctoral fellowship that he intended to use to study at the Lebedev Institute in Moscow. It was the height of the Cold War, however, and he never received the necessary Russian visa. Instead he spent the years from 1958 to 1960 at Niels Bohr's Institute of Theoretical Physics in Copenhagen. There, he said, "I discovered the $SU(2) \times U(1)$ structure of the electroweak theory." His insight needed more work, but the formula, however esoteric it is to nonphysicists, stuck as the fundamental way to express the link between the weak force and electromagnetism. It caught the attention of Murray Gell-Mann (awarded the Nobel Prize in physics in 1969), who invited Glashow to Caltech.

After Glashow's return to the United States, his career advanced rapidly. He was a research fellow at Caltech (1960–61), then an assistant professor at Stanford (1961–62). Glashow was an associate professor at UC Berkeley from 1962 until he returned to Harvard in 1966, where he stayed for the rest of his career. He became the Higgins Professor of Physics in 1979, a chair he continued to hold after Harvard also named him Mellon Professor of the Sciences in 1988. Until his retirement he was among Harvard's most famous teachers, participating in its Core Curriculum Program and offering, in addition to his specialized courses, a course for nonscientists entitled "From Alchemy to Quarks."

In 1979 Glashow shared the Nobel Prize in physics with Steven Weinberg and Abdus Salam. They were cited for their complementary contributions in formulating the electroweak theory, or the theory of the unified weak and electromagnetic interaction between elementary particles. A great advance in particle physics, among other things it predicted a new type of weak interaction in which the reacting particles do not change their charges from positive to negative. The behavior is similar to what happens in the electromagnetic interaction, prompting scientists to say that the interaction proceeds via a neutral current.

Although Weinberg and Glashow had long been friends (they were classmates at Bronx Science and at Cornell) as well as colleagues at Berkeley and Harvard, they had never really collaborated. Glashow, who had been working independently on electroweak theory since graduate school, extended work published by Weinberg and Salam to cover elementary particles known as baryons and mesons. In doing so he invented a new property for quarks (the fundamental constituents of baryons and mesons) that he called "charm." "Charm," which belonged to

a then unknown fourth quark, represented the culmination of research that Glashow began during a trip back to Denmark in 1964.

In addition to the Nobel Prize Glashow has received the J. Robert Oppenheimer Memorial Medal in 1977, the George Ledlie Prize in 1978, the Castiglione di Sicilia Prize in 1983, and the Ettore Majorana-Erice Science for Peace Prize in 1991. A member of the American Academy of Arts and Sciences and the National Academy of Sciences, Glashow holds many honorary degrees. The author of some three hundred scientific papers, he has also written several books for the general reader. These include *The Charm of Physics* (1990) and *From Alchemy to Quarks* (1994). Glashow's career has taken him all over the world, with many visiting appointments that for a time took him away from Harvard. None of the dedication to his work has detracted from his family life. Glashow married Joan Alexander in 1972. They have four children.

Like Einstein, Glashow imagines a day when physicists will have a theory unifying all four fundamental forces—the strong and weak subatomic forces, electromagnetism, and gravity—in a single mathematical framework. These forces manifest themselves in very different ways, but Glashow agrees with speculation that they were indistinguishable at the high energies generated by the Big Bang, which produced the universe. However, in Glashow's mind, physics has a considerable distance to travel before this final theory comes together. The age of great discovery is not at an end, for "nature," he said in his Nobel lecture, "must still have some surprises in store for us."

With a modesty that he thinks befits all researchers, Glashow in 1995 arrived in a leopard skin outfit at Harvard's annual satiric awarding of the "Ig Nobel Prizes," an occasion to "honor" research that "cannot and should not be reproduced." He participated, apparently with a major role, in the "Interpretive Dance of the Nucleotides" while paper airplanes whizzed past his head. Glashow regrets that his parents did not live to hear the Royal Swedish Academy of Sciences announce his Nobel Prize. But in the United States, the adopted homeland of his parents, homage is rendered in many ways. They might have appreciated the delight of their much-decorated son, supremely confident about his contributions, on this occasion as well.

David B. Goodstein
✺ CLASS OF 1954

When he died in 1985 at the age of fifty-three, David Goodstein was a wealthy man, a prominent horseman, a collector of priceless paintings, and one of America's most important gay activists.

The wealth came from family steel and oil interests in Colorado where David was born on June 6, 1932. Growing up in Denver, David never seemed to live up to his parents' expectations. His father, Julius, wanted an athlete and David was a self-described "klutz." He felt neither wanted nor loved by either Julius or Sayda Goodstein and attributed childhood overeating to his unhappiness. Julius wanted David to go to college in Colorado and to take over the family business. David wanted a college far from home and chose Cornell. Although his father refused to give him any money beyond what he needed for tuition, David went to Ithaca in 1950.

At Cornell Goodstein studied economics in the College of Arts and Sciences while putting what he learned to practical use in an antique business. He and a friend bought furniture and bric-a-brac at country auctions near Ithaca and sold them to dealers in New York City. The business did well enough to allow David to devote himself to gentlemanly equestrian pursuits at Cornell. He was president of the Saddle Club and a member of the equestrian team and the Cornell Horse Show committee.

After graduating from Cornell in 1954, Goodstein spent two years in the U.S. Army, rising to the rank of lieutenant. Then came Columbia Law School, followed by a clerkship with a judge. Reluctant to practice law, however, he took a year off to live and study in Britain and South Africa.

Goodstein inherited a substantial sum of money from his grandfather in 1960. Concluding that New York brokerage firms, banks, and investment advisors were incompetent, he became his own full-time portfolio manager. One of the early pioneers in using computers in financial analysis and a co-founder of the first mutual fund, Goodstein flourished on Wall Street.

A closeted gay man, his homosexuality known only to a small set of close friends, Goodstein personified New York City success in the 1960s. He had an office in Rockefeller Center and a house on East Sixty-second Street. He kept horses, owned an art gallery, and became involved in liberal politics, advocating civil rights for blacks and Puerto Ricans and advising the city's mayor, John Lindsay. His life changed in 1971. A large West Coast bank, with which he had concluded a lucrative joint financial venture, offered him an executive position in its San Francisco office. Relishing a new challenge, Goodstein returned to the West for the first time since coming to Cornell.

Two months into his new job he invited one of the bank's officers and his wife to dinner. In the course of the evening Goodstein's sexual orientation became apparent. He was fired two days later. Goodstein realized, as he put it, that despite his involvement in the civil rights struggle he "had never thought seriously about my own civil rights as a gay person." Reestablished in the investment business, Goodstein went public with his sexuality and committed himself and his fortune to the service of gay rights. "If they can do this to me," he reasoned, "what can they do to some poor devil without any clout?" He soon became a central player in California politics, working tirelessly for the 1974 state legislation that decriminalized homosexual activities between consenting adults. He was a founder of Concerned Voters of California, one of the groups that defeated a 1978 ballot initiative to bar homosexuals from working or teaching in public schools. Goodstein was appointed to Jerry Brown's Advisory Council on Economic Development, the California governor's first openly gay appointee.

His 1975 purchase of *The Advocate,* a Los Angeles–based gay newspaper, brought Goodstein national prominence in the gay movement. Pouring hundreds of thousands of dollars into it, he transformed a local newspaper that featured tips on how to avoid police entrapment alongside articles on male fashion and pictures of nude or nearly nude men into the largest circulation gay and lesbian biweekly magazine in America. Replacing the titillating torsos were interviews with nationally known gays and lesbians and noted personalities sympathetic to the gay cause as well as articles about safer sex.

Another important Goodstein contribution to the gay movement was the "Advocate Experience," personal growth seminars for homosexuals and lesbians that he founded in 1978 and financed for years. In the wake of Anita Bryant's successful campaign to repeal Dade County, Florida's gay rights law in 1977, Goodstein became convinced that the real problem for gays was not political but

emotional—their horrible self-image. With the help of his friend Werner Erhard, the Bay Area self-esteem and human potential guru and founder of Erhard Seminars Training (later known as "est"), Goodstein set up weekend workshops in convention centers and first-class hotels, where for twelve hours a day mainly middle-class men talked about gay pride and coming out to a life of integrity and expanded consciousness. When they finally came to an end in 2001, more than fifty thousand people had gone through the Advocate Experience, or "Goodstein 101," as the workshop was dubbed. These workshops long outlived Goodstein himself, who died in San Diego on June 22, 1985 at the age of fifty-three from complications following surgery for bowel cancer. He was survived by his partner in life, David Russel.

Goodstein remained close to Cornell as an alumnus. He funded scholarships for students who studied economics and for students from underdeveloped British Commonwealth countries. A member of the Cornell University Council, he was also one of the founders in the early 1970s, and the chair, of the Friends of the Art Museum. In a lecture to Cornell students the year before he died, Goodstein acknowledged how important his business success was for his political activism. He encouraged Cornell students, who he predicted would soon enter "the inner circles of power," to change those circles from within, "because I'm not sure we can change those things from without."

Goodstein left his personal art collection, which included, among other works, a Rembrandt, a Constable, and a Hogarth, to the Herbert F. Johnson Museum of Art. He also left his books and extensive archival material on human sexuality in general and homosexuality in particular to Cornell University. It is one of the most important research collections on these subjects in the world. In offering this collection to the university in 1984, Goodstein, who thirty-five years earlier had come to Cornell to get away from his family, wrote: "Imagine a world in which all the absurd myths and superstitions about human sexuality can be lessened even a little bit because serious scholars can begin to discover their biological, psychological, sociological, and ethical bases. . . . If the collection for human sexuality can relieve the ignorance for humanity, it will become one of the most valuable and important resources for human well-being."

Steven Weinberg
ᴥ CLASS OF 1954

In 1896 Andrew Dickson White's book *History of the Warfare of Science with Theology in Christendom* was published. Had Cornell's first president written his massive book a century later, he would surely have included the perspective of Steven Weinberg, Nobel laureate in physics and a profound skeptic of all religious attempts to assign meaning to the universe. "The more comprehensible the universe becomes," he wrote, "the more pointless it seems." The rules that govern natural phenomena are utterly impersonal.

Born on May 3, 1933, in New York City, the son of Frederick and Eva Israel Weinberg, Steven recalled that he was "not a prodigy" at school. Nonetheless, his father, a court stenographer, encouraged his scientific talents, which were sufficient to win Weinberg a place at the Bronx High School of Science. By his mid-teens his interests became focused on theoretical physics: "I felt that if I could understand theoretical physics I could understand anything."

In 1950 Weinberg entered Cornell where he spent "a lovely four years" balancing academics with an active social life. Shortly after he received his degree in 1954 he married another Cornell graduate, Louise Goldwasser. Almost "as a lark" the newlyweds traveled to Copenhagen where Weinberg enrolled as a graduate student at the Institute of Theoretical Physics founded by Niels Bohr. It proved to be an important year for him: "Before I went to Copenhagen the idea of sitting down and writing a paper was about as foreign to

me as becoming President of the United States." At the end of his stay Weinberg knew that he was capable of designing a research project in physics with publishable results.

Weinberg returned to the United States to begin a Ph.D. program at Princeton. He regretted that he never met Einstein, who died just before his arrival, but he completed his thesis quickly, in 1957. Weinberg characterized his dissertation as "undistinguished," but the subject, the application of renormalization theory to the effects of strong interactions in weak interaction processes, established his interests in particle physics and quantum field theory. No one doubted his formidable talents.

After Princeton, Weinberg spent two years as a research associate and instructor at Columbia. In 1960 he accepted a position at Berkeley and became a full professor there in 1964. He was thirty-one. Weinberg and his wife enjoyed the Bay Area, where their daughter Elizabeth was born in 1963. Nonetheless, they returned to the East Coast in 1967 where she went to Harvard Law School and he served as the Loeb Lecturer at Harvard and then as a visiting professor at MIT. In 1969, Weinberg joined the physics department at MIT. He stayed there until 1973 when he became the Higgins Professor at Harvard. He was also the Senior Scientist at the Smithsonian Astrophysical Observatory, an appointment that reflected the expanding range of his investigations. Astrophysics was the subject of his first book, *Gravitation and Cosmology* (1972).

His academic peregrinations were not over. In 1980 Louise Weinberg, a distinguished legal scholar and authority on the federal courts, accepted a position at the University of Texas Law School where today she holds the William B. Bates Chair for Administration of Justice. Two years later, in 1982, Weinberg followed his wife to Austin as the Josey Regental Professor of Science with positions in both physics and astronomy. Although warned about "potbellied bubbas in their pickups [with] shotguns in the rack behind the seat looking for hippies to kill," Weinberg liked Texas. Even though he has held visiting appointments elsewhere, he has stayed for two decades in Austin where he has gone horseback riding in the Glass Mountains and danced the Cotton-eyed Joe at the Broken Spoke.

For his work in developing the electroweak theory, which explains the unity of electromagnetism with the weak nuclear force, Weinberg shared the 1979 Nobel Prize in physics with Abdus Salam and Sheldon Glashow. That was only twelve years after Weinberg had published his ideas in a typically dense article in the *Physical Review.* Weinberg had worked with Salam in London. With Glashow he had a longer history; they had been classmates both at the Bronx High School of Science and at Cornell. Few non-physicists can follow Weinberg's mind into the world of W and Z particles, broken symmetries, quantum chromodynamics, and string theory. Nonetheless, Weinberg believes passionately in the simplicity of the physical world and shares with Stephen Hawking and Glashow the dream of finding a final theory that unites the interactions of all four fundamental forces of nature—the weak and strong subatomic forces, electromagnetism, and gravity. His *Quantum Theory of Fields,* pub-

lished in three volumes between 1995 and 1999, is a step in that direction.

Universities around the world have conferred honorary degrees on Weinberg in recognition of his achievements. The list of prizes he has won, aside from the Nobel, is long and includes the J. Robert Oppenheimer Memorial Prize in 1973, the Elliott Cresson Medal of the Franklin Institute in 1979, the Madison Medal from Princeton in 1991, and the National Medal of Science from the National Science Foundation in 1991. Elected to the American Academy of Arts and Sciences in 1968 and the National Academy of Sciences in 1972, he has served on many government and scholarly advisory boards and as a consultant for the U.S. Arms Control and Disarmament Agency.

Weinberg claims that many of his best ideas came while, when engaged in "unhappy worrying" about something he did not understand, he doodled on a pad of paper and watched a television set propped on his desk. He has much enjoyed time spent in England and credits as a special inspiration the British soap opera *Dixon of Dock Green.* For relaxation he reads medieval English history. His interest in communication has led him to work tirelessly to promote an appreciation for science among the general population. He has written several books for educated laypersons. His explanation of the Big Bang theory, *The First Three Minutes: A Modern View of the Origins of the Universe,* appeared in 1977 and has been translated into more than twenty languages. Author also of *Dreams of a Final Theory* (1992) and *Facing Up: Science and Its Cultural Adversaries* (2001), in 1999 Weinberg received the Lewis Thomas Prize, which is awarded to the researcher who best embodies the "scientist as poet." The award was appropriate. Weinberg has said that if he had the talent, he would become a poet.

In his role as public intellectual Weinberg has strenuously rejected arguments that scientific knowledge is relative, "affected by the social setting" of the research. In his opinion scientific inquiry, unlike research in history and the social sciences, moves in a clearly marked way toward a final, objective understanding of reality. Postmodern theories about the "indeterminacy of meaning" strike him as dangerous. In articles for the *New York Review of Books,* Weinberg has not been kind to religion: "With or without religion good people can behave well and bad people can do evil. But for good people to do evil, that takes religion." When confronted with the argument that science has also brought evil into the world, Weinberg has replied that science merely "amplifies the capabilities of human beings." If people apply science badly, that is not the fault of science but of their moral sense, which is often poorly instructed by reli-

gious leaders. Disagreement about a scientific principle, he notes, has never caused a war. Without the aid of religion, he refused to involve himself in work related to the war in Vietnam and during the Cold War campaigned against the proliferation of nuclear weapons.

For Weinberg no god guarantees a happy ending for human projects. At the same time no god condemns women and men to misery. The universe is pointless, a fact that leaves it up to human beings to make life worth living. They do that, Weinberg believes, by loving one another, creating works of art, striving to build peaceful communities, and seeking to understand the world they accidentally inhabit.

Richard Jay Schaap

ᏚᏢ CLASS OF 1955

A fixture in American Journalism for more than four decades, covering civil rights, politics, and the theater as well as sports, Dick Schaap loved both the written and the spoken word. The author of almost three dozen books, he was the first sportswriter to become a television star, winning six Emmys in stints for NBC, ABC, and ESPN. Fun loving and hard working, a self-proclaimed world-class name-dropper, Schaap so embodied the "as told to" autobiography that the byline for his own memoir, *Flashing before My Eyes,* reads: Dick Schaap (As Told to Dick Schaap).

Richard Jay Schaap was born on September 27, 1934, in Brooklyn, New York. Maurice Schaap, his father, was a Cornell graduate, a salesman at Bloomingdale's and then for a silverware company, and a fanatic Brooklyn Dodgers fan. His mother, Leah Lerner Schaap, went to college in her forties and became a French teacher. At age twelve, Dick decided to become a sportswriter. While a high school junior in Freeport, Long Island, he covered sports for the *Nassau Daily Re-*

view-Star, working alongside the night editor, Jimmy Breslin, then a student at Long Island University. Schaap entered Cornell in 1951 and was assigned to a World War II Quonset hut as his freshman dorm. He began in the College of Arts and Sciences, and then transferred to the School of Industrial and Labor Relations to save money. Schaap was a standout lacrosse goalie at Cornell, but he "majored" in the *Cornell Daily Sun,* staying out of the nets in his junior year so that he could serve as editor in chief of the newspaper. He graduated in 1955, got a master's degree from the Columbia School of Journalism a year later, and landed a job with *Newsweek.* Learning quickly to "write short and tight," Schaap became the youngest senior editor in the magazine's history. While at *Newsweek* he cast his first ballot for the Heisman Trophy, the most prestigious award in college football. When Jim Brown, the running back from Syracuse University, placed fifth, Schaap concluded that the selection process was hopelessly racist. He boycotted the Heisman until 1981.

In 1964, Schaap moved to the *New York Herald Tribune,* serving first as city editor, where he supervised the work of Breslin and Tom Wolfe, and then as a columnist. He broke the story of heavyweight boxer Cassius Clay's conversion to the Nation of Islam, and covered the race riots in Watts, California, and the New York City mayoral election of 1965. When Mayor John Lindsay asserted during a transit strike in 1966 that New York was still a "fun city," Schaap "grabbed the words, capitalized them and ran with them." The nickname stuck. Schaap never abandoned his interest in American politics and culture. "The journalistic principles are the same for covering a pennant race or a race riot," he maintained. "You use your eyes, your ears, . . . and your legs." Schaap wrote books about drug addiction, Robert F. Kennedy, and (with Breslin) a fictionalized account of the Son of Sam murders. A theater critic for ABC *World News Now* later in his career, he boasted that he was the only person to vote for both the Heisman Trophy and the Tony Awards.

In 1969, Schaap wrote *Instant Replay* with Jerry Kramer, an offensive lineman for the Super Bowl-champion Green Bay Packers. The best-selling sports book of its time, it was

Schaap's first in a bevy of "as told to" sports biographies. Schaap's collaborators included Hank Aaron, Tom Seaver, Dave DeBusschere, Joe Montana, Bo Jackson, Phil Simms, Frank Beard, and gay Olympian Tom Waddell. Schaap even set up a company to publish books using the formula, complete with a manual that advised writers to "make sure your tape recorder is working properly." Schaap's prodigious output prompted *Spy* magazine to run a cartoon showing a book jacket on which was written: "Ulysses, by James Joyce with Dick Schaap." Without a collaborator, Schaap wrote biographies of Mickey Mantle, Paul Hornung, George Steinbrenner, the Mets, the Masters, and the 1984 Olympics.

In the 1970s, Schaap worked as the editor of *Sport* magazine and sports anchor for WNBC-TV, the network's New York affiliate. On at least one occasion, his tart television commentary got him in trouble. In 1974, he offended thousands of Catholics when he called the thoroughbreds Secretariat and Riva Ridge "the most famous stablemates since Joseph and Mary." He was forced to deliver an on-air apology. Despite this faux pas, Schaap's career on the small screen took off. He reported on sports and culture for the NBC and ABC national evening news programs and for the ABC news magazine, *20/20.*

In 1989, Schaap moved to ESPN, where he hosted an interview show, *Dick Schaap's One on One,* and a radio show with his son Jeremy, also a Cornell graduate. For more than a decade, he served as anchor, traffic cop, and first among equals on *The Sports Reporters.* With its concluding segment, "Parting Shots," the program brought the equivalent of political punditry to sports commentary, making print journalists into television celebrities. Schaap taped his last episode of *The Sports Reporters* on September 16, 2001. His "Parting Shot" praised the firefighters, cops, and residents of New York City for "working and hoping and joining together" following the attack on the World Trade Center. By then, he had completed his memoir,

Flashing Before My Eyes: Fifty Years of Head-lines, Deadlines, and Punchlines, three hundred pages of anecdotes about Schaap's thousands of friends. It was easier to write about taking Lenny Bruce to a Pittsburgh Pirates game or escorting Cassius Clay on his first tour of New York City, he admitted, than to look inward: "Maybe if you don't reflect, you don't hurt as much." Schaap insisted that the book have no index, "so that my friends have to read it all the way through to see if I mention them."

Schaap moved back to a house on the west side of Cayuga Lake in Ithaca with his third wife, Patricia McLeod Schaap, and their two children (he had had two children with each of his previous wives, Barbara Barron Schaap

and Madeleine Gottlieb Schaap, and once quipped that he should have "married less and slept more.") He turned the barn on his property into a writer's studio, ready for several books he planned to write. Schaap hoped that Cornell, which had inducted him into its Athletic Hall of Fame in 1985, might ask him to lecture. It was not to be. On December 21, 2001, he died of complications following hip surgery. The speakers at his memorial service included Muhammad Ali, Jimmy Breslin, Billy Crystal, David Halberstam, Herb Gardner, Patti Lupone, Martina Navratilova, and Gene Shalit. The ubiquitous reporter whose favorite sport was collecting people would have been pleased.

Sanford I. Weill

≈ CLASS OF 1955

Sanford Weill lives to do deals, a friend once said: "That's what he does. It means no endgame." After decades in which he demonstrated the audacity to "merge up," Weill engineered a $76 billion stock swap in 1998 that brought together the financial-services group Travelers Inc. with the credit card giant Citicorp. At the time the biggest merger in history, the deal prompted journalists to call Wall Street "Weill Street."

Sanford Weill was born in Brooklyn, New York, on March 16, 1933. His mother, Etta Kalika Weill, was a homemaker; and his father, Max Weill, a dress manufacturer, was a Damon Runyonesque character who married three times and ended his working life in the Miami offices of companies run by his son. Known as Sandy, Weill acknowledged recently that he was "sort of a sissy as a little kid. When we used to play and fight in the streets of Brooklyn and I would get hurt or something, my mother would always come out and save me." To teach him to take pun-

ishment and learn when (and how) to dish it out, Etta and Max Weill sent Sandy to the Peekskill Military Academy for high school. He flourished there, both academically and athletically, becoming captain of the school's tennis team and a member of the Junior Davis Cup tennis team in New York City.

In 1951 Weill entered the College of Engineering at Cornell. It took only a few difficult science courses to convince him to switch to the College of Arts and Sciences and major in government. A member of Alpha Epsilon Pi fraternity, Weill continued to play tennis throughout his undergraduate years. An Air Force ROTC cadet, he considered a career as a military pilot but after graduation in 1955 he took a job as a runner for the Bear Stearns brokerage firm in New York City. Weill married that year as well. Joan Mosher proved to be the ideal helpmate, putting her husband and their two children first while stoking Sandy's ambitions and advising him on key business decisions.

Weill loved the securities business. He could not wait to get up in the morning, read the papers, and speculate about how world events would affect stock prices. Moving up quickly from messenger to broker, he pooled money with three friends in 1960 to establish Carter, Berlind, Potoma, and Weill. Stationed at first in the back rooms, where he watched the tapes, a cigar clenched between his teeth, Sandy soon demonstrated that he could acquire customers. Eventually, his client list would include Sonny Weblin (owner of the New York Jets), Joe Namath, Wilt Chamberlain, and Howard Cosell. Weill also proved adept at acquiring brokerage houses with name recognition greater than his own—"like a mouse swallowing an elephant," Leslie Eaton and Laura Holson wrote in the *New York Times*.

At one time, his firm was colloquially known as "Corned Beef With Lettuce," the first letters of the last names of its partners, Cogan, Berlind, Weill, and Levitt. In 1970 it became CBWL-Hayden Stone Inc; then Shearson Hayden Stone in 1974; then Shearson Loeb Rhoades in 1979. With each merger, Weill, who "managed by gossip," cut costs. "No one can con me," he claimed. "I know everything that goes on in every department." Weill's daughter and sometime professional colleague, Jessica Bibliowicz, described his method: "Most people ask questions to prove a point; he asks questions to learn." Celebrated for socializing with his employees, Weill also acquired a reputation as a man who did not hesitate to eliminate duplication in combined firms. "Sandy Weill takes no prisoners," said one of the three thousand employees of the Loeb Rhoades research department shortly after he got his pink slip.

In 1981, hoping to "go beyond Wall Street to build a great American institution," Weill

sold Shearson Loeb Rhoades to American Express for about $930 million in stock. This time Weill's intuitive genius had betrayed him. Constantly at odds with James D. Robinson III, the chief executive officer of American Express, Weill resigned from the company in August 1985. Written off by many as abrasive and washed up, Weill began his comeback almost immediately. Investing $7 million of his own money in Commercial Credit, a subsidiary of Control Data Corporation, he became CEO in 1986. Weill drastically cut costs at Commercial Credit, and resumed his strategy of "merging up," acquiring Gulf Insurance in 1987, Primeamerica Corporation (the parent of Smith Barney) the next year, and the retail brokerage outlets of Drexel Burnham Lambert in 1989.

In 1993 he put an exclamation point on his resurgence by reacquiring Shearson (then Shearson Lehman) from American Express Bank and then taking over Travelers Corporation in a $4 billion stock deal. By then, as Eaton and Holson put it, Weill was an elephant swallowing elephants. For another $4 billion in 1996, he took over Aetna Life and Casualty. Salomon Inc., the jewel in the Travelers' crown, was next, in 1997, for $9 billion. The CEO of a "Weillopoly," he made the mergers work by persuading thousands of employees that they were part of a team. "The enemy is the guy down the street," he repeated, "not the one in the next office." He reminded members of the staff to return internal calls before external ones, and forbade managers to sell their stock in the company. "It's hard to think of any other corporation in America that has woven so many companies into a single framework," Roger Lowenstein wrote in the *New York Times*.

Travelers' Group's next merger made Sandy Weill a legend. The dowry for the deal with Citicorp (the parent of Citibank, the second largest bank in the United States) in 1998 was twice the size of the merger between MCI and WorldCom, which had been the largest corporate marriage in history. "The Deal of a Life of Deals," as the *New York*

Times put it, the merger established a financial supermarket, offering an extraordinary menu of financial services. At a time when many of his peers were retiring, Weill became co-CEO, managing Citigroup's businesses and finances. Asked at a shareholders meeting in April 2001 about his health and Citigroup's succession plans, Weill gleefully reeled off statistics about his health: his blood pressure was 120/80, his cholesterol 183, lungs clear, and "my prostate number is close to zero."

When Weill left American Express in 1985, he found that he "was able to be very effective in philanthropic things." During his tenure at Travelers and Citigroup he spent a considerable amount of time and money on improving the quality of life in New York City. A substantial benefactor of Carnegie Hall, he served as chair of its board of trustees. In 1986 the Carnegie Recital Hall was renamed Weill Recital Hall. Weill also supported education

at all levels. He is a principal sponsor of the High School of Economics and Finance in New York City and one of the founders of the Academy of Finance program, which teaches high school students about the financial services industry. Weill has served as a member of the Cornell Board of Trustees. In 1998, the Weills committed $100 million to the Cornell University Medical College, located in New York City. The institution, renamed the Joan and Sanford I. Weill Medical College and Graduate School of Medical Sciences of Cornell University, received another gift of similar magnitude from the Weills in 2001. The Weills maintain homes in Manhattan; Greenwich, Connecticut; and Saranac Lake, New York, where, as Roger Lowenstein has observed, Weill indulges his passion for food and sports, and "tracks his share price as keenly as a heart-attack survivor monitors his blood pressure."

Floyd Abrams

∞ CLASS OF 1956

"Journalists are a hard group of people to love, but they're an easy group to defend," claims Floyd Abrams, who has argued more First Amendment and media cases before the U.S. Supreme Court than any other lawyer in history. Few of Abrams's cases, however, have been easy.

Born on July 9, 1936, in New York City, the son of Isidore Abrams, a businessman, and Rae Eberlin Abrams, a homemaker, Floyd Abrams grew up in Forest Hills, a prosperous section of Queens. Abrams was precociously bright, and graduated from high school at age fifteen. He entered Cornell in 1952, majoring in Government. A member of Delta Sigma Rho fraternity, he was active in the Debate Association, serving as its president and publicity manager. For his senior thesis, Abrams examined judicial restraint of the press in criminal

cases, lavishing praise on the English for placing strict limits on reporters. The United States, he recommended, should permit judges to hold journalists in contempt "for out-of-court commentary during a trial." His views on these matters would change.

After graduation in 1956, Abrams attended Yale University Law School, completing his degree in 1960. After a stint as a clerk for a U.S. district court judge in Delaware, in 1963 he entered into two long-lasting unions that were to endure beyond the twentieth century: marriage to Efrat Surasky and work at Cahill, Gordon & Reindel. At Cahill, Abrams toiled away as a corporate litigator. While on a trip to India, he learned that he was destined for greatness. Before Abrams was thirty-five, a soothsayer in New Delhi predicted, he would "go to his country's capital and do something famous." Shortly after he returned to the United States, Abrams was asked to do some legal work for NBC. His most interesting assignment involved a television journalist, Paul Pappas, who declined to reveal to a Massachusetts grand jury the sources of a story he had done on the Black Panthers. Convinced that the First Amendment protected Pappas, Abrams was pleased when the Supreme Court agreed to hear the case, along with two others, one involving a journalist for the *New York Times* and the other a reporter for a newspaper in Kentucky.

As *Pappas et al.* moved toward the Supreme Court, James Goodale, the in-house counsel for the *New York Times,* turned to Abrams and Yale professor Alexander Bickel to defend the newspaper's publication of material from the Pentagon Papers. An account of the U.S. role in the Vietnam War commissioned by Secretary of Defense Robert McNamara in 1967, the Pentagon Papers consisted of three thousand pages of analysis and four thousand pages of official documents, most of them labeled top secret, some of them revealing evidence of foreign policy blunders. Daniel Ellsberg, a disaffected former government official who had worked on the Pentagon Papers, leaked them to the *Times,* which began to publish excerpts on June 13, 1971. The Justice Department moved to stop publication, arguing that the *Times'* action posed a threat to national security. On June 15, a temporary re-

straining order was issued. It ws the first time in American history the press had been silenced in this way. Goodale had tried to get the Lord, Day & Lord law firm to represent the *Times,* but the senior partners rebuffed him. They believed that the newspaper had probably violated the Espionage Act of 1917 and was in any case unpatriotic.

New York Times v. the United States "radicalized" Abrams's understanding of the First Amendment. Lawyers for the government maintained that the executive branch had virtual autonomy in judging what information might breach national security. Abrams came to believe that the government was using national security to censor not protect, to avoid embarrassment not harm. On June 30, 1971, ten days before Floyd Abrams's thirty-fifth birthday, the Supreme Court, in a 6–3 decision, ruled in favor of the *Times* and the *Washington Post,* which had also published portions of the Pentagon Papers. Guardians of the First Amendment, Abrams concluded, no longer needed hypothetical cases to teach the potential harm of government control over the press: "Here you had a president in power, supported by the people around him, who quite literally wanted to suppress speech" because he did not want "revelations about how we became involved in the war in Vietnam to be made public." After the decision, newspapers published more material from the Pentagon Papers, disillusionment with the war grew, and Richard Nixon approved illegal actions to discredit Ellsberg, who joined many prominent Americans on the president's "enemies list."

A year later, in a 5–4 ruling in the Pappas case, the Supreme Court refused to establish a special privilege for reporters protecting their sources. Despite a warning from Potter Stewart, in his dissent, that the decision might encourage public officials to "annex the journalistic profession as an investigative arm of government," the majority found that the public interest in pursuing and prosecuting crimes was greater than the danger that reporters might find their capacity to gather news impaired if they could not guarantee confidentiality.

In the three decades since the Pentagon Papers and Pappas rulings, Abrams has represented media clients in numerous high-profile First Amendment cases. *Time, Business Week, The Nation, Reader's Digest,* ABC, NBC, and CBS television, and America Online have turned to him. So have Mary McCarthy and Bob Woodward. He persuaded the courts to vacate a $5.2 million damages award against NBC for newscasts linking entertainer Wayne Newton to organized crime. When Nina Totenberg of National Public Radio broke the story of Anita Hill's allegation that Clarence Thomas sexually harassed her, and a lawyer for the U.S. Senate tried, unsuccessfully, to force her to reveal her sources, Abrams "was brilliant, supportive, patient," Totenberg said. "He was my lawyer, my advisor, my psychiatrist, my friend." Abrams represented the Brooklyn Museum of Art after Mayor Rudolph Giuliani withheld municipal funds from the institution to protest a show with paintings that he believed desecrated religion. After a U.S. district court enjoined the city from taking any steps in "retaliation, discrimination, or sanction of any kind," Giuliani agreed to stop litigation, suspend efforts to evict the museum, and add $5.8 million to the budget for physical improvements to the building.

Abrams's genius, according to fellow First Amendment lawyer Robert Sack, lies in his ability to give the issue at hand "an immediacy and three-dimensionality that's very, very persuasive." He trained himself to do so by rehearsing his case in front of his young children who had "just about the right attention span, three or four minutes, like a lot of judges."

Abrams is in demand as a media commentator, public speaker, and visiting professor, as well as a courtroom advocate. "The First Amendment has no better friend," concluded William J. Brennan, who served on the U.S. Supreme Court from 1956 until 1990. The triumph of "good speech" over "bad speech" is cause for celebration, Abrams believes, but only a society that is willing to permit the circulation of bad speech can be truly free.

Charles Francis Feeney

CLASS OF 1956

When the identity of the man who had given away $600 million anonymously was revealed by the *New York Times* in 1997, Charles Feeney might have thought that his life would change forever. But, somehow, it did not. Even many of his beneficiaries still know little about him.

Charles Francis Feeney was born on April 23, 1931, in Elizabeth, New Jersey. His father, Leo Feeney, was an insurance underwriter, and his mother, Madeleine Mary Davis Feeney, was a nurse. Feeney received a traditional Catholic education, dividing his high school years between Regis High School in Manhattan and St. Mary's in Elizabeth, New

Jersey. After graduation, he enlisted in the Army and served as a flier in the Korean War. His tour of duty gave him a lifelong fascination with Asia. It also allowed him, through the G.I. Bill, to enter Cornell in 1952.

Feeney was a member of Alpha Epsilon Phi and earned extra money selling sandwiches at other fraternity houses. He graduated from Cornell in 1956 with a bachelor's degree in hotel administration and a notion that he might make his fortune selling tax-free merchandise to Americans returning home from overseas. His first venture, Cars International, offered automobiles to U.S. servicemen, who at the time had been granted a customs exemption amounting to several thousand dollars. Then, with his Cornell classmate Robert Miller and two acquaintances, Feeney opened a duty-free shop at Honolulu Airport, stocking it first with cigarettes and liquor and later with clothing and gift items. The venture was so successful that in 1960 Feeney and Miller formed Duty Free Shoppers, Ltd., with retail outlets throughout the Far East. The partners paid "commissions" to tour guides to lead their charges to a DFS store and keep them there. They also negotiated with governments in the region for exclusive rights to the duty-free business. Consequently, DFS's profits grew and grew for decades and decades. *Forbes Magazine* estimated in 1988 that its best store, in Waikiki, generated $20,000 a square foot; by contrast, Bloomingdale's in Manhattan brought in $800. When Feeney and Miller sold their interest in DFS in 1997 to LVMH (Moet Hennessy-Louis Vuitton) of France, their corporation had annual sales of more than $3 billion, greater than Saks Fifth Avenue and Neiman Marcus combined.

Starting in the 1970s, through the General Atlantic Corporation, Inter-Pacific Group Inc., and General Atlantic Partners, Feeney acquired many more properties, including Pacific Island Clubs, with resorts in Guam, Thailand, and Saipan; hotels, retail shops, and real estate in Hawaii; a shopping center in Tahiti; a golf club in Bali; a health club chain in California; a London retailer specializing in cashmere apparel; commercial and residential properties in San Francisco and New York; and oil and gas field services in the United States and the Gulf of Mexico. He was home just long enough to produce five children with Danielle Juliette Morail-Daninos—whom he married in 1959.

In the 1970s, as his companies continued to generate far more money than he needed, Feeney began to think about how to best use his fortune. He was appalled, he told a friend, by "the competition that the Forbes 400 list creates for people to get more and more." Feeney had always been involved with charitable projects, helping young people brought to his attention by business associates or friends and making major contributions to camps for deaf children. In 1981 he made one of his first large gifts. For its twenty-fifth reunion, the Cornell class of 1956 set a goal for the entire class of raising $250,000. Feeney gave $700,000. He then decided to stop making open donations, which inevitably attract requests for more, and to give anonymously. With the help of Harvey P. Dale, a member of the Cornell class of 1958 and a tax law professor at New York University, he made an irrevocable gift in 1984 to two charitable foundations that were incorporated in Bermuda to avoid disclosure laws in the United States. Feeney set up trusts for his children, and retained less than $5 million for himself. No other philanthropist has ever relinquished so high a percentage of his assets while still alive. "Money has an attraction for some people," he said, "but nobody can wear two pairs of shoes at one time." According to Dale, Feeney does not own a house or a car, flies economy class, and wears a fifteen dollar watch.

Feeney could be humorous about his passion for secrecy. Shortly after the foundations were created, he lectured the staff about the need for confidentiality. Later, when Dale and several colleagues returned to the boardroom, "Chuck and the rest of the trustees were all sitting there wearing those glasses with big noses and moustaches." But for almost fifteen years, "the anonymous donor" retained his anonymity. Even his partner Bob Miller did not know that Feeney's holdings in DFS had been turned over to charitable foundations. Grants were paid by cashier's check to conceal the identity of the benefactor. Recipients were told that the funds came from several generous "clients."

In 1997, when Feeney realized that a lawsuit launched over the sale of DFS would reveal his donations, he decided to make a public acknowledgment of his philanthropy. The

New York Times' front-page story was picked up by newspapers and magazines throughout the world. With assets then estimated at $3.5 billion, Feeney's foundations were among the best-endowed in the world. The principal beneficiaries, in addition to Cornell, were Dublin City University, Trinity College, and the University of Limerick, all in Ireland—Feeney's grandparents had emigrated to the United States from County Fermanagh. But other universities, scholarship funds, medical centers, urban affairs institutes, alliances for the aging, children's centers, housing partnerships, crime prevention councils, libraries, and dozens of other organizations throughout the United States received grants—all after a rigorous evaluation by the small staff of about twenty professionals. "Ed McMahon did not knock on my door," said Chuck Supple, president of Public Allies, which finds interns for nonprofit organizations. "These guys really kick the tires."

The *New York Times* also revealed that Feeney was the largest single American donor to Sinn Fein, the political wing of the Irish Republican Army (IRA). After a bombing in Enniskillen, Northern Ireland (in the county where Feeney's grandparents were from), which showed him that the violence needed to end, he concluded, "This is ridiculous. I must do something." Feeney's gift of $280,000 from his personal funds made possible the creation of a Washington office for Sinn Fein. He acknowledged that support for a group connected to the IRA was controversial, but insisted that he had taken steps to ensure that his donations supported nonviolent activities. According to the Irish journalist Conor O'Clery, Feeney was one of a small group of Irish Americans who served as intermediaries between Sinn Fein and the Clinton administration, helping to arrange a cease-fire in Northern Ireland in 1994.

Since 1997, Feeney has managed, once again, to resume his life beneath the radar, as a self-acknowledged "shabby billionaire," avoiding photographers, slipping into small apartments on several continents, dining alone in Tommy Makem's Irish Pavilion (a decidedly untrendy restaurant on East Fifty-seventh Street in Manhattan), and renting a house in Australia in 2000 for friends who wanted to watch the Olympic games. Divorced in 1991, he married Helga Flaiz in 1995. If anything, philanthropy now plays an even larger role in his life than before, with support for higher education, the reconstruction of Vietnam, and environmental reform in Australia among the projects that engage him. Among the most generous philanthropists in history, he remains, to the public at large, and to recipients of his largesse, "the anonymous donor."

Richard Alan Meier

❧ CLASS OF 1956

"Buildings are not organic, in that they don't grow, they don't change, and they don't [turn] green every spring," Richard Meier insists. "That which is man-made is different from that which is natural . . . And I think architecture should reflect that." The high priest of late-twentieth century modernism, and a premier architect of museums in Europe and the United States, Meier has won interna-

tional acclaim for his elegant "white houses" and austere, high-tech buildings that balance light, forms, and space, and that stand out from, rather than blending in with, the environment.

Richard Alan Meier was born in Newark, New Jersey, on October 12, 1934, the son of Jerome Meier, an electrical engineer, and Carolyn Kaltenbacher Meier, a homemaker. Educated at Columbia High School in Maplewood, New Jersey, he chose Cornell University in 1952 because its architecture students had the opportunity to take many liberal arts courses. Although he was wary of being influenced by a "single master," Meier found John Hartell, his first architectural design studio professor, "a great teacher." His multidisciplinary curriculum included a literature course with Vladimir Nabokov, a painting course with the talented and eccentric J. O. Mahoney, a planning course with John Reps, and lectures on Picasso and Matisse by Alan Solomon, later director of the Jewish Museum in New York City. Through his fraternity, Zeta Beta Tau, Meier met professors Arch and Esther Dotson, who became one of his first clients. They commissioned him to design a barn (and insisted that it be painted red) with a small attached residence on a hill near Cornell.

After receiving his bachelor's degree in architecture in 1957, Meier spent some time in Europe, where he met Le Corbusier, the French architect who provided the philosophical underpinnings of modern architecture, which he defined as "the masterly, correct, and magnificent play of mass brought together in light." Meier returned to the United States and apprenticed with Frank Grad and Sons; Davis, Brody and Wisniewski; Skidmore, Owings and Merrill; and Marcel Breuer and Associates. After work, he painted large abstract-expressionist canvases and made collages in the studio of his friend Frank Stella. In 1963, he opened his own firm, Richard Meier and Associates. His first professional commission, a home for his parents in Essex Falls, New Jersey, showed that he also had been influenced by the Kaufmann residence ("Falling Water") of Frank Lloyd Wright, the apostle of organic architecture. Wright and Le Corbusier, he claimed, shared a commitment to organizing space on a human scale. Meier's mentors had an influence as well on his presentation of self. "Meier has Wright's hair, Corb's eyeglasses, Philip Johnson's clothes, and Stanford White's social life," one wag observed. "If you think that isn't a very well-thought-out image, you don't know how architects' minds work."

In designing private houses in the 1960s, Meier tested his architectural vocabulary and values. He gained national attention with the Smith House in Darien, Connecticut, and an eleven-bedroom home in Old Westbury, New York, which *Newsweek* declared "a joy to see and romp in." By the 1970s Meier was designing commercial buildings and public structures that made him a poster boy of modern architecture, one of "the New York Five" (the others were Peter Eisenman, Michael Graves, Charles Gwathmey, and John Hejduk) who were dubbed "the whites" by cultural critic and novelist Tom Wolfe. "White is the ephemeral emblem of perpetual movement," Wolfe declared. "The white is always present but never the same, bright and rolling in the day, silver and effervescent under the full moon of New Year's Eve. . . . White is the light, the medium of understanding and transformative power." Meier transformed the thirteen-story Bell Telephone Building in Greenwich Village into 383 loft-style apartments. An early effort in "adaptive reuse," the Westbeth Artists Housing was at the time the world's largest artists' residence. Equally innovative were the several structures Meier designed for the New York State Department of Mental Hygiene. Completed in 1977, the largest was the Bronx Developmental Center, a facility providing total care for up to four hundred mentally handicapped individuals, which won the praise of critic Ada Louise Huxtable in the *New York Times* for bringing a "rigorous intellect and sensitive aesthetic" to "nearly insoluble problems." Meier followed with the Ave Simon Reading Room in the Guggenheim Museum in Manhattan (1978) and the Atheneum (1979), a visitor's center in the restored town of New Harmony, Indiana, on the banks of the Wabash River. The white porcelain enamel-clad structure, a reminder of the utopian visions of the town's founders, was a sharp contrast to its existing buildings. It was, Huxtable wrote, "as radical an addition to the rural American landscape as Le Corbusier's Villa Savoie was to the French countryside at Poissy half a century ago." In 1983 Meier completed the High Museum of Art in Atlanta. Two years later, his Museum of Decorative Arts opened in Frankfurt, Germany.

In 1984 Meier became the sixth recipient of the Pritzker Prize, the so-called Nobel Prize for architecture. Among his many other awards are the Royal Gold Medal of the Royal Institute of British Architects and the gold medal of the American Institute of Architects. During the 1980s and 1990s Meier designed an astonishing array of buildings in Europe and the United States. His work on the Continent included a new city hall and library for The Hague; the exhibition, training, and dining quarters for Max Weishaupt, GmbH, in Schwendi, Germany; the Ulm Exhibition and Assembly Building in Germany; and television studios and corporate headquarters for Canal+ in Paris. In the United States his projects included the Bridgeport Center in Connecticut, the Eye Center in Portland, Oregon, the Des Moines Arts Center addition, the Museum of Television and Radio in Beverly Hills, SwissAir's North American headquarters in Melville, New York, and the Madison Square Towers in New York City.

In 1984, after an eighteen-month competition that involved almost every master architect in the world, Meier was commissioned to design the J. Paul Getty Center in Los Angeles, a six-building complex (the world's richest museum and five art-related institutions) situated on 110 acres. Fourteen years in the making, at a cost of one billion dollars (the most expensive art institution of the century), the Getty opened in 1997. "If museums are the cathedrals of modern architecture," Bob Colacello gushed in *Vanity Fair,* "Richard Meier is completing his Chartres." The complex is not white. "They put it in my contract," Meier admits, because white was thought to be too jarring for a building under the bright Los Angeles sun. Criticized by some as an "overblown, overdesigned fortress" and as the architect "Meiering Meier," the Getty has also been praised as a masterful, even spiritual orchestration of "light and shadows, materials and volumes, views and human movements."

Six feet tall, with a shock of white hair, and a uniform of black suit, white shirt, and dark tie, Meier is restless and relentless. His marriage to Katherine Gormley in 1978 lasted long enough to produce two children, but the couple divorced within a few years. Although he spent two weeks of every month for ten years in Los Angeles, working on the Getty, Meier found time to design the Contemporary Art Museum of Barcelona, which opened in 1995. As the new millennium began, the commissions have kept coming, including one to build the Church of the Year 2000 in Rome and another to design the Life Sciences building at Cornell. Still, at the peak of his career, Meier, according to a friend, can never get "enough adulation, never enough commissions. If you're a builder, you want to build the world. You want to put your stamp on everything."

Stephen Michael Reich

~~ CLASS OF 1957

Steve Reich never liked the "minimalism" label that many critics attached to his music. Although many of his compositions depend on two or more instruments "playing the same melodic pattern one or more beats out of phase with each other," his music has evolved in complex ways that reflect Reich's education in Western classical music and his affinity for non-Western and vernacular American music, especially jazz.

Stephen Michael Reich was born in New York City on October 3, 1936. His parents, both from upper-middle-class Jewish families, separated when Reich was one year old. He stayed mostly with his father, Leonard, a successful New York lawyer, and was placed under the care of a governess. Frequent train trips carried him alone across the country to visit his mother, who became well known in the 1950s as the Broadway singer and lyricist June Carroll. Reich's father, expecting his son to become a lawyer or doctor, bothered with music only to the extent of providing his son with what Reich later called "middle-class piano lessons." At age fourteen Reich first heard music that would "end up motivating me to become a composer—jazz, Bach, and Stravinsky." At the same age he studied drumming with Roland Kohloff, who later became the principal timpanist with the New York Philharmonic. He formed a jazz ensemble in high school and made pocket money playing drums in dance bands, which he continued to do after he entered Cornell in 1953, just before his seventeenth birthday. In Ithaca, he was a member of the Joe Kurdle quintet. One listener observed that "Steve really swung on drums, but blew a little too loudly when the piano was soloing."

Reich chose Cornell with no intention of becoming a composer. He majored in philosophy and developed a particular interest in Ludwig Wittgenstein. However, as a student in several music courses he fell under the influence of Cornell's extraordinary musicologist William Austin, who combined his classical training with, for the time, an unusual academic interest in American popular music (he wrote a book on Stephen Foster) and non-Western music. Austin, who remained friends with Reich long after Reich received his bachelor's degree in 1957, encouraged him not to seek a postgraduate degree in philosophy at Harvard. Reich did not quite forget Wittgenstein, setting Wittgenstein's sentence "How small a thought to fill a whole life" in his 1996 work *Proverb*.

Instead of Harvard Reich returned to New York City where he studied privately for one year with Hall Overton, a composer who had worked with Thelonius Monk. From 1958 until 1961 he enrolled at Juilliard where his fellow students included Peter Schickele (later famous as PDQ Bach) and Philip Glass. Critics sometimes mention Glass and Reich in the same breath, but the two collaborated only briefly in the late 1960s. Judging Juilliard "conservative," in 1961 Reich "ran away from home" to San Francisco.

At first things out West did not go well. He had recently married Joyce Barkett, but the couple, who quickly had two children—an infant who died shortly after birth and a son, Michael—divorced in 1963. Reich drove a taxi, and enrolled in an M.A. program at Mills College to study composition with the eminent contemporary composer Luciano Berio. One of his classmates was Phil Lesh, later the bass guitarist for the Grateful Dead. Although he received an

M.A. from Mills in 1963, Reich was disappointed with his studies with Berio and found himself unsympathetic with the aims of the most famous names in modern music. "Everybody," he said, "was under the influence of music that was not 'pulsitile.' You can't tap your foot to either Boulez or John Cage." He was least kind to Elliott Carter who, he said, "should beg for forgiveness on Charles Ives' grave."

In his rejection of atonal music and his search for new ways to construct melodic patterns, Reich felt very much alone in the music world. He began to experiment with electronic music and formed an important contact with the composer Terry Riley. He also listened to John Coltrane at San Francisco's Jazz Center. Of the work he wrote and performed at the time, nothing has survived except *It's Gonna Rain,* his first demonstration of what he called "phasing." Reich said that he hit on phasing by accident while trying to get two tape recorders to play back a repeated fragment of taped music simultaneously. Small variations between the two machines caused one frame to slip slightly ahead of the other as they played back. Reich liked the effect, and in *It's Gonna Rain* he used it to emphasize the musical quality of the words of a black preacher he had recorded in San Francisco's Union Square. Phasing remained a trademark of Reich's work after he lost interest in electronic music and composed directly for the human voice and musical instruments.

In 1965 he moved back to New York City and took a loft in Tribeca. Most of his associates were sculptors, painters, and filmmakers rather than musicians. They were people "swimming in the same soup" who became his audience and his measure of what was working in his music. Although he recognized his limits as a performer, he decided that it was essential for him to play in all his compositions. "The pleasure I get from performing is not the pleasure of expressing myself," which he related to the misleading idea of improvisation, but of "subjugating myself to the music." In 1966 he organized Steve Reich and Musicians, which made its first European trip in 1971 and has since traveled the world, once even to Cornell where in 1972 they performed two of Reich's early phased pieces.

Reich's fame beyond a small circle of sophisticates began with *Drumming,* a composition that premiered at the Museum of Modern Art in late 1971, the same year that Michael Tilson Thomas led the Boston Symphony in a controversial performance of Reich's *Four Organs. Drumming* took an hour and a half to perform and marked the first time Reich employed a mixed ensemble of instruments and human voices. In 1970, he had traveled to Africa to study with the Ghanaian drummer Gideon Alorwoye. Malaria shortened his intended stay, but from then on Reich pursued an interest in world music, not to become an "exotic" composer contemptuous of Western traditions (a pose he caustically rejected) but to learn from unfamiliar ideas. In 1973 and 1974 he studied gamelan music with the recognized master of Balinese music and dance, I Nyoman Sumandhi, and in 1976 went to Jerusalem to study Hebrew cantillation. In Israel he became so involved in his Jewish roots that he almost left music to become a rabbi. Instead, he set a Hebrew text from Psalms for voice and ensemble in *Tehillim,* a composition that premiered in West Germany in 1981.

Reich has often worked in collaboration with his second wife, Beryl Korot, a pioneer in video art whom Reich married in 1976. In addition to a son, Ezra, they have produced a multimedia/audiovisual opera, *The Cave,* which uses a text from the Torah; and *Three Tales: A Documentary Video Opera,* which explores the implications of technology. The entire work, composed of the three parts "Hindenburg," "Bikini," and "Dolly," premiered at the Vienna Festival in May 2002. Other works have been commissioned and performed by major orchestras in the major music centers of Europe and the United

States. *Different Trains,* premiered and then recorded by the Kronos Quartet in 1988, won the Grammy Award in 1989 for the year's Best Contemporary Composition. In 1997 Nonesuch Records released the ten-disc *Steve Reich Works 1965–1995.*

The recipient of awards and grants from many of America's major foundations, including the Koussevitsky Foundation Award in 1981, Reich has moved a long way from the isolation he felt early in his career and plays to sold-out houses both at Carnegie Hall and the Bottom Line jazz/rock nightclub. Although one writer in the *New York Times* called Reich's output "extended navel-observation," England's *The Guardian* more accurately placed Reich among "a handful of living composers who can legitimately claim to have altered the direction of musical history."

Thomas Ruggles Pynchon Jr.

ᔛ CLASS OF 1959

Unlike some other famous novelists associated with Cornell—Pearl S. Buck, Toni Morrison, William Gass, and Kurt Vonnegut—Thomas Pynchon Jr. has an undergraduate degree. Relatively few other facts about his adult personal life are as certain. Pynchon does not live in seclusion but neither does he give interviews or have friends who talk about him. His life, like his fiction, poses puzzles.

Pynchon was born on May 8, 1937, in Glen Cove, Long Island. On his father's side, his lineage stretches back to the founding of the Massachusetts Bay Colony. William Pynchon, who serves as a model for William Slothrop in *Gravity's Rainbow,* crossed the Atlantic in 1630, became one of the founders of Springfield, and wrote an anti-Calvinist tract that was the first book publicly burned in Boston. The first Thomas Ruggles Pynchon lived in the eighteenth century, and another of that name wrote Nathaniel Hawthorne in the nineteenth century to complain about his defaming of the family in *The House of the Seven Gables.* Pynchon's mother, Katherine Frances Bennett Pynchon, was Catholic and reared Thomas and his two siblings, a sister and a brother, in that faith. His father, an industrial surveyor, became town supervisor of Oyster Bay.

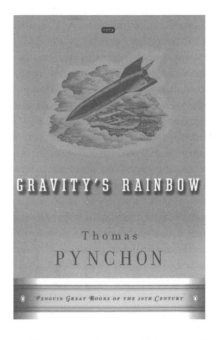

In 1953, at the age of sixteen, Pynchon graduated from Oyster Bay High School as the class salutatorian and winner of an award given to the student with the highest average in English. With a scholarship, he entered Cornell in the fall of 1953 to study engineering physics. After his sophomore year, he left Cornell to join the Navy, but returned to Ithaca in 1957, switching his major to English. He took a course with Vladimir Nabokov and joined the staff of *The Cornell Writer,* the undergraduate literary magazine, which published Pynchon's first story, "The Small Rain," in 1959. He read constantly and, according to one friend, skimmed through mathematics books for fun. Pynchon kept his picture out of the 1959 *Cornellian,* the year he took a bachelor's degree in English "with distinction in all subjects," and no photograph of him, except for a high school snapshot, has ever been published.

Because of his friendship with Richard Farina, we know something about Pynchon's Cornell years. Farina was a gregarious social activist whose second marriage was to Mimi Baez, the sister of Joan. He had a career as a singer-songwriter until 1966, when, shortly after the publication of *Been Down So Long It Looks Like Up to Me,* he was killed in a motorcycle accident. Pynchon credited Farina with introducing him to women and to a social life at Cornell. They "hung out" together at Johnny's Big Red Grill, where Peter Yarrow had a "standing gig." They once attended a masquerade party together, with Farina dressed as Hemingway and Pynchon as F. Scott Fitzgerald. "1958," Pynchon wrote, "was another planet. You have to appreciate the extent of sexual repression on that campus at the time." In May of that year Pynchon followed Farina in a student-led protest against Cornell's parietal rules. The students marched to the home of the president, threw eggs at him, and deployed a smoke bomb. Some say the Sixties at Cornell began that night.

After graduation Pynchon turned down a Woodrow Wilson Fellowship for postgraduate study, a position teaching creative writing at Cornell, and a job at *Esquire* magazine. Instead, he moved to Greenwich Village to work on his first novel. He continued to write it after he left New York to work as an engineering aide for Boeing Aircraft in Seattle. Finally, after more work on the novel while he lived in California and Mexico, Pynchon published *V* in 1963. It won the William Faulkner Foundation award for the year's best first novel. Three years later, a second, shorter novel appeared, *The Crying of Lot 49.* It received the Rosenthal Foundation Award of the National Institute of Arts and Letters. However, it was in 1973, with the publication of *Gravity's Rainbow,* that Pynchon secured his position as a major American writer. Dedicated to Farina, the novel begins with the chilling sentence "A screaming comes across the sky." The letter "V" reappears in *Gravity's Rainbow* in the destructive form of a German V-2 rocket.

Named co-winner that year with Isaac Bashevis Singer of the National Book Award, Pynchon protected his now famous anonymity by sending the comedian Irwin Corey, a master of double-talk, to accept the prize. He turned down the Howells Medal of the American Academy of Arts and Letters, saying it "is a great honor . . . but I don't want it." What he would have done about the Pulitzer Prize for *Gravity's Rainbow,* the unanimous choice of the jury, is anyone's guess since the Pulitzer advisory board overruled the jury, calling Pynchon's novel "unreadable, turgid, overwritten, and obscure."

Asked about the difficulty of his work, Pynchon simply said, "Why should anything be easy to understand?" The world he evoked was shapeless, chaotic, and ruled, if that is the right word, by mysterious forces that never quite revealed themselves. Pynchon had many vocabularies to throw at his reader—that of physics, mathematics, world literature, music from opera to jazz, and every variety of pop culture. Pynchon loved *The Wizard of Oz* and, according to his sister, watched "cruddy TV." The situations faced by his characters, an army of them, are comic and sinister at the same time. Salman Rushdie, whose own novels pose dizzying and exhilarating enigmas to their readers, identifies entropy as a central metaphor in Pynchon's work—"entropy, seen as a slow, debauched, never-ending party, a perpetual coming down."

Pynchon followed *Gravity's Rainbow* with a long silence. A collection of five stories, *Slow Learner,* appeared in 1984, and he received a MacArthur Fellowship award in 1988, an unsolicited award made in recognition of "genius." Only in 1990, however, after many mistaken rumors had circulated about the author, did Pynchon publish *Vineland,* a long novel set in California whose characters included Prairie Wheeler, Brock Vond, and a music group named Billy Barf and the Vomitones. That was followed in 1997 by *Mason and Dixon,* a novel based on the imagined exploits of the two men who drew the famous line separating Pennsylvania from Maryland.

Although he was deeply influenced by the radicalism of the 1960s ("every weirdo in the world is on my wavelength"), Pynchon never imagined an easy way out of modern social problems. In an article he wrote for the *New York Times Magazine* in 1966, "A Journey into the Mind of Watts," Pynchon attacked American racism. His novels are political insofar as they suggest the absurdity of a world that deliberately courts its own destruction and tolerates the cynical greed of its leaders. Some critics have seen a glimmer of hope in his more recent novels. That may be so, but in Pynchon's fictional landscapes the odds against redemption are very high. A 1984 article he wrote for the *New York Times Book Review,* "Is It OK to Be a Luddite?", suggested that no one could survey the human prospect with an easy conscience. A "succession of the criminally insane" had held power since 1945. Even President Eisenhower saw the problem when he left office. "There is now a permanent power establishment of admirals, generals and corporate CEOs, up against whom us average poor bastards are completely outclassed," Pynchon wrote. Even without power Pynchon's poor bastards enjoy a few good things, perhaps the most important of which is the gift of laughter.

Peter Yarrow

✌ CLASS OF 1959

Less than two years after he sang to enthusiastic crowds during a six-week engagement at Johnny's Big Red Grill in Collegetown, Peter Yarrow became part of a trio whose "songs of conscience" would make them icons in the civil rights and anti-Vietnam War crusades.

The principal influence on Peter, who was born on May 31, 1938, in New York City, was his mother, Vera Yarrow, a teacher of English, speech, and drama in the public schools and a diction coach to singers and authors. "A progressive with a capital P," he recalls, "she believed deeply in the possibility of a more just society." Vera also encouraged Peter to take up music. Infatuated with folk music by the time he was ten, he gave up the violin for the guitar. Always ready with a song, he spent his "four happiest years" at Manhattan's High School of Music and Art.

At Cornell from 1955 to 1959 as a psychology major, Yarrow encountered conservative, complacent students who were more interested in panty raids, fraternity parties, and a brew or two at Zinck's than in fighting "for something they felt was important." As a freshman, he was stung when a fraternity rejected him, with one member commenting, "I think you're in the wrong room." Yarrow found another fraternity, but recalls that he joined only because he was lonely. But it was at Cornell that he began to understand the power of music to move people. As a teaching assistant in Professor Harold W. Thompson's

course, "Folk Ballads and Folk Literature"—
dubbed "Rompin' and Stompin'" by undergraduates—he sang songs at the end of each
Saturday class to almost one thousand students. During sing-alongs and other events he
organized as president of the Folk Song Club,
students became "sensitized and connected
with each other." More than entertainment,
Yarrow wanted music to be "a transformational process."

After graduation, Yarrow planned to sing
in nightclubs for a year or two to help finance
graduate study in psychology. In Greenwich
Village, Yarrow's manager, Albert Grossman,
thought of teaming him with Mary Travers,
another folk musician from New York. When
their voices did not blend, Grossman added
(Noel) Paul Stookey, a one-time rock 'n'
roller and aspiring stand-up comedian from
Birmingham, Michigan. The trio tried "Mary
Had a Little Lamb" for an hour during their
first session, rehearsed for seven months in
Travers's three-flight walk-up apartment, then
debuted at the Bitter End in 1961 as Peter,
Paul and Mary. After appearances at the fa-
bled Gate of Horn in Chicago, the Hungry i
in San Francisco, and the Blue Angel in Manhattan, they embarked on a touring schedule
of about two hundred dates a year that would
last a decade. By 1970 they had produced
eight gold and five platinum albums.

In the confident days of 1964 Yarrow believed that the group could "mobilize the
youth of America in a way that nobody else
would." Their version of "If I Had a Hammer" (which Yarrow had heard the Weavers
sing in Carnegie Hall when he was a high
school student) became an anthem for propo-
nents of racial equality. Their versions of Bob
Dylan's "Blowin' In the Wind" and "The
Times They Are A-Changin'" helped spark
the passions of young men and women committed to social justice. Peter, Paul and Mary
tried to practice what they preached. They
joined Martin Luther King Jr. for the March
on Washington in 1963 and two years later
marched with King again in Selma, Alabama.
Deeply involved in the antiwar movement,

they performed at demonstrations, fund-rais-
ers, and teach-ins. In 1968, while on a nationwide tour to support Eugene McCarthy's
campaign for the Democratic Party nomination for president, Yarrow met Mary Beth
McCarthy, a niece of the Minnesota senator.
He married her in 1969, the year he helped
organize an antiwar March on Washington
that attracted half a million people. They have
two children.

Intense, idealistic, and didactic, Yarrow
showed a whimsical and wistful side in "Puff
the Magic Dragon," a song he wrote while
still at Cornell. In the spring of 1959 Yarrow's
friend Lenny Lipton, a physics major who
would later invent the stereoscopic display
used in computer work stations, read Ogden
Nash's poem "Really-o-Truly-o-Dragon"
while browsing in the library at Willard
Straight Hall. As he walked home, he
dreamed up his own poem, banged it out on
a typewriter, and showed it to Yarrow, who
set it to music. "Puff" is a simple story, told
in 156 words, of a dragon that has an adventure with a little boy, and then gets depressed
and retires to a cave when his friend leaves.
Audiences respond to it, Yarrow believes, not
because it allegedly has a subtext about
drugs—an idea that Yarrow called "ludi-
crous"—but because adults still hope and
dream and have adventures with their drag-
ons. In 1962, after Yarrow tracked down Lipton and added his name as coauthor, Peter,
Paul and Mary recorded the song. "Puff the
Magic Dragon" sold half a million copies
within a month of its release. Versions of the
song exist in German, Yiddish, Japanese, and
Hawaiian. A children's book extended the
story and in the 1970s CBS TV produced a series of animated features based on "Puff,"
which earned Yarrow an Emmy nomination.

In 1970 Peter, Paul and Mary decided to
pursue individual interests and disbanded.
Yarrow continued his political activism, while
completing solo music projects, cowriting
and producing the No. 1 hit "Torn Between
Two Lovers." But before the decade ended
the trio reunited for Survival Sunday, an anti-

nuclear benefit at the Hollywood Bowl to stop the Diablo Canyon nuclear power plant from going on line. Since 1978, they have played as many as forty dates a year, recorded several albums, and produced specials for PBS. Hoping to give children, "who are so frequently marginalized," a voice, in 1993 they recorded the album *Peter, Paul and Mommy, Too* (the name Mary's daughter Erica gave the group). In 1996 Yarrow earned another Emmy nomination, this time for the group's *Great Performances* special "Lifelines Live."

"The ethic behind songs of conscience doesn't change," Yarrow believes, "even though the issues are altered from generation to generation." His song "Light One Candle" has become an anthem for Judaism's commitment to a better world, while "No Easy Walk to Freedom" contributed to the struggle against apartheid and "The Great Mandala" was a protest against war. By himself, or with Mary Travers and Paul Stookey, Yarrow has been a part of virtually every progressive cause in the United States for four decades — reproductive freedom; gun control advocacy; the United Farm Workers; the sanctuary movement for refugees from Nicaragua and

El Salvador; advocacy for the homeless; the Children's Defense Fund; the fight for a cleaner environment. He has also encouraged new artists and performers through his work with the Guggenheim Museum's "Learning Through Art" program; the Newport Folk Festival, which he helped launch in 1962; and the Kerrville Folk Festival, which he co-founded more than a quarter of a century ago. Among the numerous awards he has won is the Allard K. Lowenstein Award, bestowed on him in 1982 for "remarkable efforts in advancing the causes of human rights, peace, and freedom."

Although the social activism that characterized the 1960s is not as prevalent as it was then and although "signs of poverty and inequity are everywhere," Yarrow remains an optimist about the prospects for "repairing the world." "We're part of a long train ride," he says. "People can overcome their differences, and when united, move toward a world of greater fairness and justice. As in folk music, each person has a unique role to play." Until that happens, Yarrow will not declare, as he did in one of his most popular songs, that his "Day Is Done."

Janet Reno

CLASS OF 1960

When news broke of the disaster at Waco, Texas — with approximately eighty dead, about twenty of them children — U.S. Attorney General Janet Reno spoke simply and with evident anguish to the national television audience: "I made the decision. I am accountable. The buck stops here." She was acclaimed a national hero for a candor almost unprecedented in a political figure. A child of the palmetto scrublands on the edge of south Florida's Everglades, who had early taken Abraham Lincoln as one of her models, Janet Reno has long preferred a kind of rugged

honesty to pretension and display.

She was born in Miami on July 21, 1938 to journalist parents. Her father, a Danish immigrant who had changed his name from Rasmussen to Reno, worked the police beat for the *Miami Herald* for forty-three years; her mother was an investigate reporter who liked alcohol, alligator wrestling, and poetry.

When the family moved near the Everglades, Jane Reno dug the foundation of the family home while Henry installed the plumbing in the evenings. Resourceful, intellectual, and principled, Jane and Henry Reno raised four independent children. Permitted no TV, Reno and her sister and two brothers roamed the scrubland, camping, canoeing, and visiting the Miccosukees, a neighboring Indian tribe. Almost six feet tall at eleven years old, young Janet Reno never slouched. She dreamed of being a baseball pitcher but settled on becoming a lawyer when she was fifteen because she "didn't want anybody telling me what to do."

Her parents sold pieces of the family property to finance Reno's education at Cornell; the university appealed to Reno because its academic excellence was accompanied by a longstanding commitment to women's education. Reno majored in chemistry because her mother thought women had difficulty making it in the law. The south Florida freshman remembers freezing in the upstate New York winters. She kept her distance from the social life of fraternities and sororities, working hard and often "staying up all night writing papers." She waited on tables and worked as a dorm monitor. In her senior year Reno was elected president of the Women's Student Government Association. What she particularly remembers of her years at Cornell, however, is introducing former President Harry Truman at a Cornell appearance.

After receiving her degree in 1960 and deciding she was not "cut out to be a scientist," Reno applied to and was one of sixteen women (another was Pat Schroeder from Colorado) in a class of five hundred accepted to Harvard Law School. After graduating in 1963, Reno returned to Miami and was promptly denied a position in a large Miami law firm because of her gender. She joined a smaller firm, Brigham and Brigham, where she specialized in eminent domain law. In 1967 she became the junior partner in the Miami firm of Lewis and Reno.

Five years later, after an unsuccessful campaign for the Florida State legislature, Reno, a Democrat, entered public service as an assistant state attorney in the Magistrate and Juvenile Court in Dade County. From 1973 to 1976 she was the administrative assistant to the state attorney in Dade County but then returned to private practice as a partner in a prestigious Miami law firm, Steel, Hector, and Davis.

Reno's big break occurred in 1978 when the state attorney for Dade County, elected in 1976 to a four-year term, decided to retire and suggested that Governor Reuben Askew appoint her to complete his term. Reno, the first woman to head a county prosecutor's office in Florida, had a staff of 900 employees, including 238 attorneys who handled more than 120,000 cases a year. She was elected to the position in her own right in 1980 with 74 percent of the vote, even though she ran as a Democrat in a predominantly Republican county, and was reelected in 1984, 1988, and 1992.

The most difficult and controversial episode in her years as prosecutor occurred early in 1980 when she was accused of mishandling the prosecution of four white police officers charged with beating to death Arthur McDuffie, an unarmed and handcuffed black insurance salesman. Following the acquittal of the officers rioting broke out in the Liberty City section of Miami, leading to eighteen deaths and $200 million in property damage. Stung by charges that her own racism explained why she had failed to present a convincing case to the all-white jury, Reno, a lifelong member of the NAACP, angrily denied the accusation but also took positive action. Her office aggressively tackled issues important to minorities, while appointing more blacks and Latinos to high positions in the State Attorney's office. Reno became one of Dade County's most respected public servants, respected by both minorities and whites.

In her fifteen years as chief prosecutor for Florida's most populous county, Reno acquired a reputation as a hands-on administrator with a no-nonsense, albeit compassionate, manner. "A tough, tough lady. She has a soft genteel way about her, but she is an adversary of steel," is how Seymour Gelber, the former mayor of Miami Beach, remembers those years. Reno established one of the first sexual battery units in a prosecutor's office in the country, which included a support center for children who were victims of sexual abuse. She established an innovative drug court that steered first-time offenders into counseling, not prison; it became a model for others around the country. Her vigorous prosecution of deadbeat fathers who did not pay child support was celebrated in a rap song.

In late 1992 the transition team for President-elect Bill Clinton, looking for a woman, sounded out Reno about becoming U.S. Attorney General. Wanting to be with her mother, who was dying of lung cancer, Reno said she was not interested. However, by February 1993, when Clinton's first two choices for attorney general, Zoë Baird and Judge Kimba Wood, had drawn public criticism for employing illegal immigrants in their homes, Reno changed her mind. Her mother had died and she could move to Washington. Confirmed unanimously by the Senate, she was sworn in on March 12, 1993, as the seventy-eighth, and first female, United States Attorney General.

She immediately faced a crisis. David Koresh and his Branch Davidian followers had been locked in a tense confrontation with federal law enforcement officials for several weeks. They had barricaded themselves in their compound outside Waco, Texas, after federal officials had tried to serve a search warrant. After becoming convinced that the children inside the compound were being physically abused, Reno ordered an FBI tear gas attack, intended to force the cult members out of the building. Instead, one of the Branch Davidians set fire to the compound and some eighty people were killed, including about twenty children. (Critics say the government caused the fire with its use of pyrotechnic tear gas and incendiary flares.) The candor and obvious anguish with which she addressed a news conference that day, taking full responsibility for the tragedy, and her distraught appearances later on several TV news programs, won admiration from the American people.

Despite their occasionally stormy relationship, Reno proved to be President Clinton's most resilient cabinet member, remaining attorney general through his entire two terms. She was always the center of controversy whether under attack from Democrats for referring too many cases dealing with Clinton's cabinet secretaries to independent counsels or from Republicans for protecting President Clinton and Vice President Gore from investigations of alleged fund-raising improprieties. She was responsible for the arrest of the Unabomber, Theodore J. Kaczynski, at his Montana shack in 1996, and for the antitrust suit against the Microsoft Corporation in 1998. And it was Reno who made the controversial decision in 2000 to seize six-year-old Elián González, the Cuban refugee, and reunite him with his father in Cuba.

Through the glitzy and excessive Clinton years Americans saw a no-frills Reno, a six-feet two-inch utterly unpretentious woman with little makeup, big glasses, and plain dresses. She avoided private dining rooms, taking her meals with fellow employees in the Justice Department cafeteria. Instead of chauffeured limos she walked from her apartment on Connecticut Avenue to her office. A serious woman, but capable of surprising playfulness, she delighted TV watchers by unexpectedly showing up on NBC's *Saturday Night Live* and joining the comics who had regularly and mercilessly lampooned her.

When she stepped down as attorney general in 2001, Reno, who has never married, told the press that she was "going to sit on her front porch and do nothing, perhaps take a kayak trip in the Everglades, maybe write a book or practice law." But the lure of politics won out and Reno decided to try to unseat Jeb Bush in 2002 and become governor of Florida. She was defeated, alas, in the Democratic Party primary. Meanwhile, Reno has been appointed a Frank H. T. Rhodes occasional visiting professor by her alma mater for five years. Cornell's distinguished chemistry major has come back to East Hill.

Jane Ellen Brody

❧ CLASS OF 1962

Jane Brody put on ten pounds in her first year at Cornell. The woman later crowned America's "high priestess of health" by *Time* magazine couldn't resist the all-you-can-eat cafeterias she found in college, and she left East Hill a lot chubbier than when she arrived.

Born on May 19, 1941, Brody described her early family life in the Prospect Park area of Brooklyn as "liberated." Her mother, Lillian, an elementary school teacher, always worked. Sidney, her father, a lawyer and civil servant, was a "woman's libber" who helped do the shopping, cooking, and washing. He always liked having healthy foods like bread and fresh fruit around the house. Jane was taught to eat her serving "and that was it." The Brodys encouraged their daughter to be whatever she dreamed of. After she announced at four that she wanted to be a veterinarian her father talked to her for years about the veterinary college at Cornell. At Brooklyn's James Madison High School Brody was a cheerleader, star student, and the editor of the school newspaper her senior year. That same year, a month before graduation, her mother died of ovarian cancer.

Brody didn't go to the vet school, but to the College of Agriculture, where she majored in biochemistry to prepare for a career as a research scientist. She was a member of the Pi Delta Epsilon sorority and took physical education classes every semester at Cornell, but most of the time she studied. She has described herself in college as a "super-achievement-oriented, all-work-no-play student." It paid off—she graduated number two in her Cornell class.

A summer internship as a National Science Foundation fellow at the College of Agriculture's Experiment Station in Geneva, New York, turned her against laboratory research. "What was fun for ten weeks," she decided, "when projected to ten years was not so enticing. I could see myself shortly talking to test tubes." Her ultimate vocation emerged unexpectedly from a Gannett counselor's advice. Brody had sought help for what she describes as an undergraduate "emotional meltdown." The counselor told her that she was studying too hard and should relax more, perhaps by joining a campus club. She promptly joined the staff of the *Cornell Countryman,* the ag college's publication, and became editor in chief her senior year. "I woke up one day and said, 'I love this,'" she remembers. "Why don't I do this?" She had found her calling as a journalist and writer.

Still interested in science, however, she went from Cornell to the University of Wisconsin's science journalism program. From there she got her first job as a journalist for the *Minneapolis Tribune,* where for two years she covered some science in between stories on murders and city parks. She felt lonely and different during these years in the Midwest; finding the locals too reticent, Brody turned to food. The ten pounds she'd put on at Cornell had become forty by 1965. That November, in a supreme act of will, she stopped snacking and binge eating and confined herself to three healthy meals a day. To her amazement, she started shedding weight.

Her life took an even more dramatic turn that year. On a trip back to New York she learned of an opening for a science writer at the *New York Times*. After what she thought would be a perfunctory interview, the twenty-four-year-old Brody was hired by editor Abe Rosenthal. For the next eleven years she was a general science reporter for the *Times*, specializing in articles on medicine, health, and biology. She was given her own column, "Personal Health," in the new "Living" section of the *Times* in November 1976, and her first piece was on jogging. Her column was soon syndicated in over one hundred newspapers and Brody received more mail than any other regular columnist for the *Times*. Doctors photocopied her articles for their patients.

Brody's "Personal Health" column brought significant changes to the staid and proper prose of the *New York Times*. She wrote on sensitive topics such as impotence, masturbation, and frigidity. She was the first writer to have the term *sexual intercourse* on page one of the *Times* and to get the words *ejaculation* and *penis* in the paper. Her story on how the overwhelming majority of women fail to achieve orgasm without direct stimulation of the clitoris made it into the paper only after the wife of editor Arthur Gelb told her husband how important it was for men to know this.

In the 1970s and 1980s the name Jane Brody became synonymous with healthy living. *Jane Brody's Nutrition Book* (1981) *and Jane Brody's Good Food Book* (1985) stayed on the best-seller lists for weeks, while her *Family Circle* articles expanded her audience to millions. She was widely sought after on the lecture circuit, some years speaking as many as fifty times. In 1986 she did a ten-week healthy cooking show on PBS.

Her message in the *Times* and in her books was simple: Healthy eating means cutting back on fats and sugar, increasing the intake of the complex carbohydrates in pasta, potato, bread, and rice, and eating more peas and beans, fruits and vegetables. Brody urged Americans to eat in moderation, to drop the "I deserve it" view, in which, for example, people reason that they worked hard all week and deserve some treats on the weekend. Good nutrition and regular exercise is her antidote to stress. She is up at five daily to take a four-mile jog or to go on a ten-mile bike ride.

The secret of Brody's success as a popular writer on health and food is her unique talent for translating complicated and technical material about medical subjects and nutrition into the language of her everyday readers. Doctors take her seriously. They recognize the exhaustive research behind her articles—she reads some thirty medical journals and trade publications weekly. The editor of *American Health,* Robert Barnett, believes that "she has done more than any other journalist to bring accurate information about nutrition and health to the public." Dr. Ernst Wynder, president of the American Health Foundation, goes further: "When it comes to preventive advice she is more on target than most doctors."

The new frontier for the woman who made pasta respectable is writing about aging and preserving youthful energy and enthusiasm. She still writes for the *Times,* now often about life for sixty–somethings. And she still lives in Brooklyn, in a brownstone in Park Slope, minutes from where she was born. She has been married since 1966 to Richard Engquist, a theatrical lyricist who was coauthor of some of her earliest books. Her twin sons are grown and now the feisty, dynamic Brody, a trim five-feet, 105 pounds, comes back to campus occasionally to talk to Cornellians about good health and well-being, hers and theirs. She tells the students about the Gannett counselor and the *Cornell Countryman.* "That's how," Brody proudly announces, "I got to be a journalist."

Peter Kornel Gogolak

❧ CLASS OF 1964

"All Cornell ever wants," a reporter wrote, "is Pete Gogolak with the wind behind him in the fourth quarter." A decade after Gogolak's graduation, every college and professional football team wanted a soccer-style place-kicker.

Peter Kornel Gogolak was born on April 18, 1942, in wartime Budapest. When John Gogolak, a dentist and a physician, returned from the army, he and his wife Serolta provided a comfortable life for Pete and his younger brother, Charlie. A good student, Pete could not remember a time when he did not have a soccer ball. At thirteen, he made the prestigious Ferencvaros team, popularly known as Fradi, which often played before fifty thousand fans. Pete's happiness, and that of his family, however, was tempered by their conviction that the communist regime in Hungary limited freedom and opportunity. When the government forced the Gogolaks to share their home with another family, John decided to leave. The chaos of the Hungarian Revolution in the fall of 1956 gave the family its chance. Although Serolta was pregnant, the Gogolaks walked twenty miles to the Austrian border, with rifle fire crackling around them as they escaped. When President Eisenhower eased U.S. immigration quotas for Hungarians, the Gogolaks joined thirty-eight thousand of their countrymen as "parolees" and later, as American citizens.

After a short stay at Camp Kilmer, New Jersey, Dr. Gogolak got a job at St. Lawrence State Hospital, and the family settled in Ogdensburg, New York. Pete taught himself English and completed the last three years at Ogdensburg Free Academy in two. Since there was no soccer team at his school, he tried out for football, first as an end and then as a placekicker, finding that he could generate more power by sweeping his leg across the ball, soccer-style, and kicking it with the

side of his foot rather than by kicking it straight forward. After the Big Red hockey coach, Paul Patten, stumbled across Gogolak during a visit to northern New York and recommended him to the recruiters in football, Cornell offered him an academic scholarship for the fall of 1960. He accepted, but only after Syracuse turned him down. Its coaches believed that the film clip Gogolak had sent of himself kicking the ball out of the end zone had to be a fake because such a kick of that length seemed impossible.

At Cornell Gogolak declared a zoology major, ran track, and, as a member of Delta Upsilon fraternity, became comfortable with American social mores, including dating. But he spent most of his time on the football field, experimenting with his kicking to give more lift to the ball and to control the direction. To prevent a kick from being blocked, he worked on booting the ball 1.4 seconds after it was snapped by the center to the holder. In an era when there were few if any kicking specialists, in college or the professional ranks, Gogolak became a star. He kicked three field goals in his first game for the varsity, including a forty-eight yarder. In his senior year, a fifty-yard kick against Lehigh was the longest in the nation. From 1961 until 1963 he converted on fifty-four of fifty-five extra points, including a collegiate record forty-four in a row. Before he graduated in 1964, Gogolak had decided on a career in football, not dentistry, and switched his major to art. He was probably the only kicker, he quipped, who could tell the difference between a Dürer and a Rembrandt.

The coaches of the National Football League did not know what to make of a soccer-style kicker. To Gogolak's dismay, he was not drafted by a single NFL team. Only the Buffalo Bills of the upstart American Football League were willing to take a chance on him. With an $11,000 salary and a $2,500 signing bonus, Gogolak became a pro. In his first year he helped take the Bills to the championship, kicking nineteen of twenty-seven field goals, and emerging as the second-highest scorer in the league. During what would be a second stellar season (he kicked a then-record twenty-eight field goals), Gogolak began to chafe at his paltry salary. In case his football fortunes fizzled, he continued to take courses in hotel and restaurant management at Cornell. He decided to play out his option with the Bills, hiring agent Fred Corcoran to represent him. "I believe in the free enterprise system," he explained. "That's why I came to this country." Gogolak and Corcoran met secretly with Wellington Mara, owner of the New York Giants of the NFL. Gogolak would become the first top-flight player to jump from the AFL to the NFL, igniting a "grid war" for free agents that became an incentive for owners to conclude negotiations for a merger between the rival leagues.

Gogolak spent nine years with the Giants and remains their leading scorer. More importantly, as his soccer-style kicking caught on, it revolutionized professional football. In 1966 Charlie Gogolak, who had competed against his brother as the Princeton placekicker, joined the Washington Redskins of the NFL. That same year Garo Yepremian brought his leg to the league, and in 1967 the Norwegian Jan Stenerud was signed. By the mid-1980s every kicker in professional football was a side-winder. The newcomers were far more proficient than their straight-forward predecessors. In 1963, NFL kickers made 48.6 percent of their field goals. A decade later, they converted on 63.1 percent of their attempts, and by 1993 the percentage had soared to 76.6, even though the goal posts had been moved from the front to the back of the end zone in 1974. Artificial turf and gust-free domed stadiums, which Gogolak called "a kicker's paradise," certainly contributed to the accuracy of placekickers, but most of the credit goes to the soccer style that Gogolak brought from Budapest.

Some football fans felt the kickers were so successful they had made the game duller. Rather than gambling that the offense could run or pass for a first down or a touchdown, coaches chose a relatively sure three points. By 1993 NFL teams made three field goals for every four touchdowns. The rules makers took steps to discourage field goal attempts in 1994. After a missed field goal outside of the twenty-yard line, the defensive team was awarded the ball at the spot of the kick, instead of at the line of scrimmage. And teams were given the option of passing or running for two points after a touchdown, instead of kicking for a single point. It was the first time in seventy-four years that the NFL had changed its scoring rules.

His life off the playing field gave Gogolak nothing to kick about. In 1970, he married Kathy Sauer, a stewardess for Eastern Airlines. They have two children. Gogolak prepared a career for himself after football. While he was with the Giants, he started Peter Gogolak Sports, Inc. Telling audiences about his escape from Hungary and about his kicking innovations, he booked himself as a speaker to campus and corporate audiences. More recently, Gogolak has served as vice president for sales at R. R. Donnelley Financial, a printing business. He lives in Darien, Connecticut, where he continues to receive requests to discuss his place in football history. "I don't look at soccer-style kicking as something I created," Gogolak says. "Frankly, I'm amazed nobody else saw the potential."

Thomas Jacob Peters

∿ CLASS OF 1964

He describes himself as a "gadfly, curmudgeon, champion of bold failures, prince of disorder, maestro of zest, corporate cheerleader, lover of markets, capitalist pig, and card-carrying member of the American Civil Liberties Union." Author of the most successful book on business management ever written, Tom Peters did not invent the field, but, according to the management educator and consultant Warren Bennis, he "vivified it, and yes, popularized it and legitimized it as a worthy endeavor."

Thomas Jacob Peters was born on November 7, 1942, in Baltimore, Maryland. Frank Peters, his father, worked for forty-one years for Baltimore Gas & Electric Company. Evelyn Snow Peters, his mother, had the greatest influence on Tom. A fifth-grade teacher, she was "a talker who raised a talker," instilling in her son an intellectual curiosity and love of reading. A fine student in high school, Tom excelled as well in extracurricular activities, especially debating. In 1960, he entered Cornell with a Navy ROTC scholarship to study architecture. After a semester, he switched to civil engineering. In five years at Cornell—he stayed on for a master's degree in industrial engineering—Peters played varsity lacrosse and was treasurer of Phi Gamma Delta fraternity, where he shared quarters with Ken Blanchard, whose 1983 book *The One Minute Manager* would appear with Peters on the best-seller list. Another Cornell classmate, John Naisbitt, made the list that year as well, with *Megatrends*. Although he graduated near the top of his class, Peters was "mad at Cornell because I went for five years without reading anything apart from the crap you have to read in engineering textbooks."

After graduation, Peters paid the Navy back with four years of service that included two tours of duty in Vietnam and a stint at the Pentagon. Discharged in 1970, he enrolled at Stanford, completing an MBA and a Ph.D.

While working on his doctorate, he became a consultant in the Washington, D.C., office of Peat, Marwick, Mitchell & Co. and then director of a committee on international narcotics control for the Office of Management and Budget. In 1974, Peters left Washington to join the management consulting firm McKinsey and Company in San Francisco.

In his work for McKinsey as principal practice leader in organizational effectiveness, Peters developed a model, dubbed the "magnificent seven," that was presented in a logo later called "the happy atom." Designed to help managers understand the complexities of organizational change, the model stressed attention to systems, strategy, structure, style, skills, shared values, and staff. Recommendations developed by Peters and his McKinsey colleague Robert Waterman Jr. were circulated to McKinsey clients in a 125-page "Orange Book" and summarized in an article in *Business Week* in 1980. They became the basis of *In Search of Excellence: Lessons from America's Best-Run Companies*. Published in 1982, with a practical, common sense, "can do" perspective, the book was reassuring in a time of recession and competition from Japan. Disdaining charts, bean counting, and scientific management, Peters and Waterman stressed "the soft" side of business practice, recommending attention to customers, "productivity through people," and a bias for action ("do it, fix it, try it, is our favorite maxim"). Despite an initial press run of only fifteen thousand copies, *In Search of Excellence* rocketed to the top of the best-seller lists, and within three years had sold seven million copies. Although he regretted that the book "made managing sound so incredibly easy,"

Peter Drucker, doyen of management writers, acknowledged that "When Aunt Mary has to give that nephew of hers a high school graduation present and she gives him *In Search of Excellence* you know that management has become part of the general culture."

Peters left McKinsey in 1981, although he had no idea his book would be so successful. After *In Search of Excellence,* Peters became, as he put it, "a rock star." With the creation of the Tom Peters Group in 1981 he became a corporation as well. TPG organized "Skunk Camps" for business executives, but the company's principal sources of revenue were the astronomical fees Peters charged to lecture and consult, a syndicated newspaper column, a monthly newsletter, and the videos and books he produced. A shy man, Peters comes alive on stage as a cross between a TV evangelist and a psychotherapist. More than any other person, for good and ill, he invented "the management guru." According to Ralph Ardill of the Imagination design consulting company, "He kicks ass. He is a brand."

The books Peters has published since *Excellence* have been enormously popular as well. They include *A Passion for Excellence* (1985), written with Nancy Austin, a series of profiles of managers who took risks and departed from orthodox practices; *Thriving on Chaos* (1987), whose publication date, October 19, Black Monday for the stock market, marked it as prophetic; *Excellence in the Organization* (1988), written with Robert Townsend; *Liberation Management* (1992), which admonished organizations to get rid of traditional departmental divisions and use temporary, project-based teams with decision-making authority; and *Circle of Innovation: You Can't Shrink Your Way to Greatness* (1997), a call for forgetting—not learning—as an organization's highest art in an era of rapidly evolving technology. Peters's books have been praised as pragmatic, provocative, and attentive to fundamentals. In 1990, *Business Week* included *In Search of Excellence* in a list of ten indispensable books: "You'd be hard pressed to find a better primer on the evolution and practice of management."

In contrast, critics have termed Peters's books superficial ("common sense raised to a pitch of desperation," according to the *Economist*), verbose, and inconsistent. In an article headlined "Oops," in 1984, *Business Week* revealed that many of the companies Peters had deemed excellent were foundering. Peters revels in his inconsistency, claiming that six different authors could have written his first six books. *Thriving on Chaos* opens by proclaiming, "There are no excellent companies." In *Liberation Management,* Peters asserts, "Organization structure comes first in this book; customers last. And that is quite a switch from *In Search of Excellence.*"

Ambitious and driven, married several times, with a home in northern California and a 1,000-acre farm in Vermont, Peters is a workaholic whose only hobby is reading. The best-paid management commentator the world has ever known, he claims to be revolted by his status as guru, corporate messiah, and fashion accessory. "There is something obscene about $100,000 a day," he says. "I cash the checks, but it's nutty when people in India are making 25 cents an hour." Peters feels sorry for those who come to his seminars looking for answers: "That's not my take. I just talk about stuff I've seen, try to confuse people I talk to. . . . There are no answers. Just, at best, a few guesses that might be worth a try." Those who want to understand how to run a business well, he says, "with dead seriousness," should "read Chekhov, not Drucker and Peters."

Susan Charna Rothenberg

⮌ CLASS OF 1966

Susan Rothenberg once commented, "My art is about not taking anything for granted in the world." She might have said the same thing about her life. Her enormous talent made her famous, but in her career she never took the path of least resistance. Her life has been one of unexpected, sometimes abrupt turns.

Rothenberg was born on January 20, 1945, in Buffalo, New York, the daughter of Adele and Leonard Rothenberg. Her father started in the produce business and built a chain of supermarkets in western New York. Her mother, like most middle-class women in the 1950s, was a homemaker as well as a volunteer for the local Red Cross. In one particular she was different: Adele Rothenberg also was an amateur watercolorist who encouraged the artistic talent she saw in her daughter.

Rothenberg later said, "I think you often become what you are praised for when you are very small." Encouragement for her artistic skills came not only from her parents but also from Dr. Joseph Rosenberg, a neighbor who made art a serious avocation. Although she took private art lessons, first at Buffalo's Art Museum (renamed in 1962 the Albright-Knox Art Gallery) and then with the Hungarian-born realist painter Laszlo Szabo, the pursuit of art did not consume her early years, which she recalled as "uneventful, quiet, protected, average, conventional." Rothenberg did not take art classes in high school but instead starred in theatrical productions and was a cheerleader. Dance interested her as much as painting. She loved animals and thought about becoming a veterinarian. Still, when she went away to Cornell in the fall of 1962, she entered the School of Fine Arts, intending to major in sculpture.

Rothenberg was not the first Cornell student who found her courses disappointing, although she liked studying Proust with Professor David Grossvogel. Art teachers Robert Richenberg and Alan Atwood encouraged her

ambitions. Other than that, she preferred to hang out with Mary Woronov, also an aspiring sculptor, who shared Rothenberg's love of dancing. They held a job as go-go dancers at a Collegetown bar, the Alt Heidelberg.

In the spring semester of her junior year, Rothenberg flunked a sculpture course. Impulsively, she dropped out of school and spent the next five months on the Greek island of Hydra. Finding nothing there but an uninteresting array of other college dropouts, she returned to Cornell in the fall. Things started out badly. Victor Colby, the head of the sculpture program, refused to take her back, telling her, "I don't think you have any talent whatsoever." A determined Rothenberg switched her major to painting, a change that allowed her to pursue a semester of independent work in New York City. She roomed with Woronov, who had left school without a degree and was on her way to stardom in Andy Warhol movies, most famously in *Chelsea Girls*.

With a B.F.A. from Cornell, earned in 1967, and after a summer in Spain, Rothenberg enrolled as a student in the Corcoran School of Art in Washington, D.C. Learning even less there than she had at Cornell, she dropped out of the program within weeks. With nothing better to do, she stayed in Washington for over a year, drinking, going to jazz bars, and coming close to a nervous breakdown. With vague plans to teach English in Nova Scotia, she boarded a train for Halifax in 1969. During a six-hour wait to change trains in Montreal, she decided instead to go to New York City.

New York provided her a "state of grace." She ran into some old Cornell friends, including the talented artists Alan Saret and Gordon Matta, and rented a studio. She also studied dance with Deborah Hay and Joan Jonas and learned a great deal from performance artists. In 1971 she married the sculptor George Trakas and a year later gave birth to her daughter Maggie. She decided that her own work was too imitative. So in the early 1970s she "ditched" the paintings she had started and "drew a horse." Variations on formal images of horses defined her work through the 1970s.

Most critics have called her early work minimalist. She worked in acrylics, using both bright and dark colors. What she called "Giotto blue" became a signature hue. The simplified horse images that filled her large canvases were not drawn from life. They were neither abstract nor completely real. She wanted recognizable forms but painted "exactly the way things can't be." As the work became more emotionally charged, she began to disassemble the bodies of her equine figures and distribute the parts around her canvasses. Exposed bones became a common motif. Critics now used the label neo-expressionist to describe her work, but what they in fact admired was that she was not like anyone else.

Success came quickly. Her first solo show, at the Willard Gallery in New York City in 1976, sold out. By the end of the decade, she had been exhibited in shows at the Museum of Modern Art and the Whitney. In 1980, the year she won a Guggenheim Fellowship, her work appeared at the Venice Biennale. Her personal life was less happy. When she accepted her first and only teaching job in 1977 at the California Institute for the Arts, her marriage to Trakas was falling apart. They divorced in 1979.

The 1980s brought new professional directions for Rothenberg. She abandoned horses and explored a number of other formal themes: hands and faces, her daughter's teddy bear, the painter Piet Mondrian. She switched from acrylics to oil, "just to shake things up in general." Suddenly her paintings seemed to have figures surrounded by watery space. She explored the action of dancers and jugglers in her canvases, recalling in a very fluid way the work of Marcel Duchamp. Personal references became more common, including portraits of people and things close to her, even her dog. The Stedelijk Museum in Amsterdam, the Los Angeles County Museum of Art, the Kunsthalle in Basel, and the Phillips Collection in Washington devoted solo exhibitions to her work.

In 1990 she married the versatile artist Bruce Nauman and moved with him to New Mexico where they built a house and studio in Galisteo, near Santa Fe. For the first time she encountered real horses and learned to ride. Incorporating the material of "small ranch dramas" and the unexpected violence of desert life, her work continued to evolve: "I look for the weird to liven things up." Her paintings were now exhibited around the world and in 1999 the Museum of Fine Arts in Boston put together a sensitive exhibit of the work she had done since moving to the Southwest.

In 1998 Rothenberg came back to Ithaca for a showing of her work at the Johnson Art Museum and to receive the Cornell University Alumni Arts Award. By then she was a member of the American Academy of Arts and Letters and one of the most respected American painters of her generation. She has told her admirers that she often does not know or care what her pictures mean. They are "truly mysterious to me." She knows what they are, however. She has likened them to prayers, acts of self-expression that "have to do with whatever it is that makes you want more than daily life affords."

Samuel (Sandy) Richard Berger

❧ CLASS OF 1967

At a news conference on December 5, 1996, President Clinton introduced his choices for his foreign policy team during his second term. He praised them all, but he hugged only one of them in front of the camera, his old friend of nearly twenty-five years, Sandy Berger.

Like Clinton's, Berger's journey to his White House office was the stuff of the American dream. Born on October 28, 1945, in Sharon, Connecticut, Samuel "Sandy" Berger grew up across the state border in Millerton, New York, a small town near Kingston. His father, Albert, died when Sandy was eight, and he was raised by his mother, Rose, who ran the small clothing store that had brought his parents to the Hudson Valley. Among the few Democrats in their Republican community, the Bergers were also rare Brooklyn Dodgers fans in New York Yankees territory. In high school, Berger set up pins in a bowling alley to supplement the family income.

Entering Cornell in September 1963, he majored in government and emerged as a leader in the fraternity community. A bright, ambitious, and affable member of Phi Gamma Delta and Quill and Dagger, he was elected president of the Interfraternity Council, an office he used to further his liberal politics. Berger organized a "Soul Awareness Week" on campus, arranging for civil rights activists to speak, one of whom was Stokely Carmichael, the Black Power advocate.

Three distinguished Cornell professors helped shape Berger's liberal worldview. From Walter LaFeber in history and George Kahin and Andrew Hacker in government, Berger learned that the United States was as complicit as the Stalinist Soviet Union in generating the Cold War. Kahin's course on Vietnam, Berger recounts, "had a profound effect on me. My conviction that the war was a mistake derives very directly from that course."

From Cornell Berger went to Harvard Law School, where he became a legendary schmoozer. A classmate, the erstwhile New York City politician Mark Green, calls him "the Sara Lee of our class. Nobody didn't like Sandy Berger." He didn't involve himself in the '60s counterculture and was no flower child, nor did he devote much time to marches and protests. His arena was politics from within the system. He volunteered for Robert Kennedy's presidential campaign, then worked for Eugene McCarthy's candidacy. While in law school he also married a fellow Cornellian, Susan Harrison, from Coconut Grove, Florida. The Bergers moved to Washington in 1971 and have been there ever since.

Sandy worked on Capitol Hill as a legislative aide to Senator Harold Hughes of Iowa and Representative Joseph Resnick of New York. His association with the latter, who had begun an investigation of the American Farm Bureau Federation, produced Berger's only book, *Dollar Harvest: The Story of the Farm Bureau,* which exposed the organization's poor record in preserving small family farms.

Berger left Capitol Hill in 1972 to become a speechwriter for George McGovern. At a rally at the Alamo in San Antonio, Texas, he met Bill Clinton, McGovern's Texas campaign coordinator. After McGovern's disastrous defeat, Berger spent a year in New York City as an aide to Mayor John Lindsay.

He returned to Washington in 1973, accepting a position in the law firm of Hogan and Hartson, but four years later was back in politics. He wrote speeches for President Carter and for Secretary of State Cyrus Vance and from 1978 to 1980 served as deputy director of the State Department's Policy Planning

Staff. Convinced that the administration was undermined by attacks on Vance by Zbigniew Brzezinski, Carter's national security advisor, Berger internalized the need for coordination and cooperation among foreign policy makers, which would become his signature contribution to the Clinton White House.

With Carter's defeat in 1980, Berger returned to Hogan and Hartson and launched the firm's international trade practice. He became one of Washington's premier international trade lawyers, with a long list of clients that included Toyota, foreign steel producers, and Payless Shoes. All the while he remained active in Democratic Party politics, advising a string of losing candidates: Gary Hart, Walter Mondale, Geraldine Ferraro, and Michael Dukakis.

Berger's losing streak ended with Clinton. They had remained friends through the late 1970s and 1980s when Clinton was the on and off again governor of Arkansas. Berger was one of the "Friends of Bill" who urged him to run for president. During the 1992 campaign Clinton made Berger and Anthony Lake his principal foreign policy advisors. It was Berger, however, who accompanied Clinton on the campaign plane and drilled him for his debates with President Bush.

With Clinton's victory, Berger, who headed the foreign policy transition team, could have become the president's national security advisor, but he recommended that Clinton give the post to the more experienced Lake, and he became his deputy. In his four years as deputy national security advisor, Berger coordinated and facilitated, bringing together, for example, the foreign policy deputies of the Departments of State and Defense for weekly lunches. Respected for his tactical skills, he also influenced policy, especially on China, pushing for cooperation through trade instead of confrontation on human rights issues.

In his second term Clinton made his old friend national security advisor, breaking a Washington tradition in which presidents chose academics and intellectuals for that job,

from McGeorge Bundy through Henry Kissinger, Brzezinski, and Lake himself.

The convivial, rumpled, and slightly overweight Berger routinely worked fifteen hours a day, often including weekends. He began with overnight intelligence reports and a 9:15 meeting to brief the president. The schedule left little time for his wife Susan, a real estate broker, and his three children, Deborah, Sarah, and Alexander, let alone for his passionate love of baseball, either the Baltimore Orioles or his son's team, the Berger Kings, which he had coached.

Criticized for having no grand vision or global strategy, Berger did have a consistent geo-economic worldview that emphasized free trade as the cornerstone of world peace. His conciliatory skills, observers agreed, provided the glue that held the foreign policy team together. Several times a week he brought together the "ABC Club"—Secretary of State Madeleine Albright, Berger, and Secretary of Defense William Cohen—for an informal chat or to solve a specific problem.

Berger had his foreign policy successes, working with Trent Lott to get Senate approval of the Chemical Weapons Convention, and getting the House to approve most-favored nation trade status for China. He had his failures, as well, most noticeably the February 1998 "town meeting" fiasco at Ohio State University, where CNN, there at his urging, showed the world disruptive protestors angry at administration plans to bomb Iraq, which had just expelled UN weapons inspectors. In 1999 several Republicans called for his resignation over alleged negligence in dealing with Chinese spying in U.S. nuclear labs. As national security advisor, Berger was a pragmatist, a broker of the crisis de jour, whether it was the Middle East, Bosnia, or the India-Pakistan nuclear rivalry. A grander vision might have emerged if Al Gore had become president, and, as widely rumored, instead of returning to his Washington law firm, the former president of Cornell's Interfraternity Council had become the secretary of state.

Kenneth Wayne Dryden
❧ CLASS OF 1969

When he chose to attend Cornell, Ken Dryden believed he was sacrificing his chance for a career as a professional hockey player. At a time in which 75 percent of NHL players had not finished high school, the Montreal Canadiens were willing to let him enroll at Trent University and play junior hockey in Peterborough, Ontario. But Dryden, who wanted to be a lawyer, refused to have a university experience that was "rush and cram." A Dean's List student, he won more honors than any athlete in Big Red history—and became the first Ivy Leaguer to play in the National Hockey League.

Kenneth Wayne Dryden was born on August 8, 1947, in Hamilton, Ontario, the son of Margaret and David Murray Dryden, a door-to-door, store-to-store salesman who rode to prosperity on the post-World War II boom in construction. When Ken was six, Murray Dryden paved the backyard of their new house near Toronto for a hockey rink. He built goalie nets with real metal pipes and mesh; for boards, he constructed brick and block walls as one side of "the rink," with the brick of the house as the other. Ken was hooked on hockey, emulating his older brother Dave, a goalie. Although he continued to play baseball, basketball, and run track and field in school, and practice tennis, golf, badminton, bowling, and archery for fun, "backyard time" and teen hockey took hold of his imagination. He appeared often in Toronto with a Boston Bruins sweatshirt and a makeshift goaltender's mask. "Where's that kid from?" the milkman asked Margaret Dryden. "Mars?"

Dryden entered Cornell's College of Arts and Sciences in the fall of 1965. Known as the school where you trudged through 20-degree weather, up a 30-degree hill, to get a 40 on a prelim, Cornell turned out to be "the absolute right choice." Ineligible to play varsity hockey during his first year (freshmen, Dryden recalled, played "non-games in front of nobody"), he hit .417 as an infielder on the freshman baseball team, worked as a waiter and dishwasher at a fraternity (he later joined Sigma Phi), and discovered, as a history major and by hanging out at Uris Library, that a love of learning could come through reading and writing as well as seeing and doing. In 1968–69 he was vice president of the senior honor society, Quill and Dagger.

Starting in his sophomore year, Dryden responded brilliantly to the fiercely loyal and loud fans who filled Lynah Rink game after game, setting record after record for goalies—for saves, goals against average (1.59 for his career), shutouts, and career won-lost record (an almost unbelievable 76–4–1). He took Cornell to three straight East Coast Athletic Conference (ECAC) and Ivy League championships and one NCAA title. In each of his three years minding the nets, Dryden was selected first team all-Ivy, all ECAC, and all-America. He was a charter inductee into the Cornell Athletic Hall of Fame.

When he graduated in 1969, Dryden turned down another offer from "Les Habitants" (which the Canadiens are often called) and also declined admission at Harvard Law School. He decided to register at the University of Manitoba law school and play amateur hockey with the Canadian National Team. But when Canada pulled out of world hockey and the team folded, he made an agreement with the Canadiens to play on weekends with their farm club, the Montreal Voyagers, until he graduated from McGill University Law School. In 1970 Dryden married a Cornell classmate, Lynda Curran, a teacher. They have two children. By March 1971, with the play-offs about to begin, and merely adequate goalies on the team, the Canadiens' coach, Al MacNeil, himself a rookie, called Dryden up. With only six regular season games under his belt, he helped the team win the Stanley Cup by defeating the Boston Bruins, with Bobby Orr and Phil Esposito; the Minnesota North Stars; and, in seven close contests, the favored Chicago Black Hawks, led by Bobby Hull. Dryden won the Conn Smythe Trophy as the most valuable player of the playoffs.

In seven full seasons in the nets, Dryden helped the Canadiens to five more titles. Named the NHL rookie of the year in 1972, he took home five Vezina Trophies, awarded by the league's general managers to the out-standing goaltender of the year. Ranked first in goals against average (2.24), Dryden had forty-six shutouts during his short career. He was just as good during the pressure-packed playoffs. In 112 Stanley Cup playoff contests, Dryden compiled an 80–32 record, with ten shutouts and a 2.40 goals against average. He was inducted into the National Hockey League Hall of Fame in 1983.

Resting his chin on the glove hand over his stick, Dryden has been called "the hockey version of Rodin's 'The Thinker.'" Even as a professional hockey player, he refused to abandon other, more cerebral, career goals. In the summer of 1971, he worked as one of Ralph Nader's "Raiders," studying the impact of water pollution on commercial and sport fishermen. Dryden's group recommended organizing the fishermen as a citizen's group to agitate for laws to regulate the environment. In 1973 he received his law degree from McGill. Following a contract dispute with the

Canadiens, he sat out the 1973–74 hockey season, working instead for $134 a week as a law clerk.

Feeling it was time to move on and because he wanted to have an impact on public policy, Dryden retired from professional hockey in his prime, in 1979. He held several positions with the province of Ontario, including a two-year stint as youth commissioner, helping develop training programs for high school dropouts. In 1980, as a commentator for ABC television, Dryden and Al Michaels brought to millions of homes around the globe the United States hockey team's Olympic gold medal victory over the Soviet Union. He was part of the ABC broadcast team at the 1984 and 1988 Olympics as well.

Most of his time, however, was spent writing. Early in his hockey career, Dryden wrote *Face-Off at the Summit* (1973), an account of his experiences tending goal for Team Canada in its first-ever hockey series against the Soviet Union. In 1984, he published *The Game,* a No. 1 best-seller in Canada that has been praised as the most insightful analysis of any major professional sport ever written. Dryden's third book, *Home Game,* cowritten with Roy MacGregor, examined the role of hockey in Canadian life. The book was turned into a six-part Canadian Broadcasting Corporation TV series, *Ken Dryden's Home Game,* which he wrote, coproduced, and hosted. His autobiography, *The Moved and the Shaken: The Story of One Man's Life,* appeared in 1993.

In 1997, after an eighteen-year absence, Dryden returned to the National Hockey League, this time as president of the Toronto Maple Leafs. Taking over an inept team that was in need of a new arena and still reeling from allegations that a ring of pedophiles abused dozens of children at Maple Leaf Gardens from the late 1960s through the early 1980s, Dryden appointed himself general manager as well. "I never assume I can do something," he says, "but I don't assume I can't, either."

Thomas Wade Jones
❧ CLASS OF 1969

On April 20, 1969, Thomas Wade Jones, brandishing a gun, walked out of Willard Straight Hall with eighty other African American students who had occupied the building over a parents' day weekend. The photograph of that event, which appeared on front pages across the country and won a Pulitzer Prize for the cameraman, spoke to profound changes that had transformed Cornell and American higher education during the 1960s. More than thirty years later, Jones, now a spectacularly successful leader of corporate America and a Cornell trustee, remains central to discussions about the legacy of those rancorous days.

Born on May 17, 1949 in New York City, Jones knew little about radical activism during his childhood. His father, Edward Wilfred Jones, was a physicist, and his mother, Marie Carter Jones, was a teacher. Squarely in the middle class, Jones attended largely white schools in New York City where he skipped the fourth and eighth grades. When he graduated from high school in 1965, his class voted him "most likely to succeed." He entered Cornell later that year, at age sixteen, and moved with social ease between his black and white friends. Elected president of his freshman class, named to the student judicial board, and "rushed" by a largely white fraternity, Jones was following a conventional road to success.

Events in the late '60s changed the attitudes of many university students from privileged backgrounds, Tom Jones among them. He joined the Afro-American Society (AAS) and read widely in black history and the sociology of race. Attracted to the politics of confrontation adopted by students protesting the Vietnam War, he also shared the militant attitudes of black students who no longer believed in the philosophy of nonviolence preached by Martin Luther King Jr. Committed to black separatism, he and the other leaders of the AAS demanded that Cornell establish a largely autonomous black studies program. Sharp disagreement about the academic nature of what finally became Cornell's Africana Studies and Research Center was one reason for the Straight takeover. Another was an insistence that Cornell drop disciplinary action that had been taken against students who had been involved in an earlier disruption of an authorized campus event.

Members of the AAS had no guns when they first entered Willard Straight. But when members of a white fraternity took it upon themselves to try to liberate the building, the black students procured weapons, which they said symbolized the need of African Americans to confront white Americans with arms in self-defense. They agreed to leave the student center after they had negotiated an agreement with members of the university administration. However, in a mass meeting the faculty rejected the agreement, which the majority believed had been secured through intimidation. That set the stage for a notorious speech that Jones made over the radio. In remarks heard by the entire Ithaca community, he threatened President Perkins and various faculty members, who, he said, "are going to die in the gutter like dogs." Dramatically, he announced that Cornell had three hours to live.

Jones's remarks were in fact not backed up by any plan of action. But the possibility of violence on campus was real. In a second tumultuous and bitterly divisive meeting the faculty reversed itself. It took many years to heal the scars. Allan Sindler, a professor who had taught Jones and recognized his talent but who was nonetheless one of those threatened by Jones, resigned from Cornell in disgust along with two other members of the government department, Allan Bloom and Walter Berns. Perkins, who had done more than any other Ivy League president to recognize an institutional responsibility to recruit black students, was forced to resign, reviled on the one side as a racist and on the other as Neville Chamberlain.

Jones did not immediately back down. He made a speech in late June, shortly after his graduation. Laced with anti-Semitism, it defended the action of the "Black Liberation Front." Jones, however, was already married and had a son. He stayed at Cornell to pursue a master's degree, awarded in 1972, in city and regional planning. His next stop was Boston, where he became a certified public accountant, worked for Arthur Young and Company, and finished an MBA by going to night school at Boston University. He stayed in Boston for the next eleven years.

In 1975, after he and his wife Stephanie divorced, Jones married Adelaide Knox Jones, a graduate of Tuskegee Institute and Southern Illinois University. He has one son from his first marriage and three children from his second. With deserved reputations as a workaholic and a financial wizard, his career advanced quickly. From 1982 until 1989 he was the senior vice president and treasurer of John Hancock Mutual Fund Life Insurance. Then he went to work for TIAA/CREF, the investment group that handles the pension fund for many of the nation's teachers. He rose from chief financial officer to president, enriching the retirement portfolios of many professors at Cornell whom he had once infuriated. An unforgiving Walter Berns quipped, "First he threatens my life, now he is in control of what happens after I die."

Jones left TIAA/CREF in 1997 to join the Travelers Group as vice president and director while he also served as chairman and chief executive officer of Salomon Smith Barney Asset Management. His boss and strong supporter at Travelers was Sanford I. Weill, whom he had met when both served on Cornell Medical College's board of overseers. Since 1999 Jones has been chairman of the Global Investment Management and Private Banking Group, which oversees $677 million in assets. He has largely succeeded in turning the complex collection of asset-management operations that he inherited—each with its own set of business operations—into one global wealth-management firm. "Confusion," Jones told *Forbes* magazine, "is not a good thing."

In 1980 Jones wrote a letter to James Perkins that said, in part, "I give you an apology for not having stood with you against the tide of emotionalism and racial fear, and for using my talents to mobilize forces which intimidated the faculty." In 1994 Jones made a large gift to Cornell to endow the James A. Perkins Prize for Interracial Understanding and Harmony. He and Cornell's former president returned to Ithaca and shook hands. Jones had reason to know that trying to do the right thing is never easy. Some radical students at Cornell turned out to jeer him for "selling out to the Establishment." Jones, however, was prepared to face them down and to urge them to work for a society that celebrates diversity but that also "affirms a greater sense of community, transcends our diversity, and unites us as one people despite our various colors and cultures and creeds."

On the ghastly morning of September 11, 2001, Tom Jones walked out of another famous building, not Willard Straight, with a large group of people connected to him. They were the people who worked under his direction in an office located in the World Trade Center. When the tower they had left collapsed into rubble, they were all safe and accounted for. A certain kind of radicalism claimed a great victory on that morning, but Jones was no longer an enemy of what New York City's Twin Towers had represented.

Richard Jay Price

❧ CLASS OF 1971

His literary debut, a violent and sex-filled story about teenage Italian-American gang members, was every writer's fantasy come true. The *New York Times* reported that even before its 1974 publication Samuel Goldwyn Jr. had acquired the movie rights to *The Wanderers,* a novel by Richard Price, "a 24-year-old New Yorker, an alumnus of both a Bronx gang and Cornell." *People* magazine praised the brilliant new novel by an authentic voice from the "stultifying, brutalizing Bronx housing projects," writing about his fellow "hoods who used to beat him to hamburger as a kid."

Richard Price had grown up in a Bronx project, but not everything in the press releases was true. As he later acknowledged, the only gang he belonged to was "the Goldberg gang. We walked down the street doing algebra." He was born on October 12, 1949, the son of Milton, a freelance window dresser, and Harriet, a homemaker and later a bank teller, who lived in the Parkside Housing Project, a postwar public project for blue-collar families in the northeast section of the Bronx. The tough neighborhood was similar to the setting of *The Wanderers.* Price developed his passion for reading and writing from his grandfather, an amateur Yiddish poet, and his grandmother, a gifted storyteller. Born with a mild form of cerebral palsy that affected his right side, he was unfit for the rough and tumble of street life. "I could only get so far with a bum arm and a limpy leg," he has noted, "so I began looking for something to maintain the specialness. If I had a perfectly normal hand, I wouldn't have written a word in my life."

Price wrote his first story when he was eleven. All through P.S. 41 and the Bronx High School of Science he was "the writer" or "Shakespeare" to his fellow students, leaving his short stories and poetry on girls' desks. The first person in his family to go to college, Price chose Cornell's School of Industrial and Labor Relations in 1967 because, as he put it,

"writing is just fun, but someday I will have a family to support."

At Cornell he was "hellmaster" of Tau Epsilon Phi and flirted with the radical Students for a Democratic Society (SDS). Feeling out of place, "like a Martian," and intimidated by his richer classmates, Price adopted an even stronger Bronx accent, he remembers, and "acted twice as streety." Though determined to go to law school, he found time to squeeze in creative writing courses and came under the influence of an instructor, Ronald Sukenick, who introduced him to avant-garde literature.

Two books proved crucial in his evolution as a writer. In Hubert Selby Jr.'s *Last Exit to Brooklyn* and in *The Essential Lenny Bruce* Price found his voice, the gritty realism and switchblade prose that he calls "the music of the projects." He read one of his short stories about the Bronx written in that voice at a Collegetown coffeehouse. After receiving a standing ovation, he said good-bye to law school.

After graduating from Cornell in 1971 with a B.S. from the I&LR School, Price spent a year working and then in 1972 went to Stanford on a fiction writing grant. He stayed for only three months. "It was like Westchester with palm trees," he later wrote. Insisting that he "was very much a New York person," he enrolled in the creative writing program at Columbia where he studied from 1972 to 1974, supporting himself by teaching part-time at New York area colleges.

In 1974 came *The Wanderers,* his rite of passage novel about the gang who took its name from the song by Dion and the Belmonts. With the *New York Times* reviewer praising the book, even its violence and obscenities, for its "near Chekhovian understatement" and calling it a "metaphor signifying the vitality of lower class life," Price's career was launched. He has suggested that the book did well in part "because not many alumni of housing projects become writers."

With *Bloodbrothers* (1976), his second novel, set in Co-op City, the huge apartment complex on the outskirts of the Bronx to which his parents had moved while he was at Cornell, critics proclaimed Price the "voice of the Bronx." They applauded his tale of an 18-year-old Italian American choosing between college and his father's life in the construction business as a hot new example of "lower depths chic" writing. It, too, was made into a film, starring Richard Gere.

Price's third novel, *Ladies' Man* (1978), moves from the Bronx to Manhattan and won less acclaim from reviewers. Begun as a commission from *Penthouse* magazine, the story follows a lonely door-to-door salesman on a painful weeklong odyssey through sex clubs, gay bars, and prostitutes' rooms. Price became addicted to cocaine while writing his fourth book, *The Breaks* (1983), his most autobiographical novel. Set in a college very much like Cornell, it is about a young man, the first in his family to go to college, who abandons the idea of law school to perform stand-up comedy. "You start using cocaine to help you write, then you need the writing as an excuse to do coke," he later observed. His three-year addiction ended in 1982 and Price rearranged his life. He married his long-time girlfriend, the artist Judy Hudson, in 1984. They now have two daughters, Annie and Genevieve. He began teaching writing at a drug rehabilitation center in the Bronx and after years of refusing calls from Hollywood he decided to write screenplays for movies, which he did for eight very successful years.

His gritty, urban realist writing style ap-pealed to Martin Scorsese, who hired Price to write the screenplay for *The Color of Money* (1986), which starred Paul Newman and Tom Cruise. Price was nominated for an Academy Award for the film. Commanding a fee of over $500,000 per script, Price wrote the screenplays for a string of films in the late 1980s and early 1990s, managing to write himself a small part in each one: Scorsese's *Life Lessons* with Nick Nolte; *Sea of Love* with Al Pacino and Ellen Barkin; *Mad Dog and Glory* with Robert De Niro and Bill Murray; *Night and the City* again with De Niro.

Needing structure and discipline for his writing, Price methodically worked each day on his screenplays from 10 A.M. to 4 P.M. in his rented home office in New York City, but researching his material often took him into the streets. He spent countless nights riding in police cars and sleeping in crack houses preparing for his next and best-known novel, *Clockers* (1992), which garnered him a $500,000 advance. A powerful book about teenage cocaine dealers who sell drugs "around the clock" and the police who arrest them in "the iron triangle of hell" (Price's term for the devastated slums of Jersey City), *Clockers* was nominated for a National Book Critics Circle Award and was made into a film directed by Spike Lee in 1995. Universal Studios paid $1.9 million for the movie rights and for the script written by Price and Lee.

In the years since *Clockers,* Price solidified his place as one of America's preeminent novelists. His 1999 book *Freedomland* received widespread praise, and in 2003 his novel *Samaritan* held pride of place as lead title in the catalog of Alfred A. Knopf, one of the country's most distinguished publishers. But perhaps the most personally satisfying mark of his phenomenal success was that thirty years after graduating from the ILR School and no longer feeling "like a Martian," Price returned to Cornell in the spring semester of 2001. He taught two creative writing courses in the English Department for the benefit of the aspiring Richard Prices of the twenty-first century.

Edward Francis Marinaro

❧ CLASS OF 1972

He was the only all-American college football player with a regular role on *Laverne and Shirley* and the only star of *Hill Street Blues* to catch a pass in the National Football League.

Edward Francis Marinaro was born on March 31, 1950, in New York City. His parents, Louis Marinaro and Rose Errico Marinaro, owned a sign-painting company in New Jersey. A standout football player at New Milford High School in New Jersey, Marinaro chose to matriculate at Cornell in 1968 and major in hotel administration.

In three years as a tailback for the Big Red (freshmen in those days were ineligible for varsity sports), the six-feet, two-inch, 210-pound Marinaro laid claim to every scoring and rushing mark at Cornell, while smashing eleven NCAA and twelve Ivy League records. In a twenty-seven game career, Marinaro, a workhorse, gained 4,715 yards on 918 carries, an astonishing 174.6 yard per game average. In twenty-three contests he rushed for more than one hundred yards, chalking up two hundred or more yards in ten of those games. In his final game for Cornell, Marinaro gained 230 yards in 42 carries and scored 5 touchdowns in a 41–13 win over the University of Pennsylvania that enabled the Big Red to tie Dartmouth for the Ivy League Championship.

Marinaro was a consensus choice as all-American in his senior year, when he also won the Maxwell Award as College Player of the Year. Only the biggest prize in college football, the Heisman Trophy, eluded him. With some sportswriters disdaining to vote for a player in a conference where they believed the competition was inferior, Marinaro finished second to Pat Sullivan, the quarterback at Auburn University. To that point, it was the closest vote in the history of the Heisman. Marinaro's consolation came later when he was inducted into the College Football Hall of Fame and selected as the Ivy League

Silver Anniversary Player of the quarter century from 1956 to 1980.

After graduation in 1972, Marinaro, who admitted that he "majored in macho sports" at Cornell, "thought about working in a hotel for about twenty minutes." Football took him in a different direction and the "Italian Stallion" entered the National Football League with the Minnesota Vikings. Thought to lack the speed to succeed as a ballcarrier, Marinaro served as a blocking back for Chuck Foreman, the team's rushing sensation, and caught passes out of the backfield. In 1976, he joined the New York Jets, where he ran for one hundred yards for two consecutive games, only to suffer a foot injury that threatened his career. After an unsuccessful comeback with the Seattle Seahawks and the Chicago Bears, Marinaro retired in 1978.

With a taste for the limelight, Marinaro followed Joe Namath, his friend and teammate on the New York Jets, out to Hollywood. He took some acting classes, got a few "gift" two-line parts, played a small role in an episode of the TV series *Eischeid,* and was one of three hunks on a male *Charlie's Angels* pilot that was not picked up by the network. Marinaro's break came in 1980 on the hit comedy series *Laverne and Shirley.* Cast as Laverne's cousin from Italy, Marinaro was so good the producers made him a regular. As Sonny St. Jacques, the caretaker of the girls' apartment building, he often made his entrance by hanging upside down across the window.

Buoyed by good money, fan mail from admiring women, and the prospect of success as a TV star, Marinaro was devastated when the producers of *Laverne and Shirley* declined to pick up his option for a second season. "It was like getting cut from the football team," he recalled. But within a month, the actor got a far better role on the Emmy Award–winning dramatic series *Hill Street Blues*. Officer Joe Coffey was scheduled to appear in four episodes before being killed by a deranged motorist. Marinaro worked hard at the role, developing a suggestive relationship with Lucy Bates, the tough policewoman played by Betty Thomas. Telling Marinaro that "Joe Coffey's life is in the hands of your agent," the director of *Hill Street Blues* decided that Coffey would recover from his wounds.

Although playing a blue-collar cop made him a star, Marinaro began to tire of the role. "The first four years were great," he told the *New York Times,* but after a while "you want to do a different character, stretch a little." So he asked to be written out of the series at the end of the 1985–86 season. This time, when Coffey went down in a hail of bullets, he did not get up.

Life after *Blues,* however, was not so easy. Marinaro was so identified with his character that casting directors could not picture him in another role and "yet they don't want me to play another cop." To be sure, Marinaro got work in the late 1980s—as a plastic surgeon who three women take into their hearts and their beds in the TV movie *Sharing Richard;* as a plainclothes detective in the film *Mace;* in a CBS "Schoolbreak Special," *What If I'm Gay*; and in commercials for Miller High Life beer and Fruit of the Loom underwear. Into the '90s Marinaro, who is single, continued to be cast as a ladies' man, opposite Connie Selleca in *Passport to Murder,* Alyssa Milano in *Amy Fisher: My Story,* Cheryl Ladd in *Dancing with Danger,* and Loni Anderson in *Without Warning.* Two more TV series came his way as well. He added testosterone to *Sisters* as Mitch, the current husband of one sister, the ex-husband of another, and the father of a child with a third. And in *Champs,* he was one of five forty-somethings who kept replaying the big basketball game of their lives, twenty years after they graduated from high school. "I'm not afraid of smart women," his character says before adding, "not too smart." If his career was something less than an aesthetic tour de force, it paid for a beautiful home, several cars, and a lavish lifestyle. "I've made more money on my own," Marinaro reports, than "if I'd stayed on salary" at *Hill Street Blues.*

When not working, Marinaro enjoys fly-fishing and competing in the Celebrity Players Golf Tour. "In a lot of ways," he maintains, "what I've accomplished as an actor is greater than what I did as a football player." Maybe so. But long after they have forgotten Joe Coffey, Big Red football fans will remember Marinaro in his No. 44 jersey—the only uniform retired in the history of Cornell.

Abby Joseph Cohen
❧ CLASS OF 1973

The "perma-bull," "icon," and "spiritual leader" of the 1990s stock market, Abby Joseph Cohen won *Smart Money*'s Portfolio Strategist of the Year Award in the first three years the magazine ran the contest. *Vanity Fair* put her on its list of the latest fads, along with the Lexus LX 50 and thong lingerie. And even after the Dow dropped and the NASDAQ nose-dived, Cohen remains one of the most influential investment strategists on Wall Street.

Abby Joseph was born on February 29, 1952, in New York City. Her father, Raymond Joseph, was an accountant who later became the controller of the African American magazine *Essence*. Before she got married, Abby's mother, Shirley Silverstein Joseph, worked in the controller's office at General Foods. Although she came of age during the 1960s, Abby felt no need to rebel. But she was neither docile nor deferential. Like her mother, Abby remembers, she was "willing to go against conventional wisdom. If I've done my homework and believe that I'm right, I really don't care if people agree with me or not." At Martin Van Buren High School in Queens, she was elected "girl leader" of the honor society, won two Future Scientists of America awards, and graduated twelfth in a class of 1,636. She entered Cornell in 1969 as a prospective physics major, but soon switched to economics and the relatively new discipline of computer science. Discouraged by the professor from taking an advanced computer science course because she was not an engineer, a graduate student, or a male, she persevered: "I was no computer geek, but I was just as good as anyone else." In addition to her double major, Abby was treasurer and vice president of her sorority, Delta Phi Epsilon, and active in Hillel. Soon after her graduation in 1973, she married David M. Cohen, a labor relations major she had met in Economics 101.

The Cohens moved to Washington, D.C., where David attended law school and Abby worked full time at the Federal Reserve Board and completed a master's degree in economics at George Washington University. In 1976, she joined T. Rowe Price as an economist. In seven years with the firm, she learned to build econometric models and apply them to the analysis of securities. In 1980, Cohen gave birth to the first of her two daughters and chose to become a working mom. "The culture had changed since my mother's day," she explained. "She was content with her choice, but I still wonder how far she could have gone."

In 1982 the Cohens relocated to New York City after Abby was appointed as a portfolio strategist at Drexel Burnham Lambert (David would become director of labor and employee relations at Columbia University). Promoted to chief strategist in 1987, she did not anticipate Black Monday, when the Dow fell 22.6 percent, the largest one-day drop in its history. But she did advise clients the next morning to use all available cash to jump back into the market. Those who did made a lot of money. Drexel Burnham went bankrupt in 1990, ruined by the junk bond frauds of Michael Milken. After a brief detour at a subsidiary of Barclay's Bank of Great Britain, Cohen landed on her feet at Goldman Sachs. In scores of prescient reports for the firm's investors, she took note of significant changes in the U.S. economy: American businesses were investing in productivity and identifying growth areas such as cellular phones, computer software, and financial services; Baby Boomers were beginning to save and invest more; and the federal government was reining in spending. She predicted that these developments—and a vigilant Alan Greenspan at the Federal Reserve Board—would keep inflation low and produce a long period of steady and sustainable economic growth.

"It's said that the five scariest words about the market are 'This time it is different'," Cohen acknowledged. "But sometimes it really is different." As the markets soared, price-earnings ratios skyrocketed, and other analysts flinched, Abby Cohen remained bullish. The United States, she repeated, was the "supertanker" of the global economy, "hard to knock off course." When the Hong Kong stock market capsized in October 1997, driving the Dow down 554 points in one day, she remained unfazed. It rebounded quickly, just as she said it would. A few months later, Louis Rukeyser, host of television's *Wall Street Week,* called her "the most influential market forecaster, period." With grey hair, glasses, and unprepossessing suits, looking more like the stereotypical librarian than a portfolio power broker, she was ubiquitous on PBS, CNN, CNBC, in business magazines, and on the corporate lecture circuit. "It's standing room only when she comes to talk," said Joseph McAlinden of Dean Whitter. And when she spoke, the markets moved. Dragged out of a meeting to scotch a rumor that she had turned bearish, Cohen spoke through an intercom to the investment community, single-handedly reversing a sixty-point slide on the Dow. "It was as if the world were falling," said Goldman Sachs colleague Steven Wagshal, "and Abby came in and lifted it up again."

So great was Cohen's status as a celebrity that journalist Alex Berenson speculated in a column in the *New York Times* about what would happen if she expanded her influence beyond the financial markets. Berenson played the scenario out with a series of news items: Steven Spielberg would cancel plans to make a science-fiction movie because she turned thumbs down on the project; teen pregnancy would drop when millions of teens responded to an "Abby Says No" abstinence campaign; China and Taiwan would make peace following her prediction that markets in both nations would plummet if a war between them broke out; and Cohen would become the U.S. senator from New York, winning 98 percent of the vote, although her name was not listed on the ballot.

Goldman Sachs's failure to make her a partner before 1998 was troubling to many on Wall Street. Unlike deal-making investment bankers, Goldman Sachs executives explained, Cohen did not bring in millions of dollars to the company. Others detected a gender bias in the firm's inaction. "That's a very sore subject," said Linda Strumpf, manager of the Ford Foundation's investment portfolio. After all, to the average investor Goldman Sachs was "Abby Joseph Cohen's company."

Cohen did not foresee the end of the bull market in 2000. She advised clients to take some money out of tech stocks, but her forecasts for the market and the economy in general in 2000 and 2001 were far off the mark. With her mind fastened on the future, she was, outwardly at least, unperturbed by the turbulence in the market and its impact on her reputation. She continued to spurn the Goldman Sachs limousine as an unnecessary extravagance, preferring to take the express bus to Manhattan from her unostentatious three-bedroom house in Queens. And she still loves being an investment strategist. A member of the board of trustees at Cornell, Cohen occasionally offers finance seminars at the Johnson Graduate School of Management. Offered a position on the faculty, she insisted she was "having too much fun" on Wall Street to "even think about it." Will Abby Joseph Cohen "turn out to be just one of those people who embodied a moment, rather than analyzed it?" Peter Truell asked in the *New York Times.* "The answer will be important not just to her, but also to the legions of relatively inexperienced investors who hang on her every word."

Francis Fukuyama
❧ CLASS OF 1974

As he listened to Soviet President Mikhail Gorbachev declare that the essence of socialism was competition, Francis Fukuyama got the idea for his immensely influential book, *The End of History and the Last Man*. "If Gorbachev was saying that," he concluded, then Hegel had triumphed over Marx: a constitutional state rather than communism marked the end of history. "You will be misunderstood," a friend predicted when Fukuyama showed him a draft of his argument. He was right. With *The End of History* Fukuyama became, in some quarters, a prophet of democratic capitalism, and in others, a poster boy for the smug triumphalism of post–Cold War America.

Francis Fukuyama was born on October 27, 1952, in Chicago, Illinois. He was the only child of Yoshio Fukuyama, an ordained minister in the United Church of Christ and a professor at Chicago Theological Seminary, and Toshiko Kawata Fukuyama, a potter. A native Californian, Yoshio was a seminary student during World War II, and thus was not placed, like his parents were, in a detention camp. Toshiko was born in Japan, and came to the United States on a student visa to attend college. After the war she was forced to return home briefly when her visa expired, even though she was married to a U.S. citizen. Francis spent his formative years in Manhattan. He rode the subway one-and-a-half hours each way to private school, he recalled, and found time to attend astronomy classes at the Hayden Planetarium and to frequent jazz clubs in Greenwich Village. When his father received an appointment at Penn State, the family relocated to State College, Pennsylvania. In his junior year of high school, Fukuyama was chosen to attend a Telluride Summer Program on the Civil War that was taught at Hampton Institute in Virginia. In 1970, he matriculated at Cornell as a Tellurider.

To pursue his interest in "aesthetics," Fukuyama took courses in comparative literature and classics in a College Scholar curriculum he designed for himself. Allan Bloom, translator of the works of Plato and Rousseau and a Cornell professor until 1971, became his intellectual mentor. He was not involved in sports, did not play a musical instrument, and did not participate in stage productions at Telluride House, his roommate recalled. He did not drink much and was "the only one of my friends who used a pipe—I mean for tobacco, not for drugs." Fukuyama "wanted to read books, mostly, and have ideas." He graduated from Cornell a semester early, in January 1974, and spent the spring in Paris, reading Continental literature and philosophy. Fukuyama returned to the United States to enroll in a doctoral program in comparative literature at Yale, but lasted only a year. He had developed such an aversion to the "over-intellectual approach" of postmodern literary critics that he "turned to nuclear weapons instead." Fukuyama transferred to Harvard's government department, completing a dissertation in 1981 on the involvement of the Soviet Union in the Middle East.

During the 1980s, Fukuyama worked for Pan Heuristic Systems, a consulting group specializing in national security, and then for the RAND Corporation in Santa Monica, California. He was writing as well, publishing a report on the security of Pakistan (1980), a book on the Soviet Union and Iraq (1980), and another on the Soviet Union and the Third World (1983). In 1981, a fellow Cornell Tellurider, Paul Wolfowitz, then chief of the Policy Planning Staff at the Department of State in Washington, D.C., added Fukuyama to the U.S. delegation to talks between Egypt and Israel on Palestinian autonomy. He would shuttle back and forth between RAND and the Policy Planning Staff, serving the latter as consultant and as deputy director.

By the late '80s, Fukuyama had started a family. He married Laura Holmgren in 1986. They have three children. Family responsibilities, however, did not slow Fukuyama down. He wrote articles for prominent periodicals, including *Foreign Affairs, The New Republic,* and *Commentary.* In 1989, Fukuyama captured worldwide attention with a sixteen-page essay, "The End of History?" published in the *National Interest.* Three years later he spelled out his argument in the elegantly written and learned *The End of History and the Last Man.* With the end of communism, he asserted, ideological forces were no longer created and driven by contradictions within a system or between systems: "What we may in fact be witnessing is not just the passing of a particular period of postwar history, but the end point of mankind's ideological evolution and the emergence of Western liberal democracy as the final form of government." His views were not entirely sanguine, for he recognized that violent conflicts might continue along with poverty, crime, racism, and unemployment. The post-historical world might even be a "very sad time" because the struggle "that called forth daring, courage, imagination, and idealism will be replaced by economic calculation, the endless solving of technical problems, environmental concerns, and the satisfaction of sophisticated consumer demands."

Fukuyama's timing was perfect. A few months after his article appeared, the Berlin Wall fell. The Soviet Union collapsed as his book was reviewed. Intense discussion of "the end of history" took place in dozens of countries, with Mikhail Gorbachev and Margaret Thatcher among the world leaders commenting on the phenomenon. In the United States, many newspapers and magazines devoted substantial space to Fukuyama's speculations. Praised for writing an important and intellectually challenging essay, Fukuyama was also criticized as a cheerleader for capitalism—"At last, self-congratulations raised to philosophy. The Bush years have found their Burke, or their Pangloss," wrote the journalist Christopher Hitchens—and for ignoring such forces as nationalism and religious fundamentalism. He has refused to back down. Insisting that as an ideology Islam poses no threat to the West, he has branded the attack on the World Trade Center "a rearguard action" that will not stop "this great freight train of globalization."

An internationally renowned public intellectual, a consultant on foreign policy, and a card-carrying academic (he has taught at George Mason University, and is currently on the faculty of the School of Advanced International Studies at Johns Hopkins University), Fukuyama has maintained a prodigious pace of publication. In 1993, with Kongdan Oh, he wrote a book about the security relationship between Japan and the United States. In *Trust: The Social Virtues and the Creation of Prosperity* (1995), he examined how "social capital" facilitated economic growth, comparing "high trust" nations with "low trust" nations.

Acknowledging that a failure to consider human nature and the capacity of science to alter it posed a fundamental challenge to the "end of history" thesis, Fukuyama took on the subject in his next two books. *The Great Disruption: Human Nature and the Reconstitution of Social Order* (1999), began with the social ills associated with postindustrial society, including teen pregnancy, drug abuse, crime, and the breakdown of the family. Fukuyama predicted that the disruption would be temporary, largely because humans have an innate desire to adhere to norms of behavior and build communities. If they needed help at all, he concluded, it should come from local organizations, not the national government.

In *Our Posthuman Future: Consequences of the Biotechnology Revolution* (2002), Fukuyama warned that genetic engineering could wreak havoc with these innate desires, causing us "to lose our humanity—that is, some essential quality that has always underpinned our sense of who we are and where we are going." The danger is that much greater because scientists and bioethicists "have become nothing more than sophisticated and sophistic justifiers of whatever it is the scientific community wants them to do." What Fukuyama thinks about biotechnology matters: he sits on the White House Council on Bioethics. History may or may not have ended, but, quite clearly, Fukuyama's work is far from over.

Christopher Reeve
CLASS OF 1974

When his first *Superman* movie came out, Christopher Reeve defined a hero as a person who commits a courageous act without considering the consequences. He now believes "a hero is an ordinary individual who finds the strength to persevere and endure in spite of overwhelming obstacles."

Christopher Reeve was born in Manhattan on September 25, 1952. His father, Franklin D'Olier Reeve, was a graduate student in Russian literature at Columbia. He "could do everything," Chris remembered, "from playing Parcheesi to translating Dostoyevsky." Chris's mother, Barbara Pitney Lamb Reeve, was the daughter of a prominent New York City lawyer and a student at Barnard. The Reeves separated in 1956 and remained estranged for decades. They had a tendency, Chris felt, "to use me as a chess piece." Relocated to Princeton, New Jersey, where Barbara married a wealthy stockbroker, Christopher was enrolled in Princeton Day School. In fourth or fifth grade, he took a part in Gilbert and Sullivan's *Yeoman of the Guard*. Acting became his passion. By the age of sixteen, he had appeared at the Williamstown Theatre in Massachusetts, the Boothbay Playhouse in Maine, and the San Diego Shakespeare Festival in California.

Christopher's parents agreed on one thing: before he began his career as an actor he must go to college. He chose Cornell over Princeton, mostly because snowstorms "from the end of October to the first of May" were conducive to study but not to travel to New York for an audition. With an Independent Major, specializing in English and theater arts, Reeve worked for WVBR radio, sang in the Sage Chapel choir, sailed, and played hockey. He appeared in several plays, performed in the basement of Lincoln Hall or at Willard Straight Hall, under the direction of Professor James Clancy. He had parts in *Rosencrantz and Guildenstern Are Dead*, *Waiting for Godot*, *The Winter's Tale*, and *The Good Woman of Setzuan*. A resident of Risley, Reeve was unobtrusive but ambitious. Decades later, a student who lived down the hall joked: "I didn't know how strong he was. All I can say is that there was only one gorge at Cornell until Reeve came here."

Reeve took a leave of absence to observe productions backstage at the Old Vic in London and the Comédie-Française in Paris. He then convinced Clancy and the dean of the College of Arts and Sciences to allow him to complete his degree by spending his senior year at Juilliard. After earning his B.A. in 1974, Reeve left Juilliard to play the bigamist Ben Harper on the CBS soap opera *Love of Life*. A heartthrob on the small screen for two years, he appeared on Broadway as well in 1976 as grandson to Katharine Hepburn in *A Matter of Gravity*. With one brief, forgettable film on his résumé, the submarine disaster *Grey Lady Down*, Reeve was one of two hundred actors to audition for the role of Superman. When Marlon Brando and Gene Hackman signed to play supporting parts, the producers, Alexander and Ilya Salkind, decided to cast an "unknown" in the title role. Reeve got the part, he later explained, because he had "the look. . . . The other 10 percent is acting talent." To prepare himself, he added thirty pounds to his frame, three inches to his biceps, and four to his chest. Viewing the script as a romantic comedy, Reeve modeled his Clark Kent on Cary Grant's lovable bumbler in *Bringing Up Baby* while giving the "Man of Steel" a touch of humor, wisdom, and maturity. *Superman* premiered on December 15, 1978—and was a smash hit. A cover story in *Newsweek* singled out Reeve as "a delight. Ridiculously good-looking, with a face as sharp and strong as an ax blade," his Clark Kent and Superman "are simply two sides of gallantry and innocence."

Although a *Superman II* was just about inevitable, Reeve tried to "escape the cape" with his next film. He turned down *American Gigolo, Urban Cowboy,* and *Body Heat* for the modestly budgeted *Somewhere in Time* (1980), a romance about a man who falls in love with a 1912 photograph of an actress and travels to the early twentieth century to meet her. It was an unfortunate choice. "Reeve looks like a helium-filled canary," wrote one critic. Except for a fanatical few, who established INSITE (the International Network of Somewhere in Time Enthusiasts), audiences stayed away in droves.

In *Superman II* (1981), Reeve reestablished himself as a star. With terrific special effects and a story in which Clark Kent reveals his secret identity to Lois Lane and Superman loses his powers when the couple make love, the sequel outgrossed the original at the box office.

Still leery of typecasting, Reeve returned to Broadway and to mixed reviews as a bitter, paraplegic Vietnam War veteran in Lanford Wilson's *Fifth of July* (1980). On the big screen, he had two modest successes: as a psychopathic killer, playing opposite Michael Caine, in *Deathtrap* (1982), and as Basil Ransom in the Merchant-Ivory production of *The Bostonians* (1984) with Vanessa Redgrave. But as the decade wore on, Reeve's career foundered. *Superman III* (1984), *Superman IV* (1987), *Monsignor* (1982), *The Aviator* (1985), and *Switching Channels* (1988) bombed. As Reeve's run as an above-the-line movie star ended, so did his relationship with Gae Exton, which had produced two children. Reeve returned to Williamstown for "some breathing space," and met Dana Morosini, an actress and singer. The two married in 1992. They have one son.

Reeve found rewarding work in the '80s and '90s. He was an amoral yuppie pitted against Morgan Freeman's pimp in the film *Street Smart* (1987); among his made-for-TV movies were *The Rose and the Jackal* (1990), *The Sea Wolf* (1993), and *Above Suspicion* (1994), in which he played a paralyzed cop. In the critically acclaimed Merchant-Ivory film *Remains of the Day* (1993), starring Anthony Hopkins and Emma Thompson, Reeve played an American congressman.

Active politically for liberal causes, Reeve was a member of the Creative Coalition, Amnesty International, and People for the American Way. In 1987, he traveled to Chile to demonstrate on behalf of seventy-seven actors who had been threatened with execution by the Pinochet government. For this work, he won an Obie in 1988 and an award from the Walter Briehl Human Rights Foundation.

An avid flier, skier, scuba diver, and wind-surfer, Reeve overcame an allergic reaction to horses to become an amateur show jumper. On Memorial Day weekend, 1995, shortly before he was scheduled to go to Ireland to shoot Francis Ford Coppola's remake of *Kidnapped,* he entered a competition in Commonwealth, Virginia. When his horse, Eastern Express, stopped suddenly in front of a fence, Reeve was thrown. With his hands tangled in the bridle, he could not break his fall and suffered a severe spinal cord injury. His life hung in the balance for days. Following superb medical treatment, therapy, and sheer determination, Reeve, although paralyzed from the neck down, began to breathe without a respirator and to speak.

An appearance at an October 16 dinner later that year honoring Robin Williams, his best friend and roommate at Juilliard, marked Reeve's emergence as a spokesperson for victims of spinal cord injuries. As "president of a club I wouldn't want to join"—the American Paralysis Association (now the Christopher Reeve Paralysis Foundation)—and in speeches around the country, including one at the Democratic National Convention in 1996, Reeve raised money for research, lobbied Congress to raise insurance caps on catastrophic injuries, and supported federal funding of experiments using embryonic stem cells. In an inspirational and often painfully frank memoir, *Still Me: A Life* (1998), Reeve discussed his exercise regimen, his sexual and emotional life, two mishaps from a drug reaction, the dysreflexia (caused by a blocked bowel or urinary tract) that almost killed him, and his determination to walk again: "My lesion is only twenty millimeters wide. Get across that gap, and I'm up and about." In 2002, he published a second memoir, *Nothing Is Impossible: Reflections on a New Life.*

Reeve became active professionally again, too. His first directorial effort, *In the Gloaming* (1997), starring Glenn Close, was nominated for five Emmys and won six Cable Ace Awards. The next year he directed and won a Golden Globe for acting in a remake of Hitchcock's *Rear Window,* the story of a wheelchair-bound architect with a large ego who spots a crime as he looks out from his apartment. In Reeve's film the architect learns "a lesson in humility. He starts out as a master of the universe, and goes through a profound transformation."

Credits for Photographs of Notables

Credits are given in the order in which the photographs appear in the book.

Joseph Benson Foraker, Class of 1869: from Everett Walters, *Joseph Benson Foraker: An Uncompromising Republican* (Columbus: Ohio History Press, 1948).

David Starr Jordan, Class of 1872: courtesy *Cornell Alumni News.*

John Henry Comstock, Class of 1874: courtesy Division of Rare and Manuscript Collections, Cornell University Library.

Edward Leamington Nichols, Class of 1875: courtesy Division of Rare and Manuscript Collections, Cornell University Library.

Martha Carey Thomas, Class of 1877: photograph by Frederick Hollyer, London. Courtesy Bryn Mawr College Library.

Hermann Michael Biggs, Class of 1882: wood engraving by Timothy Cole, 1927.

Florence Kelley, Class of 1882: courtesy Augustus M. Kelley Publishers.

Anna Botsford Comstock, Class of 1885: courtesy Division of Rare and Manuscript Collections, Cornell University Library.

Veranus Alva Moore, Class of 1887: courtesy Cornell University College of Veterinary Medicine.

Mario Garcia Menocal, Class of 1888: AP/Wide World Photos.

John R. Mott, Class of 1888: courtesy Division of Rare and Manuscript Collections, Cornell University Library.

William Alanson White, Class of 1889: by permission of Ayer Company Publishers.

Ida Henrietta Hyde, Class of 1891: courtesy Division of Rare and Manuscript Collections, Cornell University Library.

Myron Charles Taylor, Class of 1894: courtesy Division of Rare and Manuscript Collections, Cornell University Library.

Glenn Scobey Warner, Class of 1894: courtesy Division of Rare and Manuscript Collections, Cornell University Library.

Emily Dunning Barringer, Class of 1897: courtesy Division of Rare and Manuscript Collections, Cornell University Library.

Louis Agassiz Fuertes, Class of 1897: courtesy Division of Rare and Manuscript Collections, Cornell University Library.

Isadore G. Mudge, Class of 1897: courtesy Columbia University Archives, Columbiana Library.

Frank Ernest Gannett, Class of 1898: courtesy Division of Rare and Manuscript Collections, Cornell University Library.

Walter Clark Teagle, Class of 1900: courtesy Division of Rare and Manuscript Collections, Cornell University Library.

Willis Haviland Carrier, Class of 1901: by permission of Ayer Company Publishers.

Willard Dickerman Straight, Class of 1901: by permission of Ayer Company Publishers.

Richmond Harold Shreve, Class of 1902: courtesy Division of Rare and Manuscript Collections, Cornell University Library.

Arthur Garfield Dove, Class of 1903: courtesy Division of Rare and Manuscript Collections, Cornell University Library.

Willis Ray Gregg, Class of 1903: photograph by Fabian Bachrach, *New York Times* obituary, Sept. 15, 1938.

George Jean Nathan, Class of 1904: photograph by Underwood and Underwood, 1926.

Jessie Redmon Fauset, Class of 1905: Harmon Foundation Collection, Library of Congress Manuscript Division.

Leo Max Frank, Class of 1906: photograph originally appeared in *The Atlanta Constitution,* August 19, 1913.

Louis Robert Wolheim, Class of 1906: courtesy Division of Rare and Manuscript Collections, Cornell University Library.

Arthur Augustus Allen, Class of 1907: courtesy Division of Rare and Manuscript Collections, Cornell University Library.

Adolph Coors Jr., Class of 1907: courtesy Adolph Coors Foundation.

Kenneth Lewis Roberts, Class of 1908: courtesy Division of Rare and Manuscript Collections, Cornell University Library.

Alice Catherine Evans, Class of 1909: courtesy National Library of Medicine.

Martha Van Rensselaer, Class of 1909: courtesy Division of Rare and Manuscript Collections, Cornell University Library.

Thomas Midgley Jr., Class of 1911: courtesy Division of Rare and Manuscript Collections, Cornell University Library.

Edward L. Bernays, Class of 1912: courtesy family of Edward L. Bernays.

Millar Burrows, Class of 1912: courtesy Division of Rare and Manuscript Collections, Cornell University Library.

Georgia Elma Harkness, Class of 1912: courtesy Division of Rare and Manuscript Collections, Cornell University Library.

John Merrill Olin, Class of 1913: reprinted from *Sports Illustrated,* Nov. 17, 1958, p. 37.

Y. R. Chao (Chao Yuen Ren), Class of 1914: from *Autobiography of a Chinese Woman, Buwei Yang Chao* (New York: John Day, 1947).

William Frederic Friedman, Class of 1914: courtesy William F. Friedman Collection, George C. Marshall Research Foundation.

Hu Shih, Class of 1914: Alfred Eisenstaedt/Pix Inc./TimePix.

Leroy Randle Grumman, Class of 1916: from Richard Thruelsen, *The Grumman Story* (New York: Praeger, 1976).

Laurens Hammond, Class of 1916: courtesy Division of Rare and Manuscript Collections, Cornell University Library.

H. C. Zen (Jen Hung-chün), Class of 1916: courtesy of E-tu Zen Sun (daughter of H. C. Zen).

George Joseph Hecht, Class of 1917: courtesy Division of Rare and Manuscript Collections, Cornell University Library.

Howard Winchester Hawks, Class of 1918: from Peter Bogdanovich, *Who the Devil Made It* (New York: Alfred A. Knopf, 1997).

Arthur Hobson Dean, Class of 1919: courtesy Division of Rare and Manuscript Collections, Cornell University Library.

Isidor Isaac Rabi, Class of 1919: courtesy John S. Rigden.

Colston Estey Warne, Class of 1920: courtesy Division of Rare and Manuscript Collections, Cornell University Library.

Laura Z. Hobson, Class of 1921: courtesy Division of Rare and Manuscript Collections, Cornell University Library.

E. B. White, Class of 1921: courtesy Division of Rare and Manuscript Collections, Cornell University Library.

Barbara McClintock, Class of 1923: courtesy Division of Rare and Manuscript Collections, Cornell University Library.

Gregory Goodwin Pincus, Class of 1924: courtesy Division of Rare and Manuscript Collections, Cornell University Library.

Julian Haynes Steward, Class of 1925: courtesy Division of Rare and Manuscript Collections, Cornell University Library.

Andrew John Biemiller, Class of 1926: courtesy Division of Rare and Manuscript Collections, Cornell University Library.

Leon (Lee) Pressman, Class of 1926: courtesy Division of Rare and Manuscript Collections, Cornell University Library.

Margaret Bourke-White, Class of 1927: courtesy Division of Rare and Manuscript Collections, Cornell University Library.

Nathaniel Alexander Owings, Class of 1927: courtesy Division of Rare and Manuscript Collections, Cornell University Library.

Franchot Tone, Class of 1927: courtesy Division of Rare and Manuscript Collections, Cornell University Library.

Sidney Sonny Kingsley, Class of 1928: courtesy Division of Rare and Manuscript Collections, Cornell University Library.

Allen Funt, Class of 1934: by permission of Everett Collection, Inc.

Margaret Morgan Lawrence, Class of 1936: by permission of Stefan Merken, photographer.

Arthur Laurents, Class of 1937: by permission of Arthur Laurents.

Charles Cummings Collingwood, Class of 1939: from Stanley Cloud and Lynne Olson, *The Murrow Boys* (Boston: Houghton Mifflin, 1996), courtesy Molly Collingwood.

Jerome Heartwell Holland, Class of 1939: courtesy Division of Rare and Manuscript Collections, Cornell University Library.

Constance Knowles Eberhardt Cook, Class of 1941: courtesy Constance Knowles Eberhardt Cook.

Henry Jay Heimlich, Class of 1941: courtesy The Heimlich Institute.

Samuel Riley Pierce Jr., Class of 1944: courtesy Division of Rare and Manuscript Collections, Cornell University Library.

Joyce Bauer Brothers, Class of 1947: courtesy Division of Rare and Manuscript Collections, Cornell University Library.

James Whitman McLamore, Class of 1947: from James McLamore, *The Burger King: Jim McLamore and the Building of an Empire*, 1998, by permission of the McGraw-Hill Companies.

Robert William Fogel, Class of 1948: courtesy Division of Rare and Manuscript Collections, Cornell University Library.

Wilson Greatbatch, Class of 1950: from Wilson Greatbatch, *The Making of the Pacemaker* (Amherst, N.Y.: Prometheus Books, 2000), courtesy Royal Victorian Children's Hospital, Melbourne, Australia.

Harold Irving Bloom, Class of 1951: courtesy Division of Rare and Manuscript Collections, Cornell University Library.

Clifford Michael Irving, Class of 1951: courtesy Curt Gunther, photographer.

Ruth Bader Ginsburg, Class of 1954: courtesy *CQ Weekly,* photographer R. Michael Jenkins.

Sheldon Lee Glashow, Class of 1954: copyright the Nobel Foundation.

David B. Goodstein, Class of 1954: reprinted from *Los Angeles Times* obituary, June 27, 1985.

Steven Weinberg, Class of 1954: copyright the Nobel Foundation.

Richard Jay Schaap, Class of 1955: courtesy the Schaap family.

Sanford I. Weill, Class of 1955: by permission of Andrew Popper, photographer.

Floyd Abrams, Class of 1956: courtesy of Cornell University Photography.

Charles Francis Feeney, Class of 1956: courtesy Division of Rare and Manuscript Collections, Cornell University Library.

Richard Alan Meier, Class of 1956: courtesy Division of Rare and Manuscript Collections, Cornell University Library.

Stephen Michael Reich, Class of 1957: photograph by John Halpern, courtesy Boosey & Hawkes.

Thomas Ruggles Pynchon Jr., Class of 1959: from *Gravity's Rainbow* by Thomas Pynchon, copyright 1973 by Thomas Pynchon. Used by permission of Viking Penguin, a division of Penguin Putnam Inc.

Peter Yarrow, Class of 1959: courtesy Robert Corwin, photographer.

Janet Reno, Class of 1960: courtesy Division of Rare and Manuscript Collections, Cornell University Library.

Jane Ellen Brody, Class of 1962: from Jane Brody, *Good Food Book* (New York: Norton, 1985), copyright Thomas Victor, photographer, 1985.

Peter Kornel Gogolak, Class of 1964: courtesy Cornell Athletics Department.

Thomas Jacob Peters, Class of 1964: courtesy Division of Rare and Manuscript Collections, Cornell University Library.

Susan Charna Rothenberg, Class of 1966: by permission of Brigitte Lacombe, photographer.

Samuel (Sandy) Richard Berger, Class of 1967: courtesy of Sandy Berger.

Kenneth Wayne Dryden, Class of 1969: courtesy Cornell Athletics Department.

Thomas Wade Jones, Class of 1969: by permission of Evan Kafka, photographer.

Richard Jay Price, Class of 1971: by permission of James Hamilton, photographer.

Edward Francis Marinaro, Class of 1972: *Hill Street Blues* publicity photo, courtesy the files of Cornell Athletics Department.

Abby Joseph Cohen, Class of 1973: courtesy Division of Rare and Manuscript Collections, Cornell University Library.

Francis Fukuyama, Class of 1974: courtesy Laura Holmgren, photographer.

Christopher Reeve, Class of 1974: courtesy Bradford Herzog, photographer.

Index